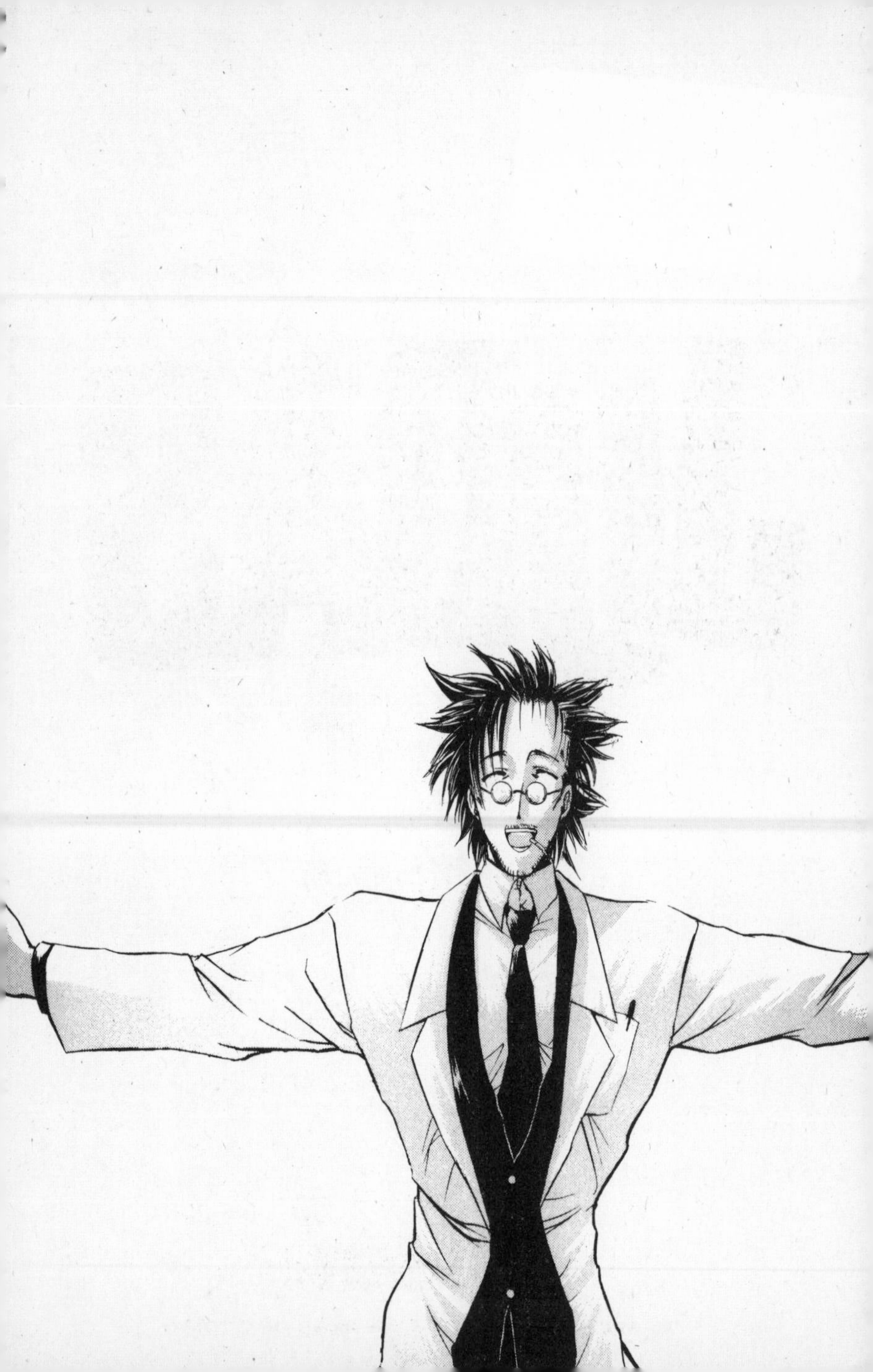

JUDAS

Volume 1
by
Suu Minazuki

HAMBURG // LONDON // LOS ANGELES // TOKYO

JUDAS Vol. 1

Created by Suu Minazuki

Translation - Nan Rymer
English Adaptation - Jay Antani
Associate Editor - Stephanie Duchin
Retouch and Lettering - Nathan Kaestle
Graphic Designer - James Lee

Editor - Paul Morrissey
Digital Imaging Manager - Chris Buford
Pre-Production Supervisor - Erika Terriquez
Art Director - Anne Marie Horne
Production Manager - Elisabeth Brizzi
VP of Production - Ron Klamert
Editor-in-Chief - Rob Tokar
Publisher - Mike Kiley
President and C.O.O. - John Parker
C.E.O. and Chief Creative Officer - Stuart Levy

A  Manga

TOKYOPOP Inc.
5900 Wilshire Blvd. Suite 2000
Los Angeles, CA 90036

E-mail: info@TOKYOPOP.com
Come visit us online at www.TOKYOPOP.com

ISBN: 1-59816-630-1

First TOKYOPOP printing: October 2006

10 9 8 7 6 5 4 3 2 1

Printed in the USA

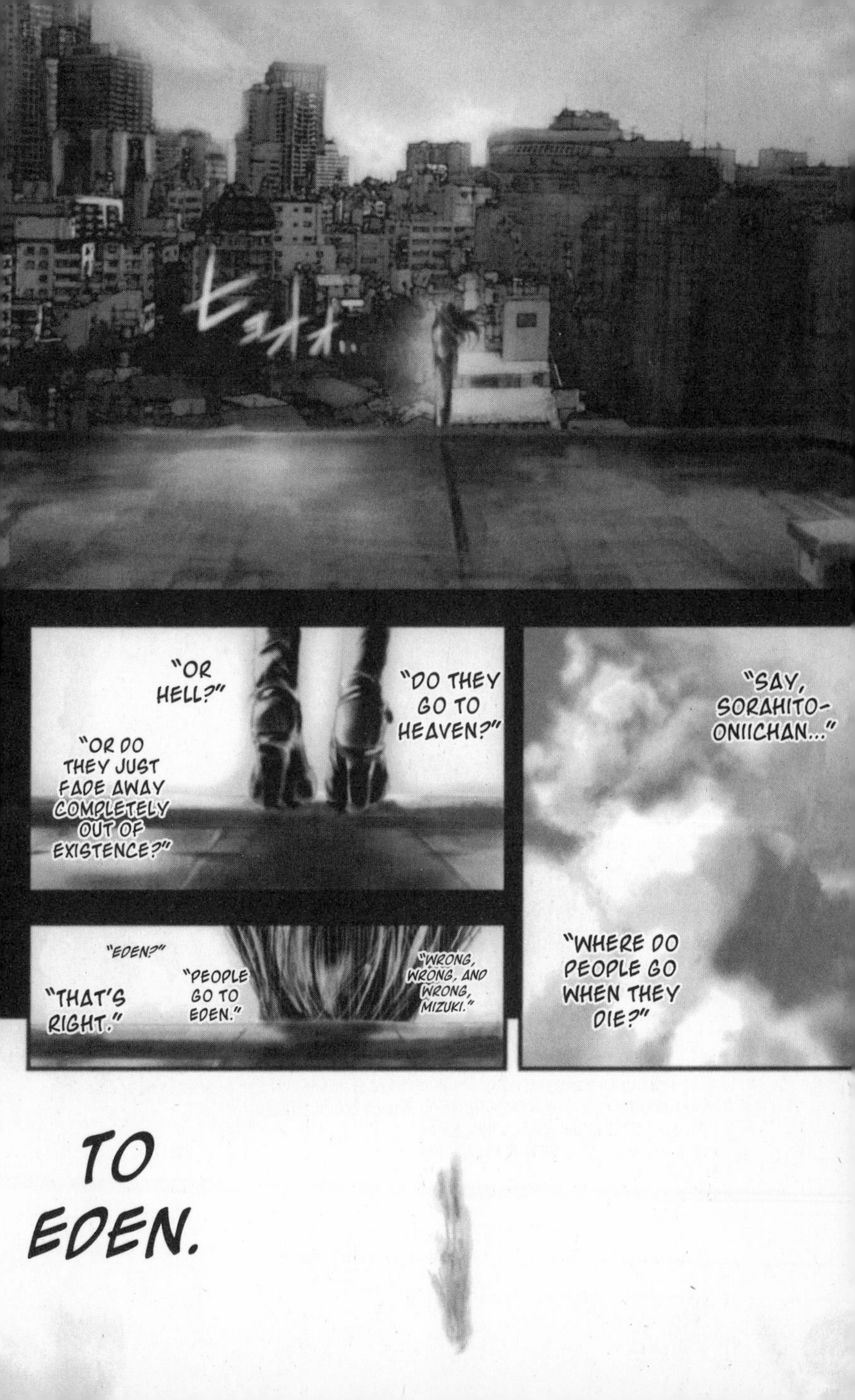
ヒョオオ
"SAY, SORAHITO-ONIICHAN..."
"WHERE DO PEOPLE GO WHEN THEY DIE?"
"DO THEY GO TO HEAVEN?"
"OR HELL?"
"OR DO THEY JUST FADE AWAY COMPLETELY OUT OF EXISTENCE?"
"WRONG, WRONG, AND WRONG, MIZUKI."
"PEOPLE GO TO EDEN."
"EDEN?"
"THAT'S RIGHT."
TO EDEN.

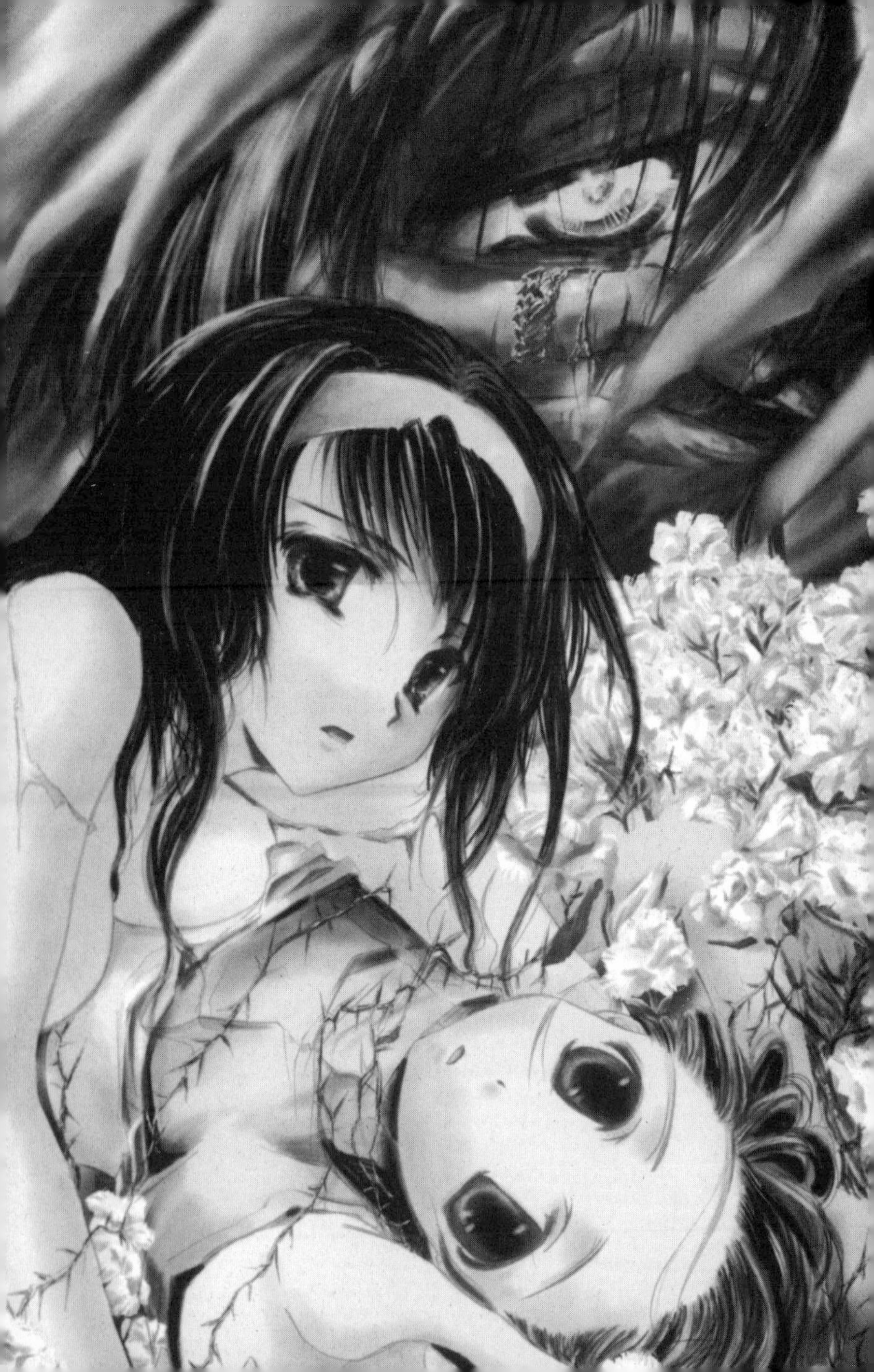

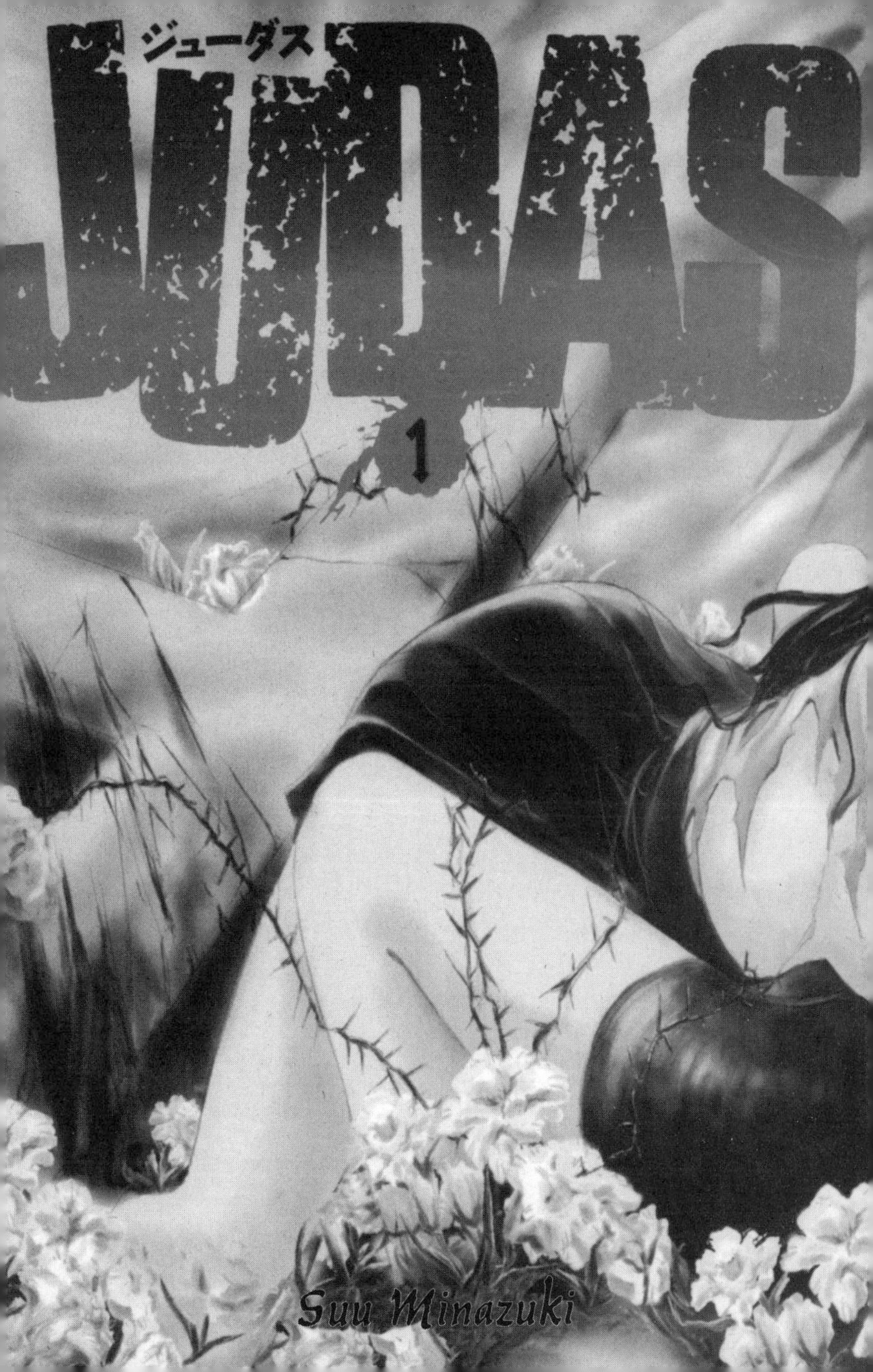
ジューダス
JUDAS
1
Suu Minazuki

JUDAS
1

contents

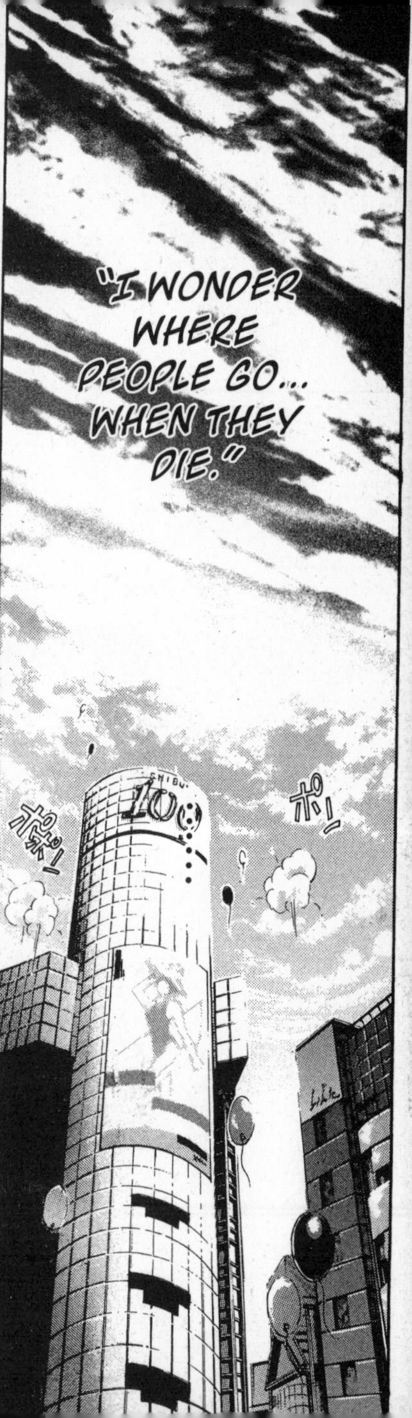
"I WONDER WHERE PEOPLE GO... WHEN THEY DIE."
ポン
ポポン!

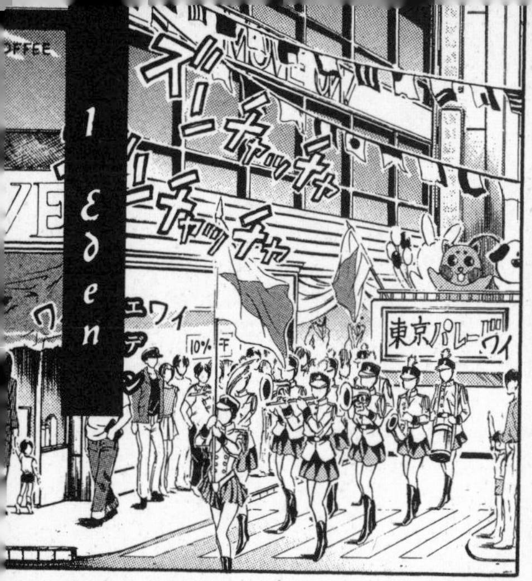
1 Eden
東京パレード
Tokyo Parade.

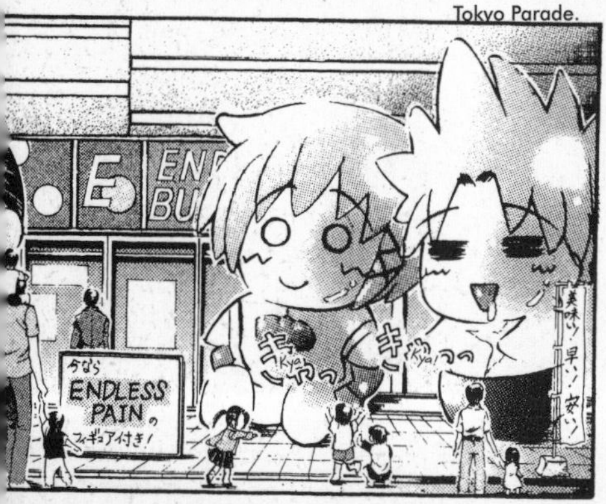
今なら ENDLESS PAIN のフィギュア付き!
美味い! 早い! 安い!
It's good! It's fast! It's cheap!

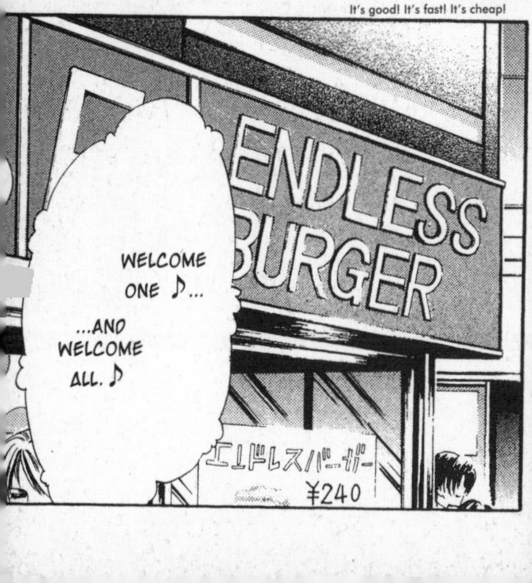
ENDLESS BURGER
WELCOME ONE ♪...
...AND WELCOME ALL. ♪
エンドレスバーガー ¥240

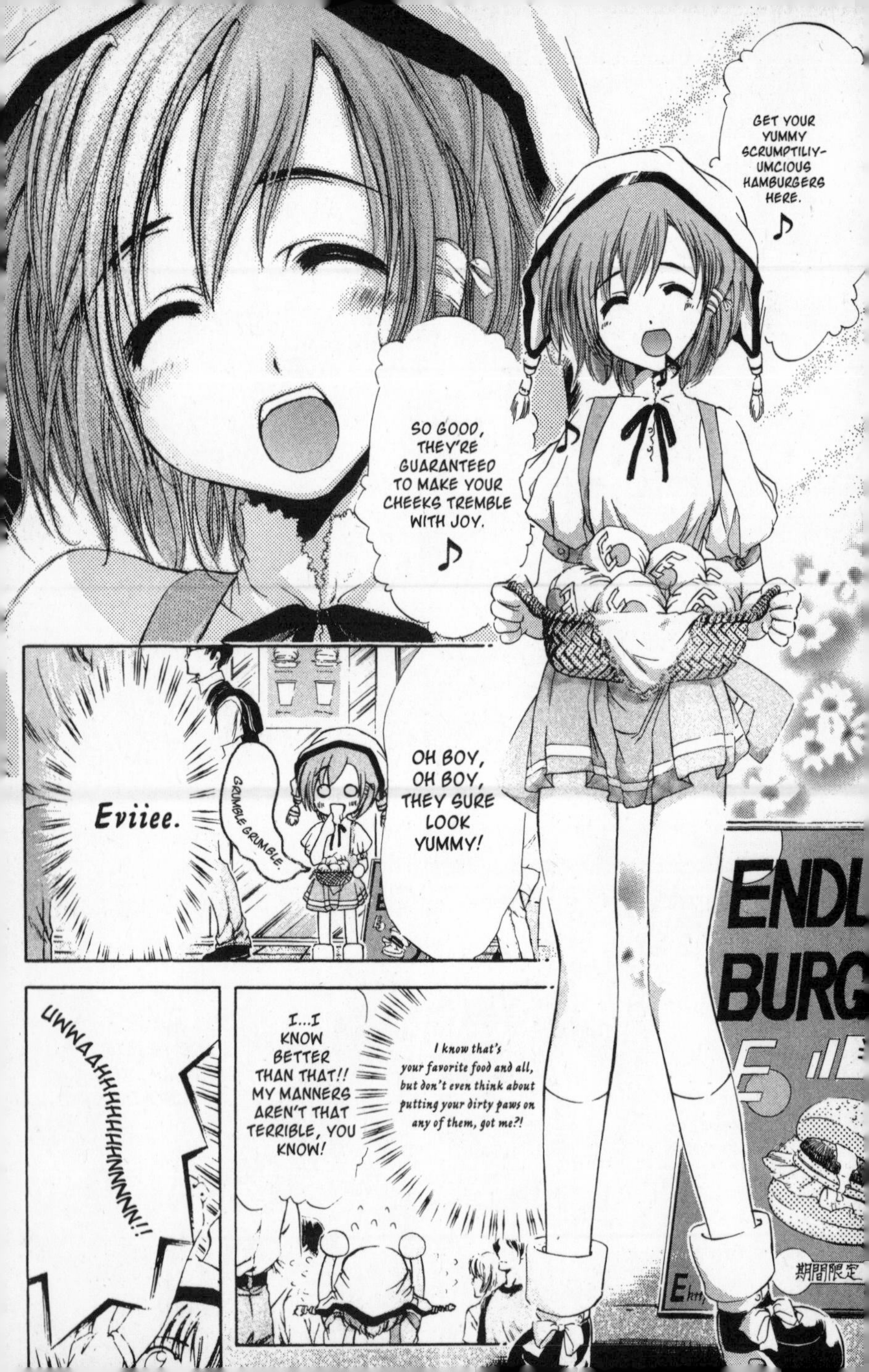
GET YOUR YUMMY SCRUMPTILIY-UMCIOUS HAMBURGERS HERE. ♪
SO GOOD, THEY'RE GUARANTEED TO MAKE YOUR CHEEKS TREMBLE WITH JOY. ♪
ENDL
BURG
期間限定
OH BOY, OH BOY, THEY SURE LOOK YUMMY!
GRUMBLE GRUMBLE.
Eviiee.
I know that's your favorite food and all, but don't even think about putting your dirty paws on any of them, got me?!
I...I KNOW BETTER THAN THAT!! MY MANNERS AREN'T THAT TERRIBLE, YOU KNOW!
UWWAAHHHHHHHHNNNNN!!

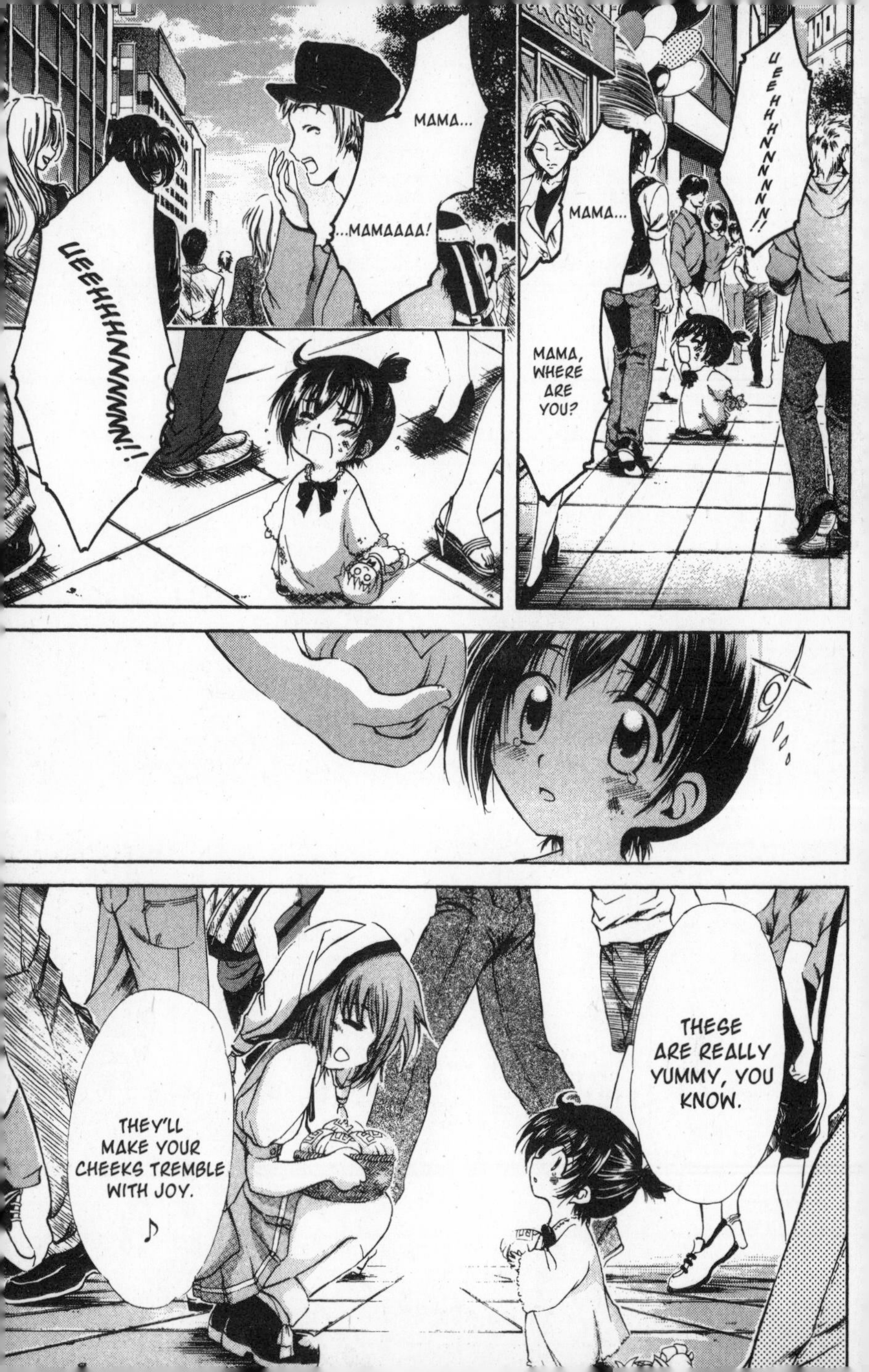

UEEHHHNNNNNN!!
MAMA...
MAMA, WHERE ARE YOU?
MAMA...
...MAMAAAA!
UEEHHHNNNNNNN!!
THESE ARE REALLY YUMMY, YOU KNOW.
THEY'LL MAKE YOUR CHEEKS TREMBLE WITH JOY. ♪

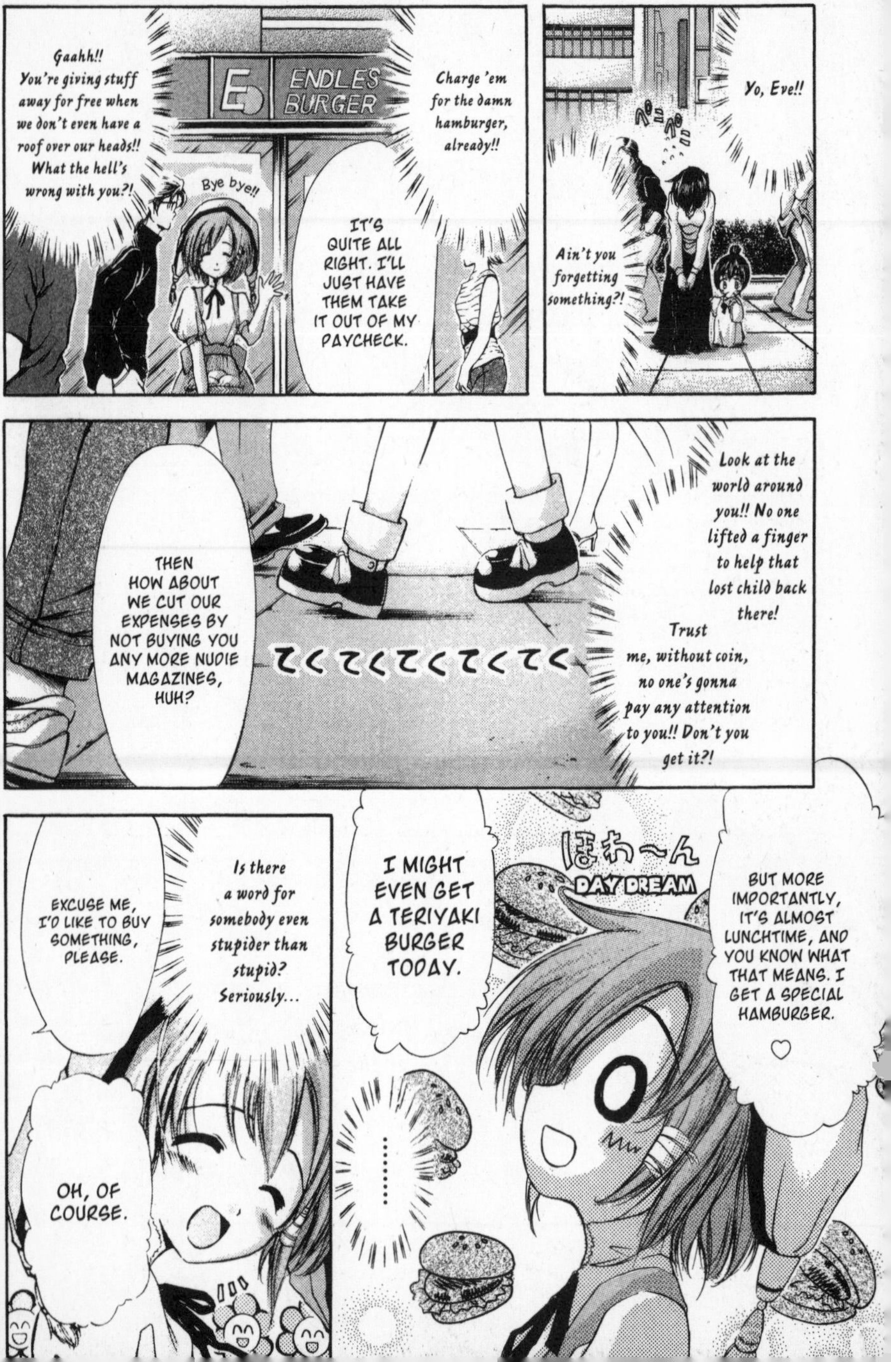
Yo, Eve!!
Ain't you forgetting something?!
Bye bye!!
Gaahh!! You're giving stuff away for free when we don't even have a roof over our heads!! What the hell's wrong with you?!
ENDLES BURGER
Charge 'em for the damn hamburger, already!!
IT'S QUITE ALL RIGHT. I'LL JUST HAVE THEM TAKE IT OUT OF MY PAYCHECK.
Look at the world around you!! No one lifted a finger to help that lost child back there!
Trust me, without coin, no one's gonna pay any attention to you!! Don't you get it?!
てくてくてくてくてくてく
THEN HOW ABOUT WE CUT OUR EXPENSES BY NOT BUYING YOU ANY MORE NUDIE MAGAZINES, HUH?
ほわ～ん
DAY DREAM
BUT MORE IMPORTANTLY, IT'S ALMOST LUNCHTIME, AND YOU KNOW WHAT THAT MEANS. I GET A SPECIAL HAMBURGER. ♡
I MIGHT EVEN GET A TERIYAKI BURGER TODAY.
......
Is there a word for somebody even stupider than stupid? Seriously...
EXCUSE ME, I'D LIKE TO BUY SOMETHING, PLEASE.
OH, OF COURSE.

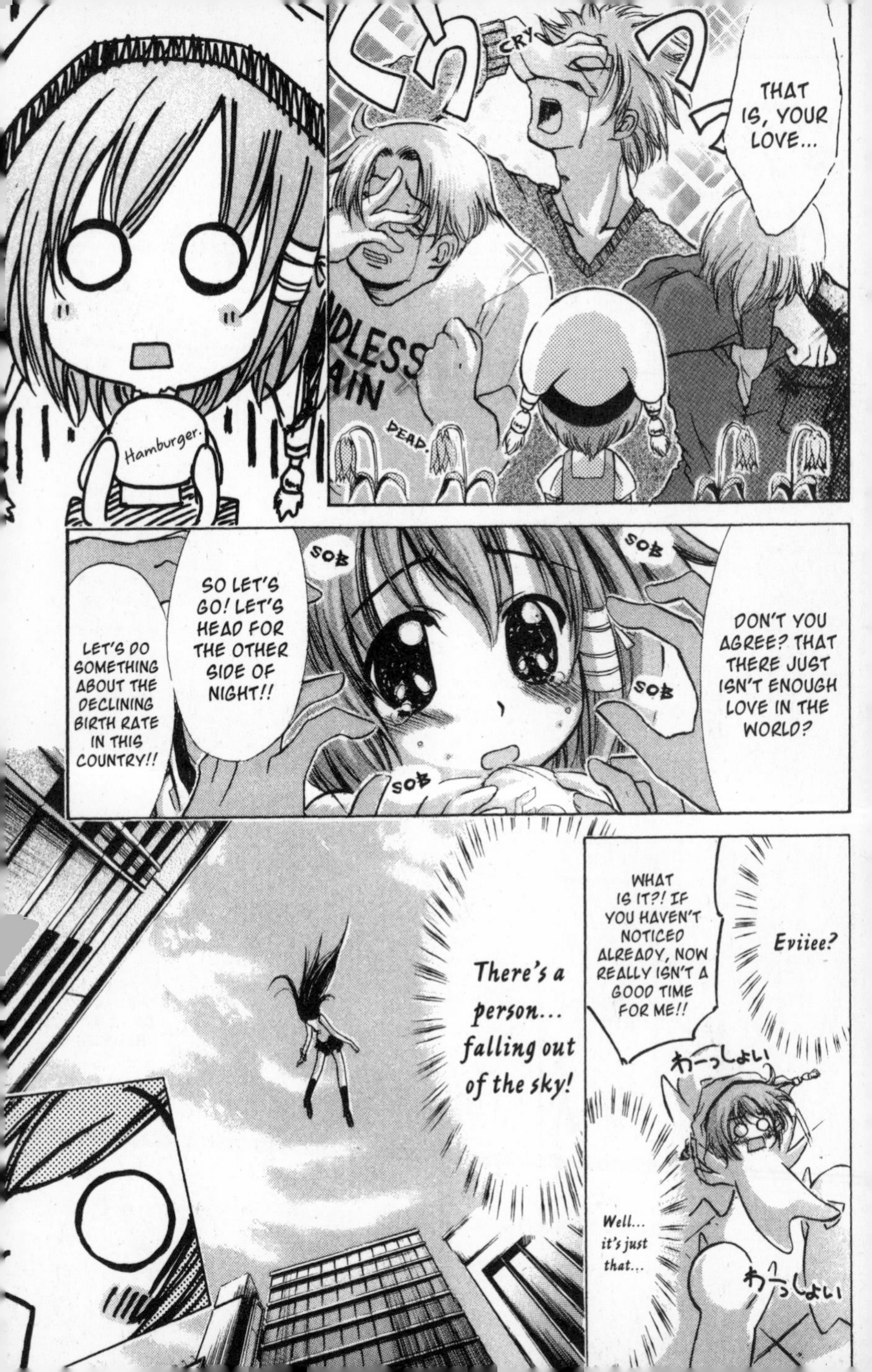
CRY
THAT IS, YOUR LOVE...
DEAD.
Hamburger.
DON'T YOU AGREE? THAT THERE JUST ISN'T ENOUGH LOVE IN THE WORLD?
SOB
SOB
SOB
SOB
SO LET'S GO! LET'S HEAD FOR THE OTHER SIDE OF NIGHT!!
LET'S DO SOMETHING ABOUT THE DECLINING BIRTH RATE IN THIS COUNTRY!!
Eviiee?
WHAT IS IT?! IF YOU HAVEN'T NOTICED ALREADY, NOW REALLY ISN'T A GOOD TIME FOR ME!!
わーっしょい
Well... it's just that...
わっしょい
There's a person... falling out of the sky!

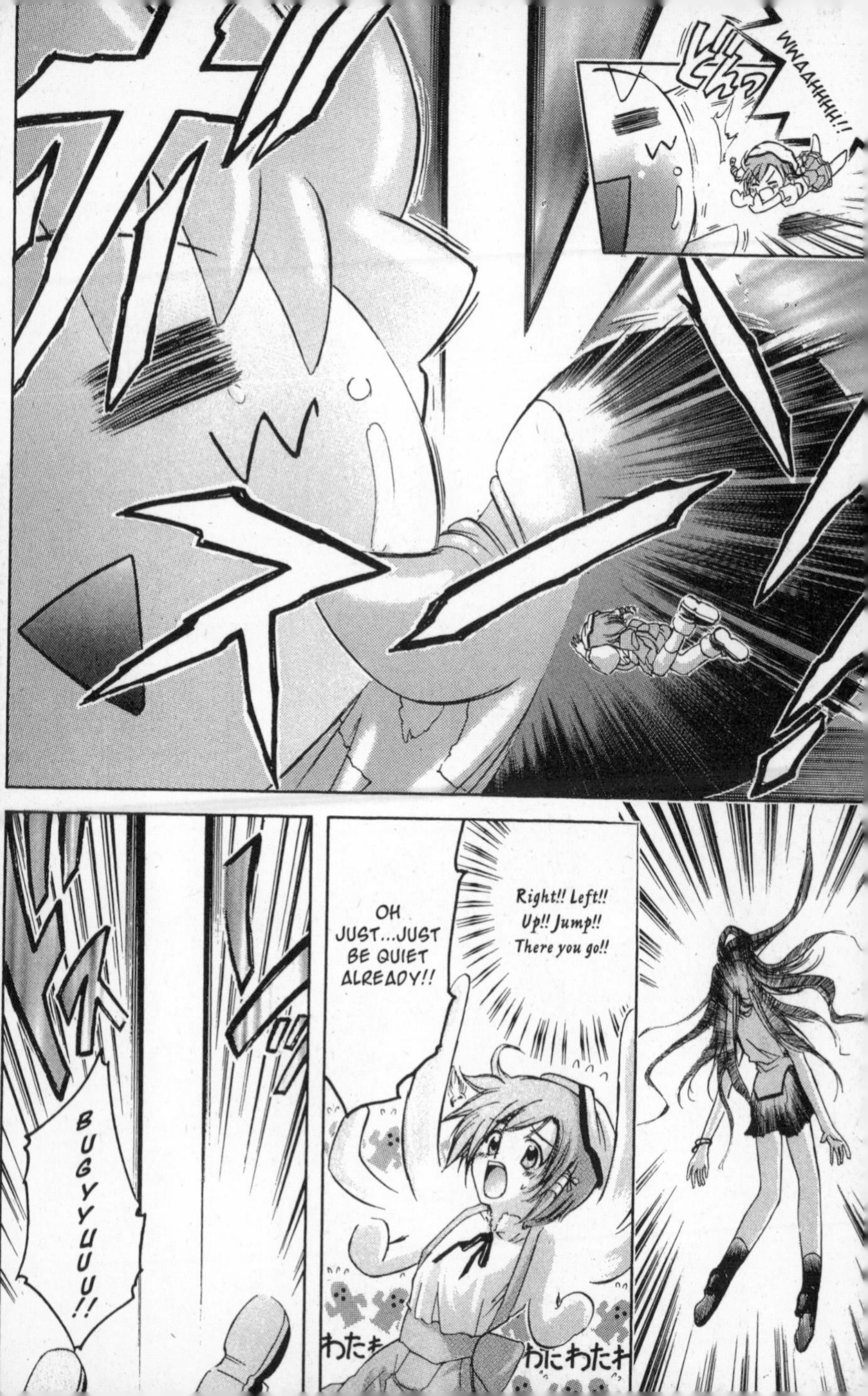
WWAAHHHH!!
Right!! Left!! Up!! Jump!! There you go!!
OH JUST...JUST BE QUIET ALREADY!!
BUGYYUUUU!!

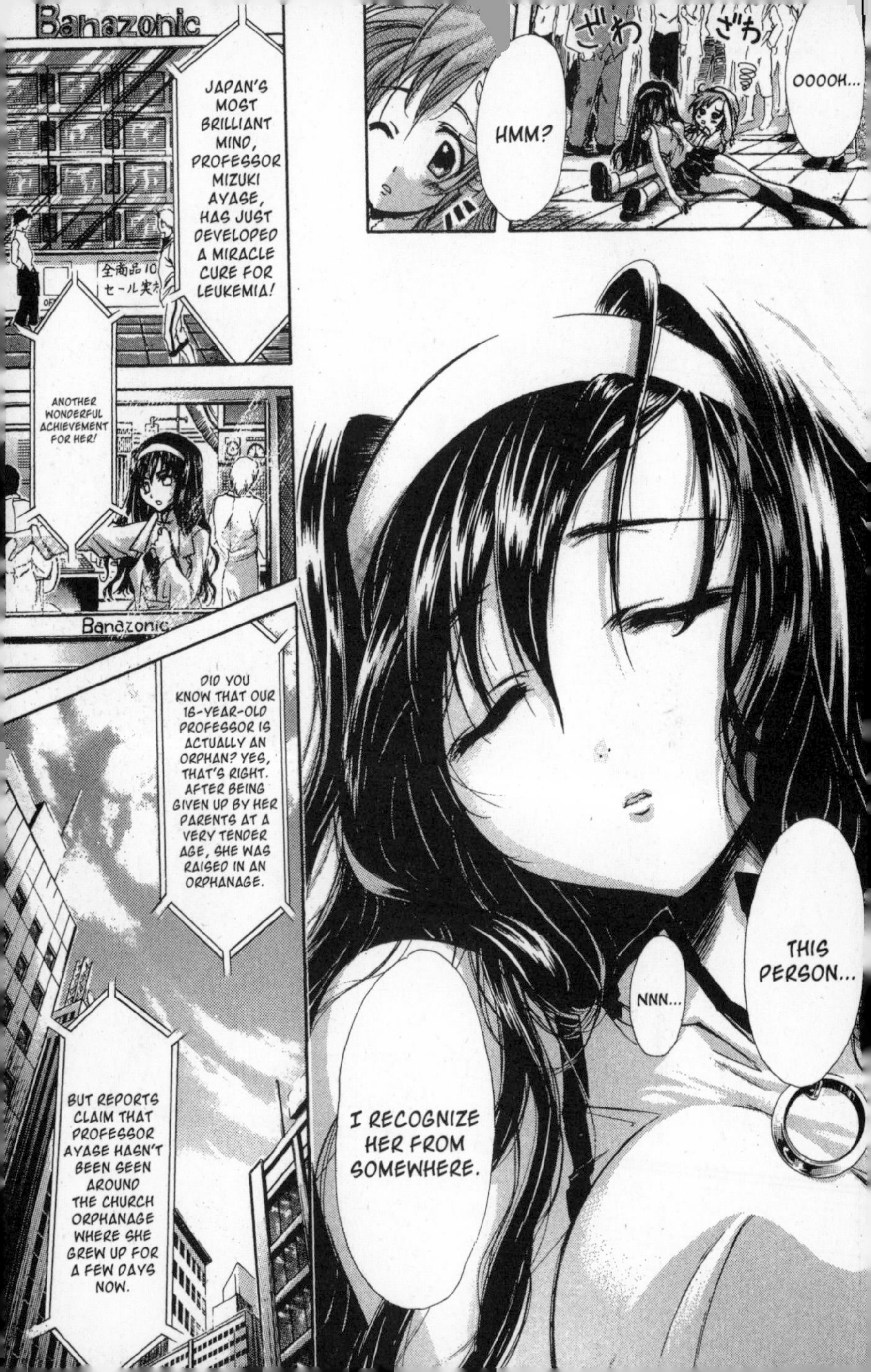
ざわ
ざわ
OOOOH...
HMM?
THIS PERSON...
NNN...
I RECOGNIZE HER FROM SOMEWHERE.
Banazonic
JAPAN'S MOST BRILLIANT MIND, PROFESSOR MIZUKI AYASE, HAS JUST DEVELOPED A MIRACLE CURE FOR LEUKEMIA!
ANOTHER WONDERFUL ACHIEVEMENT FOR HER!
Banazonic
DID YOU KNOW THAT OUR 16-YEAR-OLD PROFESSOR IS ACTUALLY AN ORPHAN? YES, THAT'S RIGHT. AFTER BEING GIVEN UP BY HER PARENTS AT A VERY TENDER AGE, SHE WAS RAISED IN AN ORPHANAGE.
BUT REPORTS CLAIM THAT PROFESSOR AYASE HASN'T BEEN SEEN AROUND THE CHURCH ORPHANAGE WHERE SHE GREW UP FOR A FEW DAYS NOW.

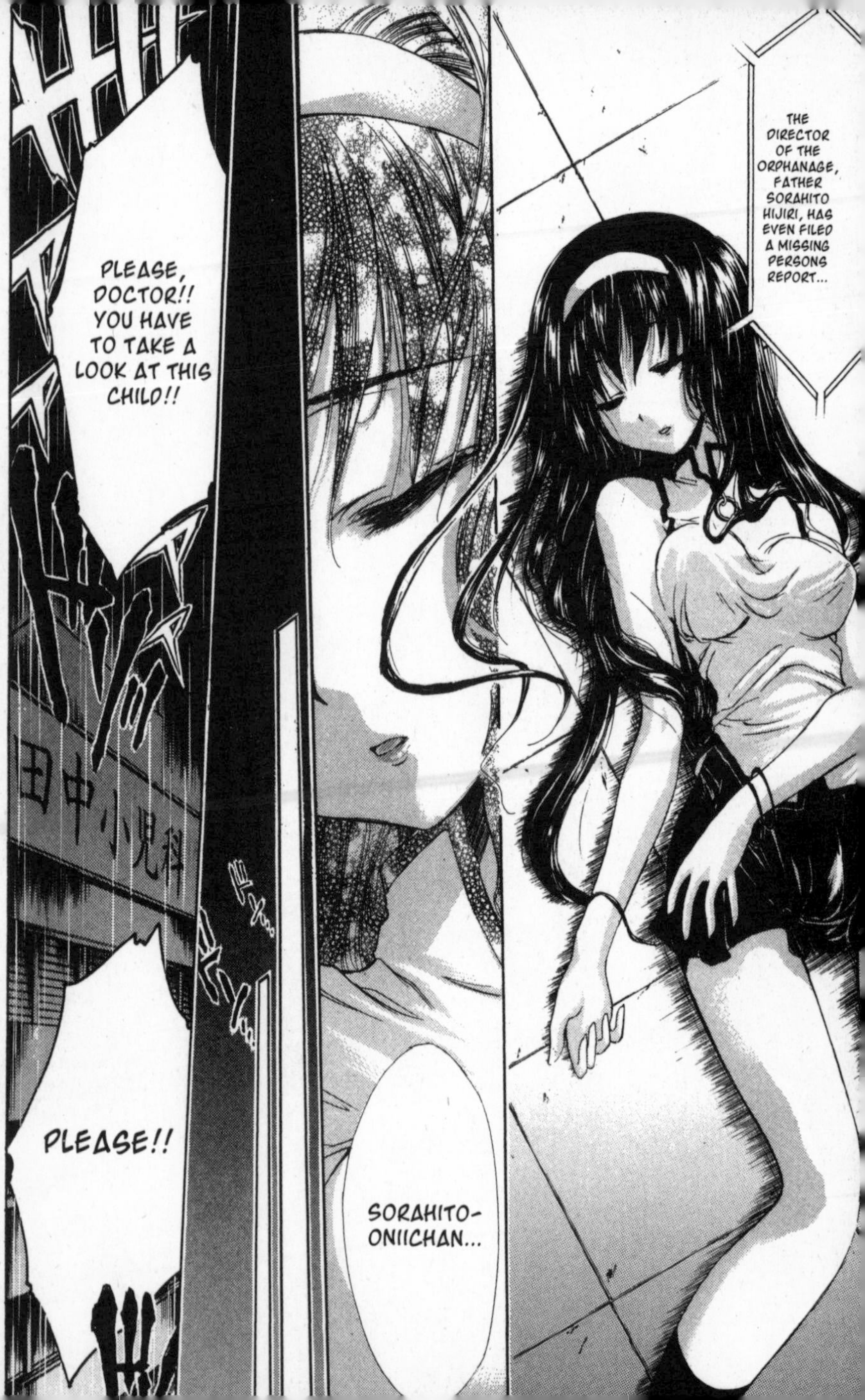
THE DIRECTOR OF THE ORPHANAGE, FATHER SORAHITO HIJIRI, HAS EVEN FILED A MISSING PERSONS REPORT...
SORAHITO-ONIICHAN...
PLEASE, DOCTOR!! YOU HAVE TO TAKE A LOOK AT THIS CHILD!!
田中小児科
PLEASE!!

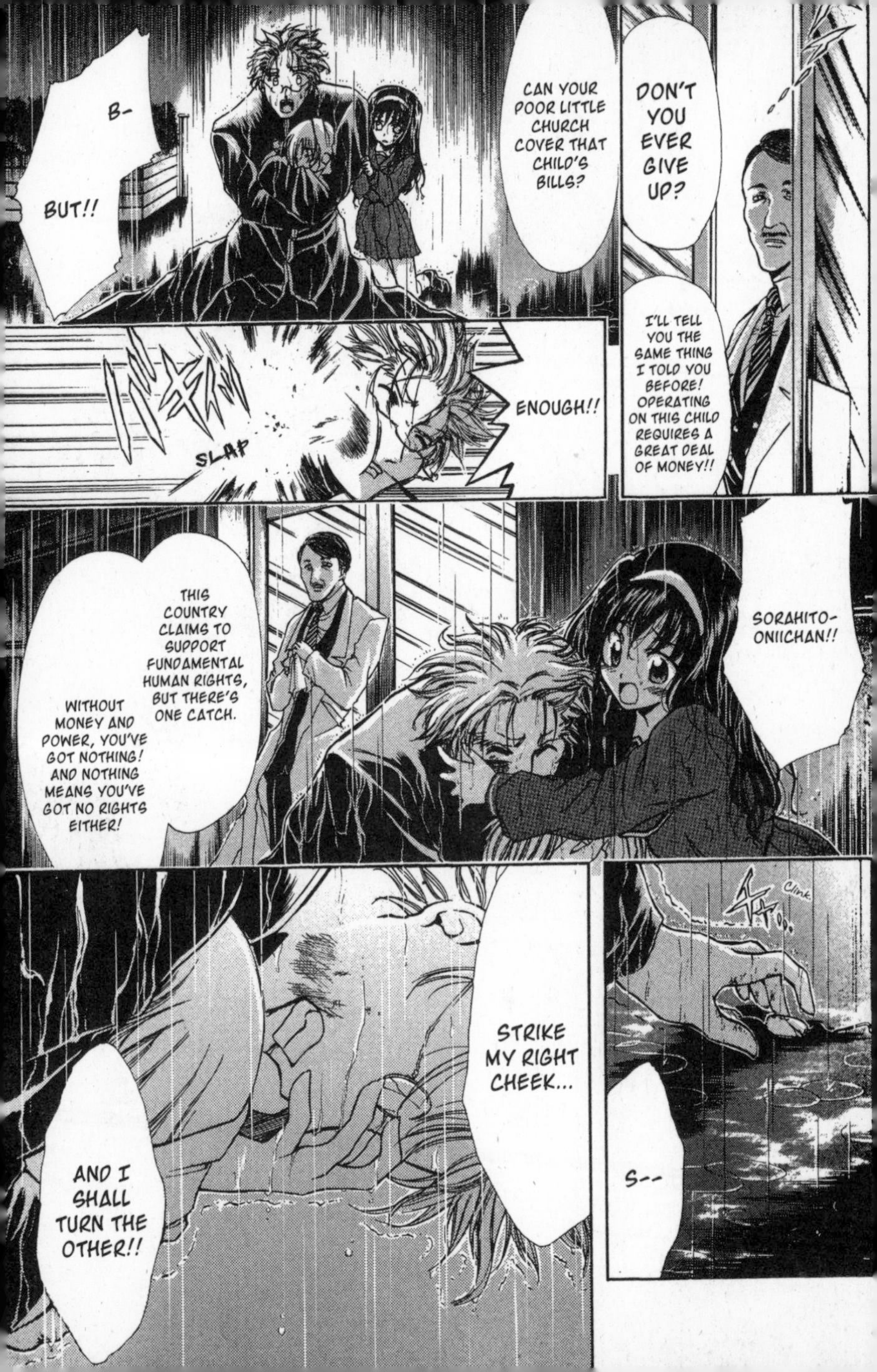
DON'T YOU EVER GIVE UP?
I'LL TELL YOU THE SAME THING I TOLD YOU BEFORE! OPERATING ON THIS CHILD REQUIRES A GREAT DEAL OF MONEY!!
CAN YOUR POOR LITTLE CHURCH COVER THAT CHILD'S BILLS?
B-
BUT!!
ENOUGH!!
SLAP
SORAHITO-ONIICHAN!!
THIS COUNTRY CLAIMS TO SUPPORT FUNDAMENTAL HUMAN RIGHTS, BUT THERE'S ONE CATCH.
WITHOUT MONEY AND POWER, YOU'VE GOT NOTHING! AND NOTHING MEANS YOU'VE GOT NO RIGHTS EITHER!
Clink
S--
STRIKE MY RIGHT CHEEK...
AND I SHALL TURN THE OTHER!!

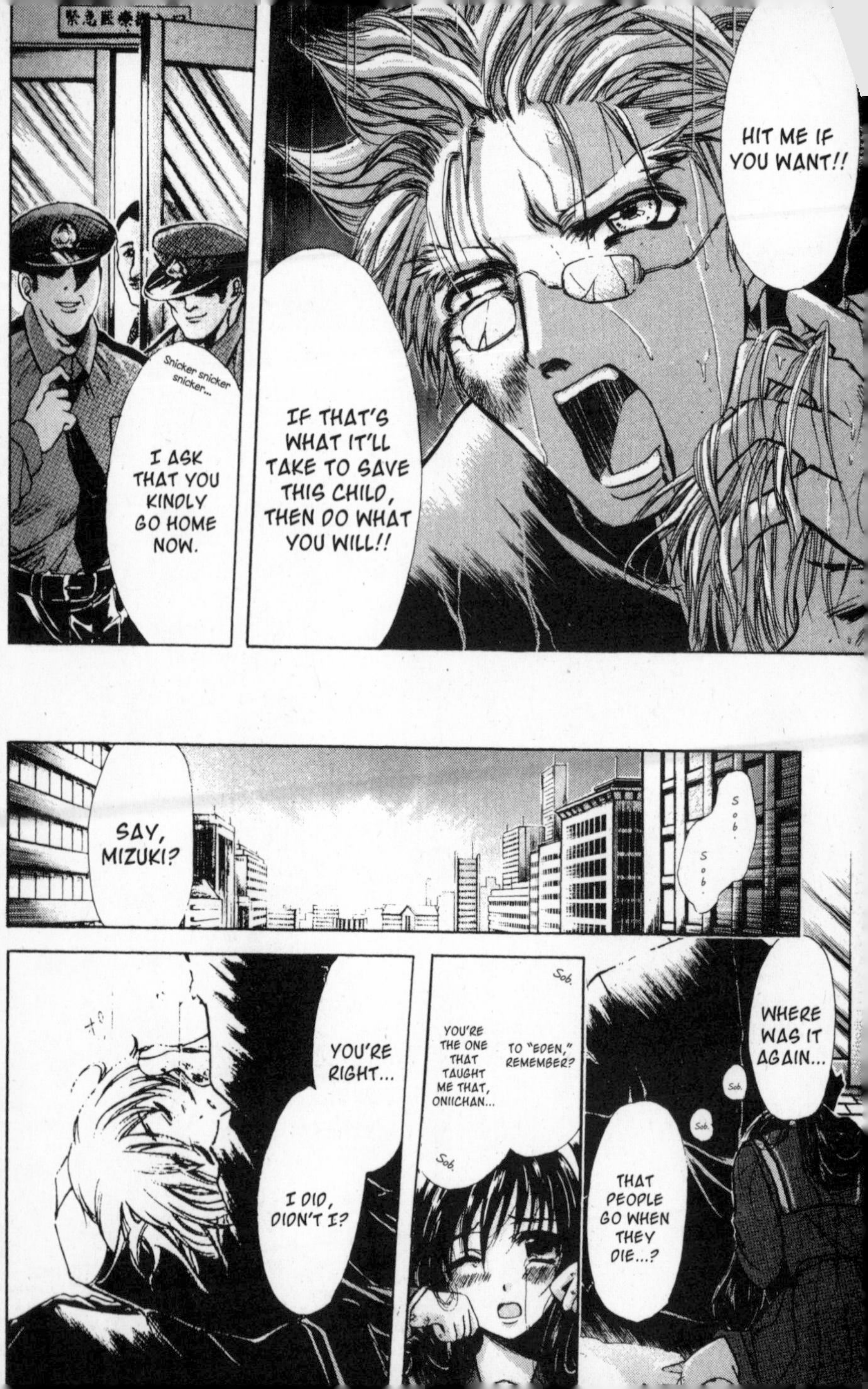
HIT ME IF YOU WANT!!
IF THAT'S WHAT IT'LL TAKE TO SAVE THIS CHILD, THEN DO WHAT YOU WILL!!
Snicker snicker snicker...
I ASK THAT YOU KINDLY GO HOME NOW.
Sob. Sob.
SAY, MIZUKI?
WHERE WAS IT AGAIN...
Sob.
Sob.
THAT PEOPLE GO WHEN THEY DIE...?
Sob.
TO "EDEN," REMEMBER?
YOU'RE THE ONE THAT TAUGHT ME THAT, ONIICHAN...
Sob.
YOU'RE RIGHT...
I DID, DIDN'T I?

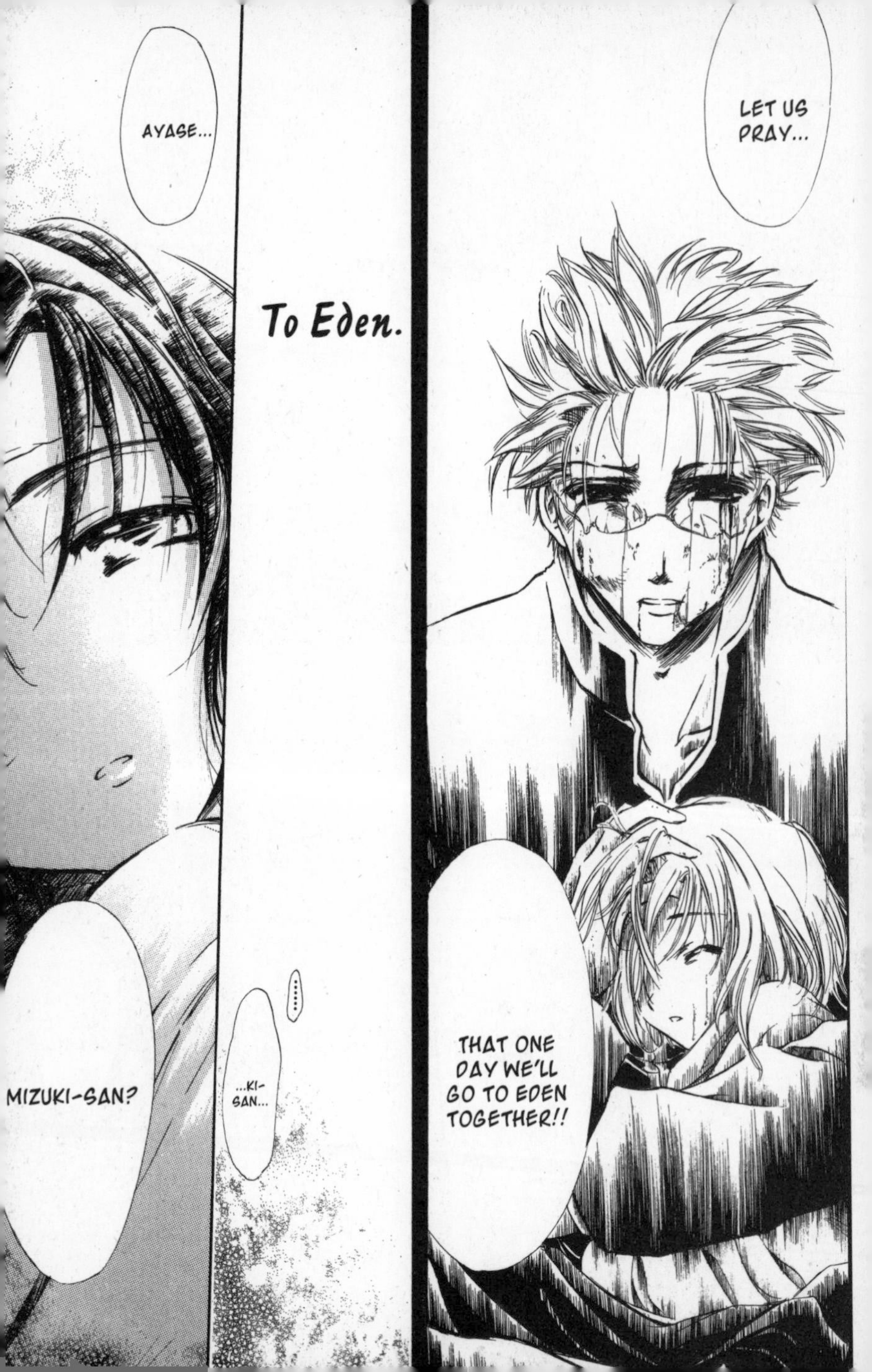
LET US PRAY...
THAT ONE DAY WE'LL GO TO EDEN TOGETHER!!
To Eden.
......
...KI-SAN...
AYASE...
MIZUKI-SAN?

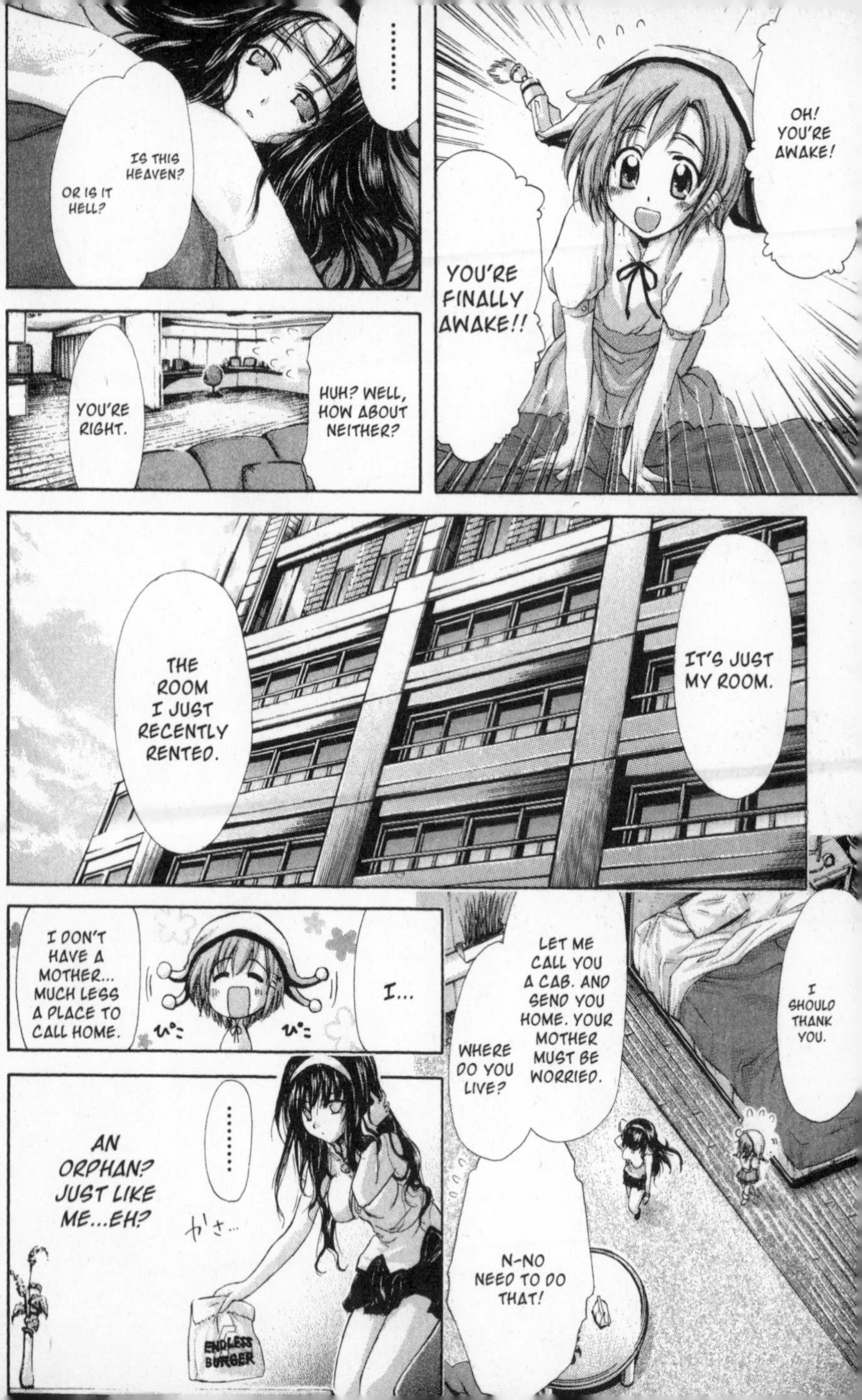
OH! YOU'RE AWAKE!
YOU'RE FINALLY AWAKE!!
......
IS THIS HEAVEN?
OR IS IT HELL?
HUH? WELL, HOW ABOUT NEITHER?
YOU'RE RIGHT.
IT'S JUST MY ROOM.
THE ROOM I JUST RECENTLY RENTED.
I SHOULD THANK YOU.
LET ME CALL YOU A CAB. AND SEND YOU HOME. YOUR MOTHER MUST BE WORRIED.
WHERE DO YOU LIVE?
N-NO NEED TO DO THAT!
I...
I DON'T HAVE A MOTHER... MUCH LESS A PLACE TO CALL HOME.
ぴこ
ぴこ
......
AN ORPHAN? JUST LIKE ME...EH?
かさ...
ENDLESS BURGER

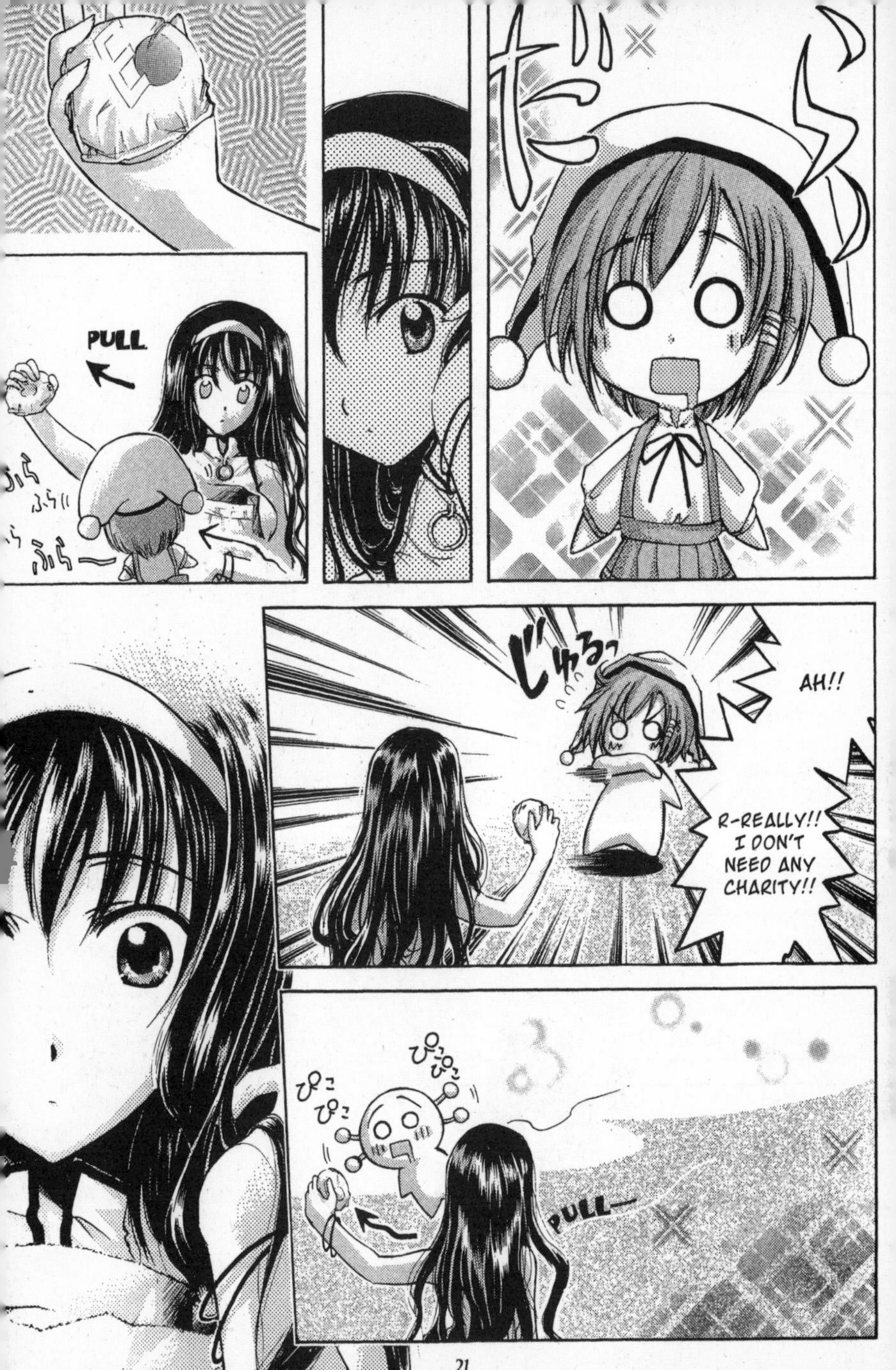
PULL
AH!!
R-REALLY!! I DON'T NEED ANY CHARITY!!
PULL—

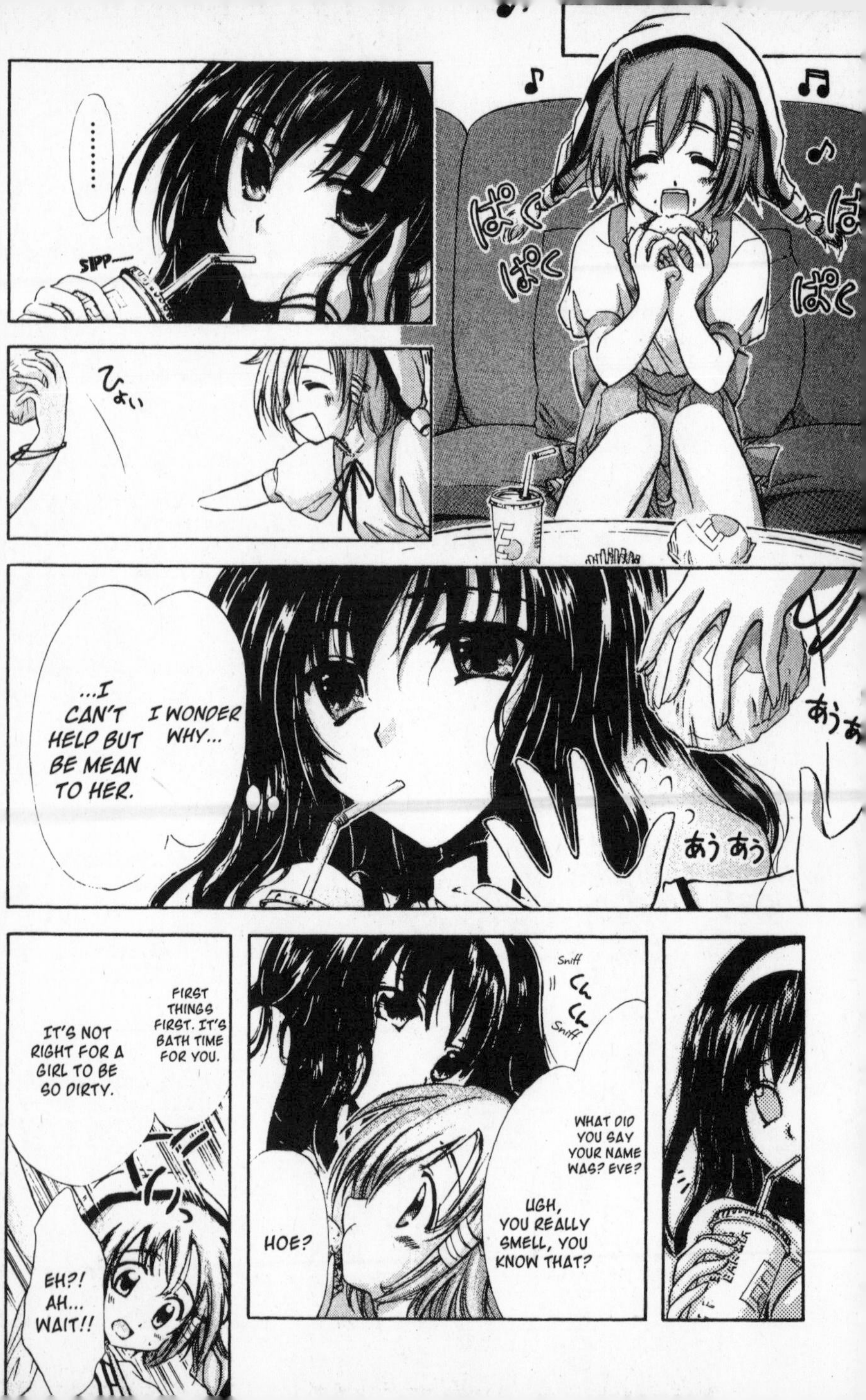
♪ ♫ ♪
は ぱく
ぱく ぱく
......
SIPP----
ひょい
あうあ
あう あう
I WONDER WHY...
...I CAN'T HELP BUT BE MEAN TO HER.
Sniff くん くん Sniff
WHAT DID YOU SAY YOUR NAME WAS? EVE?
UGH, YOU REALLY SMELL, YOU KNOW THAT?
HOE?
FIRST THINGS FIRST. IT'S BATH TIME FOR YOU.
IT'S NOT RIGHT FOR A GIRL TO BE SO DIRTY.
EH?! AH... WAIT!!

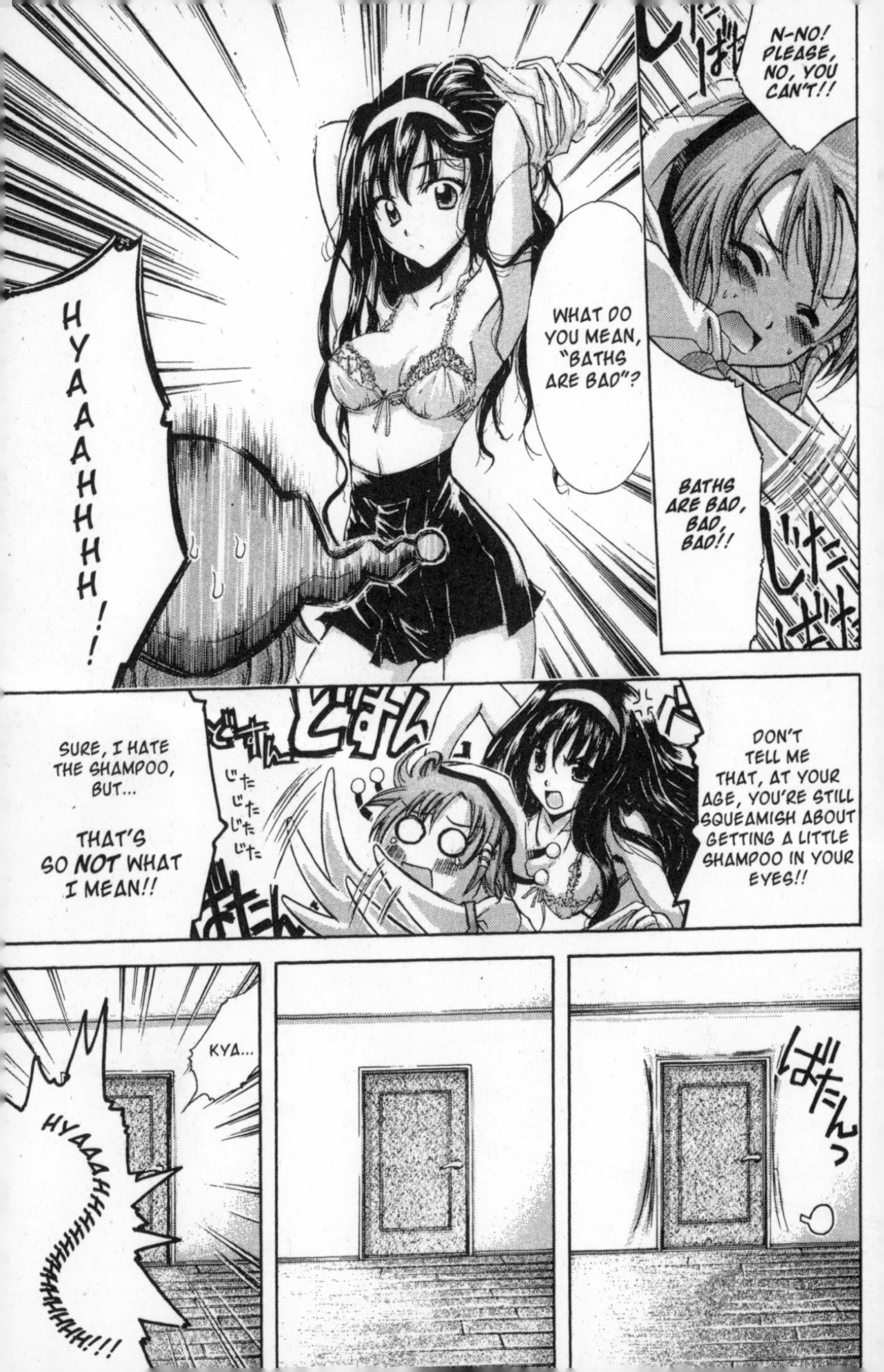
N-NO! PLEASE, NO, YOU CAN'T!!
BATHS ARE BAD, BAD, BAD!!
WHAT DO YOU MEAN, "BATHS ARE BAD"?
HYAAAAHHHHH!!
DON'T TELL ME THAT, AT YOUR AGE, YOU'RE STILL SQUEAMISH ABOUT GETTING A LITTLE SHAMPOO IN YOUR EYES!!
どすん どすん
じた じた じた じた
SURE, I HATE THE SHAMPOO, BUT...
THAT'S SO **NOT** WHAT I MEAN!!
ばたん
ばたんっ
KYA...
HYAAAAHHHHHHHHHHHHHHHHH!!!

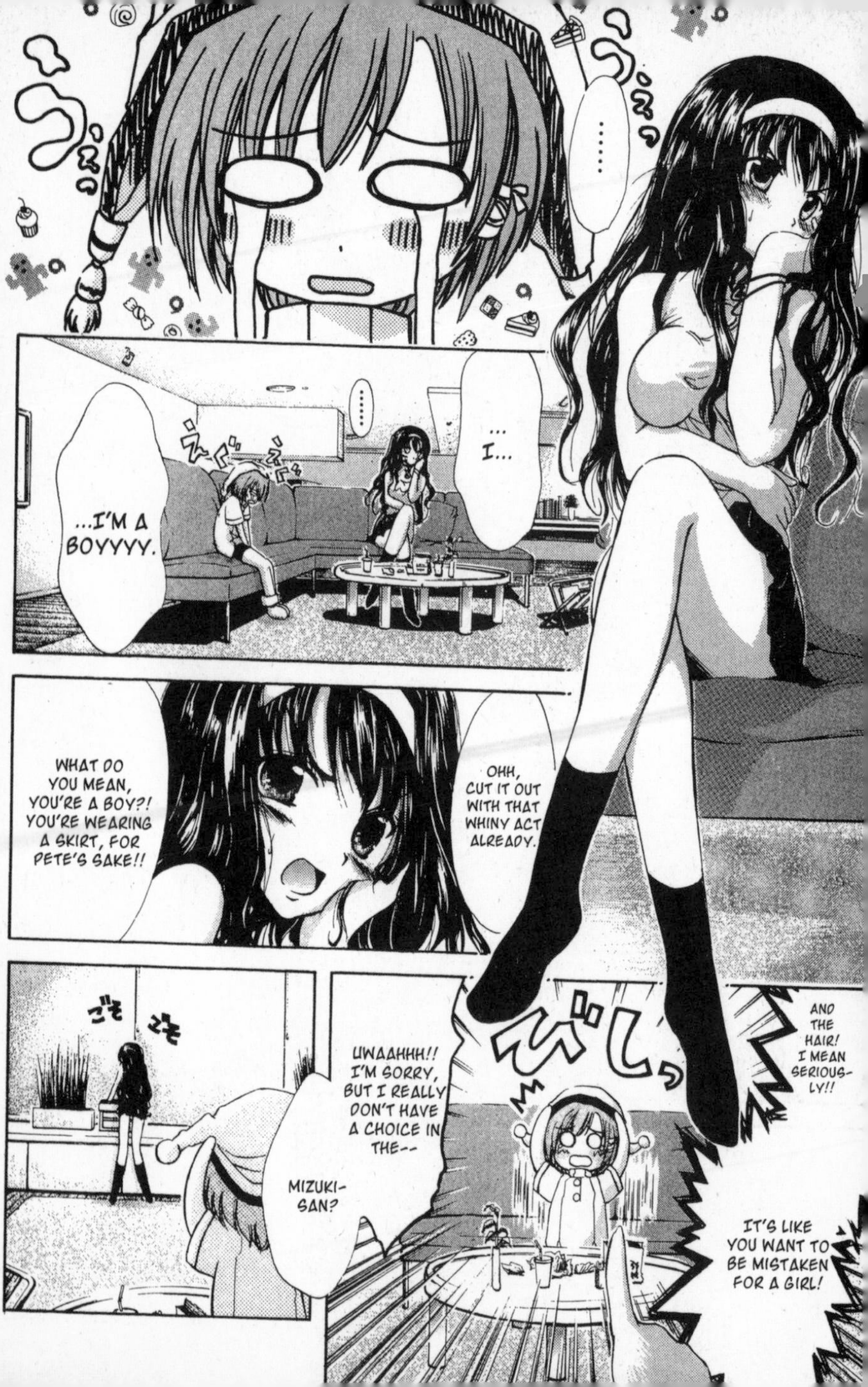
.....
.....
... I...
...I'M A BOYYYY.
OHH, CUT IT OUT WITH THAT WHINY ACT ALREADY.
WHAT DO YOU MEAN, YOU'RE A BOY?! YOU'RE WEARING A SKIRT, FOR PETE'S SAKE!!
AND THE HAIR! I MEAN SERIOUSLY!!
IT'S LIKE YOU WANT TO BE MISTAKEN FOR A GIRL!
UWAAHHH!! I'M SORRY, BUT I REALLY DON'T HAVE A CHOICE IN THE--
MIZUKI-SAN?

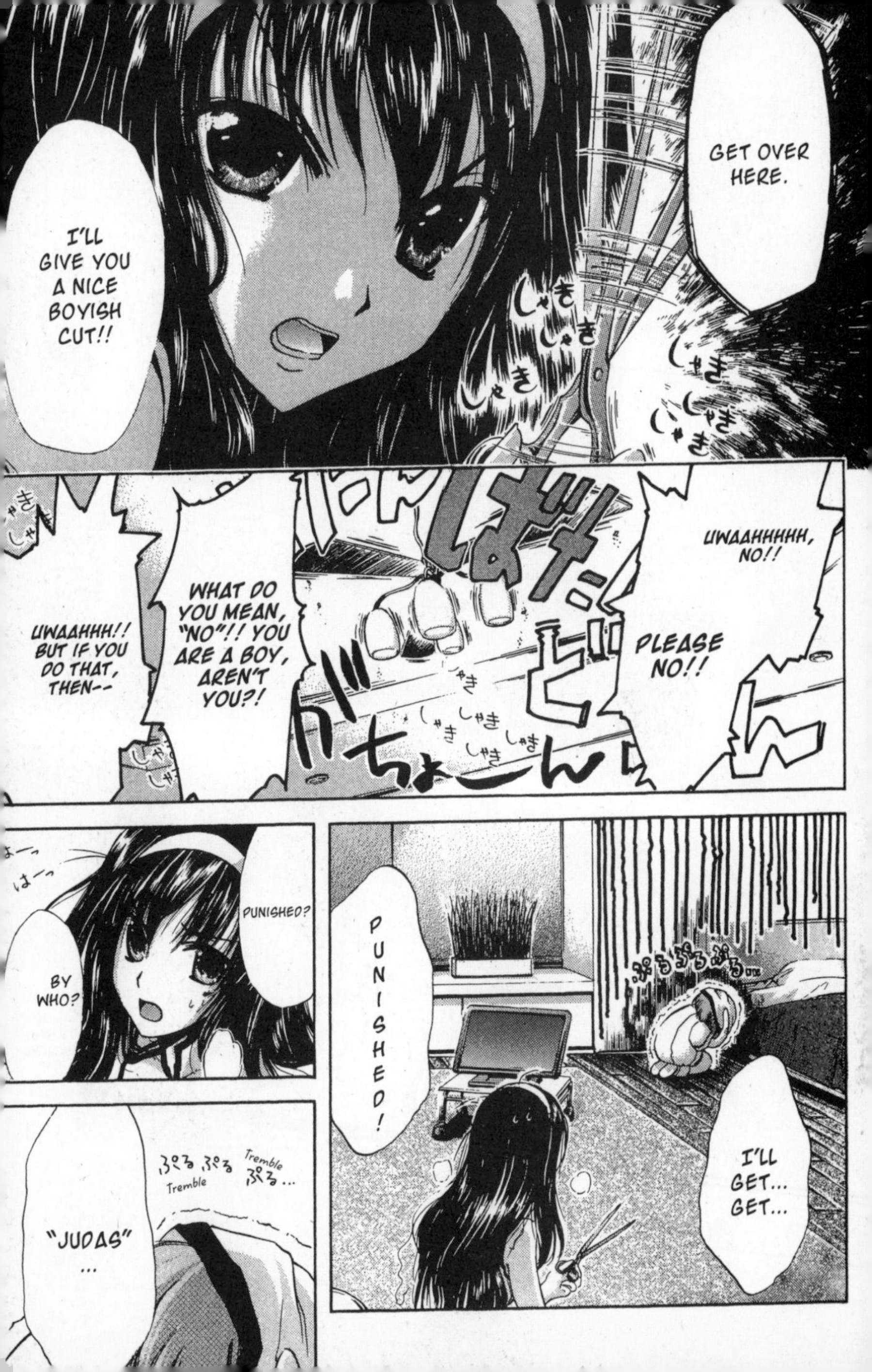
GET OVER HERE.
I'LL GIVE YOU A NICE BOYISH CUT!!
じゃき じゃき じゃき
じゃき じゃき じゃき
UWAAHHHH, NO!!
PLEASE NO!!
WHAT DO YOU MEAN, "NO"!! YOU ARE A BOY, AREN'T YOU?!
UWAAHHH!! BUT IF YOU DO THAT, THEN--
PUNISHED!
ぷるぷるぷる
I'LL GET... GET...
PUNISHED?
BY WHO?
ぷる ぷる ぷる...
Tremble Tremble
"JUDAS" ...

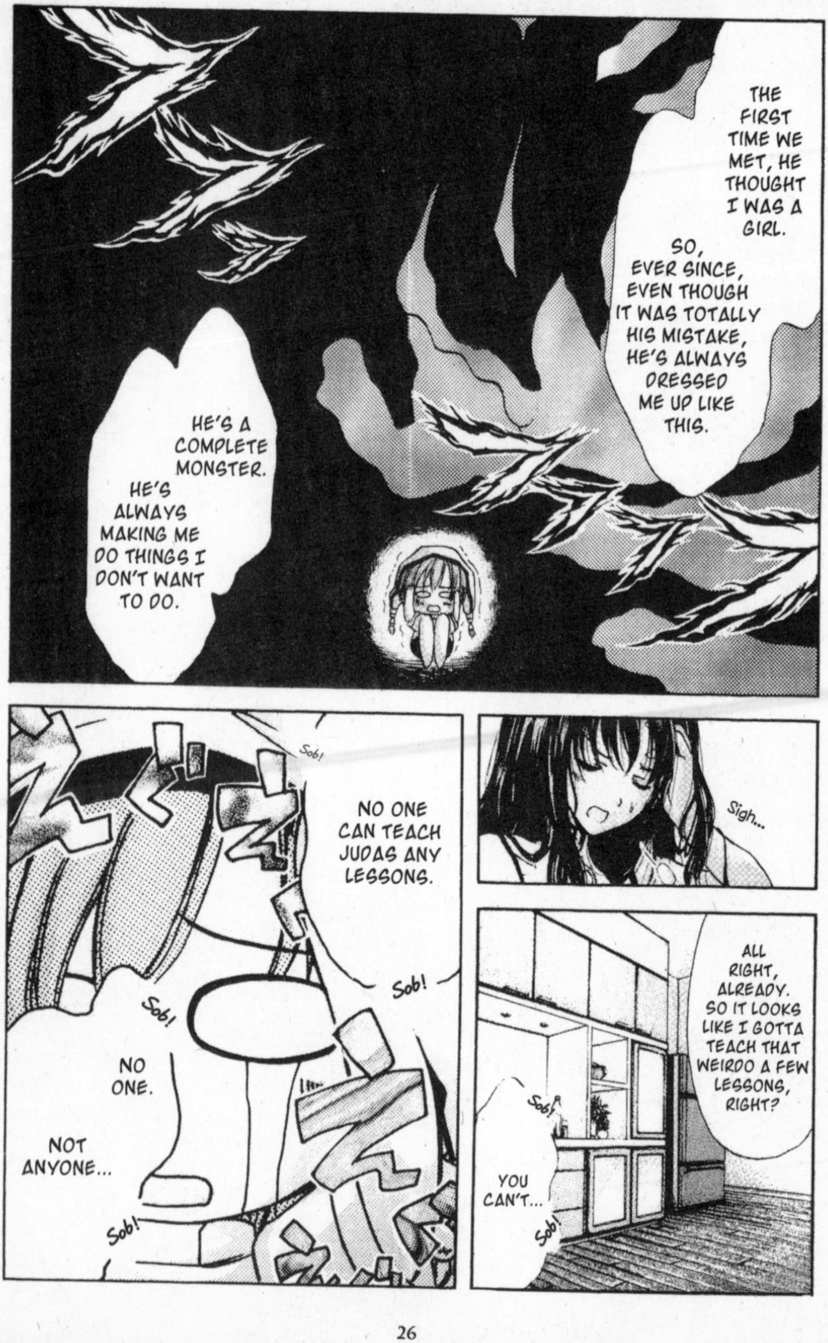
THE FIRST TIME WE MET, HE THOUGHT I WAS A GIRL.
SO, EVER SINCE, EVEN THOUGH IT WAS TOTALLY HIS MISTAKE, HE'S ALWAYS DRESSED ME UP LIKE THIS.
HE'S A COMPLETE MONSTER.
HE'S ALWAYS MAKING ME DO THINGS I DON'T WANT TO DO.
Sigh...
ALL RIGHT, ALREADY. SO IT LOOKS LIKE I GOTTA TEACH THAT WEIRDO A FEW LESSONS, RIGHT?
Sob!
YOU CAN'T...
Sob!
Sob!
NO ONE CAN TEACH JUDAS ANY LESSONS.
Sob!
Sob!
NO ONE.
NOT ANYONE...
Sob!

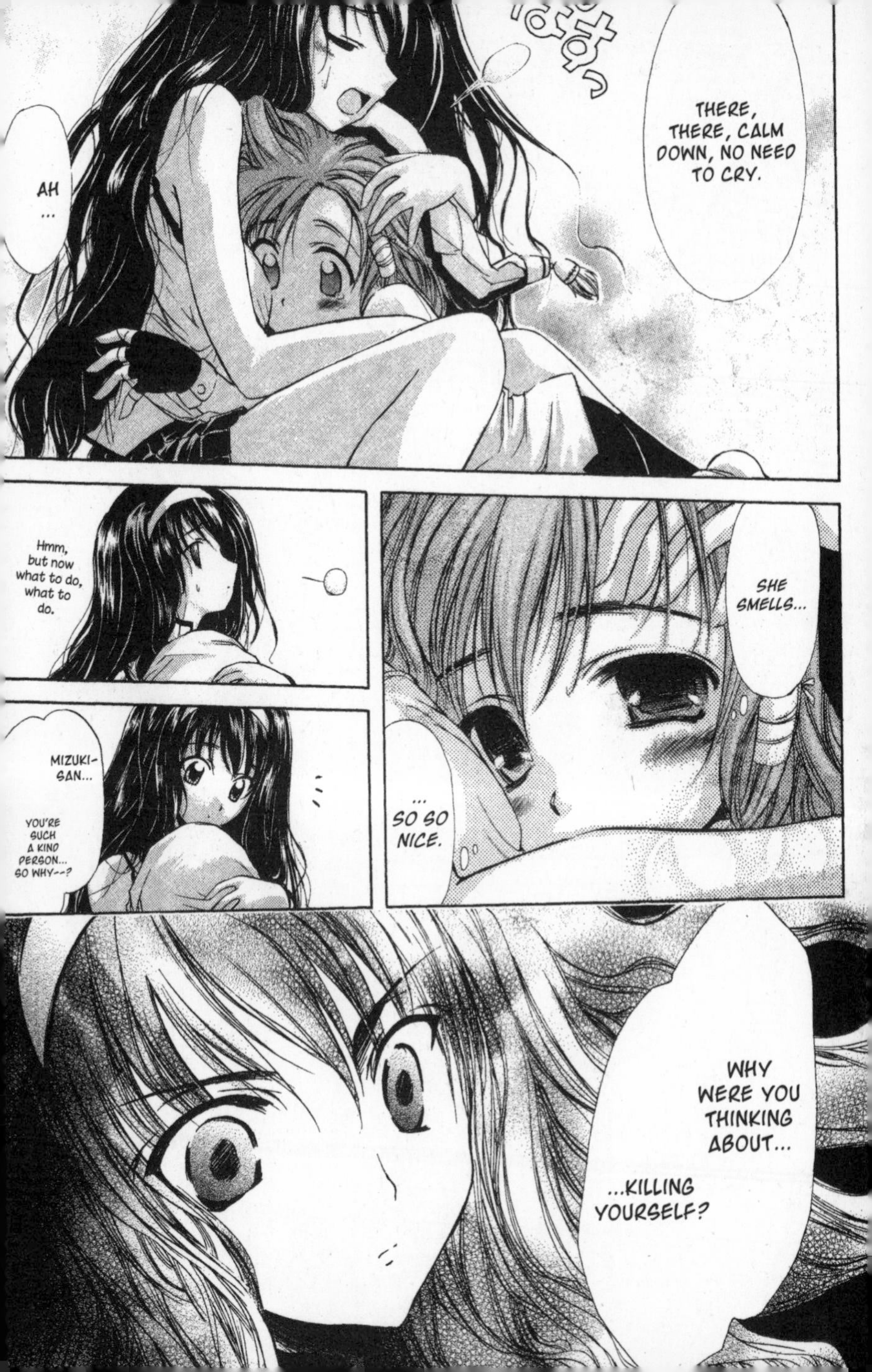
THERE, THERE, CALM DOWN, NO NEED TO CRY.
AH ...
SHE SMELLS...
... SO SO NICE.
Hmm, but now what to do, what to do.
MIZUKI-SAN...
YOU'RE SUCH A KIND PERSON... SO WHY--?
WHY WERE YOU THINKING ABOUT...
...KILLING YOURSELF?

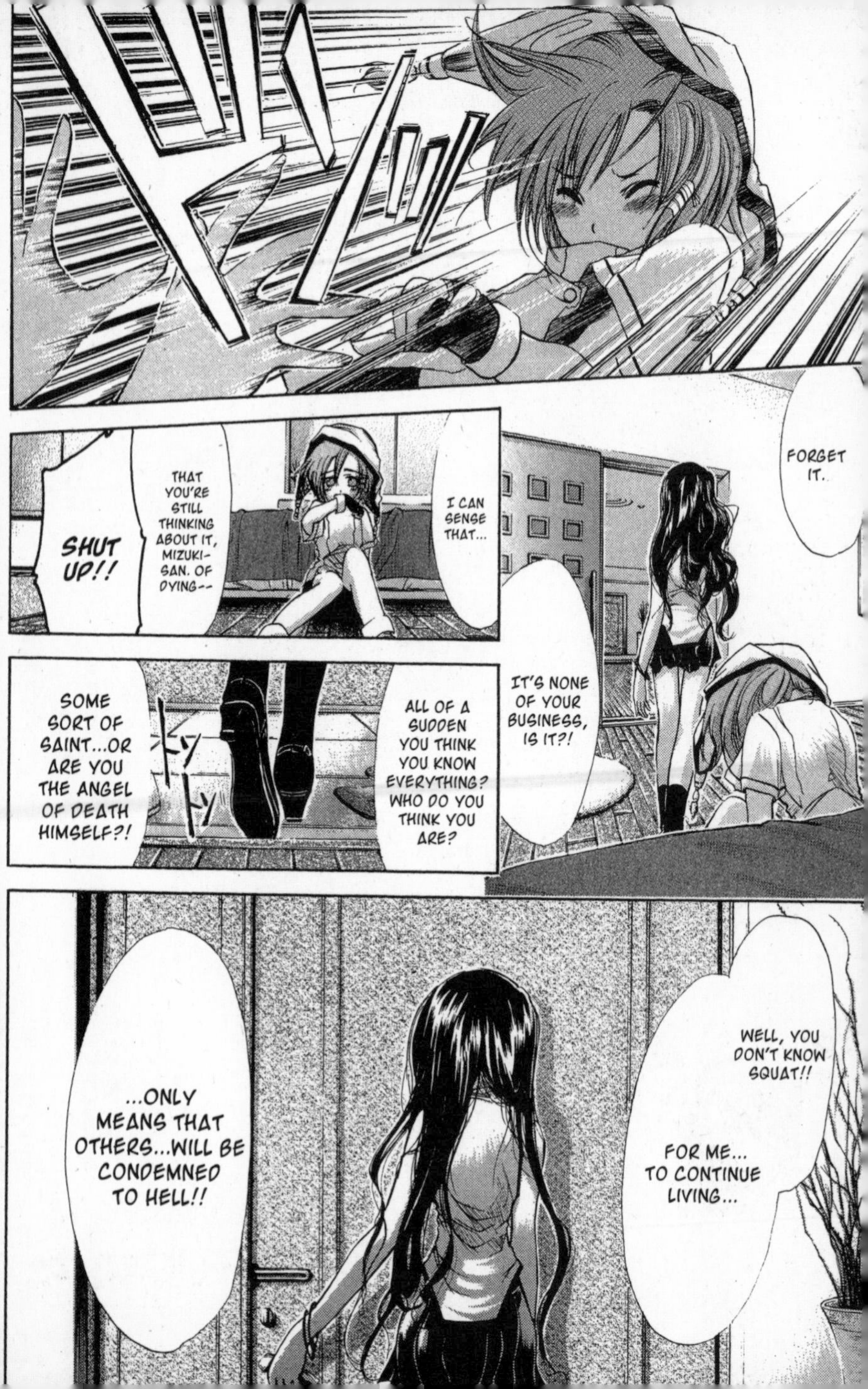
FORGET IT.
IT'S NONE OF YOUR BUSINESS, IS IT?!
I CAN SENSE THAT...
THAT YOU'RE STILL THINKING ABOUT IT, MIZUKI-SAN. OF DYING--
SHUT UP!!
ALL OF A SUDDEN YOU THINK YOU KNOW EVERYTHING? WHO DO YOU THINK YOU ARE?
SOME SORT OF SAINT...OR ARE YOU THE ANGEL OF DEATH HIMSELF?!
WELL, YOU DON'T KNOW SQUAT!!
FOR ME... TO CONTINUE LIVING...
...ONLY MEANS THAT OTHERS...WILL BE CONDEMNED TO HELL!!

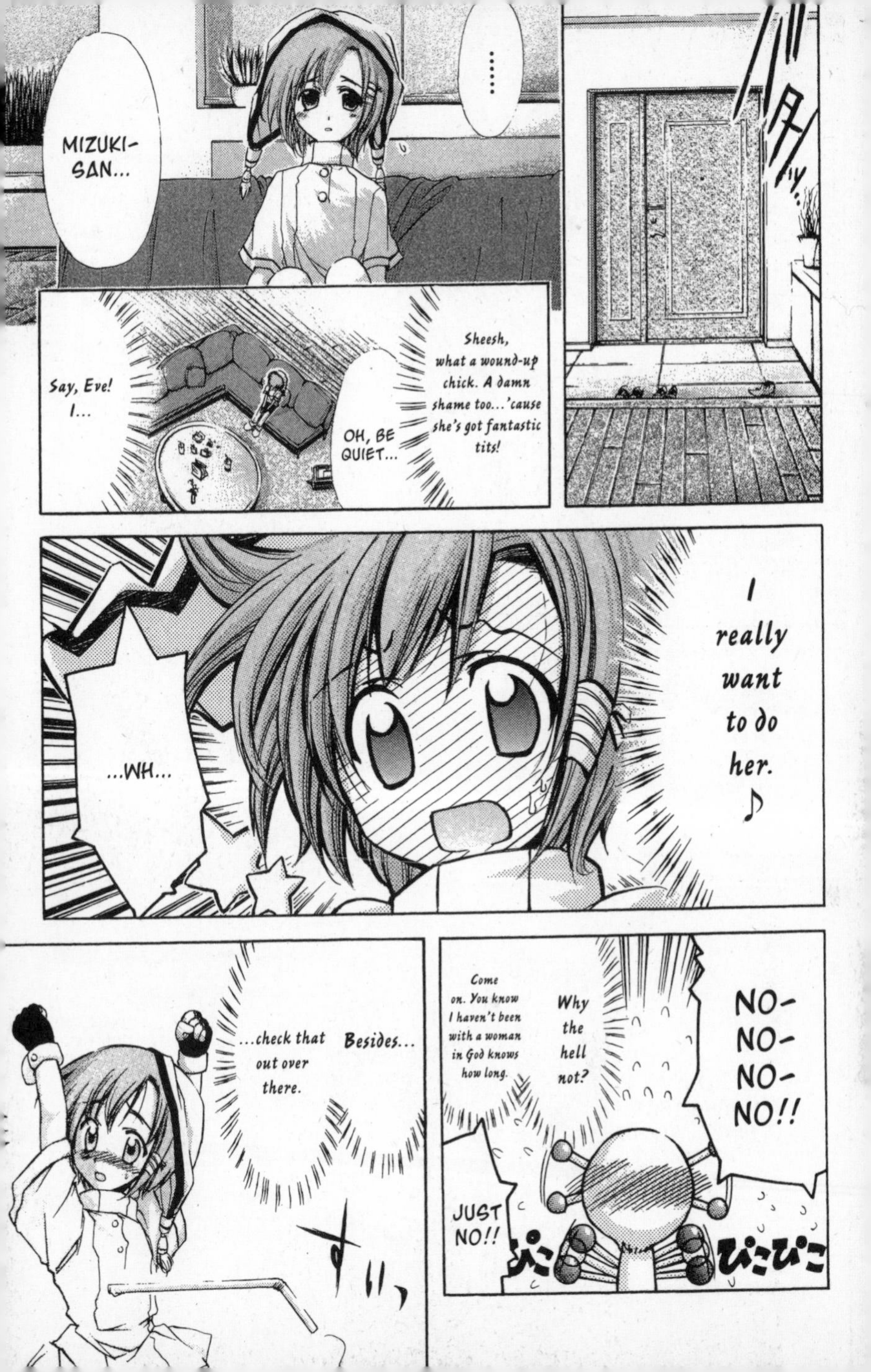

......
MIZUKI-SAN...
Sheesh, what a wound-up chick. A damn shame too...'cause she's got fantastic tits!
OH, BE QUIET...
Say, Eve! I...
I really want to do her. ♪
...WH...
NO-NO-NO-NO!!
Why the hell not?
Come on. You know I haven't been with a woman in God knows how long.
JUST NO!!
ぴこぴこ
Besides...
...check that out over there.

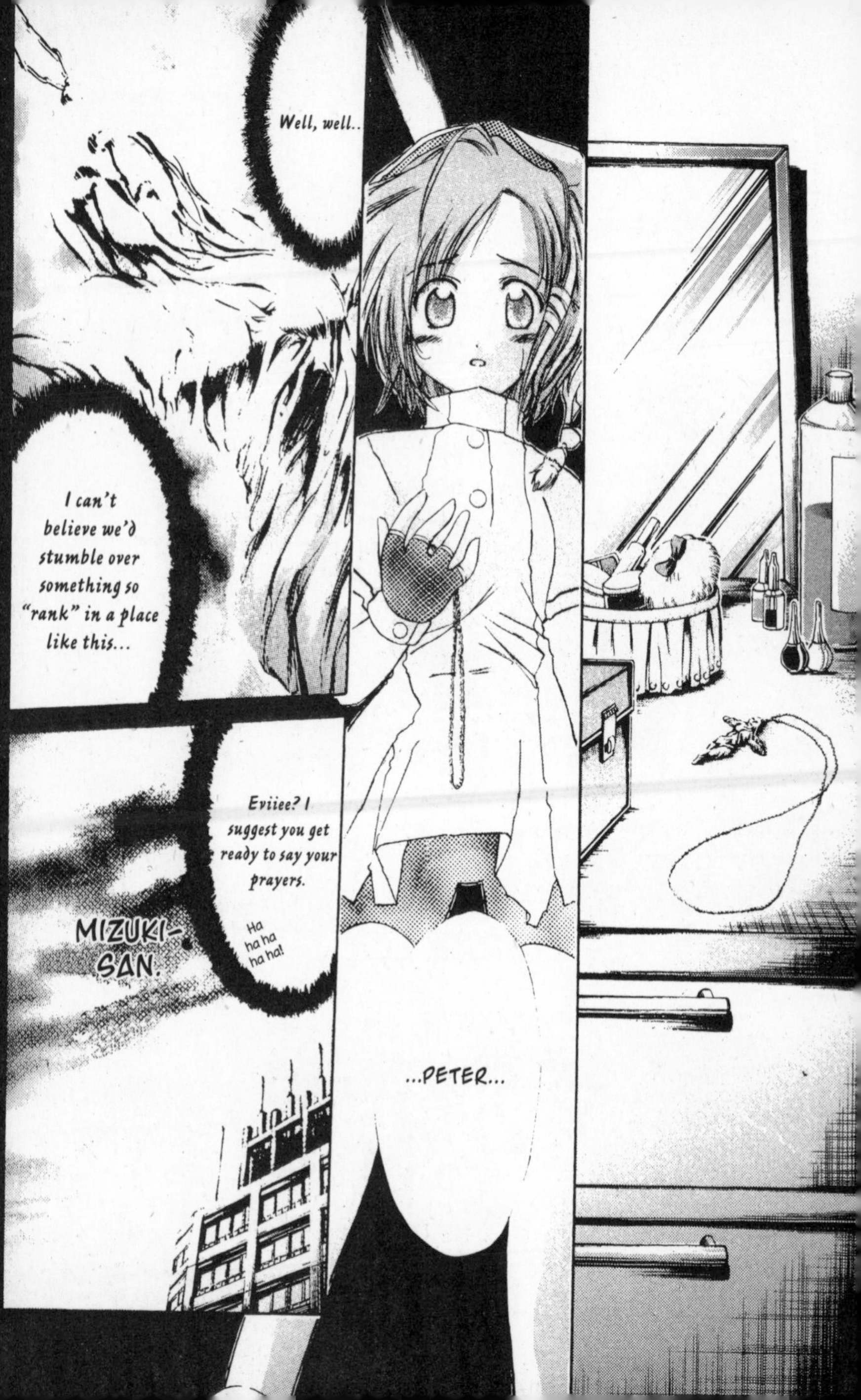
...PETER...
Well, well..
I can't believe we'd stumble over something so "rank" in a place like this...
Eviiee? I suggest you get ready to say your prayers.
Ha ha ha ha ha!
MIZUKI-SAN.

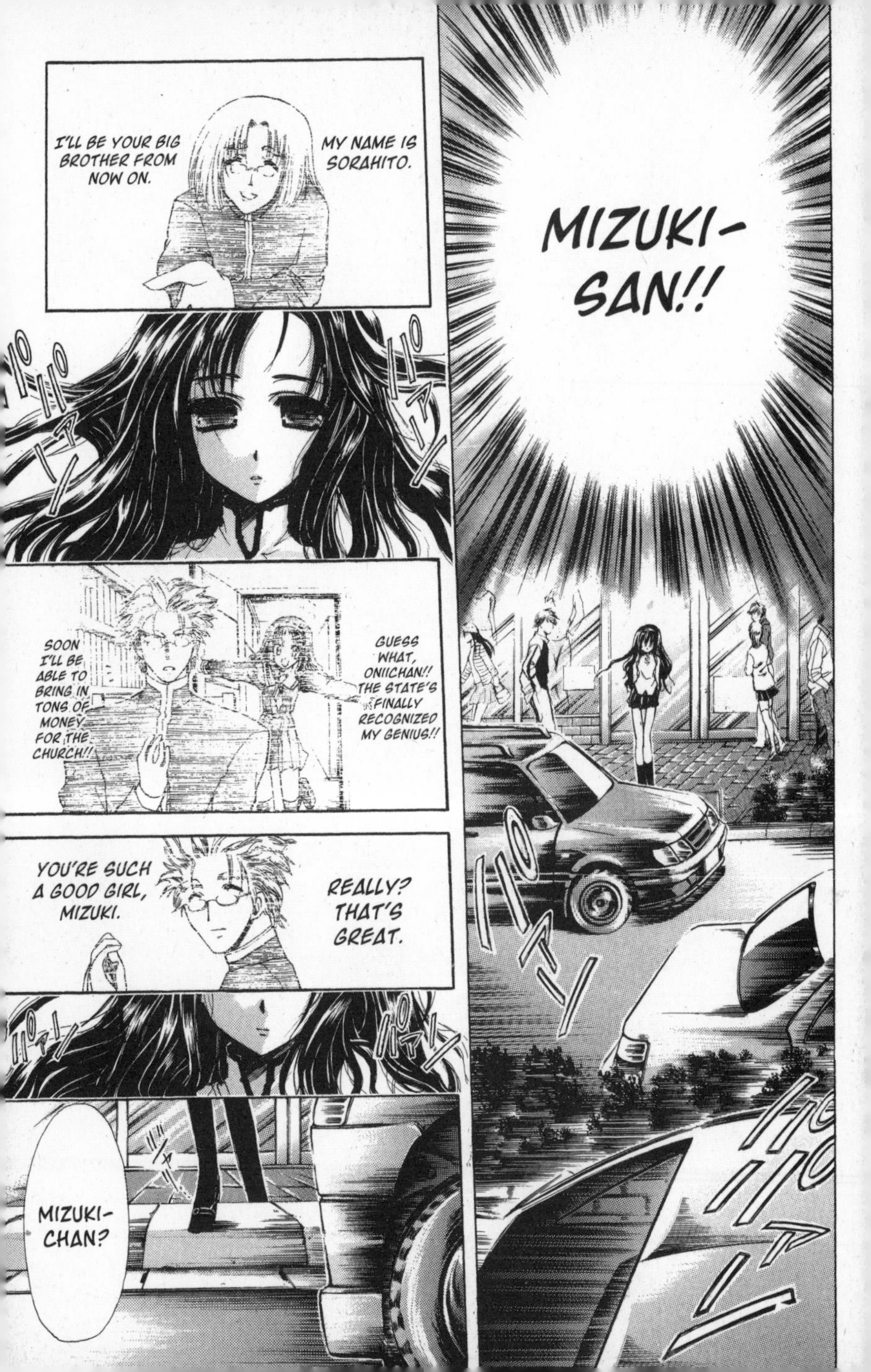
MIZUKI-SAN!!
MY NAME IS SORAHITO.
I'LL BE YOUR BIG BROTHER FROM NOW ON.
GUESS WHAT, ONIICHAN!! THE STATE'S FINALLY RECOGNIZED MY GENIUS!!
SOON I'LL BE ABLE TO BRING IN TONS OF MONEY FOR THE CHURCH!!
REALLY? THAT'S GREAT.
YOU'RE SUCH A GOOD GIRL, MIZUKI.
MIZUKI-CHAN?

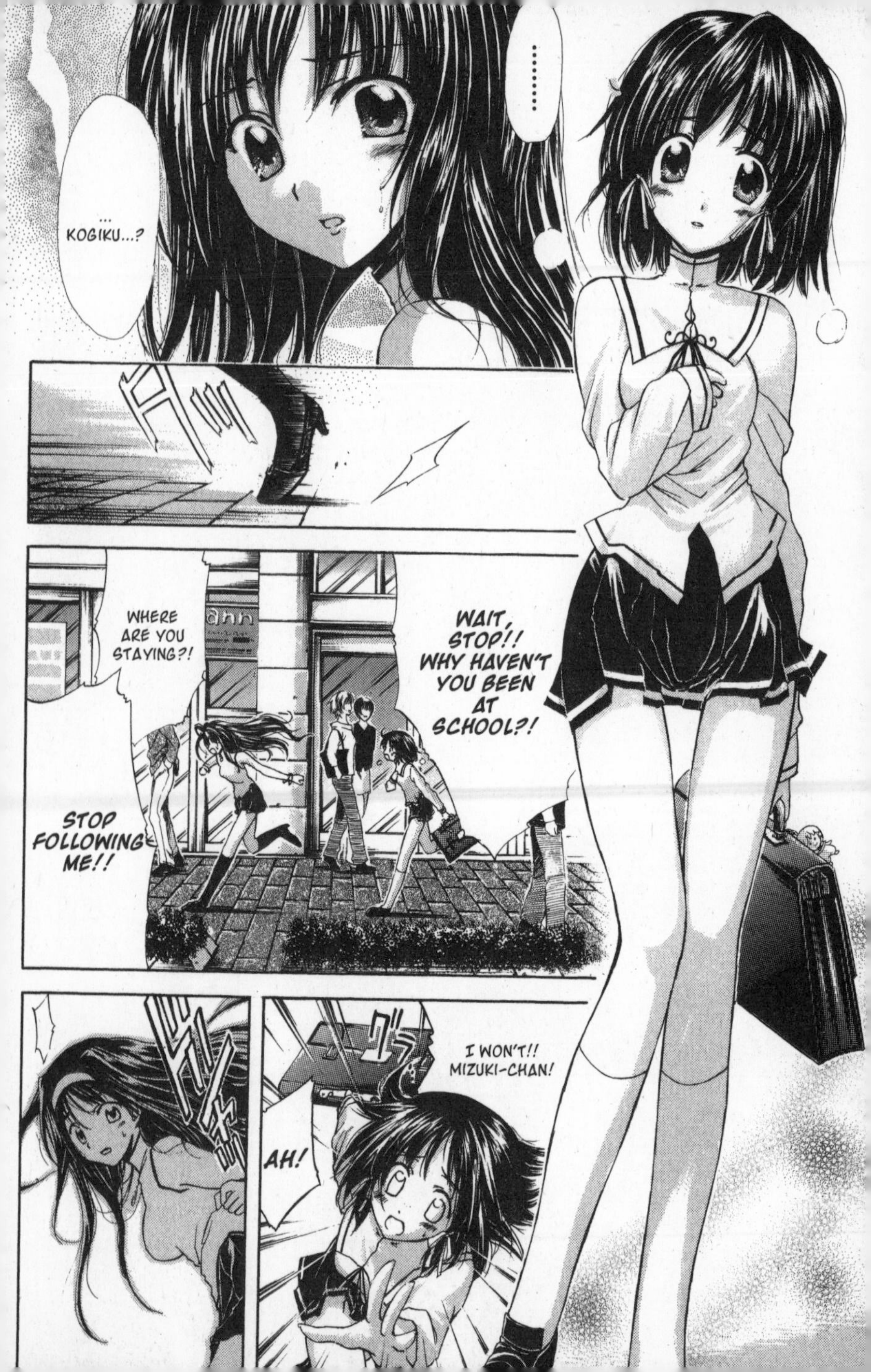
......
... KOGIKU...?
WAIT, STOP!! WHY HAVEN'T YOU BEEN AT SCHOOL?!
WHERE ARE YOU STAYING?!
STOP FOLLOWING ME!!
I WON'T!! MIZUKI-CHAN!
AH!
!

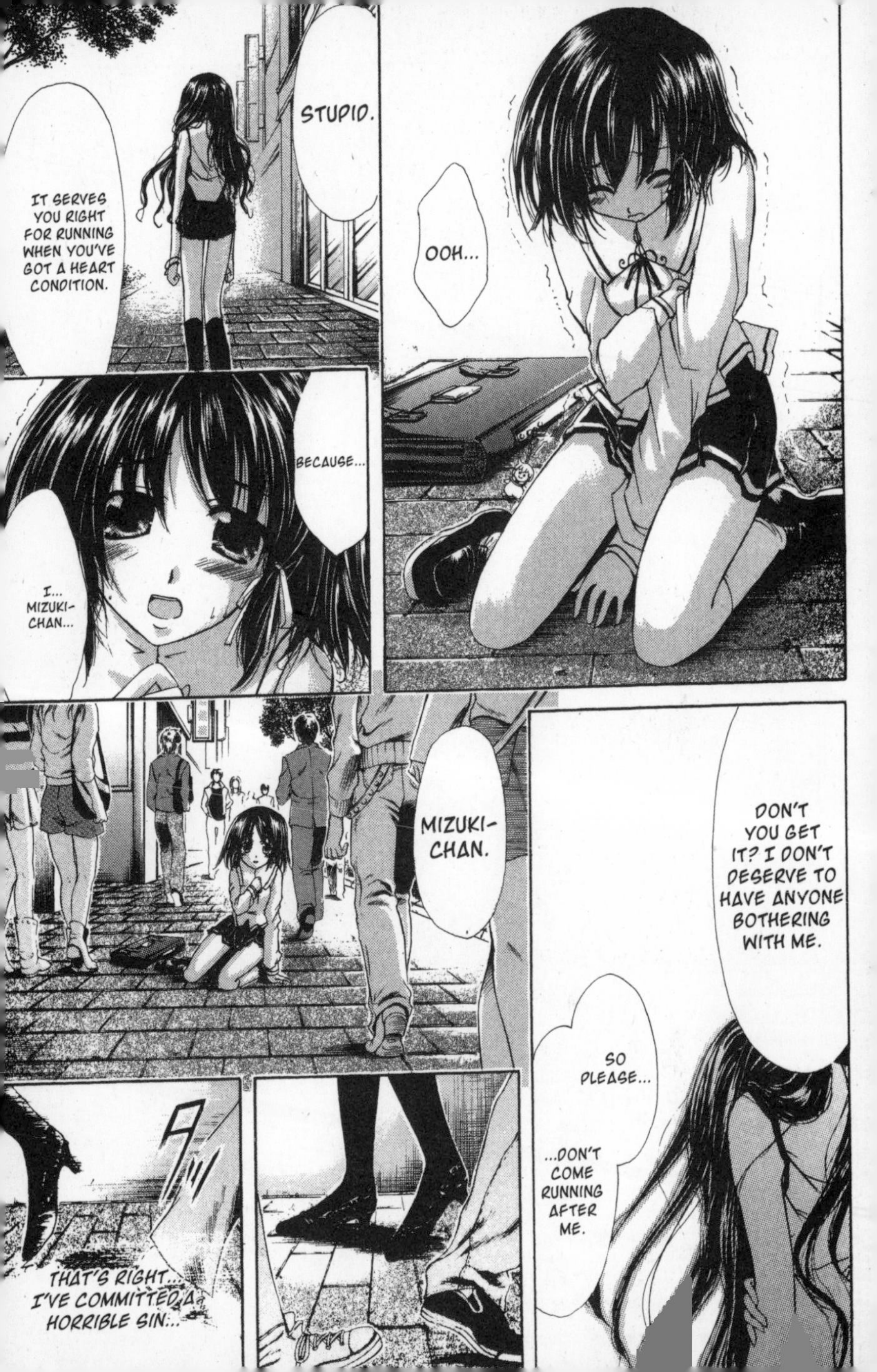
OOH...
STUPID.
IT SERVES YOU RIGHT FOR RUNNING WHEN YOU'VE GOT A HEART CONDITION.
BECAUSE...
I... MIZUKI-CHAN...
DON'T YOU GET IT? I DON'T DESERVE TO HAVE ANYONE BOTHERING WITH ME.
SO PLEASE...
...DON'T COME RUNNING AFTER ME.
MIZUKI-CHAN.
THAT'S RIGHT... I'VE COMMITTED A HORRIBLE SIN...

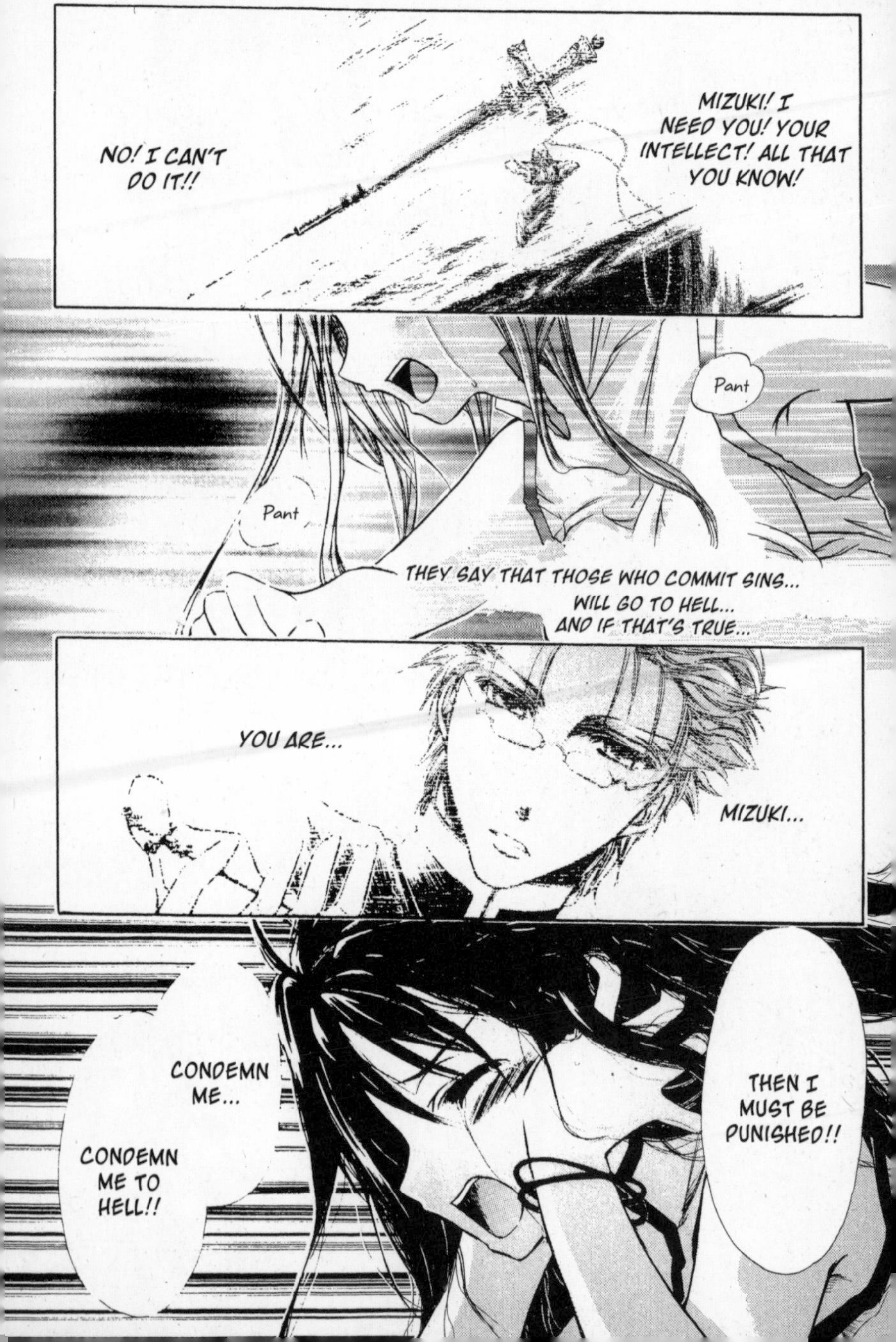
MIZUKI! I NEED YOU! YOUR INTELLECT! ALL THAT YOU KNOW!
NO! I CAN'T DO IT!!
Pant
Pant
THEY SAY THAT THOSE WHO COMMIT SINS... WILL GO TO HELL... AND IF THAT'S TRUE...
YOU ARE...
MIZUKI...
THEN I MUST BE PUNISHED!!
CONDEMN ME...
CONDEMN ME TO HELL!!

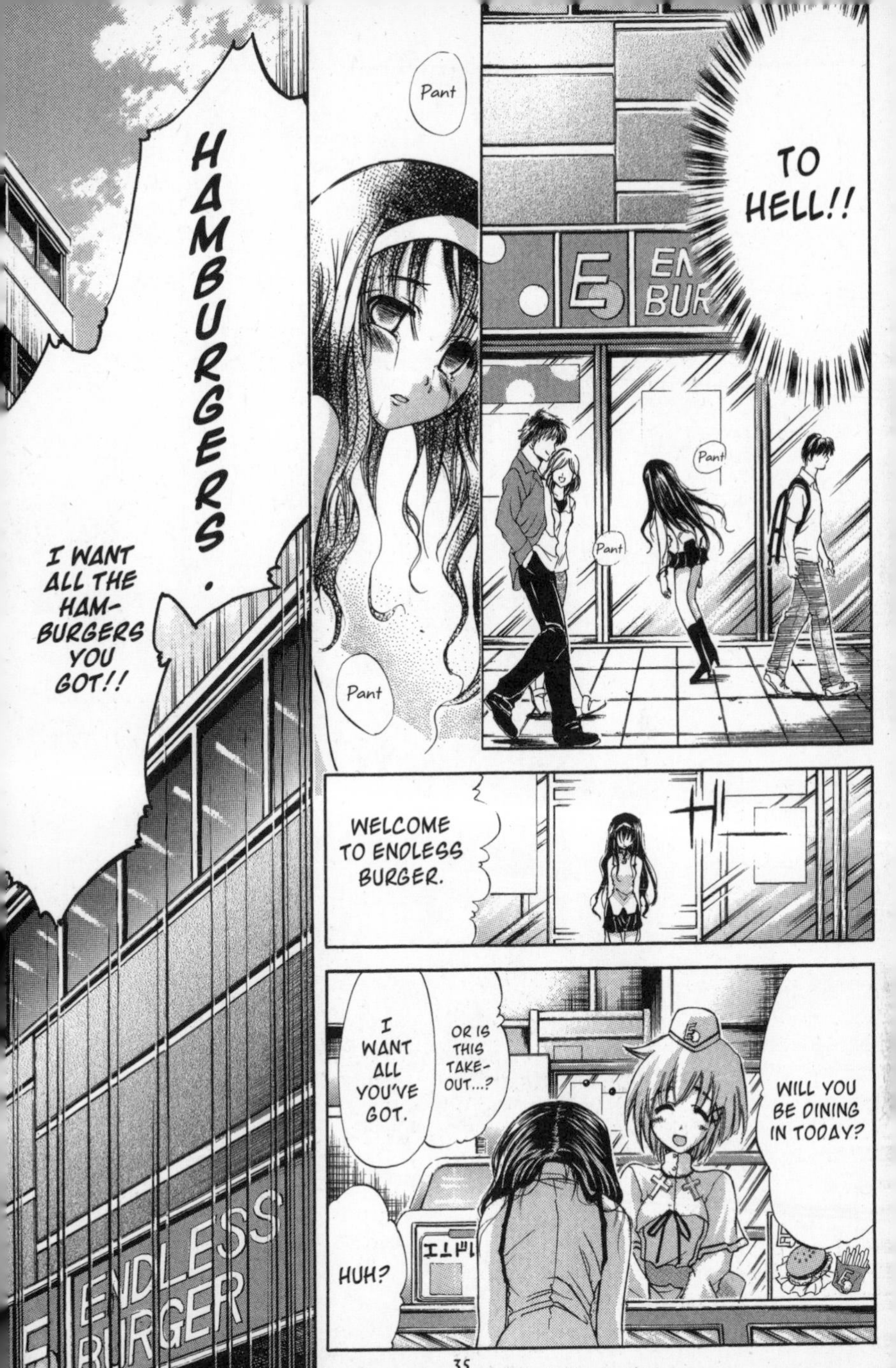
TO HELL!!
Pant
Pant
Pant
Pant
WELCOME TO ENDLESS BURGER.
WILL YOU BE DINING IN TODAY?
OR IS THIS TAKE-OUT...?
I WANT ALL YOU'VE GOT.
HUH?
HAMBURGERS.
I WANT ALL THE HAM-BURGERS YOU GOT!!
ENDLESS BURGER

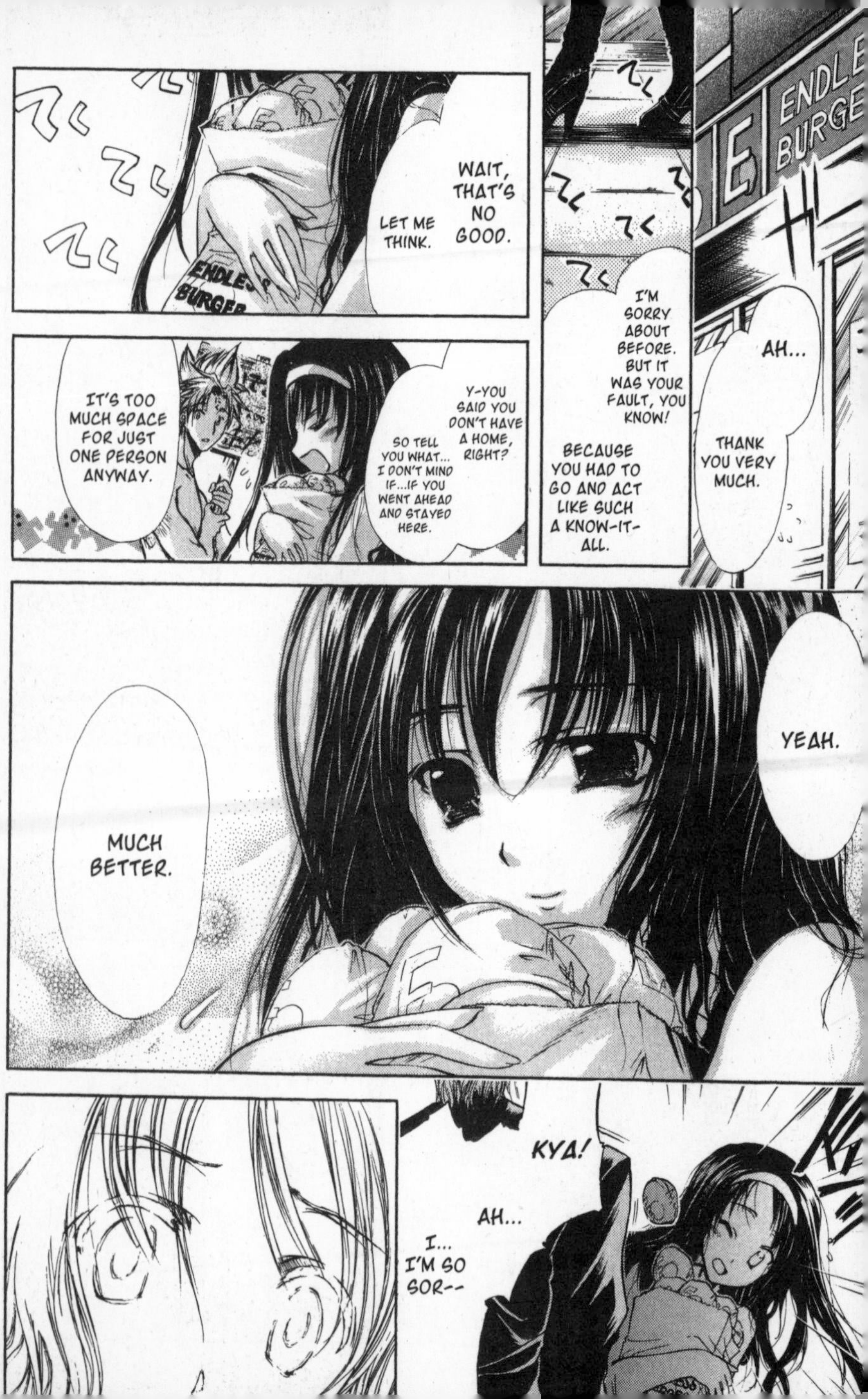
AH...
THANK YOU VERY MUCH.
I'M SORRY ABOUT BEFORE. BUT IT WAS YOUR FAULT, YOU KNOW!
BECAUSE YOU HAD TO GO AND ACT LIKE SUCH A KNOW-IT-ALL.
WAIT, THAT'S NO GOOD.
LET ME THINK.
Y-YOU SAID YOU DON'T HAVE A HOME, RIGHT?
SO TELL YOU WHAT... I DON'T MIND IF...IF YOU WENT AHEAD AND STAYED HERE.
IT'S TOO MUCH SPACE FOR JUST ONE PERSON ANYWAY.
YEAH.
MUCH BETTER.
KYA!
AH...
I... I'M SO SOR--

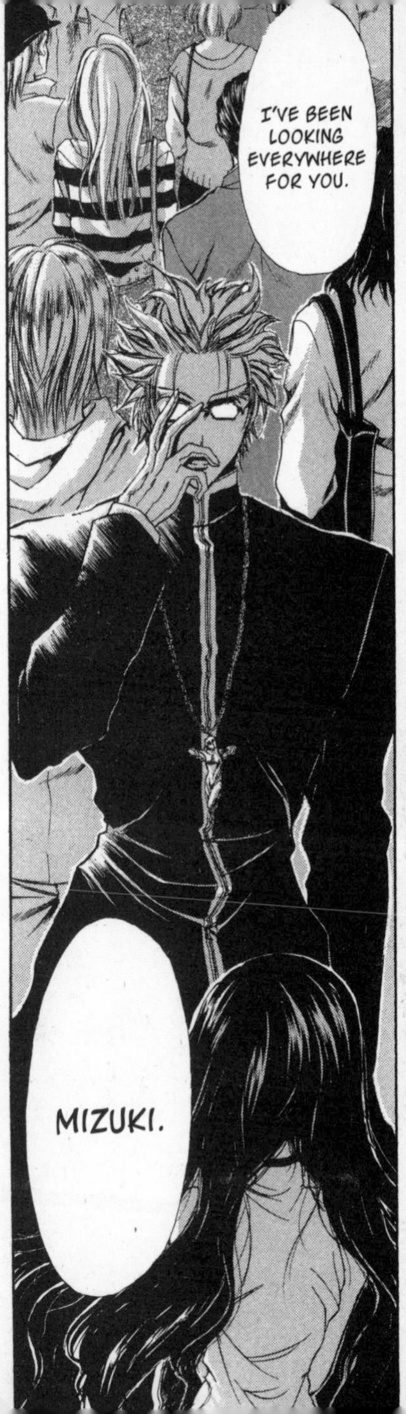
I'VE BEEN LOOKING EVERYWHERE FOR YOU.
MIZUKI.

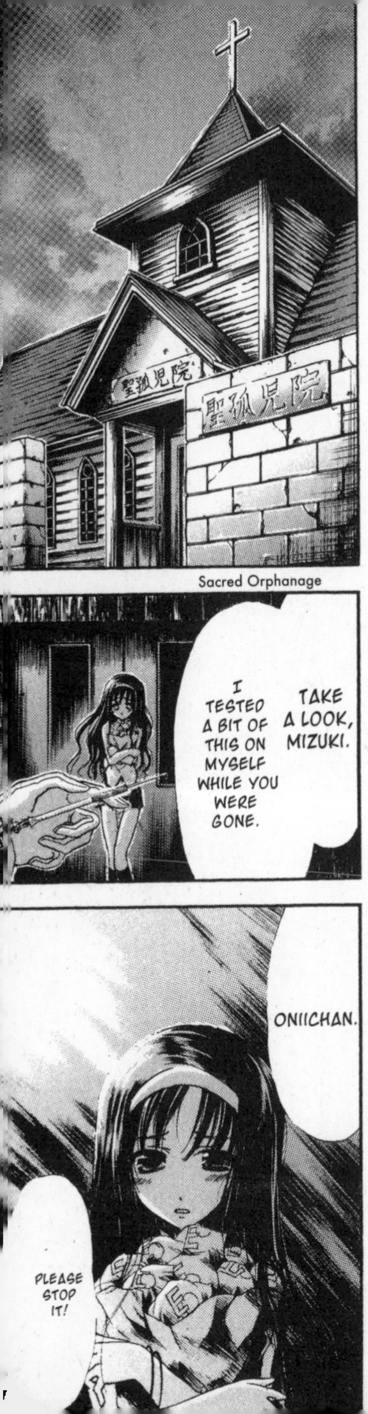
聖孤児院
聖孤児院
Sacred Orphanage
TAKE A LOOK, MIZUKI.
I TESTED A BIT OF THIS ON MYSELF WHILE YOU WERE GONE.
ONIICHAN.
PLEASE STOP IT!

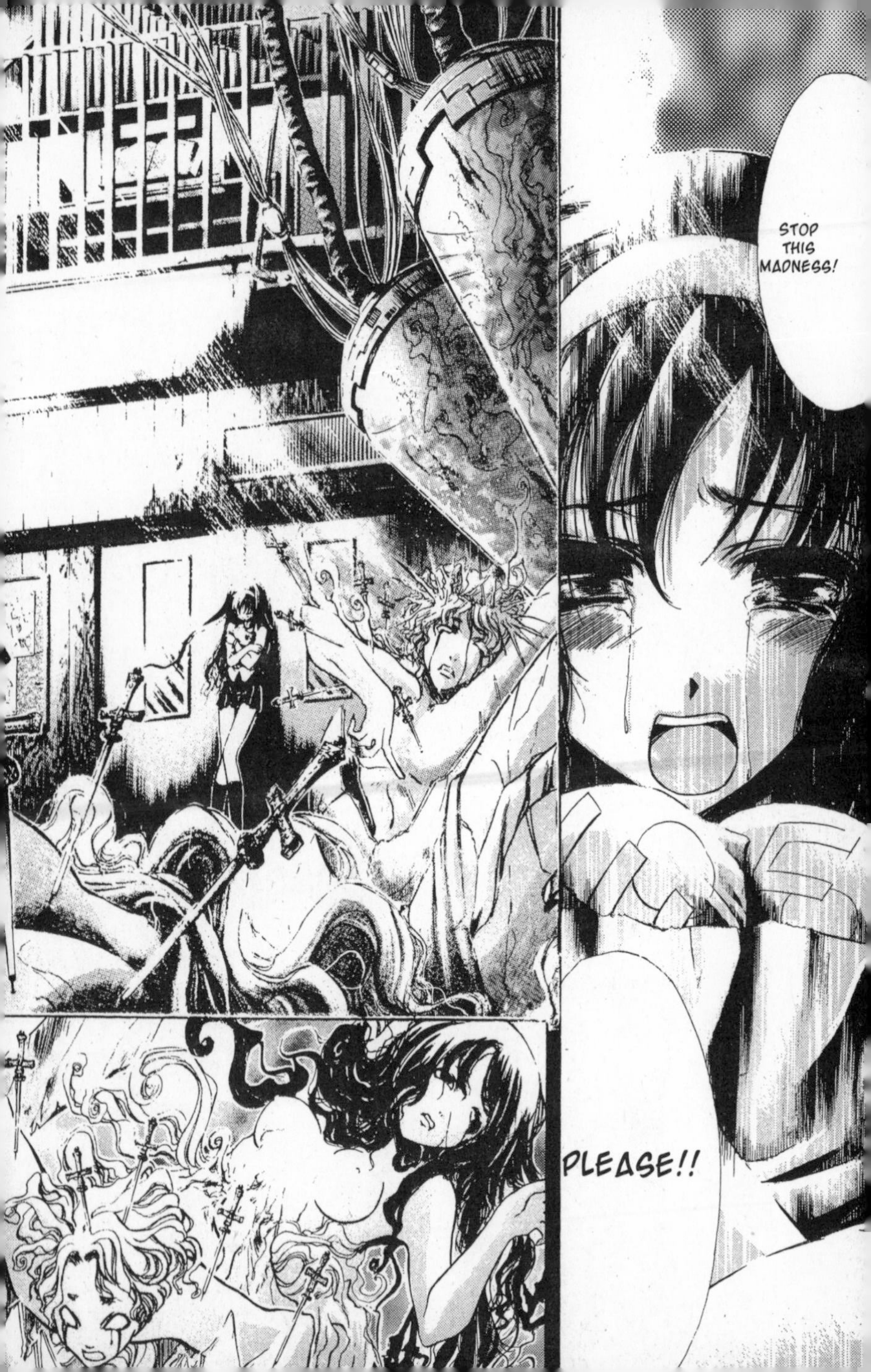
STOP THIS MADNESS!
PLEASE!!

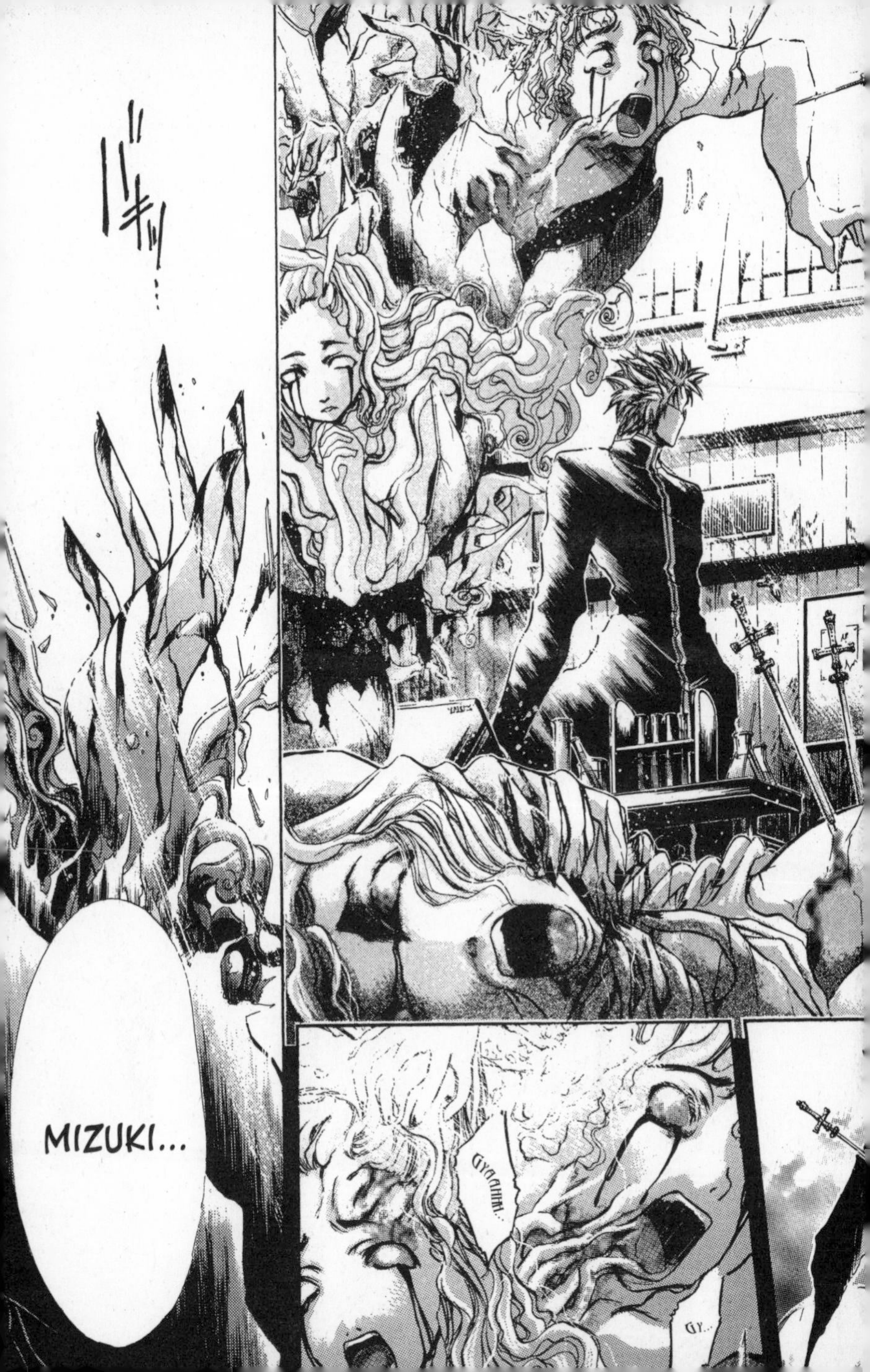
GYAAHH...
GY...
MIZUKI...

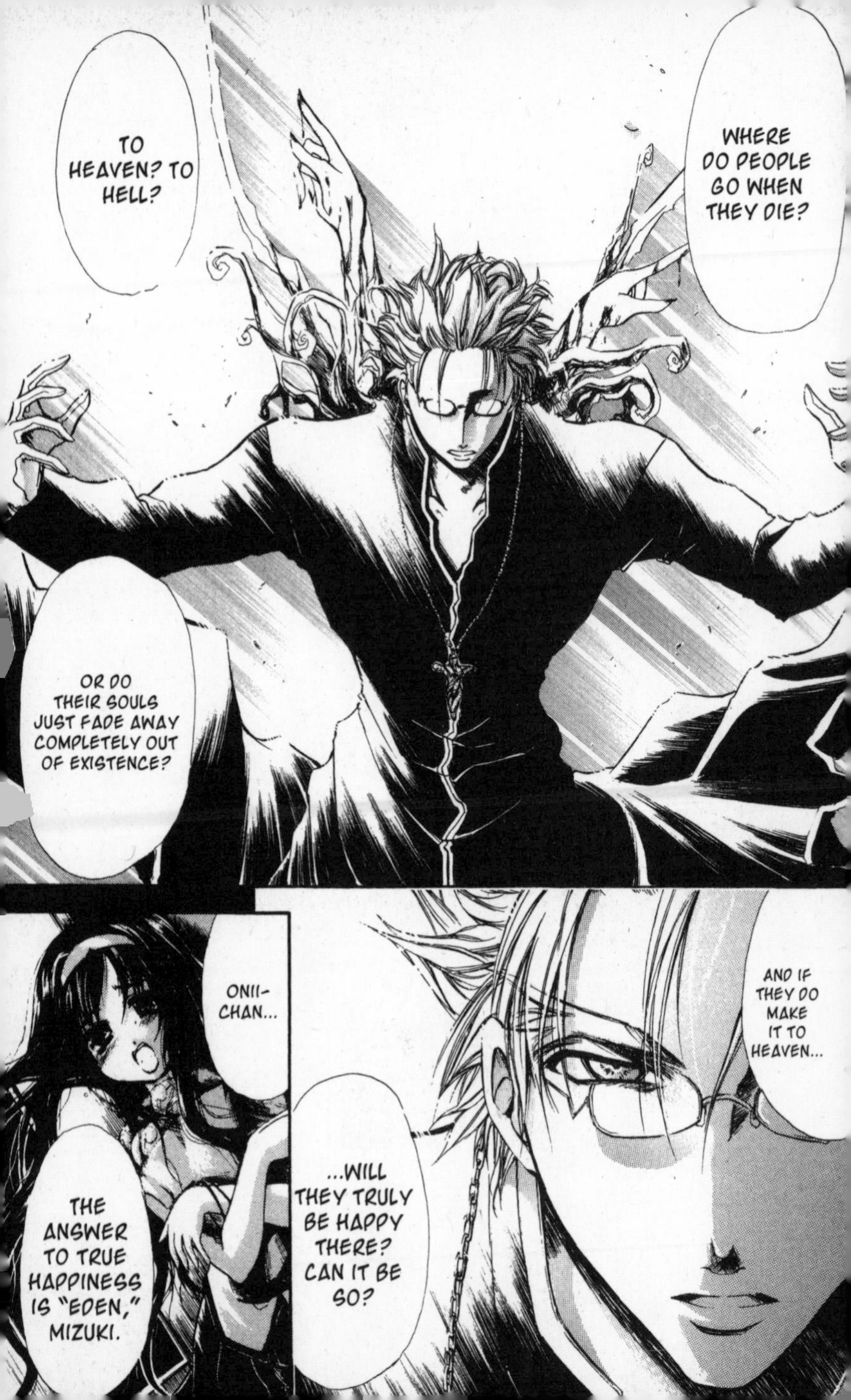
WHERE DO PEOPLE GO WHEN THEY DIE?
TO HEAVEN? TO HELL?
OR DO THEIR SOULS JUST FADE AWAY COMPLETELY OUT OF EXISTENCE?
AND IF THEY DO MAKE IT TO HEAVEN...
...WILL THEY TRULY BE HAPPY THERE? CAN IT BE SO?
ONII-CHAN...
THE ANSWER TO TRUE HAPPINESS IS "EDEN," MIZUKI.

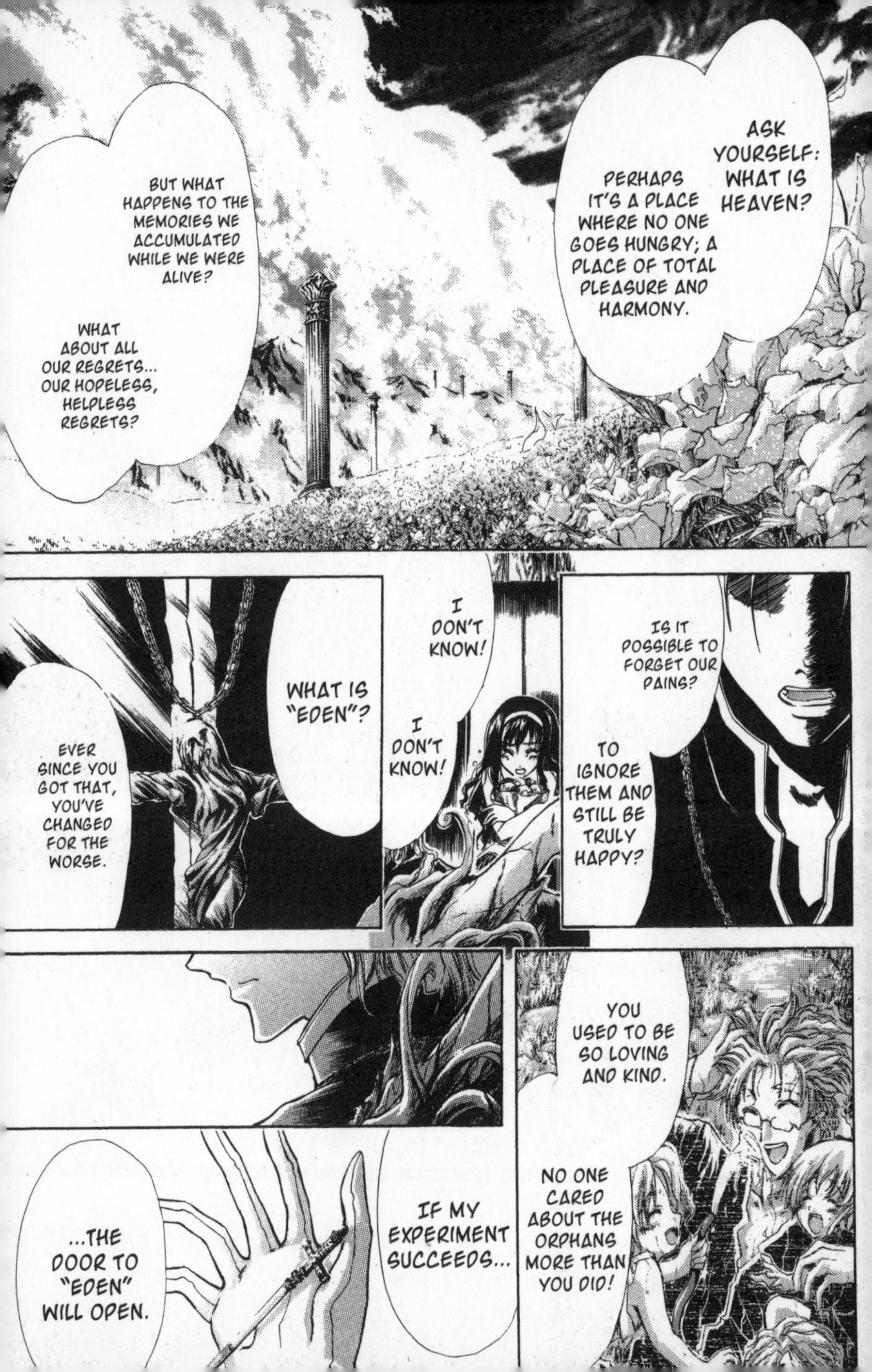
ASK YOURSELF: WHAT IS HEAVEN?
PERHAPS IT'S A PLACE WHERE NO ONE GOES HUNGRY; A PLACE OF TOTAL PLEASURE AND HARMONY.
BUT WHAT HAPPENS TO THE MEMORIES WE ACCUMULATED WHILE WE WERE ALIVE?
WHAT ABOUT ALL OUR REGRETS... OUR HOPELESS, HELPLESS REGRETS?
IS IT POSSIBLE TO FORGET OUR PAINS?
TO IGNORE THEM AND STILL BE TRULY HAPPY?
I DON'T KNOW!
I DON'T KNOW!
WHAT IS "EDEN"?
EVER SINCE YOU GOT THAT, YOU'VE CHANGED FOR THE WORSE.
YOU USED TO BE SO LOVING AND KIND.
NO ONE CARED ABOUT THE ORPHANS MORE THAN YOU DID!
IF MY EXPERIMENT SUCCEEDS...
...THE DOOR TO "EDEN" WILL OPEN.

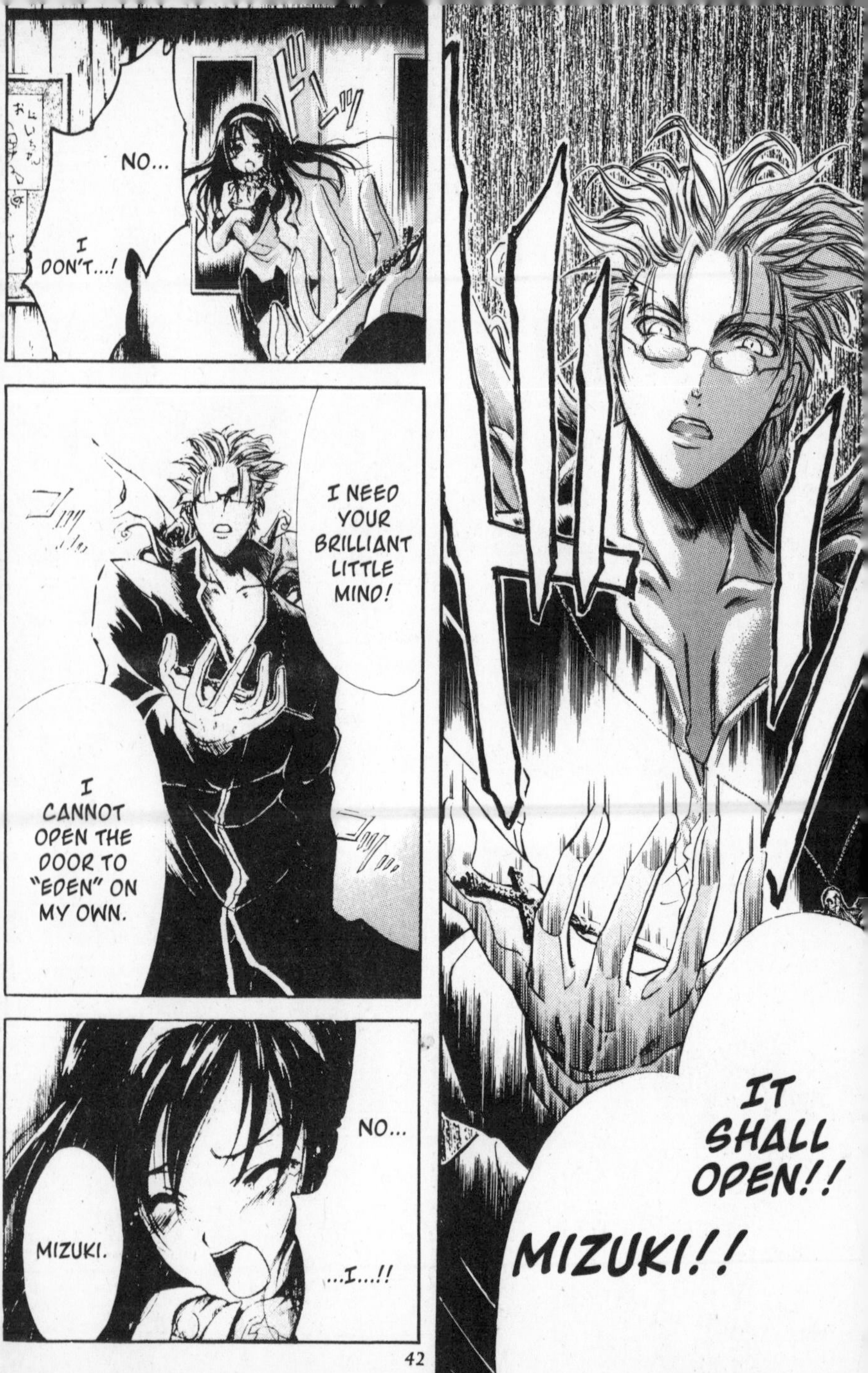
IT SHALL OPEN!!
MIZUKI!!
NO...
I DON'T...!
I NEED YOUR BRILLIANT LITTLE MIND!
I CANNOT OPEN THE DOOR TO "EDEN" ON MY OWN.
NO...
MIZUKI.
...I...!!

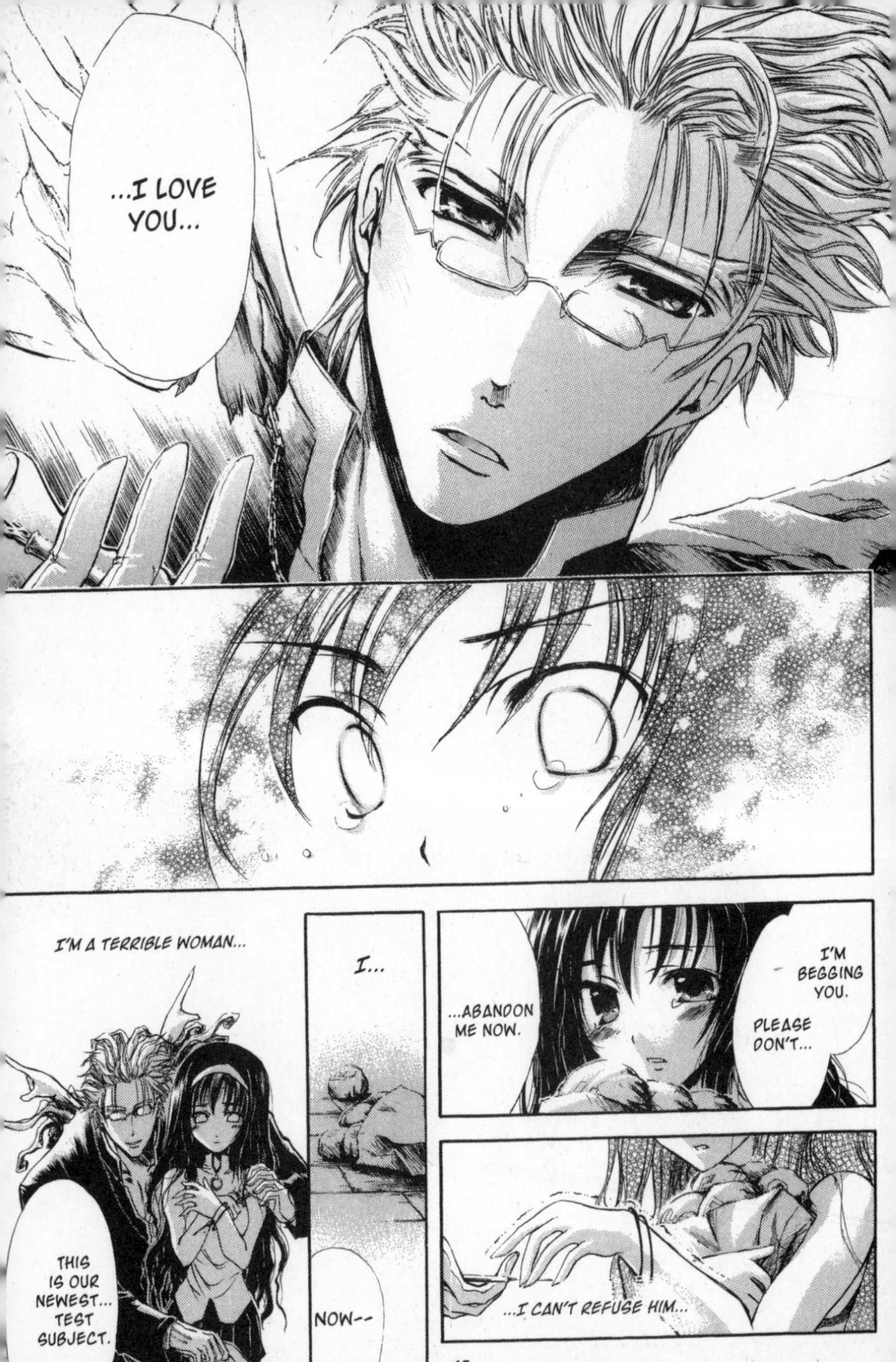
...I LOVE YOU...
I'M BEGGING YOU.
PLEASE DON'T...
...ABANDON ME NOW.
...I CAN'T REFUSE HIM...
I...
NOW--
I'M A TERRIBLE WOMAN...
THIS IS OUR NEWEST... TEST SUBJECT.

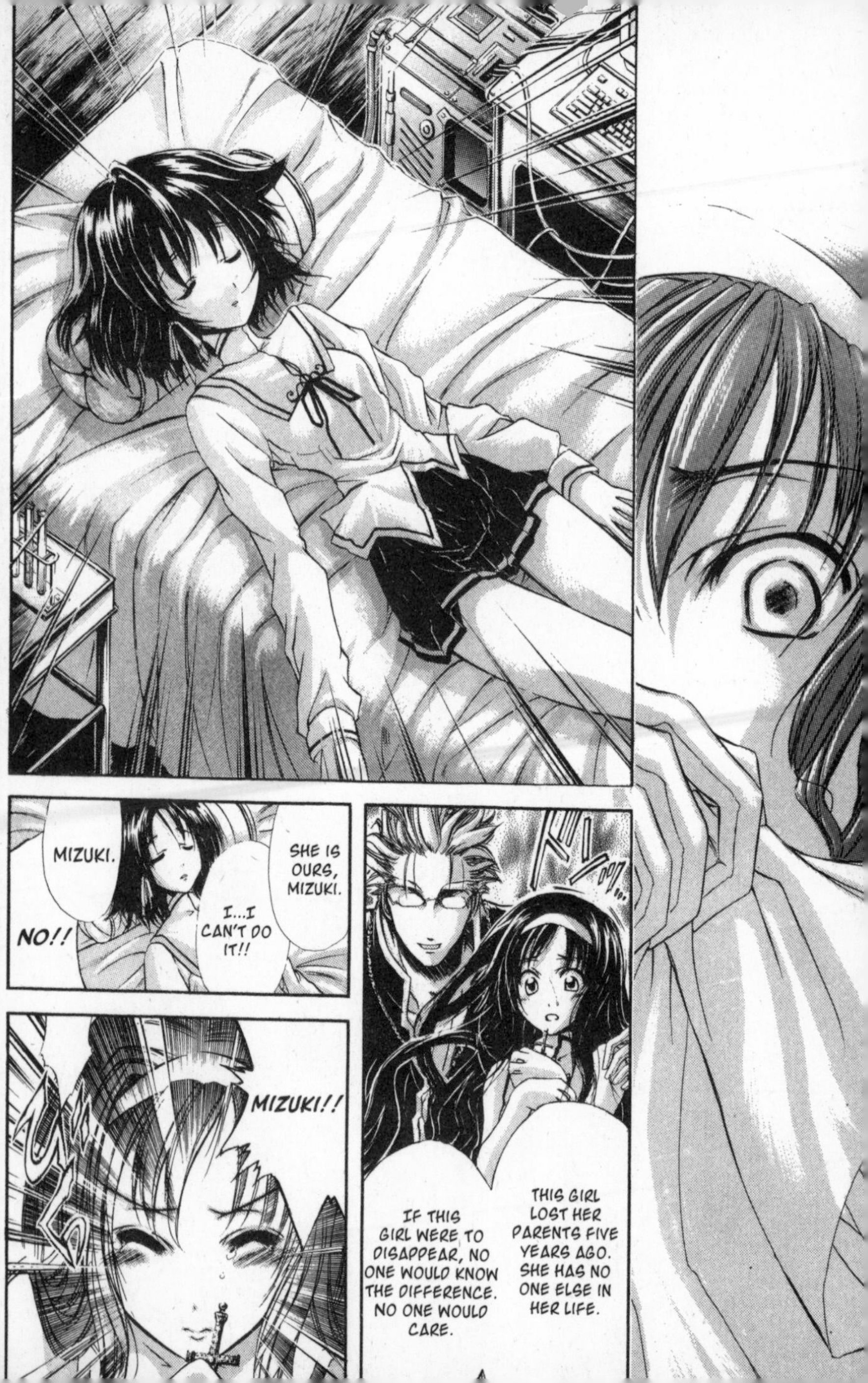
THIS GIRL LOST HER PARENTS FIVE YEARS AGO. SHE HAS NO ONE ELSE IN HER LIFE.
IF THIS GIRL WERE TO DISAPPEAR, NO ONE WOULD KNOW THE DIFFERENCE. NO ONE WOULD CARE.
SHE IS OURS, MIZUKI.
MIZUKI.
I...I CAN'T DO IT!!
NO!!
MIZUKI!!

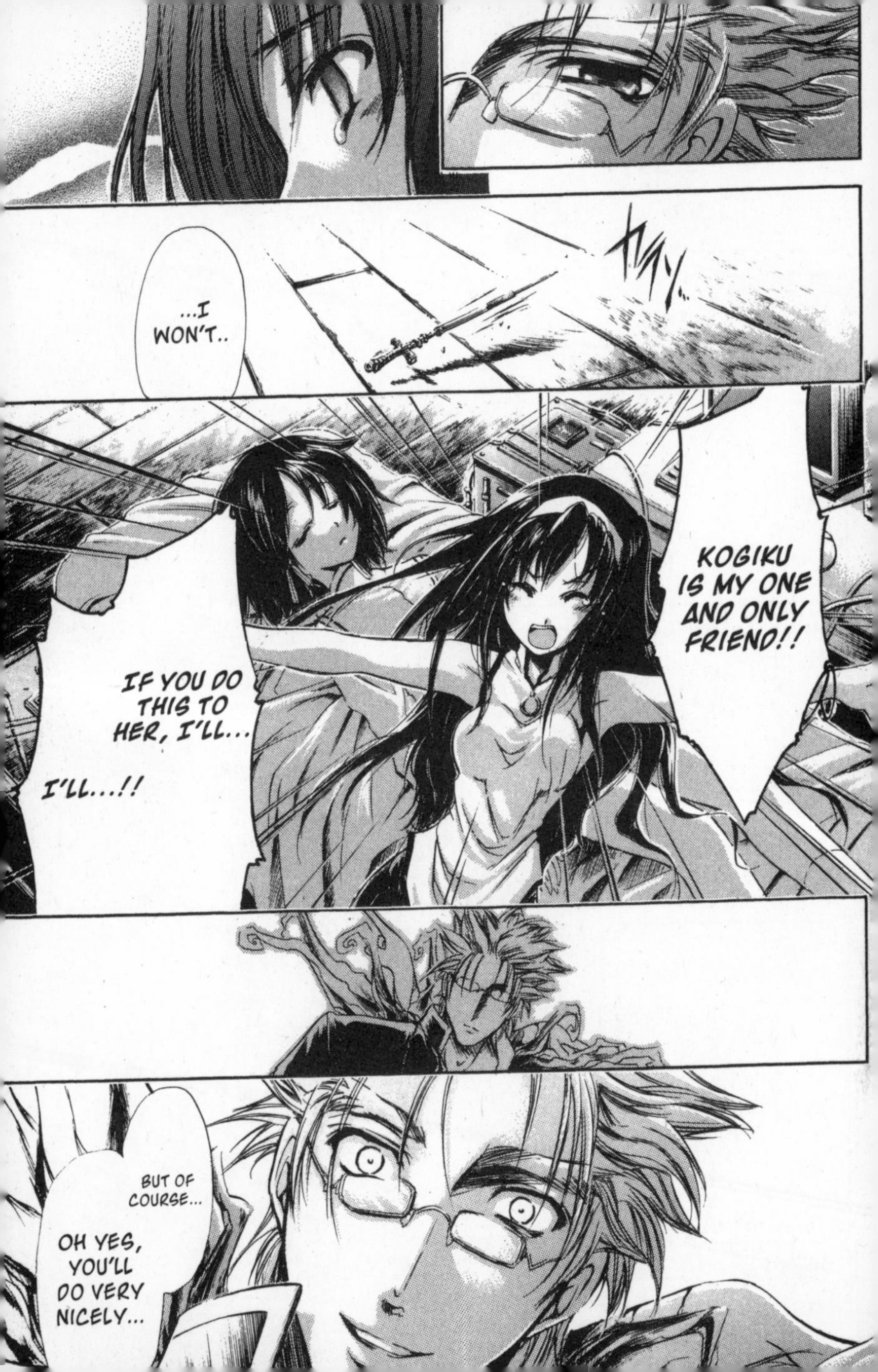
...I WON'T..
KOGIKU IS MY ONE AND ONLY FRIEND!!
IF YOU DO THIS TO HER, I'LL...
I'LL...!!
BUT OF COURSE...
OH YES, YOU'LL DO VERY NICELY...

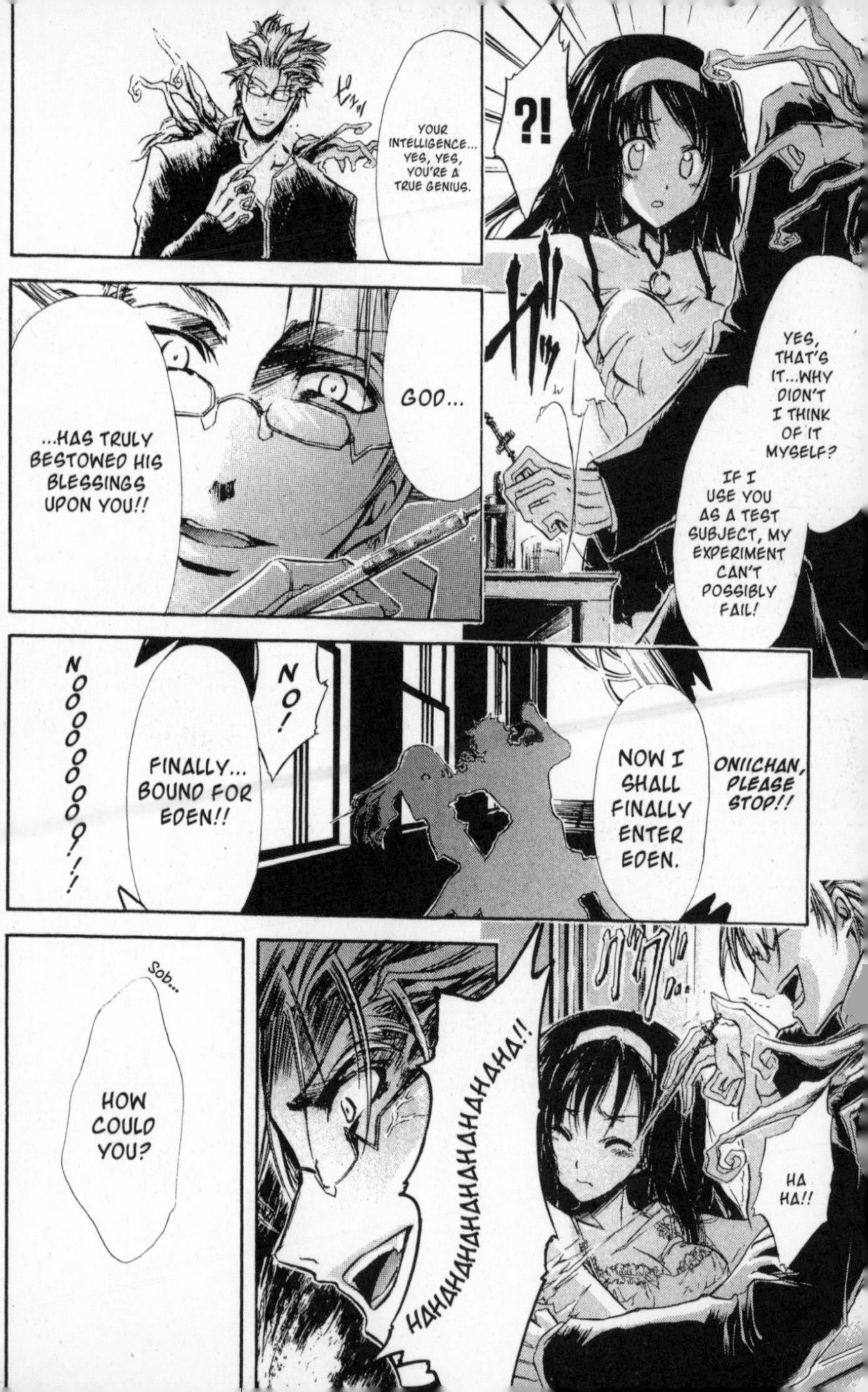
?!
YES, THAT'S IT...WHY DIDN'T I THINK OF IT MYSELF?
IF I USE YOU AS A TEST SUBJECT, MY EXPERIMENT CAN'T POSSIBLY FAIL!
YOUR INTELLIGENCE... YES, YES, YOU'RE A TRUE GENIUS.
GOD...
...HAS TRULY BESTOWED HIS BLESSINGS UPON YOU!!
ONIICHAN, PLEASE STOP!!
NOW I SHALL FINALLY ENTER EDEN.
NO!
FINALLY... BOUND FOR EDEN!!
NOOOOOOOOOO!!
HA HA!!
HAHAHAHAHAHAHAHA!!
Sob...
HOW COULD YOU?

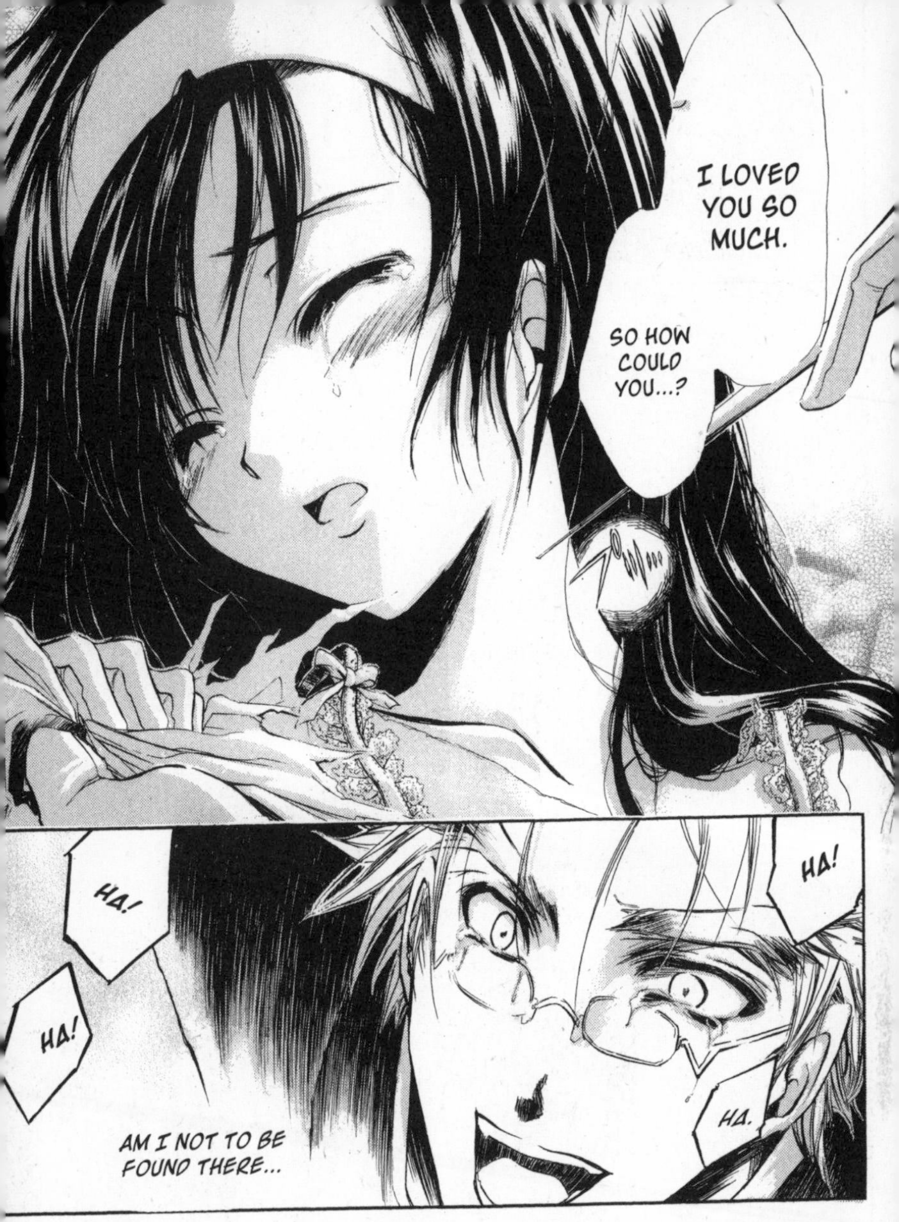
I LOVED YOU SO MUCH.
SO HOW COULD YOU...?
HA!
HA.
HA!
HA!
AM I NOT TO BE FOUND THERE...

...IN YOUR VISIONS OF EDEN...?

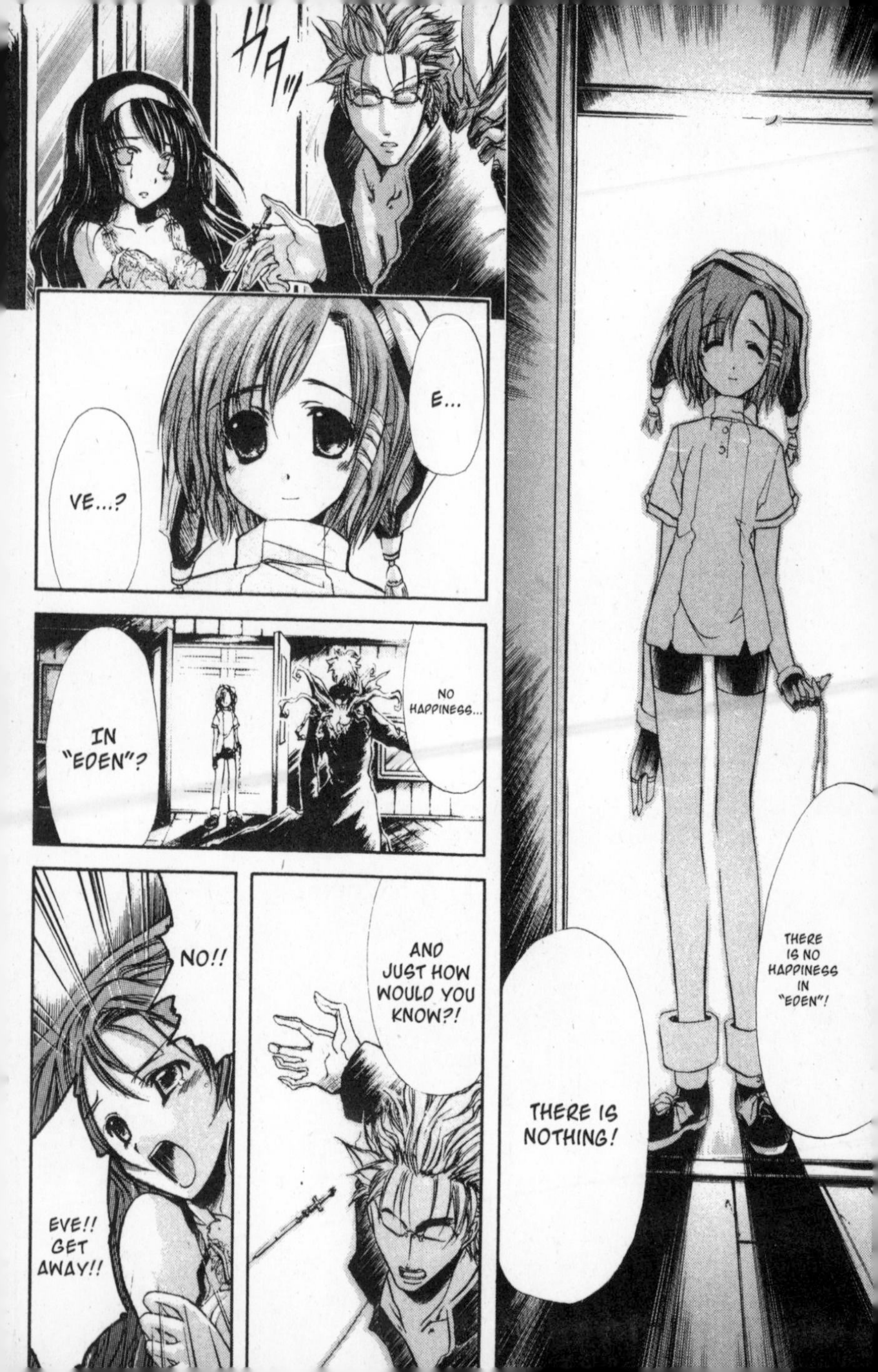
THERE IS NO HAPPINESS IN "EDEN"!
THERE IS NOTHING!
ガタッ
E...
VE...?
NO HAPPINESS...
IN "EDEN"?
AND JUST HOW WOULD YOU KNOW?!
NO!!
EVE!! GET AWAY!!

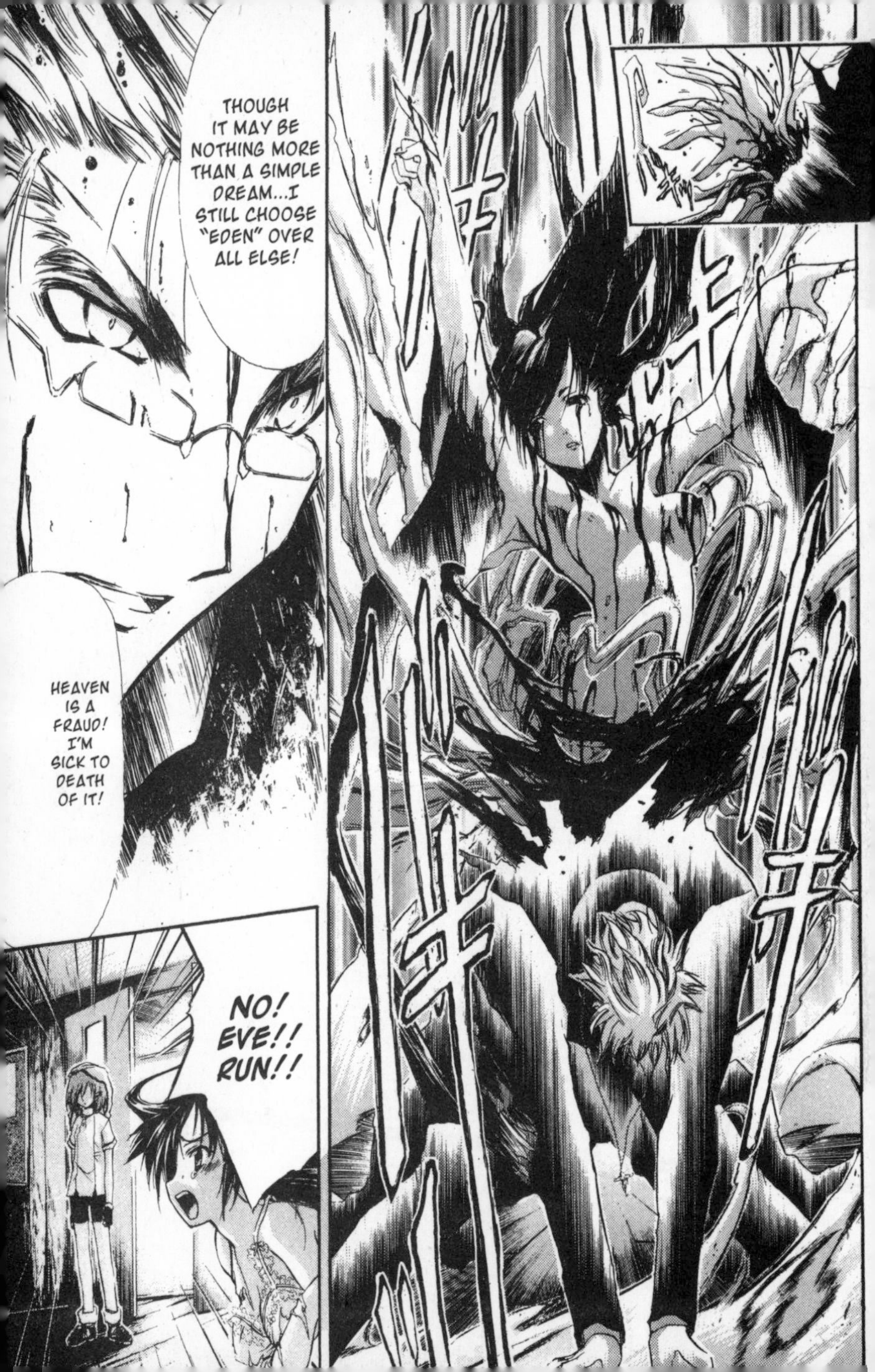
THOUGH IT MAY BE NOTHING MORE THAN A SIMPLE DREAM...I STILL CHOOSE "EDEN" OVER ALL ELSE!
HEAVEN IS A FRAUD! I'M SICK TO DEATH OF IT!
NO! EVE!! RUN!!

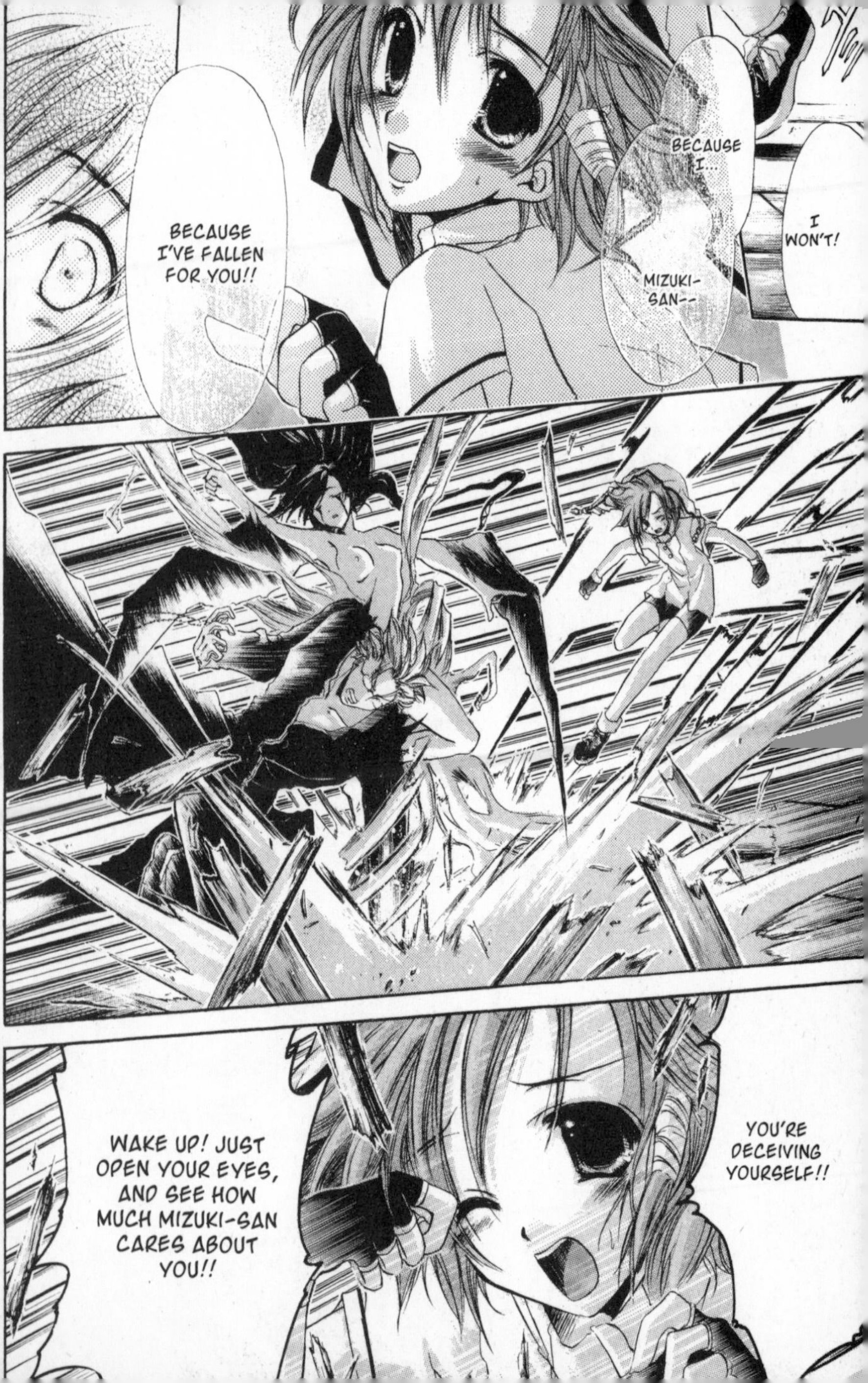
I WON'T!
BECAUSE I... MIZUKI-SAN--
BECAUSE I'VE FALLEN FOR YOU!!
YOU'RE DECEIVING YOURSELF!!
WAKE UP! JUST OPEN YOUR EYES, AND SEE HOW MUCH MIZUKI-SAN CARES ABOUT YOU!!

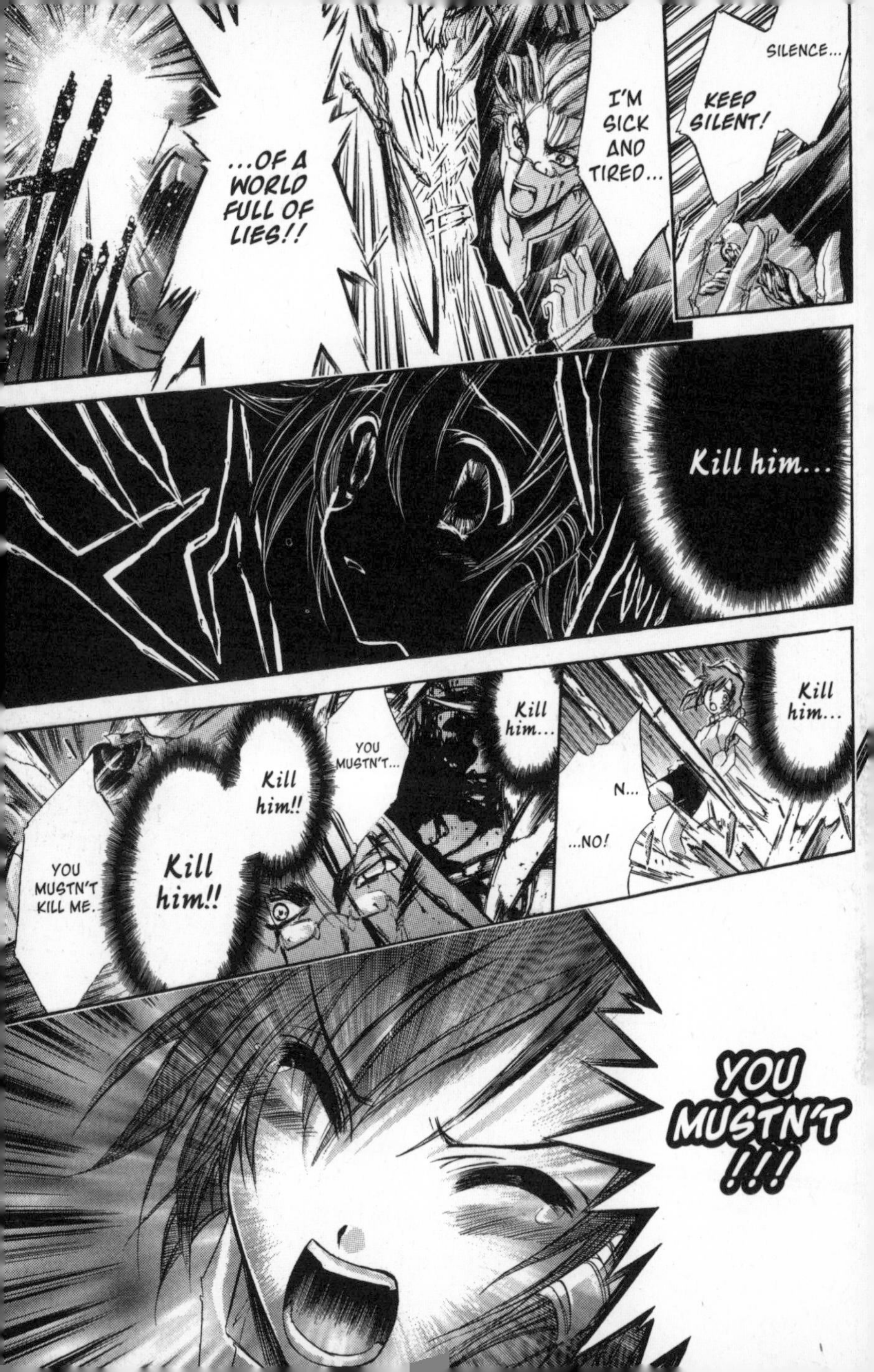
SILENCE...
KEEP SILENT!
I'M SICK AND TIRED...
...OF A WORLD FULL OF LIES!!
Kill him...
Kill him...
N...
...NO!
Kill him...
YOU MUSTN'T...
Kill him!!
Kill him!!
YOU MUSTN'T KILL ME.
YOU MUSTN'T !!!

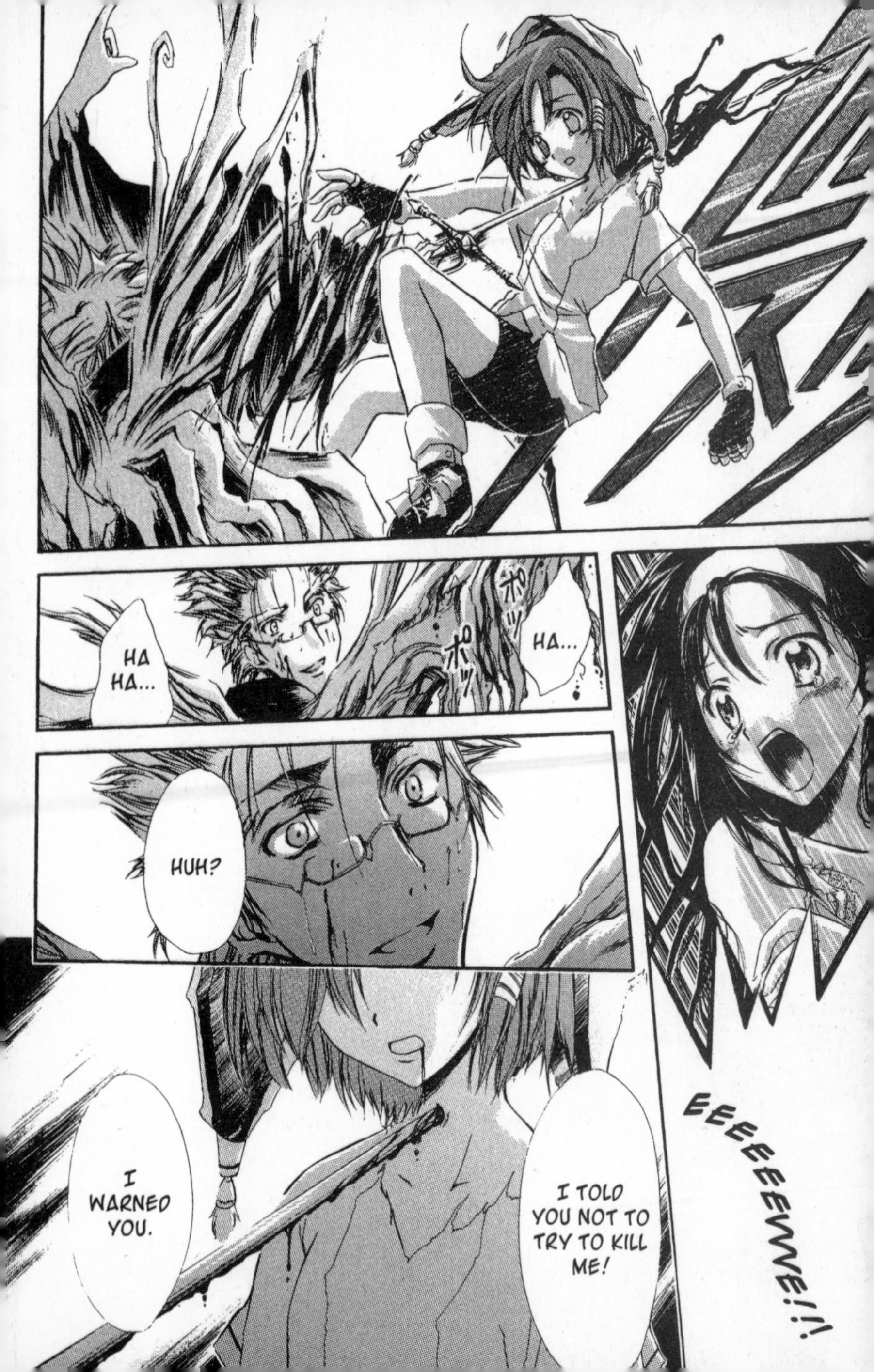
EEEEEEWWE!!!
ポッ
ポッ
HA...
HA HA...
HUH?
I TOLD YOU NOT TO TRY TO KILL ME!
I WARNED YOU.

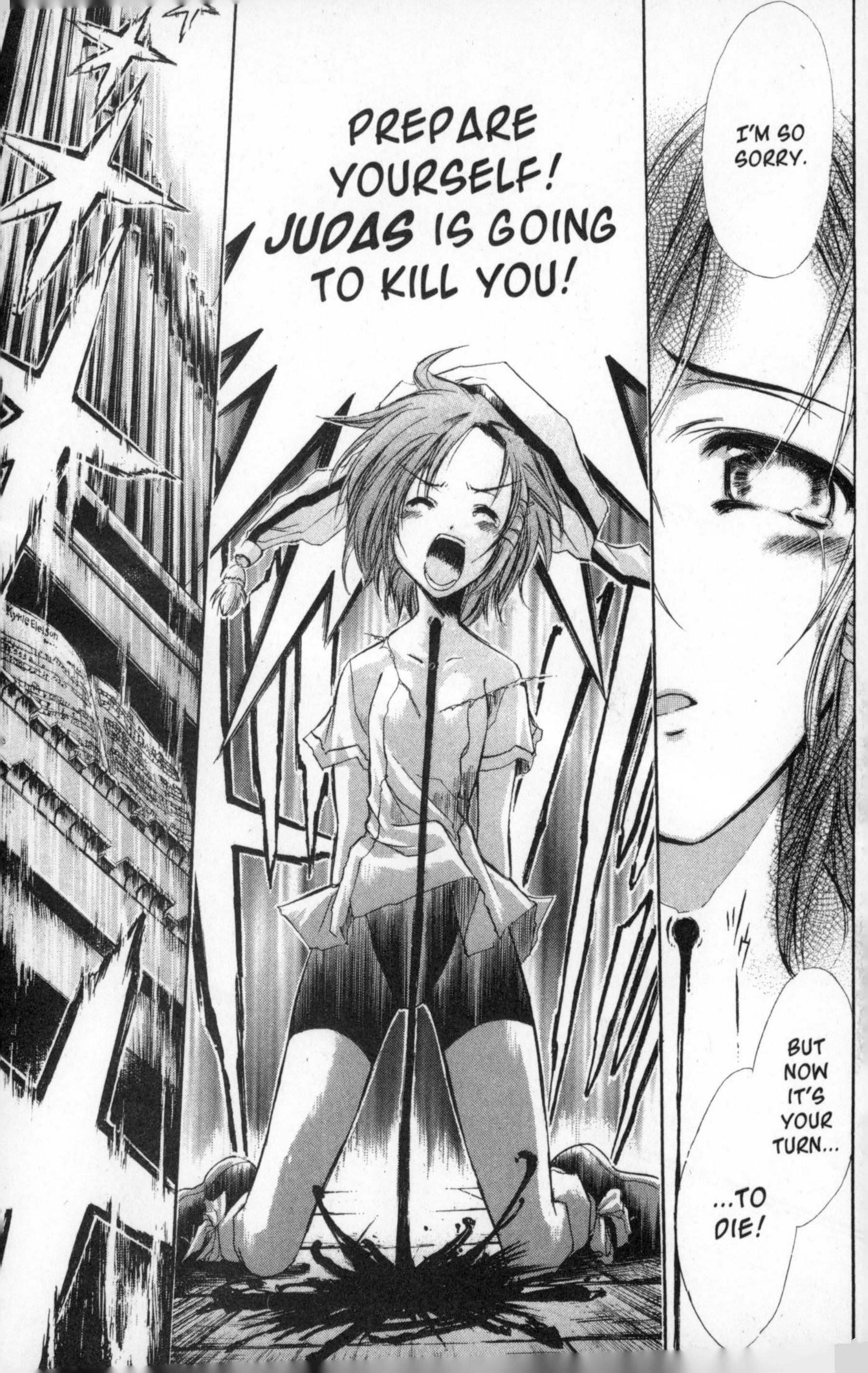
I'M SO SORRY.
BUT NOW IT'S YOUR TURN...
...TO DIE!
PREPARE YOURSELF! JUDAS IS GOING TO KILL YOU!
Kyrie Eleison

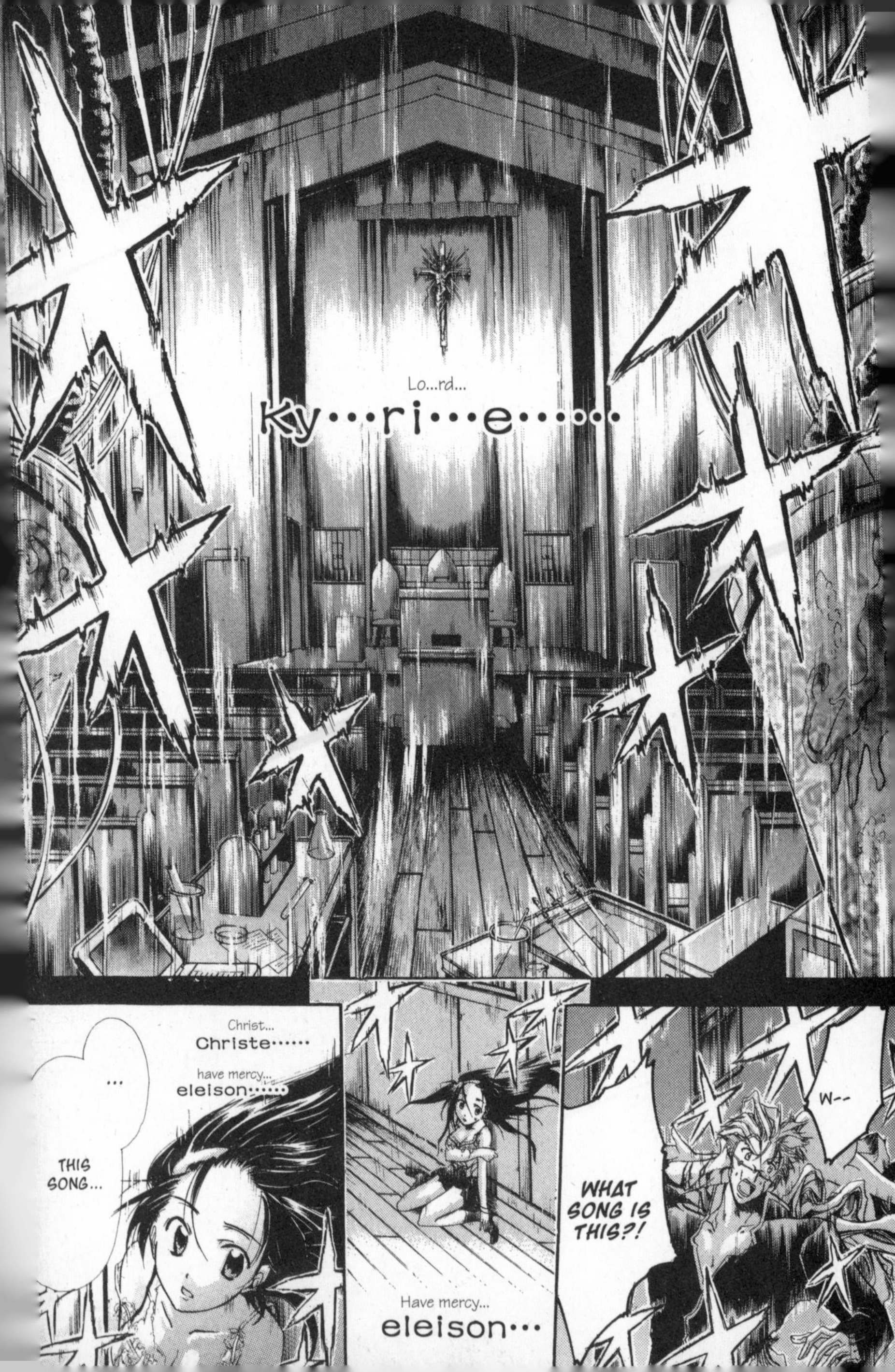

Lo...rd...
Ky···ri···e·······
W--
WHAT SONG IS THIS?!
Have mercy...
eleison···
Christ...
Christe······
have mercy...
eleison······
...
THIS SONG...

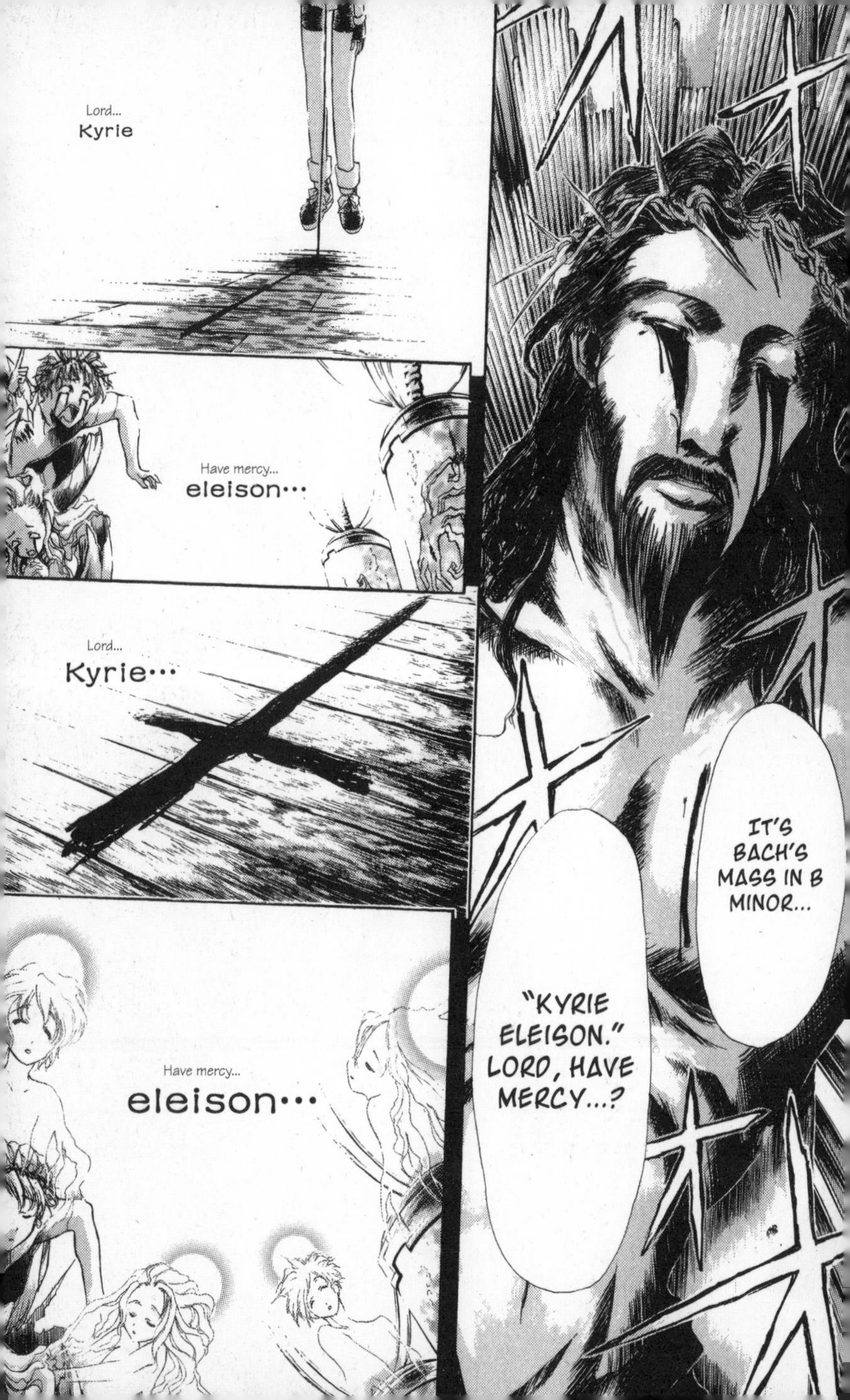
IT'S BACH'S MASS IN B MINOR...
"KYRIE ELEISON." LORD, HAVE MERCY...?
Lord...
Kyrie
Have mercy...
eleison···
Lord...
Kyrie···
Have mercy...
eleison···

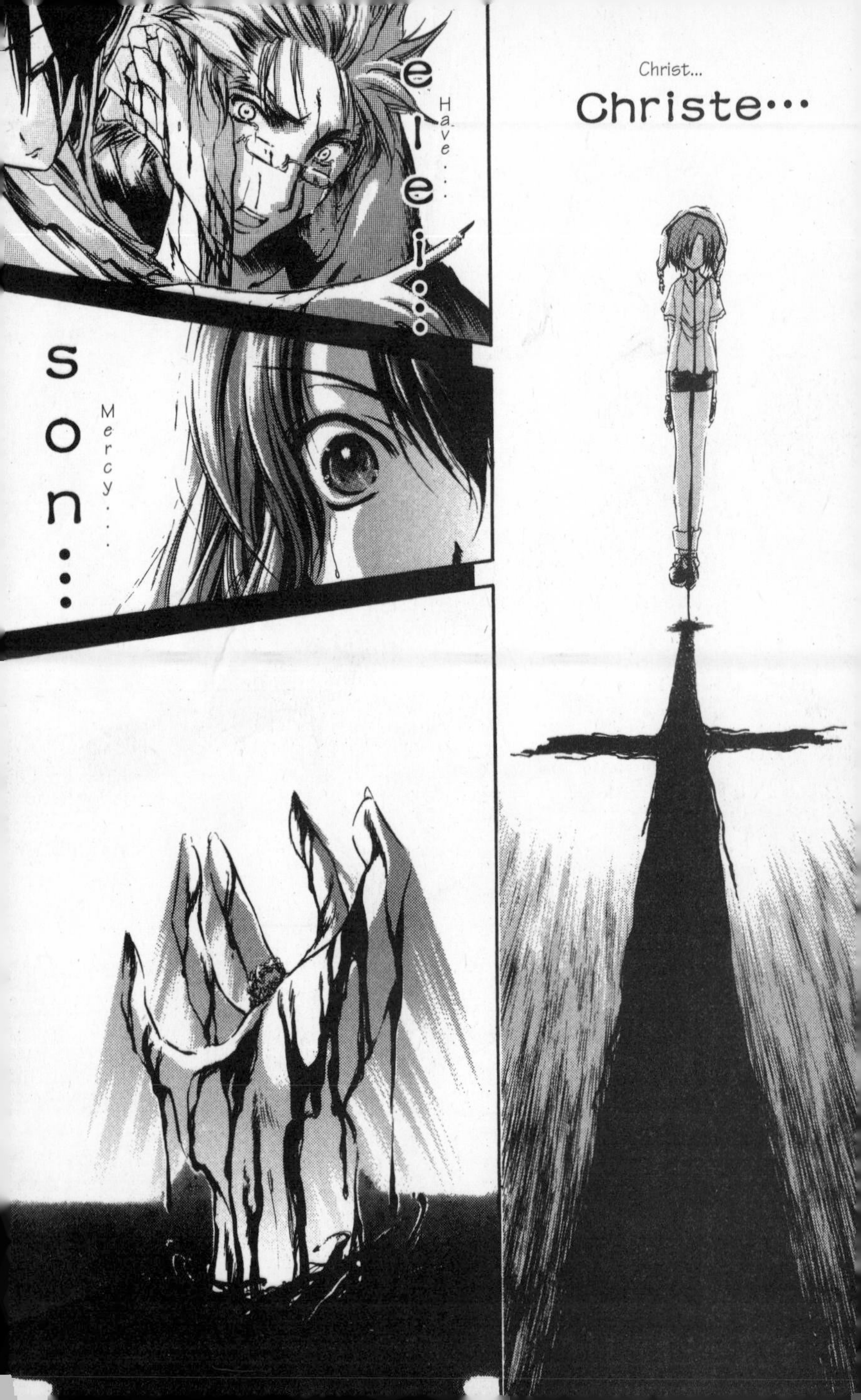
Christ...
Christe...
ele i...
Have...
son...
Mercy...

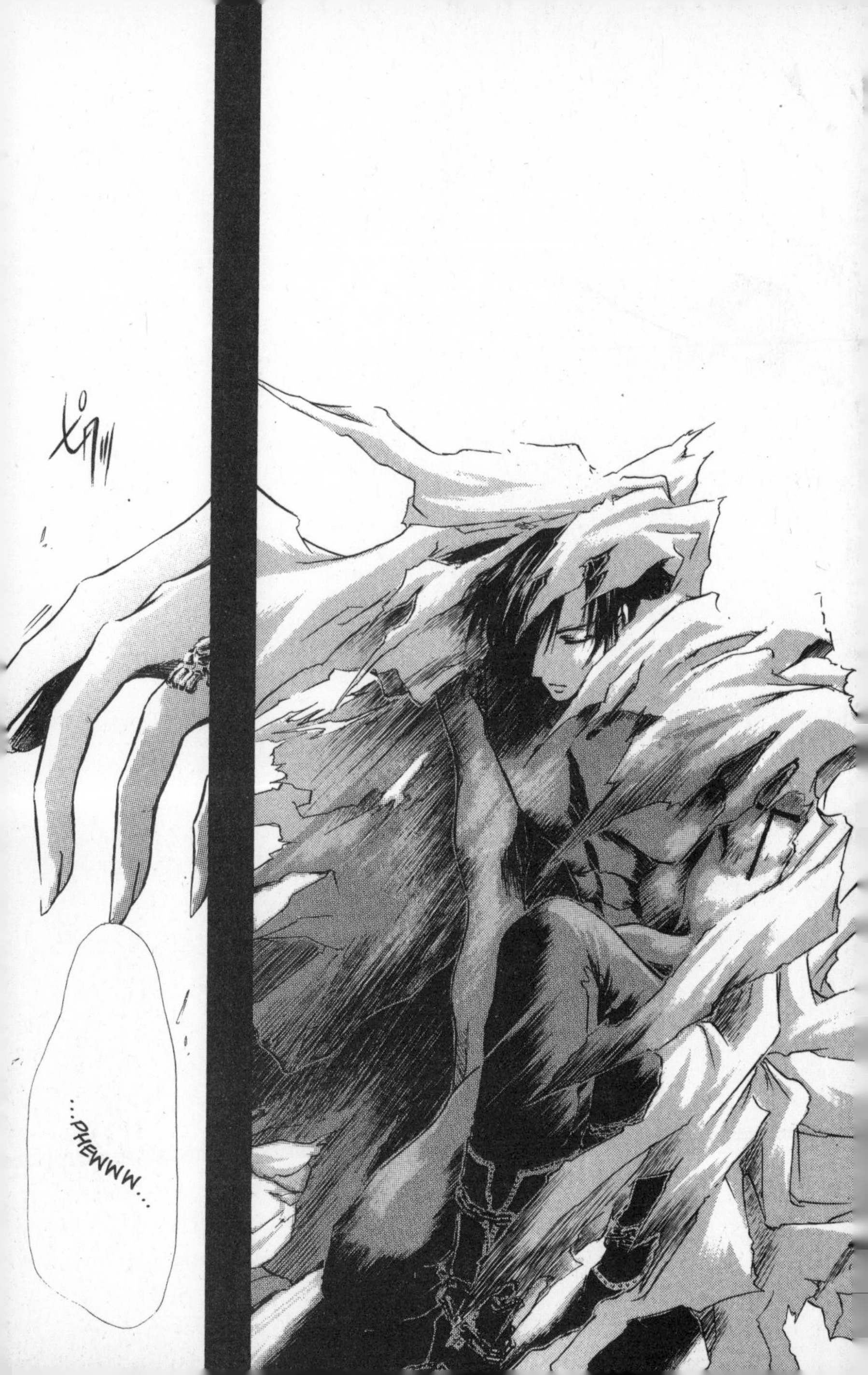
...PHEWWW...

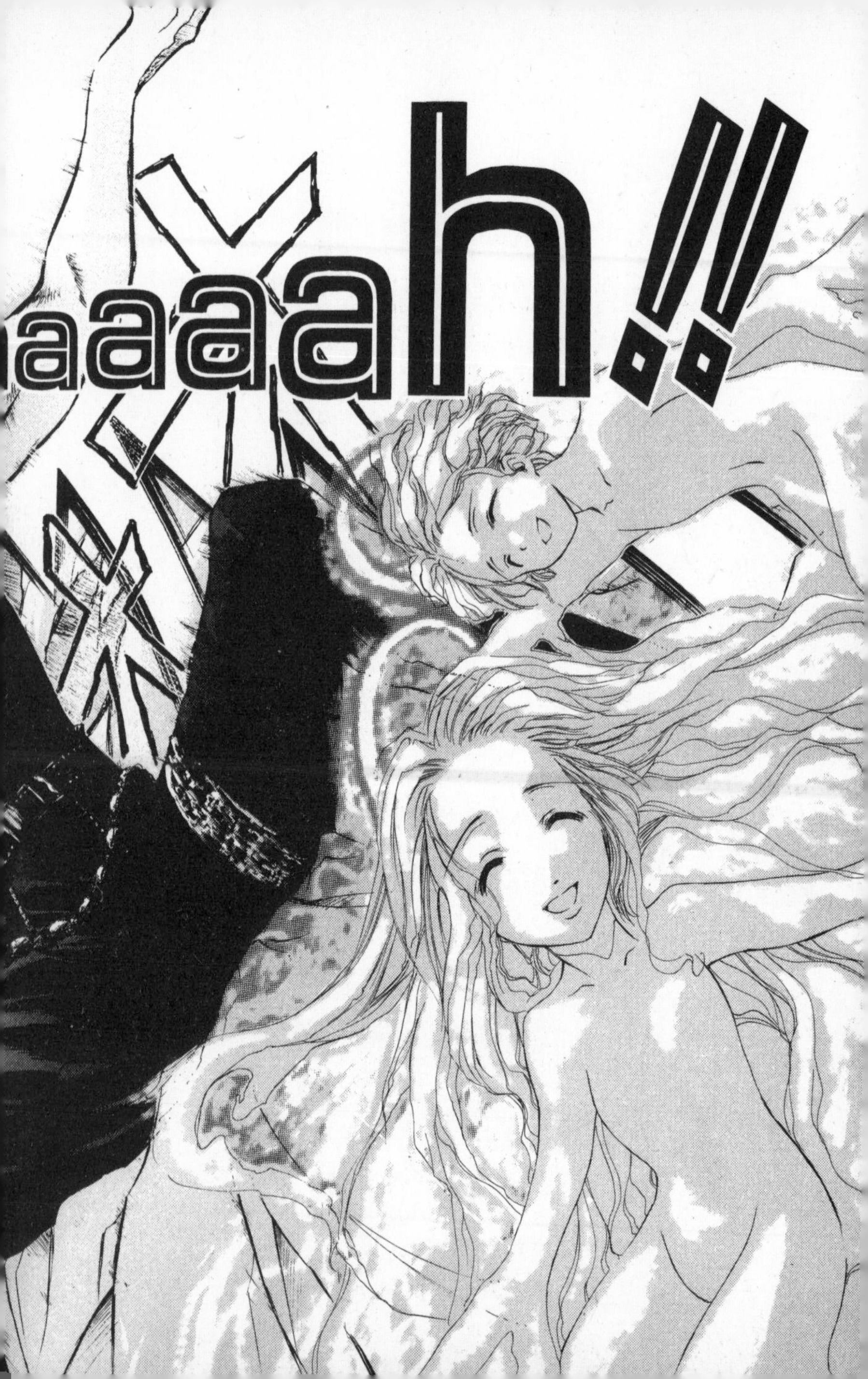
aaaaah!!

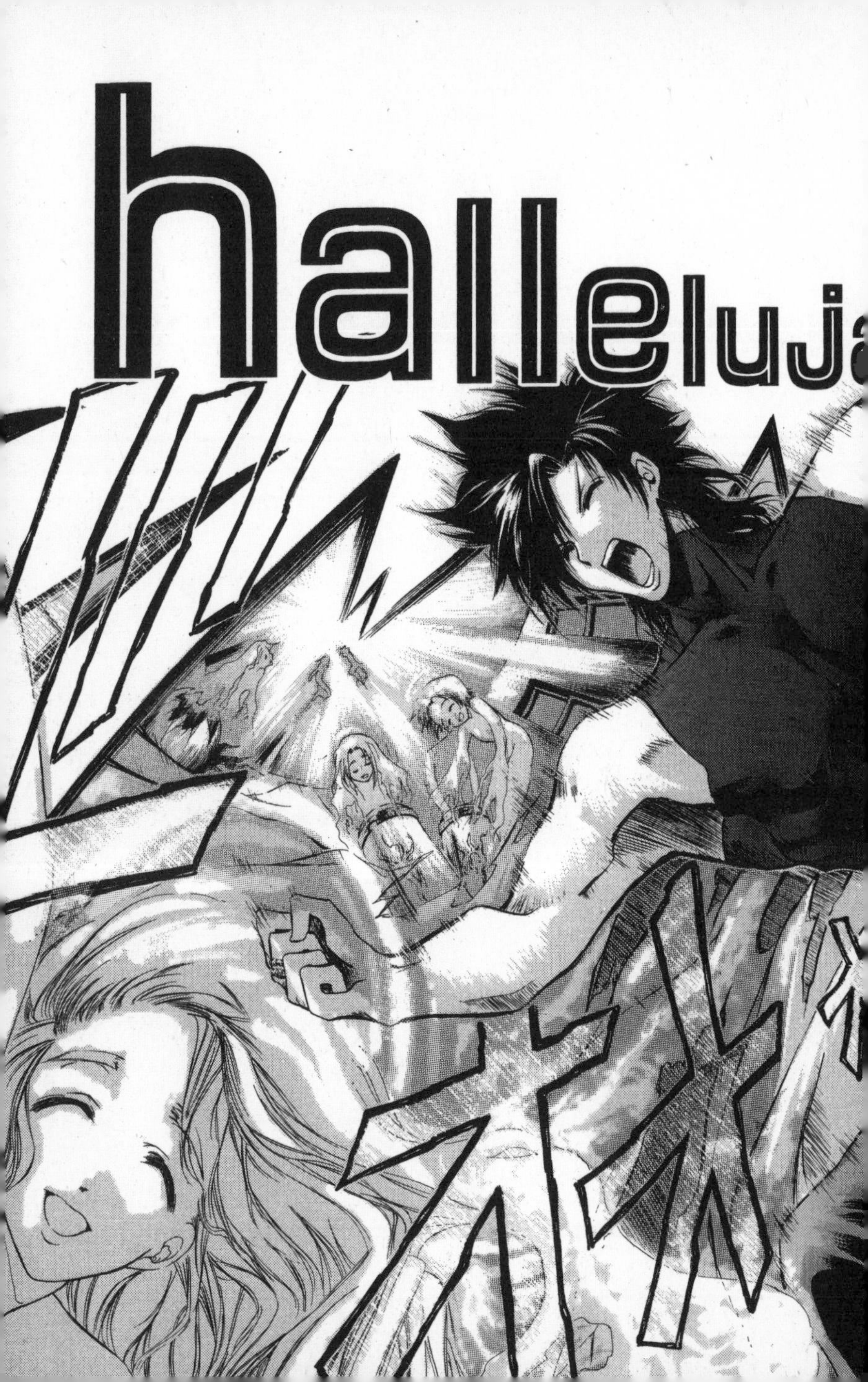
halleluja

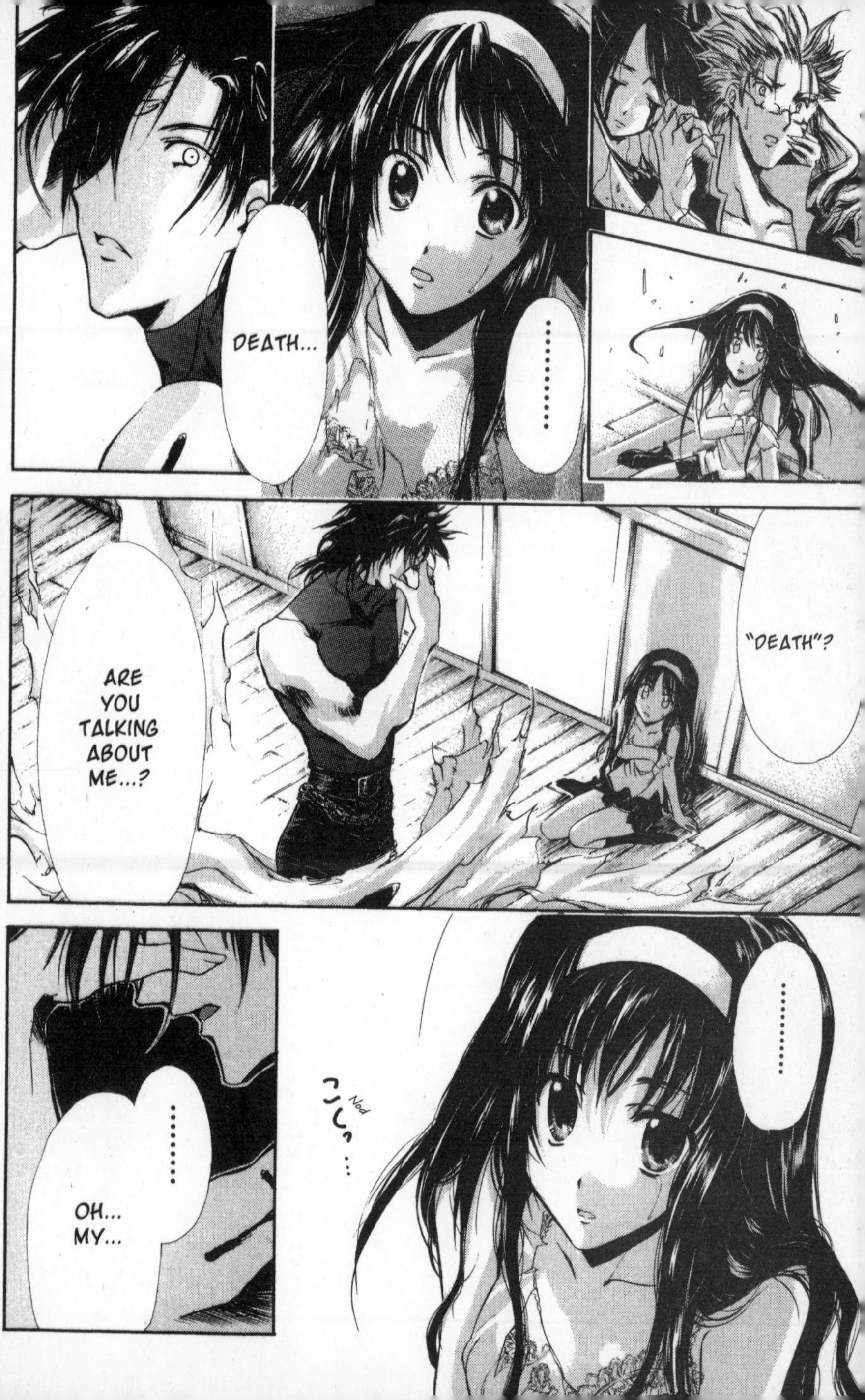
......
DEATH...
"DEATH"?
ARE YOU TALKING ABOUT ME...?
......
Nod
......
OH... MY...

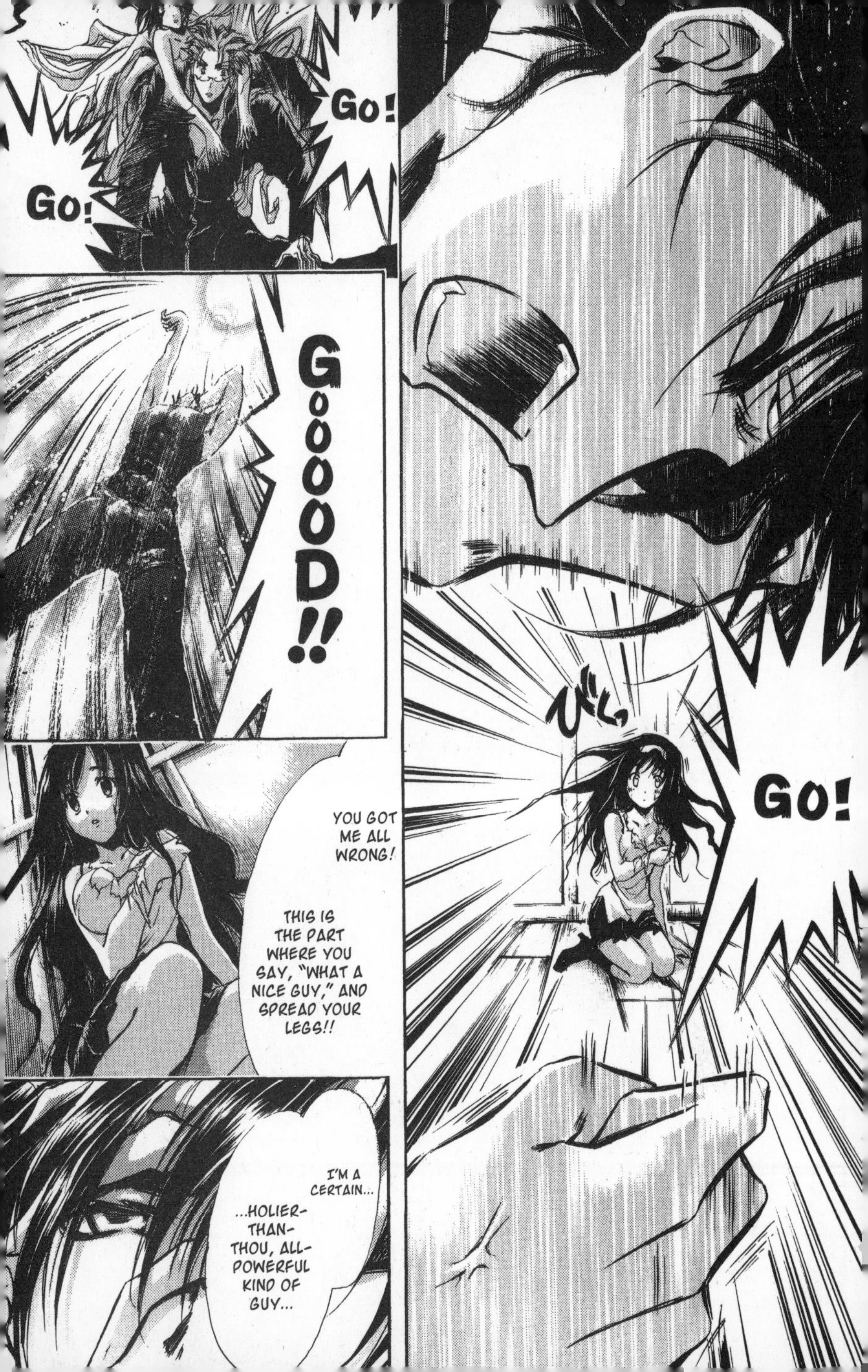

びくっ
GO!
GO!
GO!
GOOOOOD!!
YOU GOT ME ALL WRONG!
THIS IS THE PART WHERE YOU SAY, "WHAT A NICE GUY," AND SPREAD YOUR LEGS!!
I'M A CERTAIN...
...HOLIER-THAN-THOU, ALL-POWERFUL KIND OF GUY...

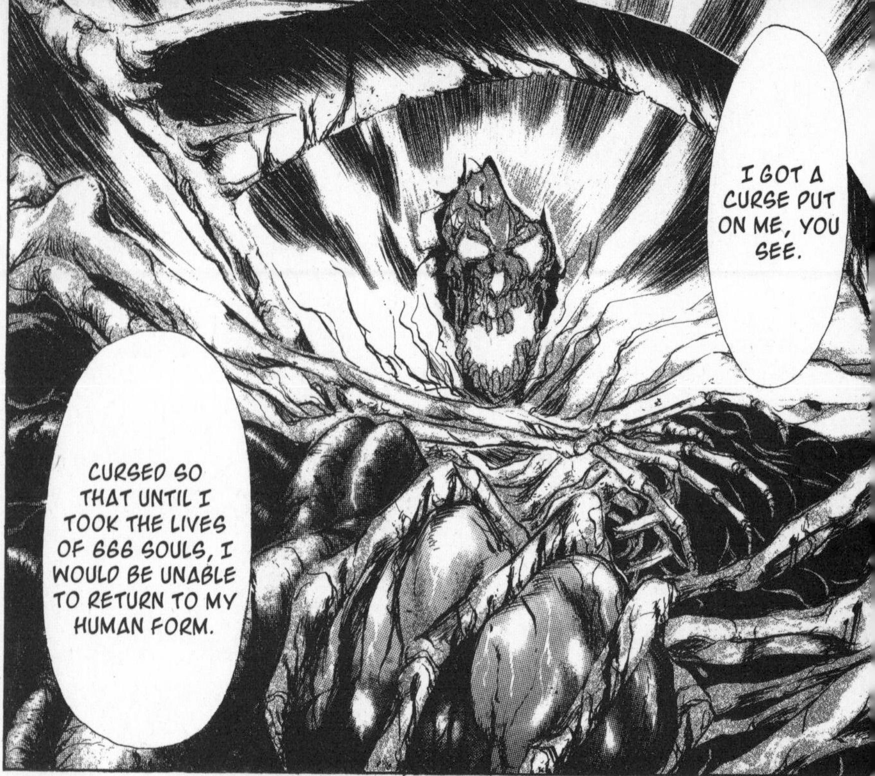
I GOT A CURSE PUT ON ME, YOU SEE.
CURSED SO THAT UNTIL I TOOK THE LIVES OF 666 SOULS, I WOULD BE UNABLE TO RETURN TO MY HUMAN FORM.

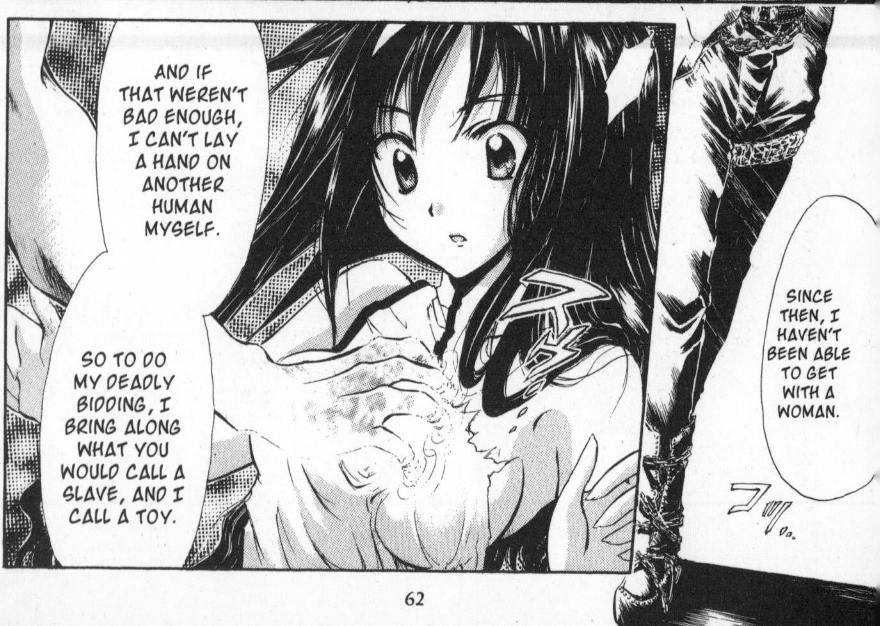
SINCE THEN, I HAVEN'T BEEN ABLE TO GET WITH A WOMAN.
AND IF THAT WEREN'T BAD ENOUGH, I CAN'T LAY A HAND ON ANOTHER HUMAN MYSELF.
SO TO DO MY DEADLY BIDDING, I BRING ALONG WHAT YOU WOULD CALL A SLAVE, AND I CALL A TOY.

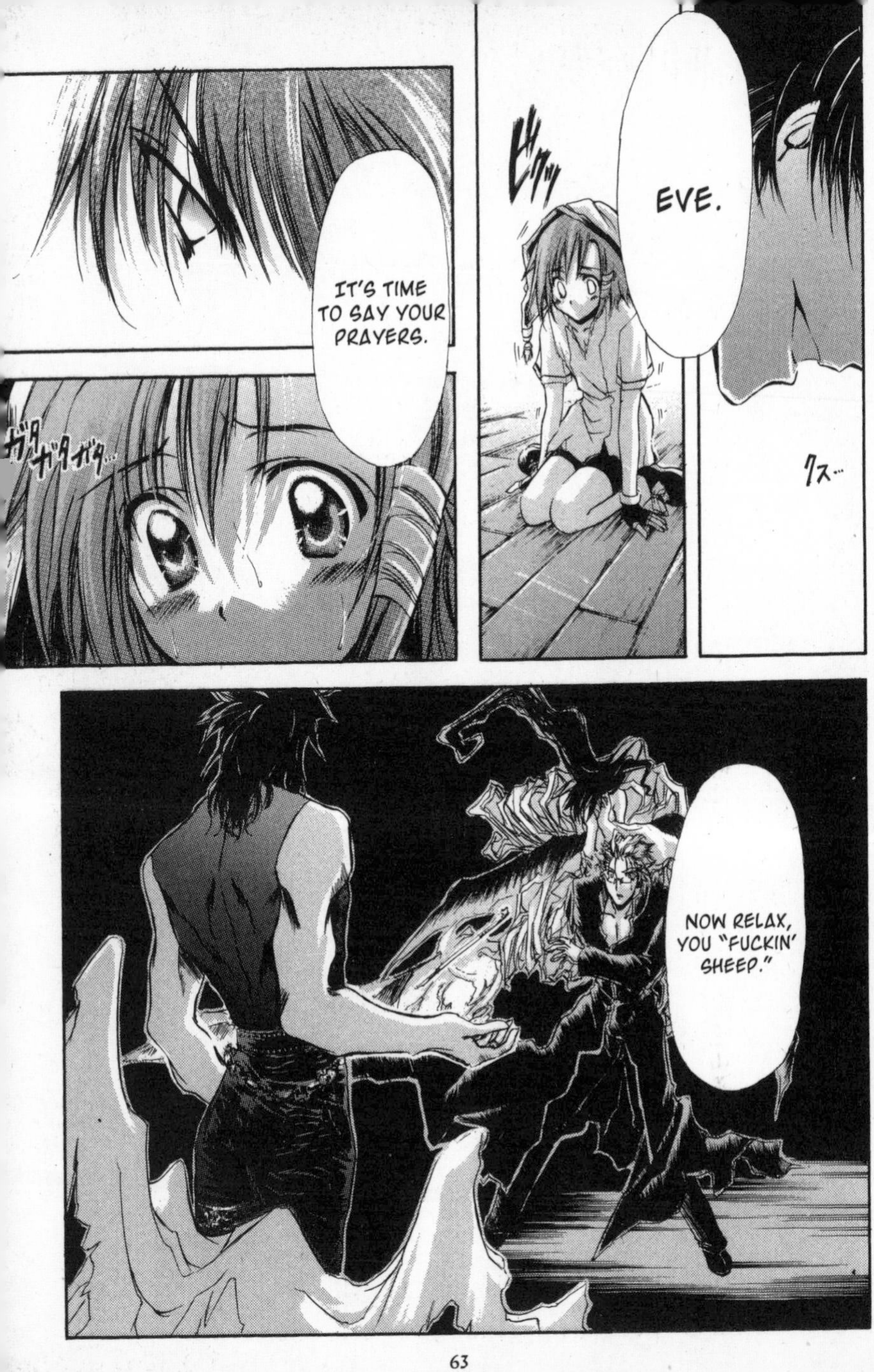
EVE.
クス…
ビクッ
IT'S TIME TO SAY YOUR PRAYERS.
ガタガタガタ…
NOW RELAX, YOU "FUCKIN' SHEEP."

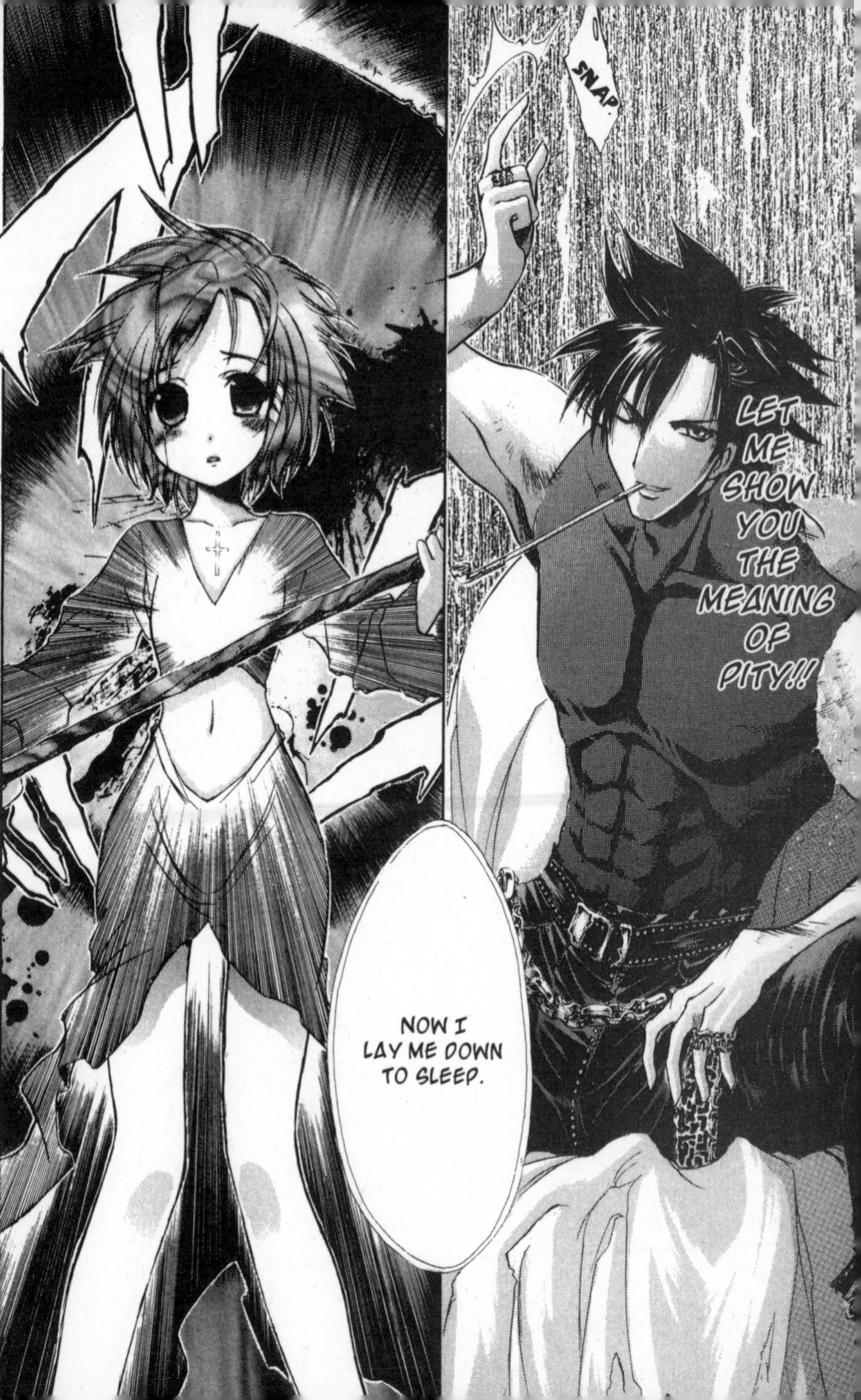
SNAP
LET ME SHOW YOU THE MEANING OF PITY!!
NOW I LAY ME DOWN TO SLEEP.

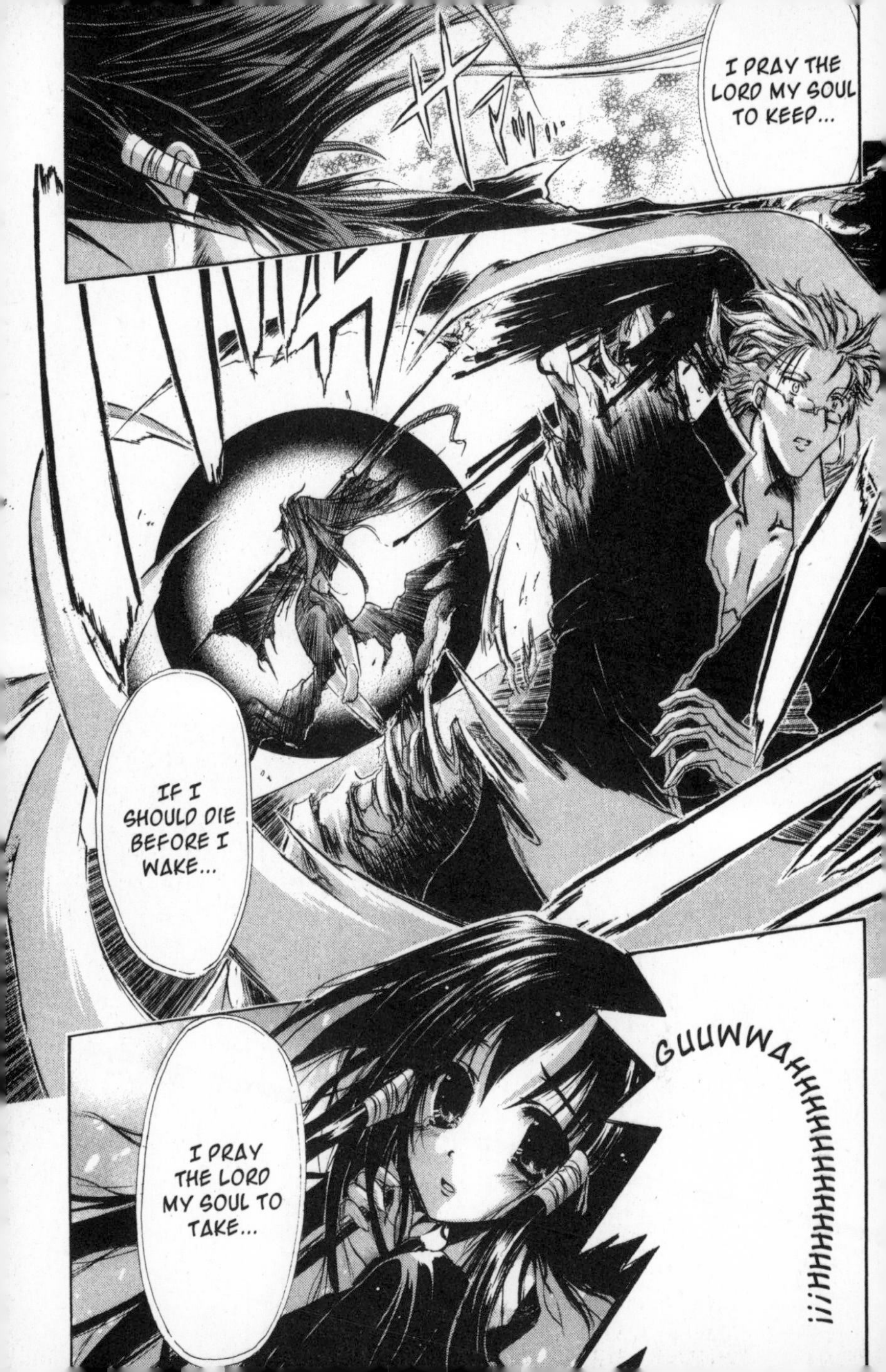
I PRAY THE LORD MY SOUL TO KEEP...
IF I SHOULD DIE BEFORE I WAKE...
GUUWAHHHHHHHHHHHHHHHHH!!!
I PRAY THE LORD MY SOUL TO TAKE...

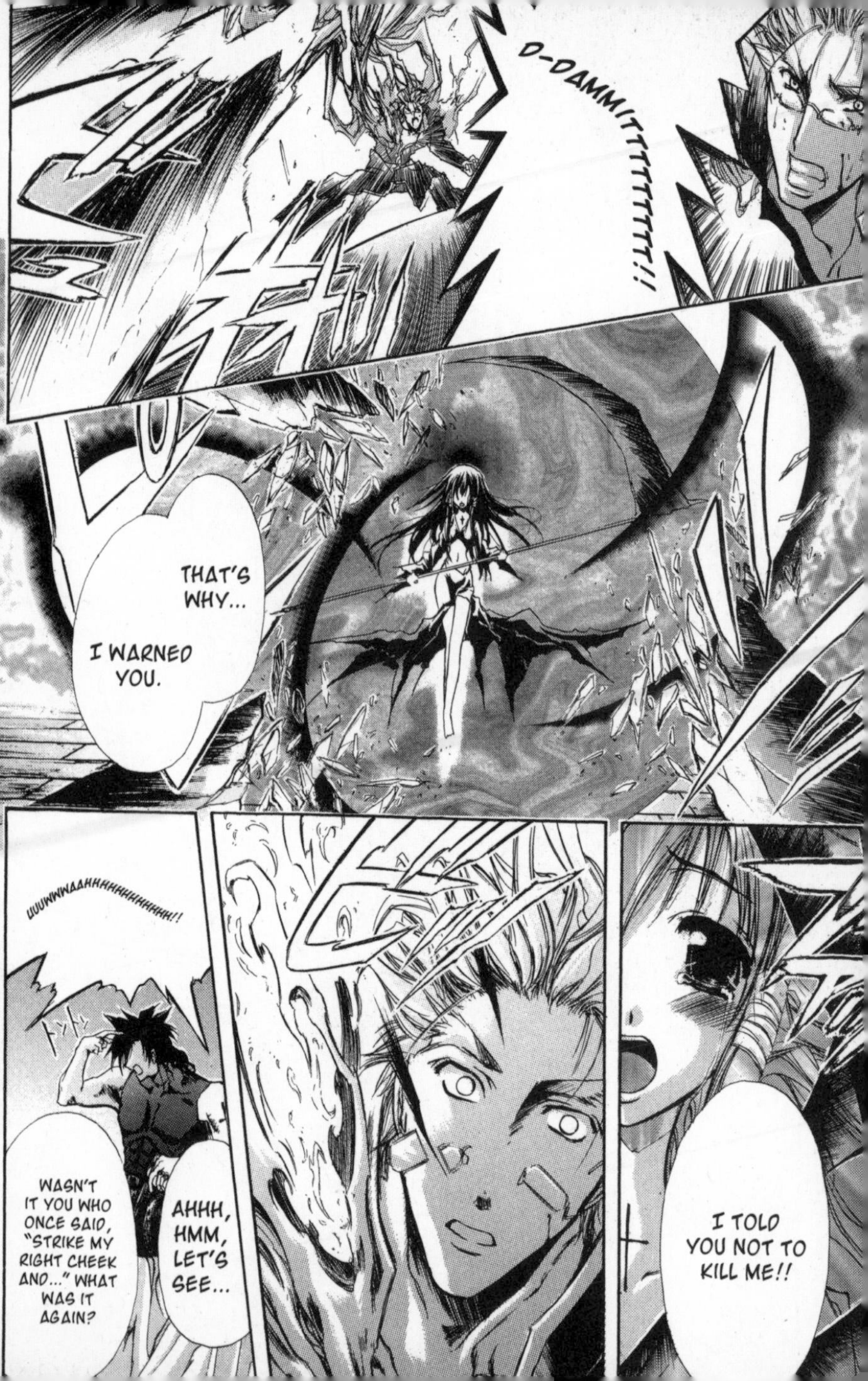
D-DAMMITTTTTTTTTT!!
THAT'S WHY...
I WARNED YOU.
I TOLD YOU NOT TO KILL ME!!
UUUWWWAAHHHHHHHHHHHHH!!
AHHH, HMM, LET'S SEE...
WASN'T IT YOU WHO ONCE SAID, "STRIKE MY RIGHT CHEEK AND..." WHAT WAS IT AGAIN?

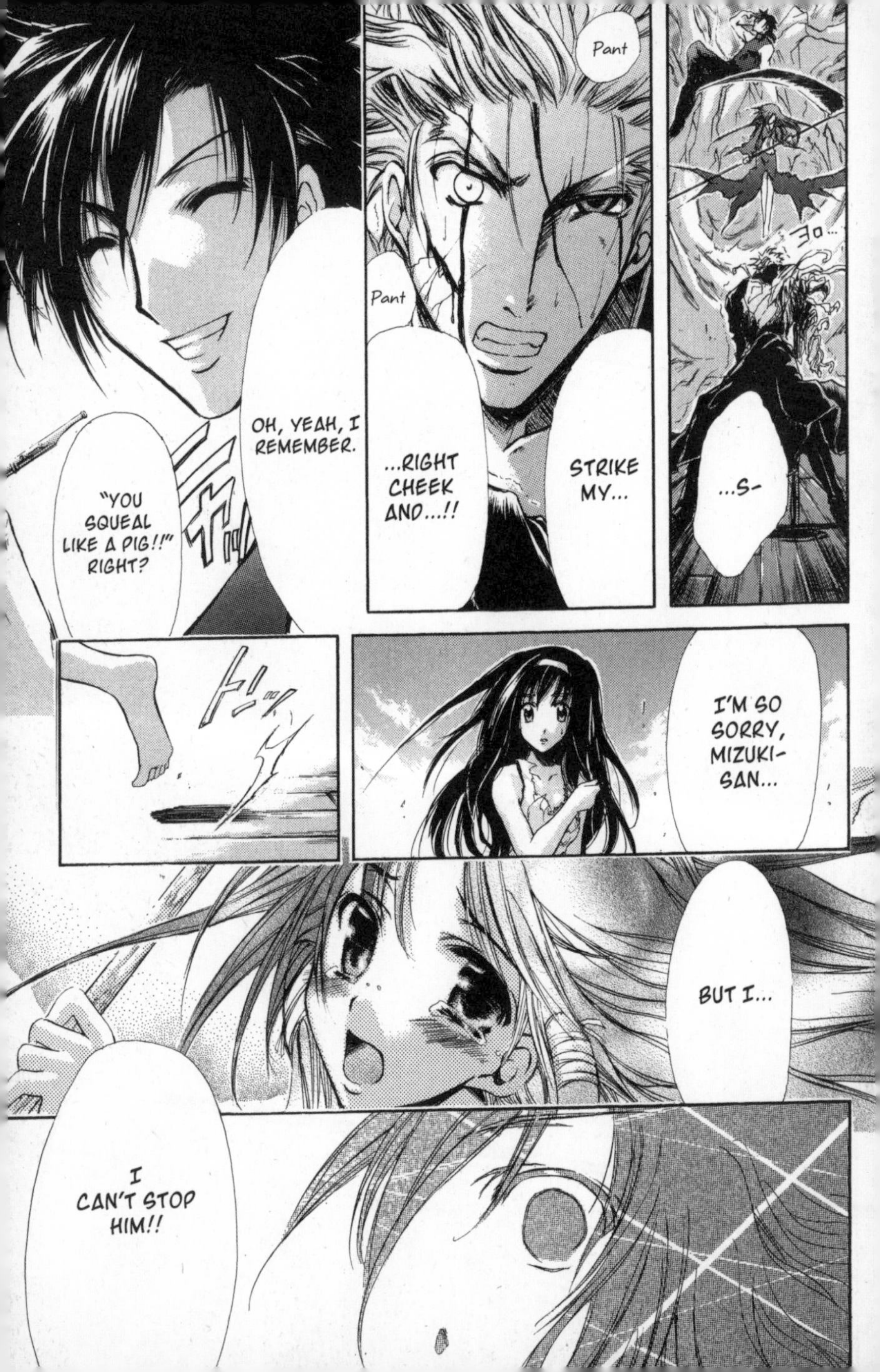
ヨロ…
...S-
Pant
STRIKE MY...
Pant
...RIGHT CHEEK AND...!!
OH, YEAH, I REMEMBER.
"YOU SQUEAL LIKE A PIG!!" RIGHT?
I'M SO SORRY, MIZUKI-SAN...
BUT I...
I CAN'T STOP HIM!!

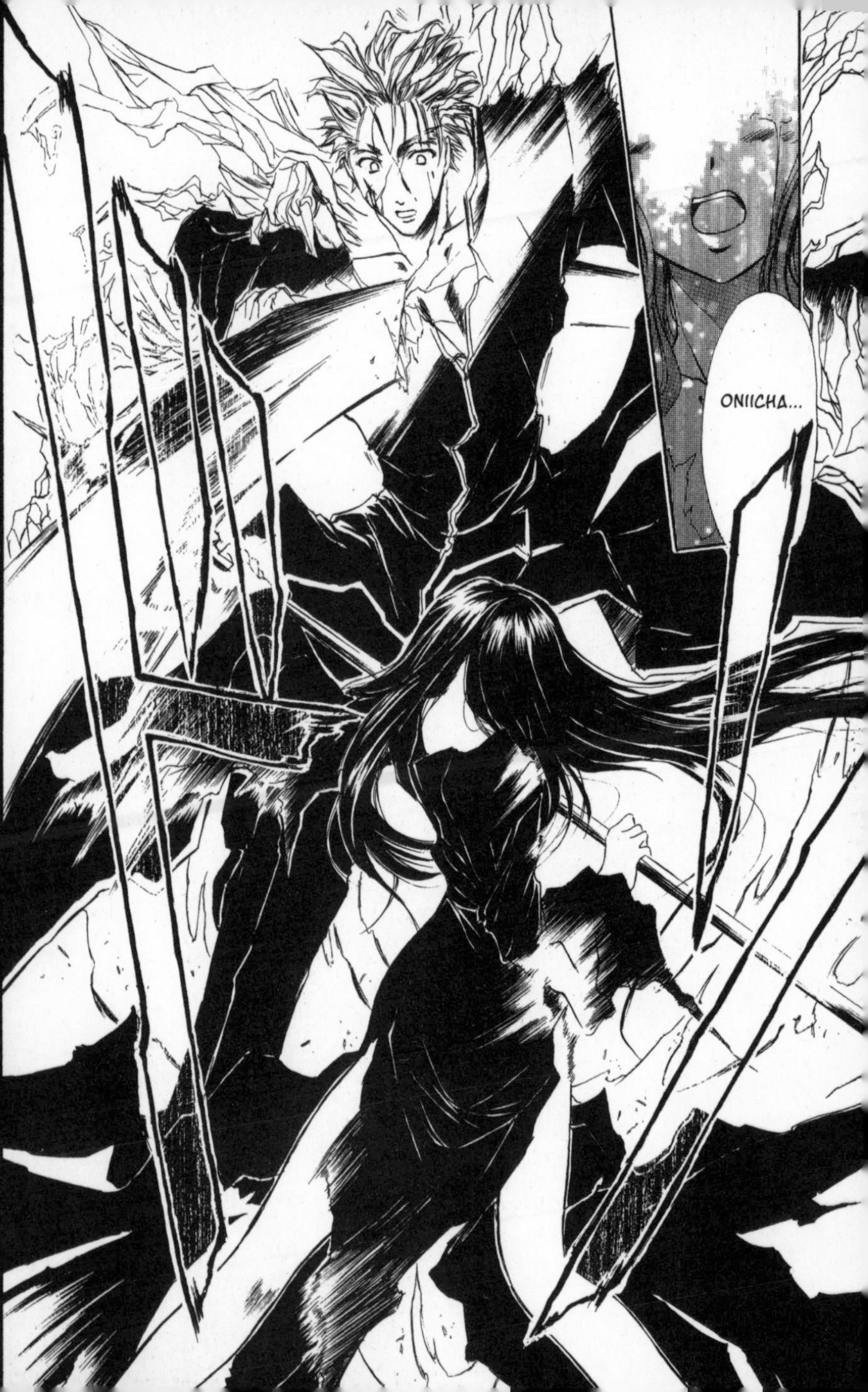
ONIICHA...

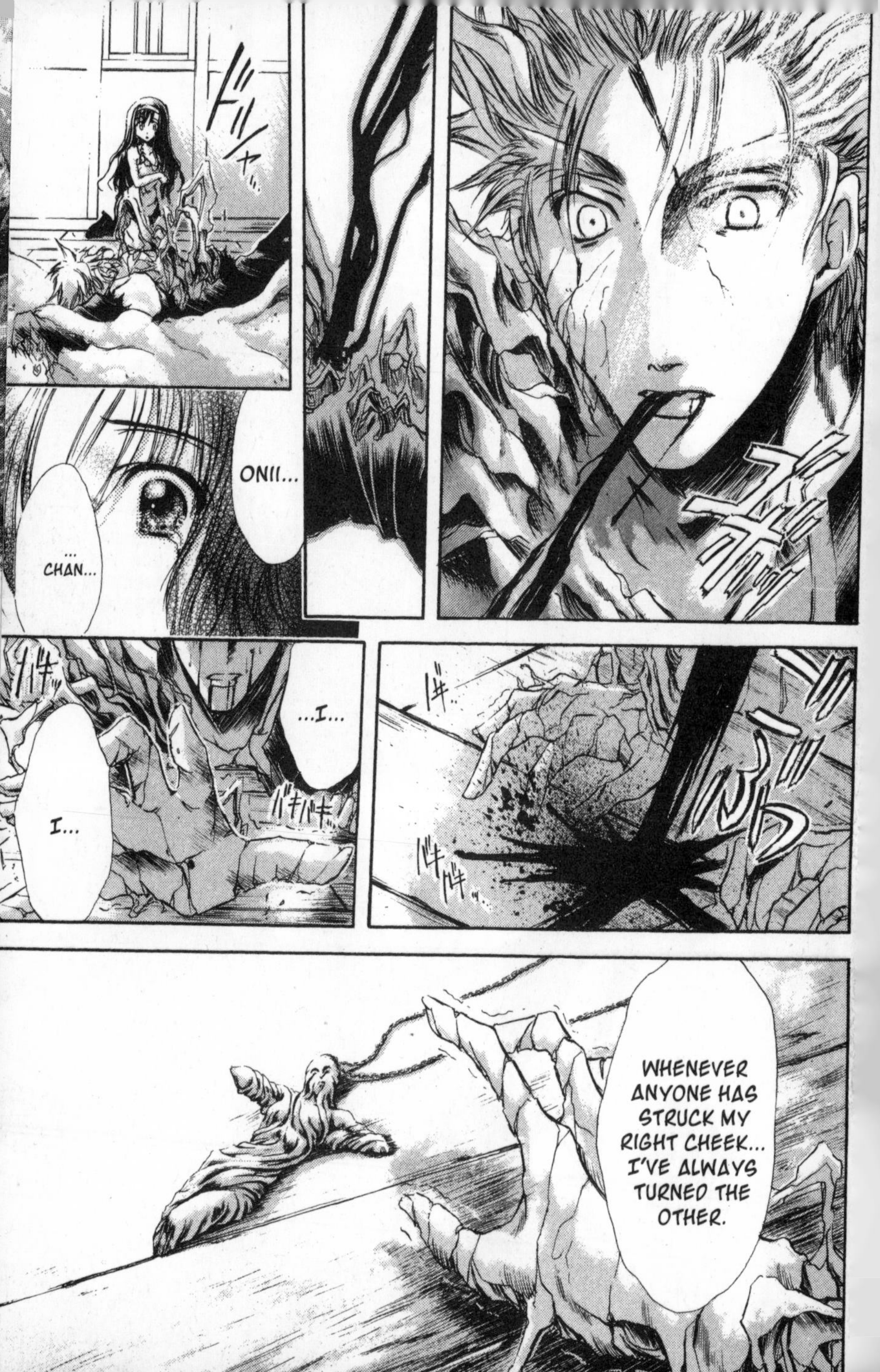
ONII...
...
CHAN...
...I...
I...
WHENEVER ANYONE HAS STRUCK MY RIGHT CHEEK... I'VE ALWAYS TURNED THE OTHER.

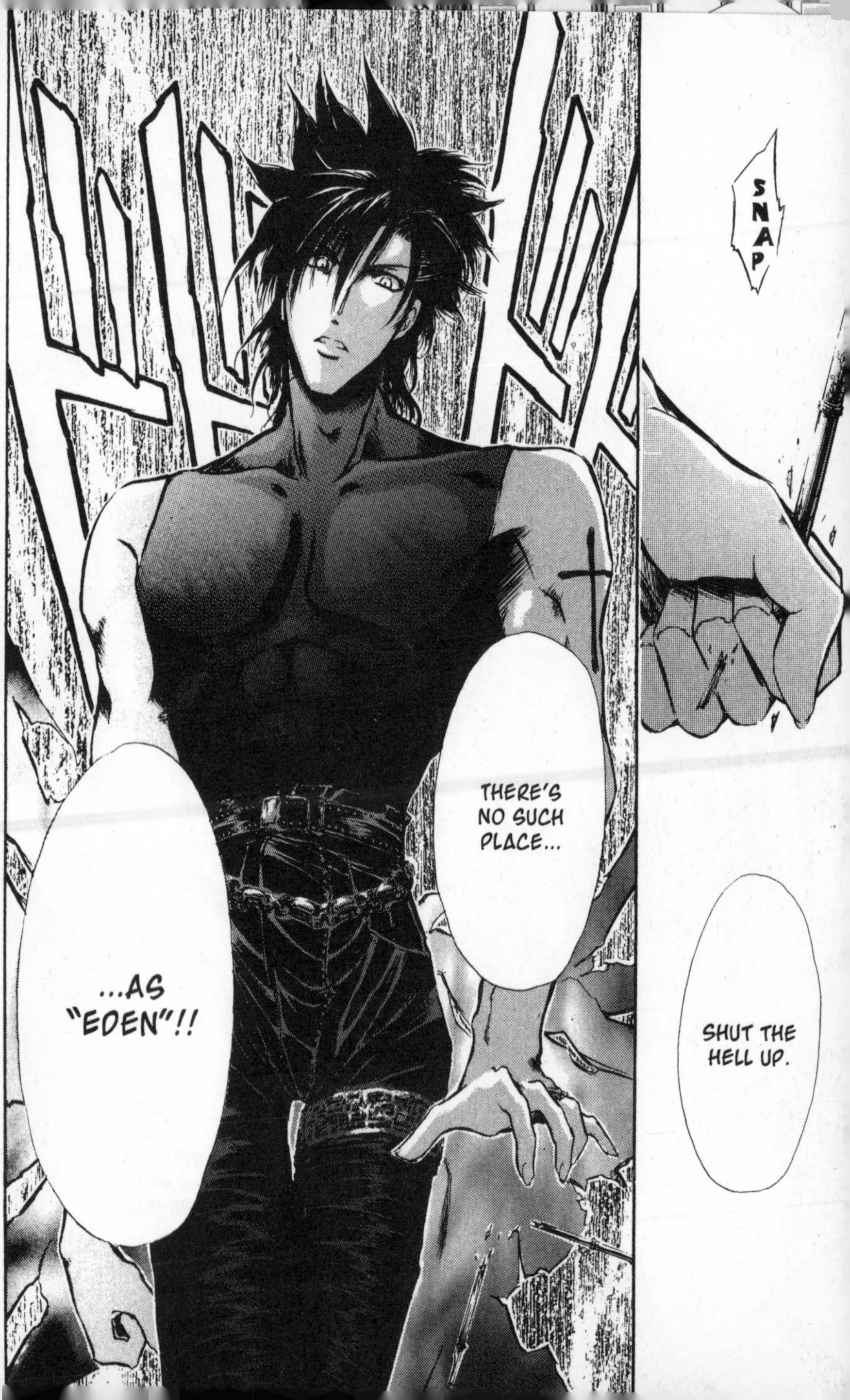
SNAP
SHUT THE HELL UP.
THERE'S NO SUCH PLACE...
...AS "EDEN"!!

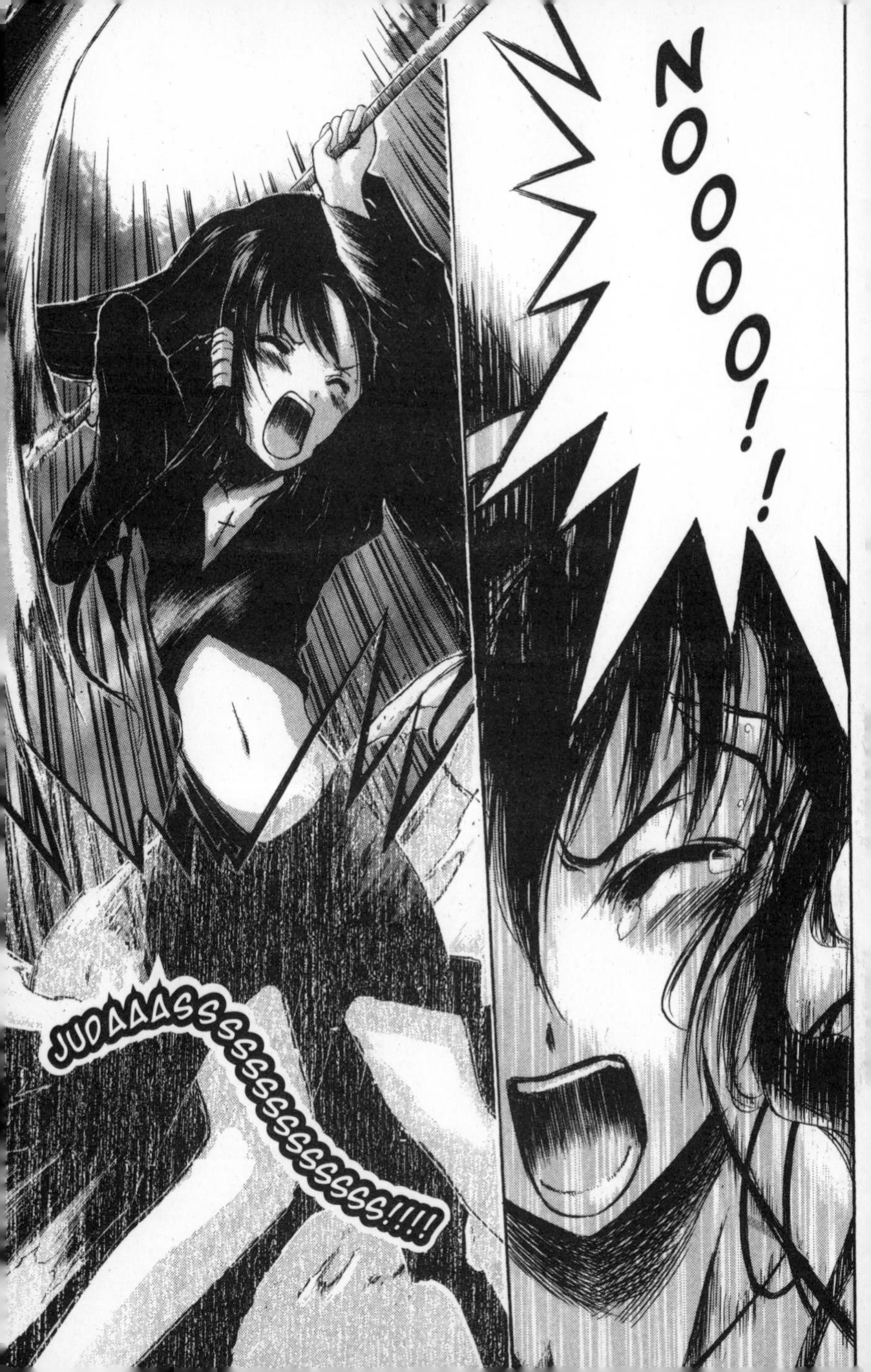
NOOOO!!
JUDAAASSSSSSSSSSSSSS!!!!

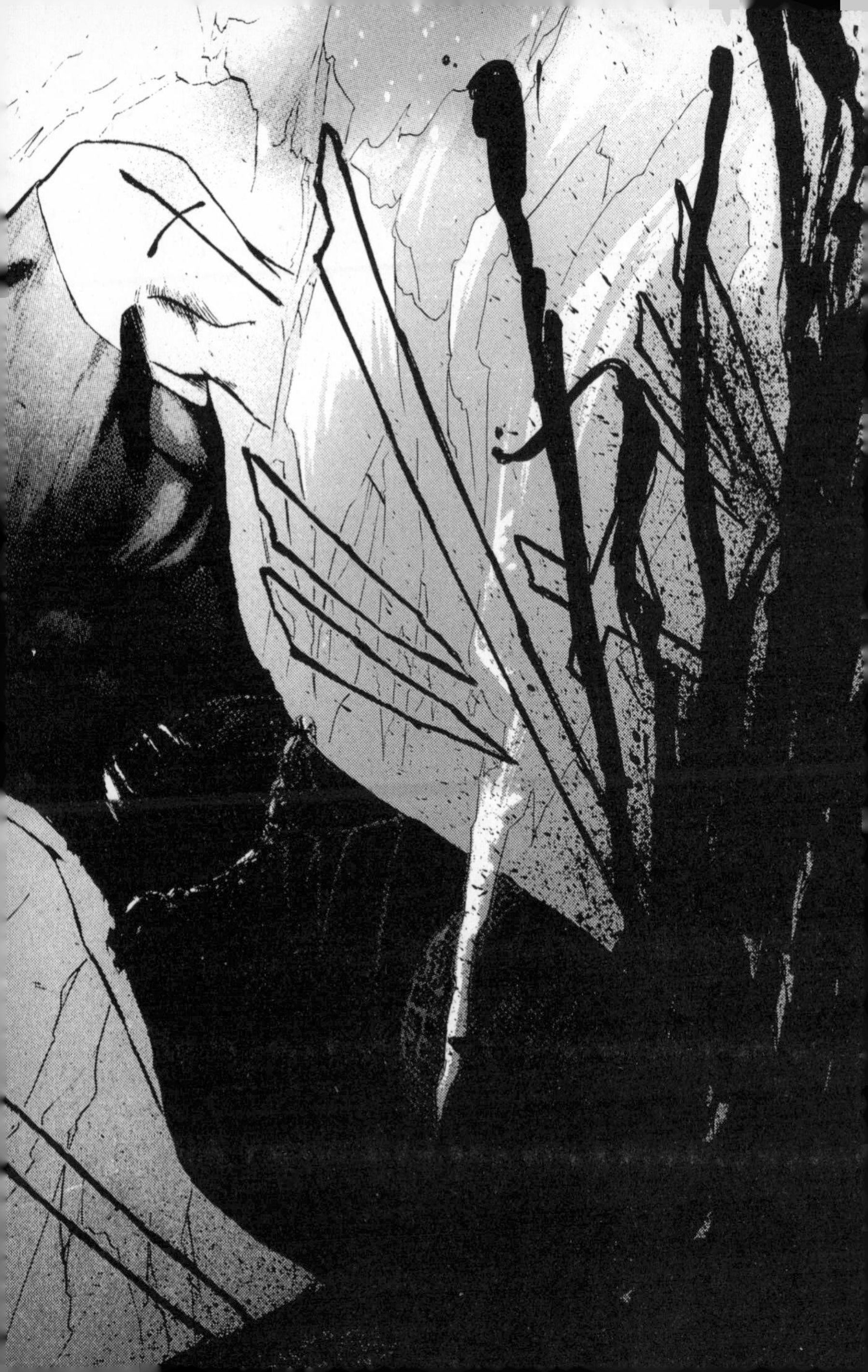

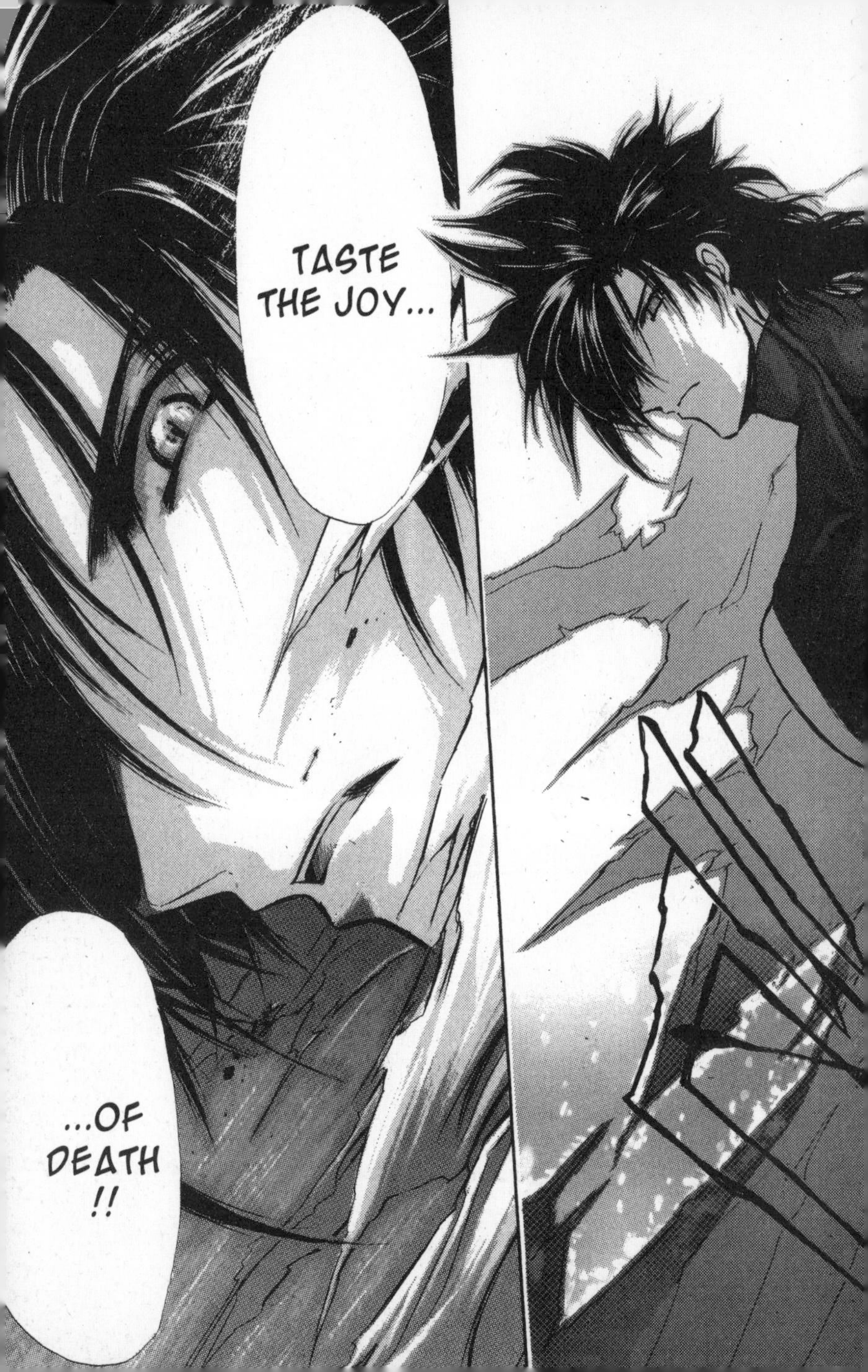
TASTE THE JOY...
...OF DEATH !!

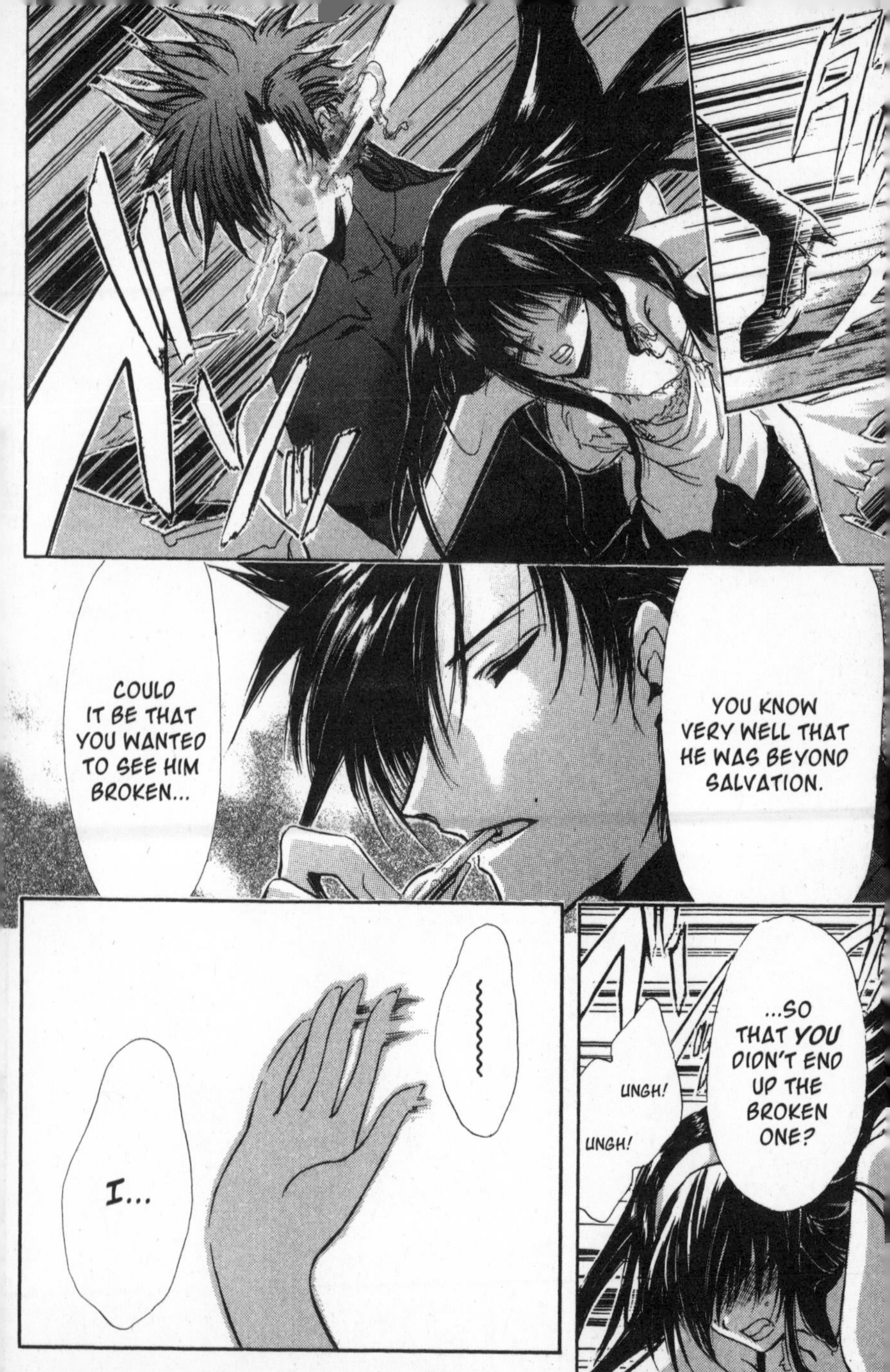
YOU KNOW VERY WELL THAT HE WAS BEYOND SALVATION.
COULD IT BE THAT YOU WANTED TO SEE HIM BROKEN...
...SO THAT YOU DIDN'T END UP THE BROKEN ONE?
UNGH!
UNGH!
I...

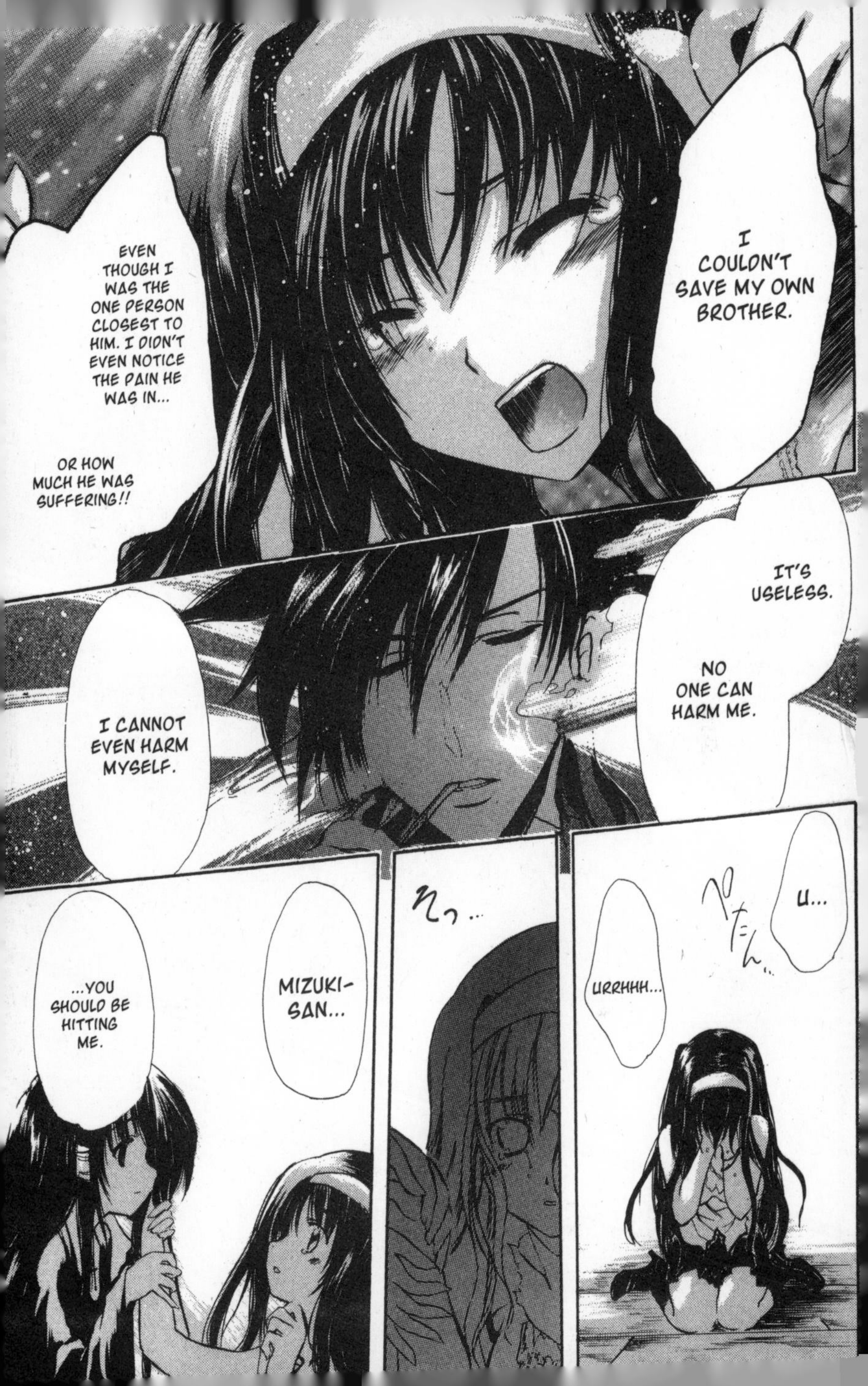
I COULDN'T SAVE MY OWN BROTHER.
EVEN THOUGH I WAS THE ONE PERSON CLOSEST TO HIM. I DIDN'T EVEN NOTICE THE PAIN HE WAS IN...
OR HOW MUCH HE WAS SUFFERING!!
IT'S USELESS.
NO ONE CAN HARM ME.
I CANNOT EVEN HARM MYSELF.
U...
ぺたん..
URRHHH...
えっ…
MIZUKI-SAN...
...YOU SHOULD BE HITTING ME.

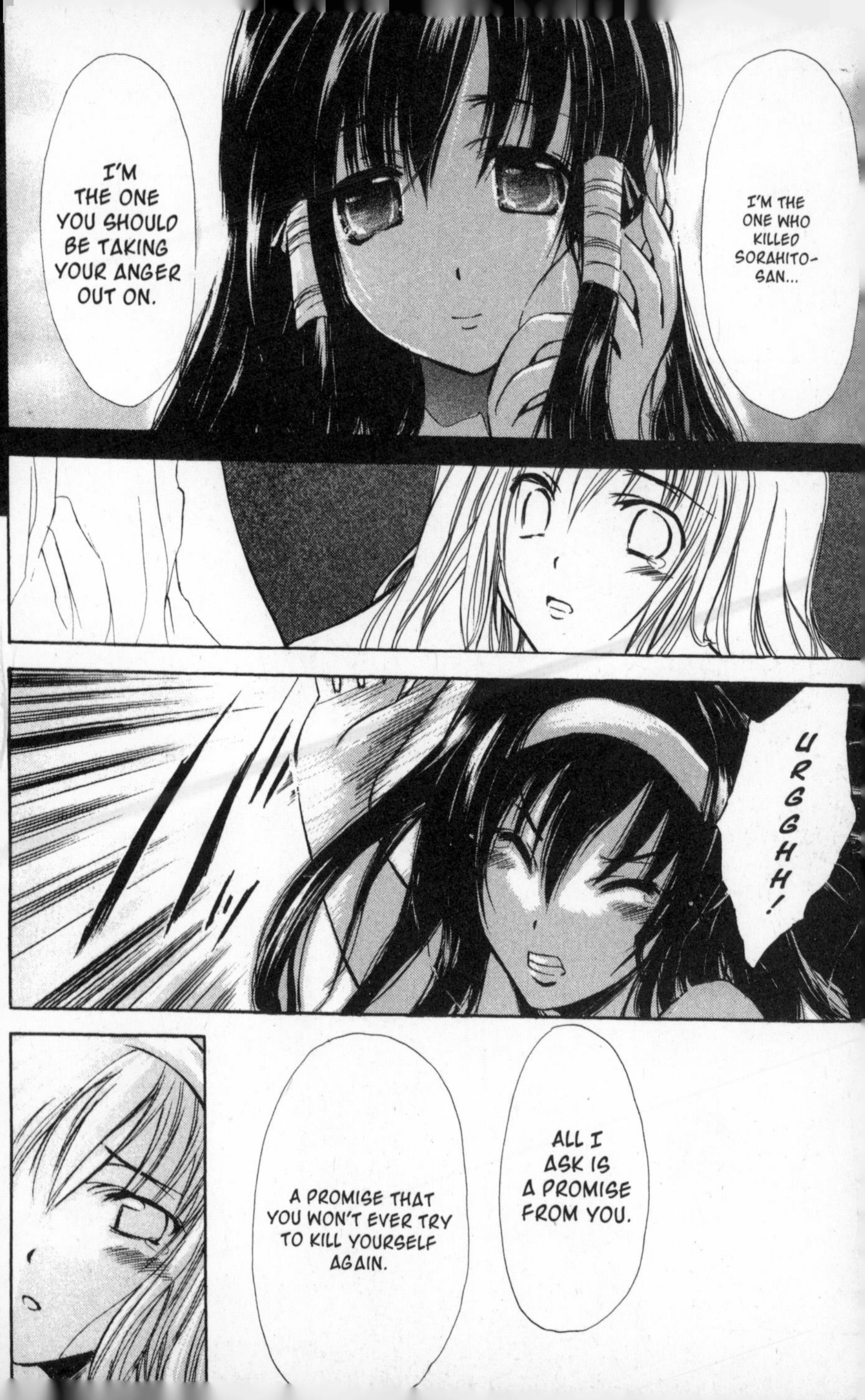
I'M THE ONE WHO KILLED SORAHITO-SAN...
I'M THE ONE YOU SHOULD BE TAKING YOUR ANGER OUT ON.
URGGHH!
ALL I ASK IS A PROMISE FROM YOU.
A PROMISE THAT YOU WON'T EVER TRY TO KILL YOURSELF AGAIN.

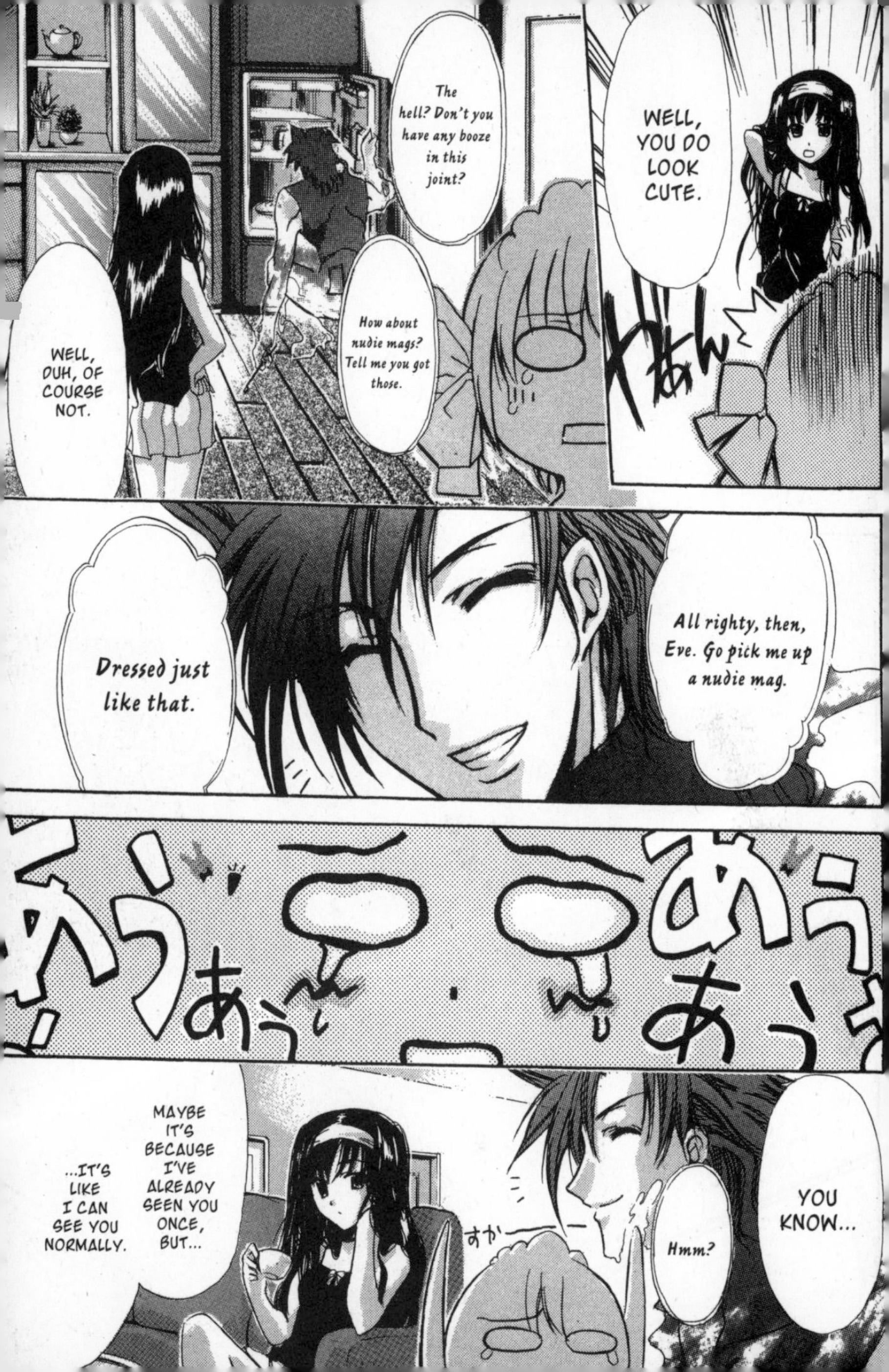
WELL, YOU DO LOOK CUTE.
The hell? Don't you have any booze in this joint?
How about nudie mags? Tell me you got those.
WELL, DUH, OF COURSE NOT.
All righty, then, Eve. Go pick me up a nudie mag.
Dressed just like that.
あうあう
あうあう
YOU KNOW...
Hmm?
すか——
MAYBE IT'S BECAUSE I'VE ALREADY SEEN YOU ONCE, BUT...
...IT'S LIKE I CAN SEE YOU NORMALLY.

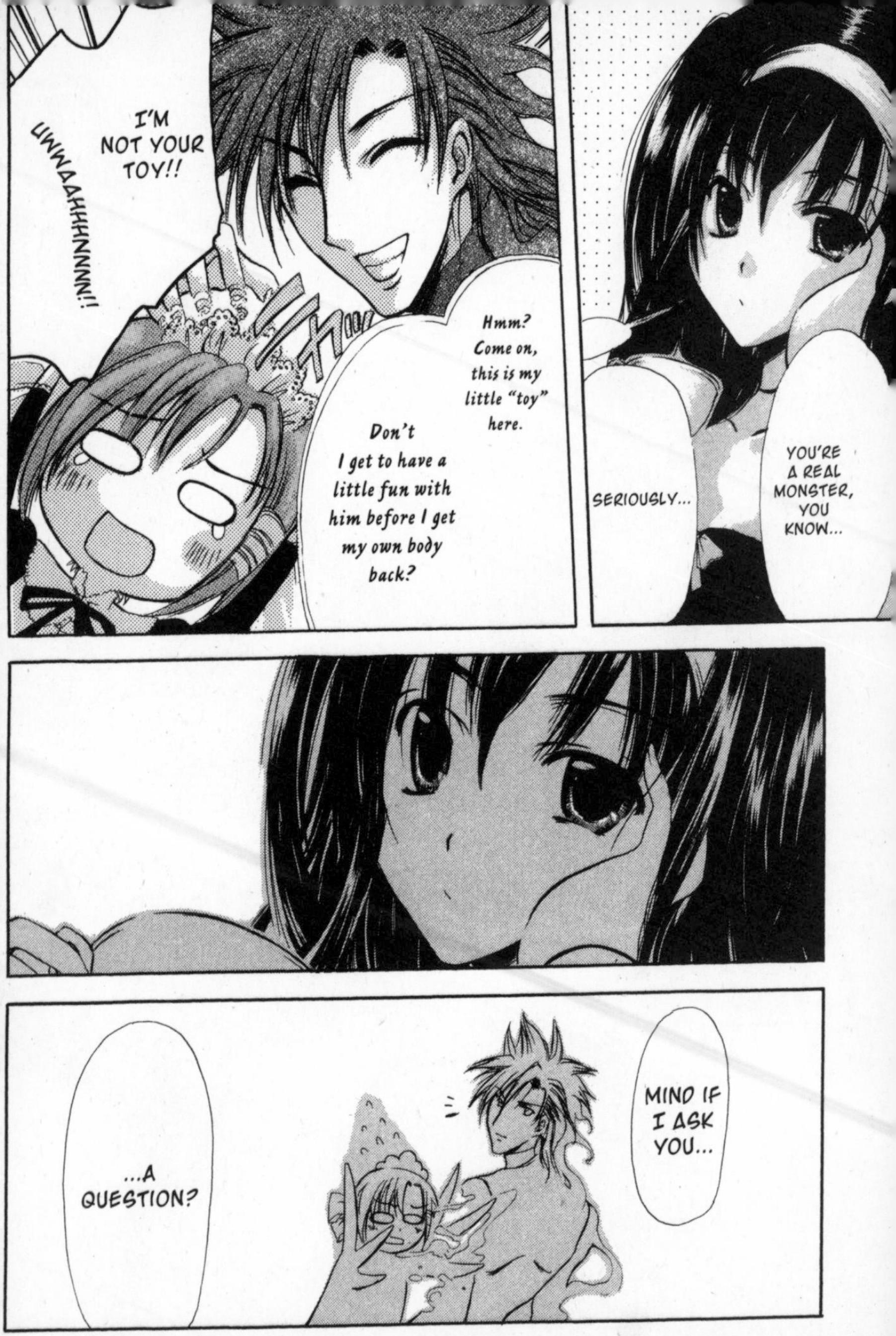
YOU'RE A REAL MONSTER, YOU KNOW...
SERIOUSLY...
Hmm? Come on, this is my little "toy" here.
Don't I get to have a little fun with him before I get my own body back?
I'M NOT YOUR TOY!!
UWWAAHHHNNNN!!
MIND IF I ASK YOU...
...A QUESTION?

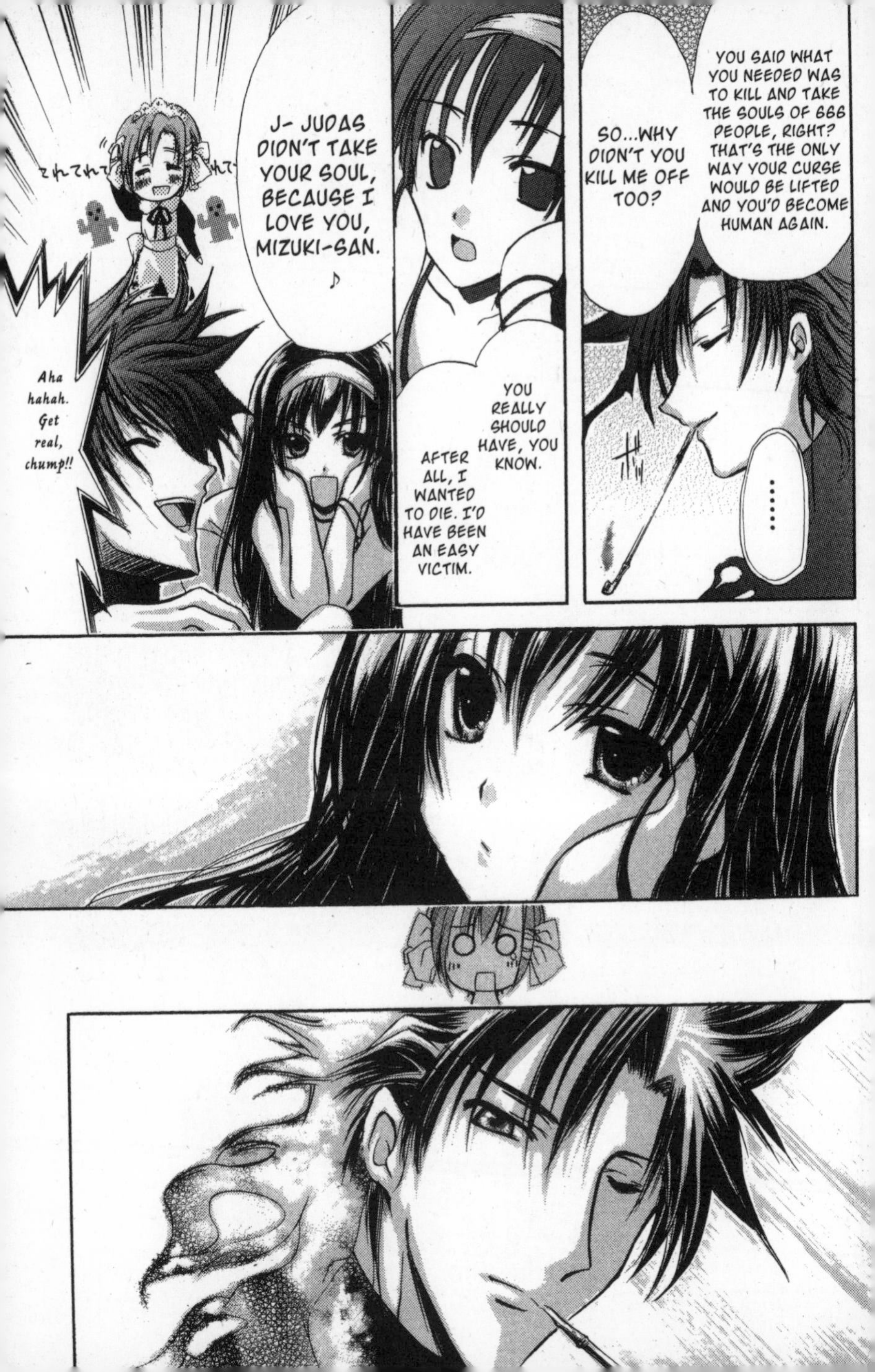
YOU SAID WHAT YOU NEEDED WAS TO KILL AND TAKE THE SOULS OF 666 PEOPLE, RIGHT? THAT'S THE ONLY WAY YOUR CURSE WOULD BE LIFTED AND YOU'D BECOME HUMAN AGAIN.
SO...WHY DIDN'T YOU KILL ME OFF TOO?
......
YOU REALLY SHOULD HAVE, YOU KNOW.
AFTER ALL, I WANTED TO DIE. I'D HAVE BEEN AN EASY VICTIM.
J- JUDAS DIDN'T TAKE YOUR SOUL, BECAUSE I LOVE YOU, MIZUKI-SAN. ♪
てれてれ
Aha hahah. Get real, chump!!

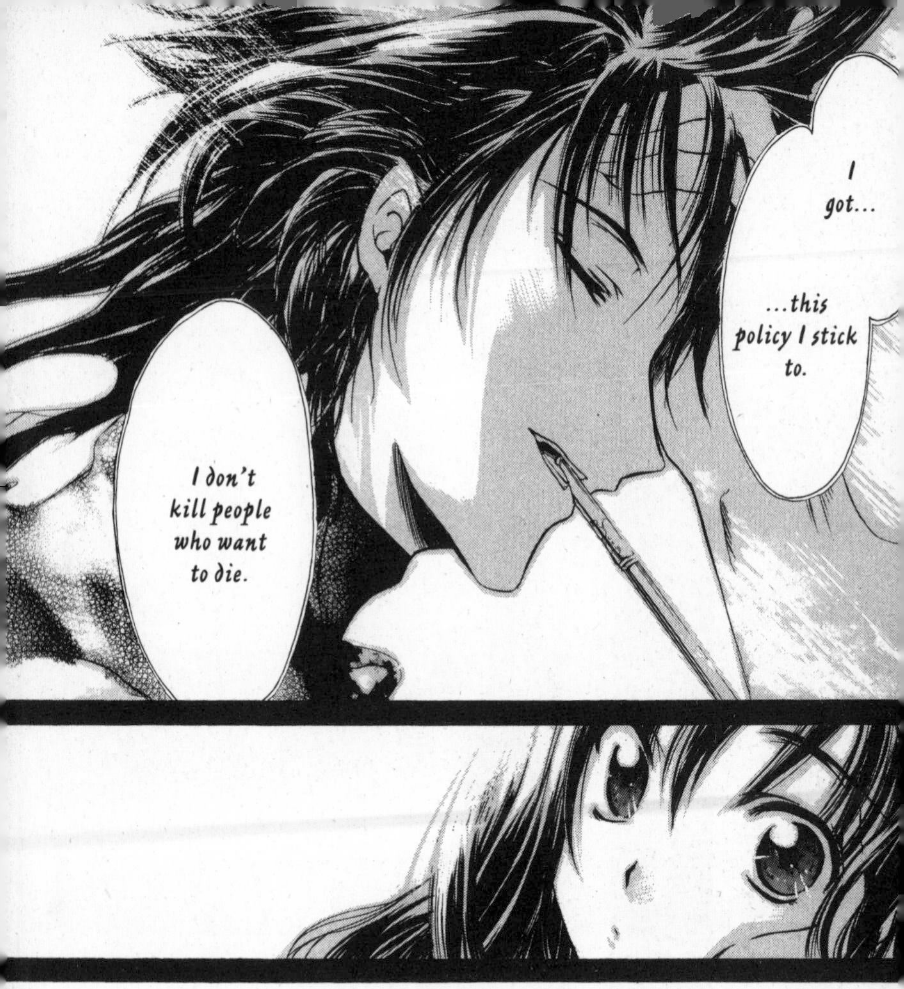
I got...
...this policy I stick to.
I don't kill people who want to die.

JUDAS

JUDAS

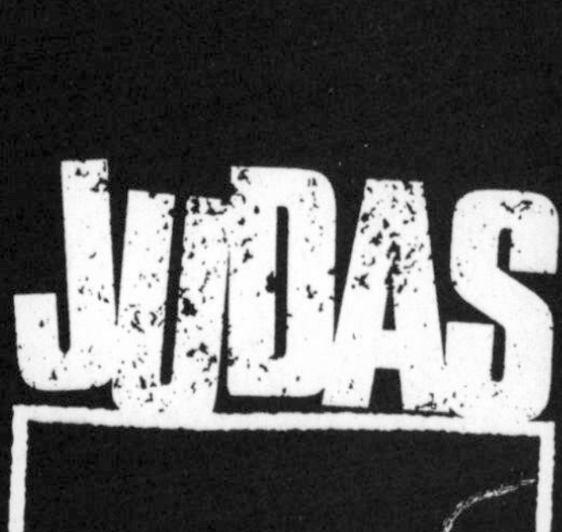

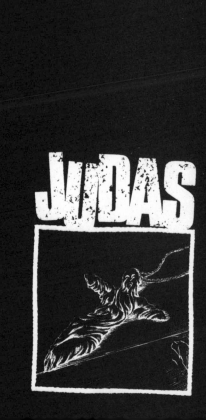

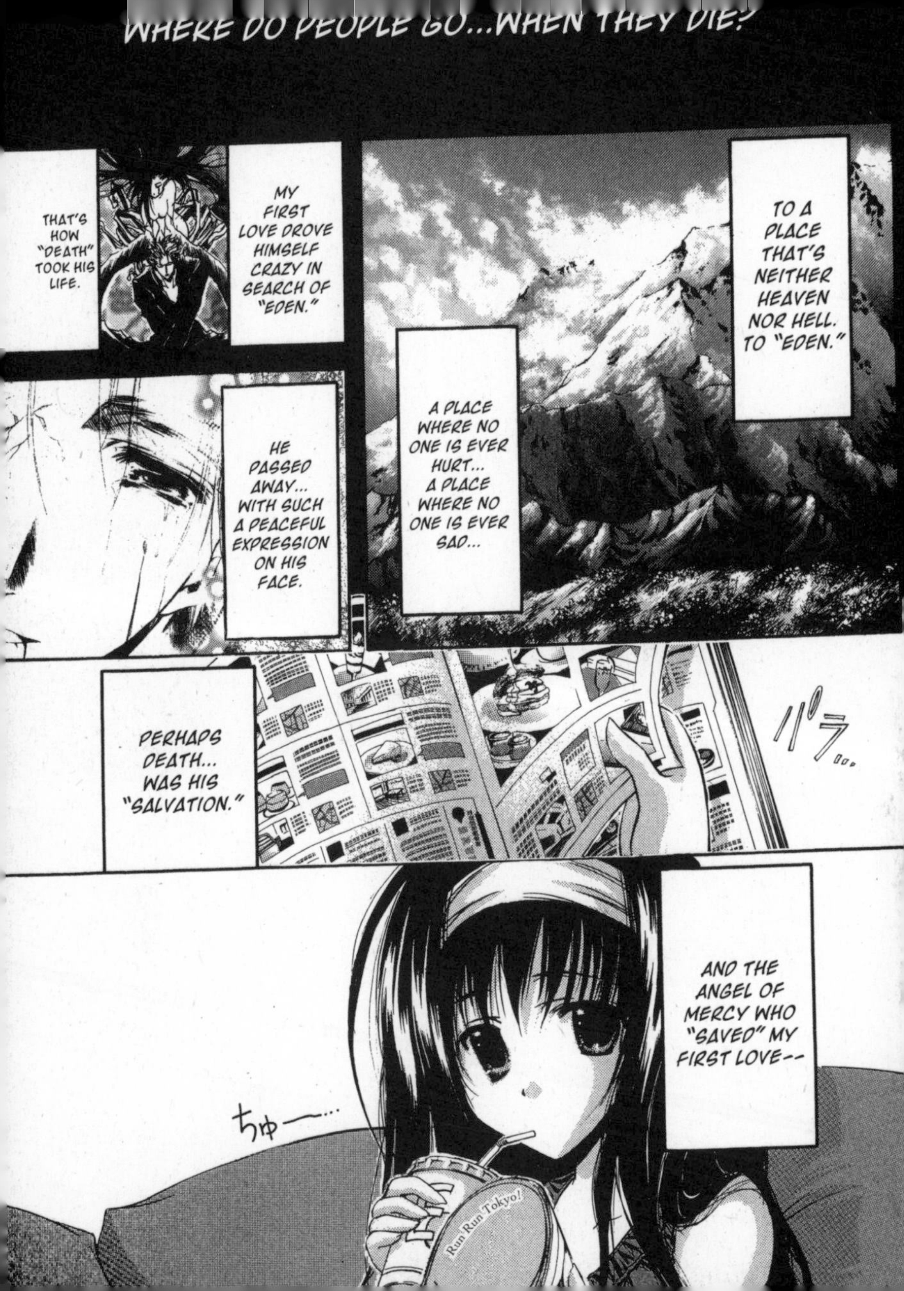

WHERE DO PEOPLE GO...WHEN THEY DIE?
TO A PLACE THAT'S NEITHER HEAVEN NOR HELL. TO "EDEN."
A PLACE WHERE NO ONE IS EVER HURT... A PLACE WHERE NO ONE IS EVER SAD...
MY FIRST LOVE DROVE HIMSELF CRAZY IN SEARCH OF "EDEN."
THAT'S HOW "DEATH" TOOK HIS LIFE.
HE PASSED AWAY... WITH SUCH A PEACEFUL EXPRESSION ON HIS FACE.
パラ…
PERHAPS DEATH... WAS HIS "SALVATION."
AND THE ANGEL OF MERCY WHO "SAVED" MY FIRST LOVE--
ちゅー…
Run Run Tokyo!

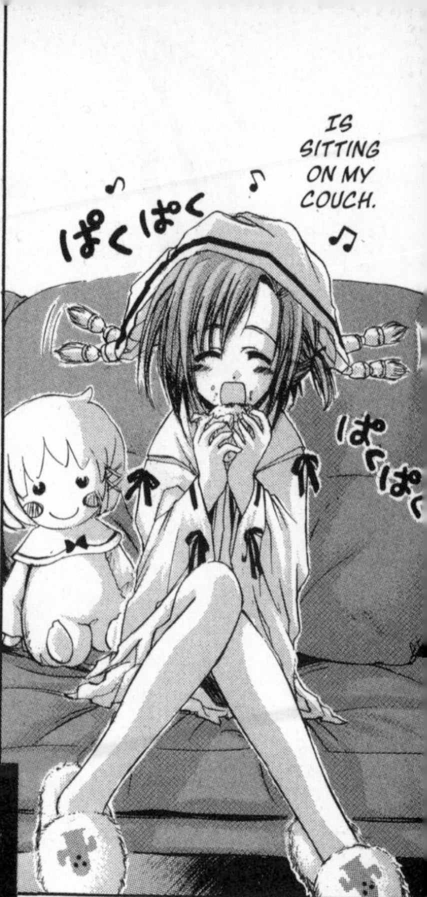
IS SITTING ON MY COUCH.
ぱくぱく
ぱくぱく

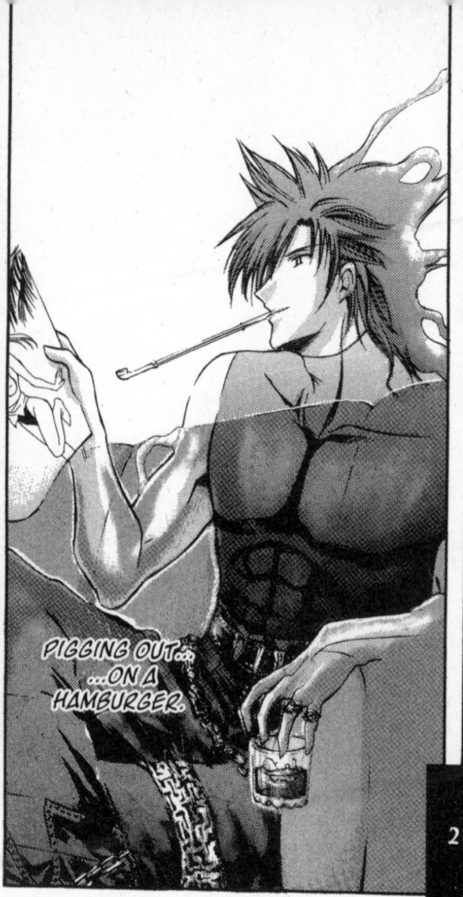
PIGGING OUT...
...ON A HAMBURGER.

2 He Who Defies Death

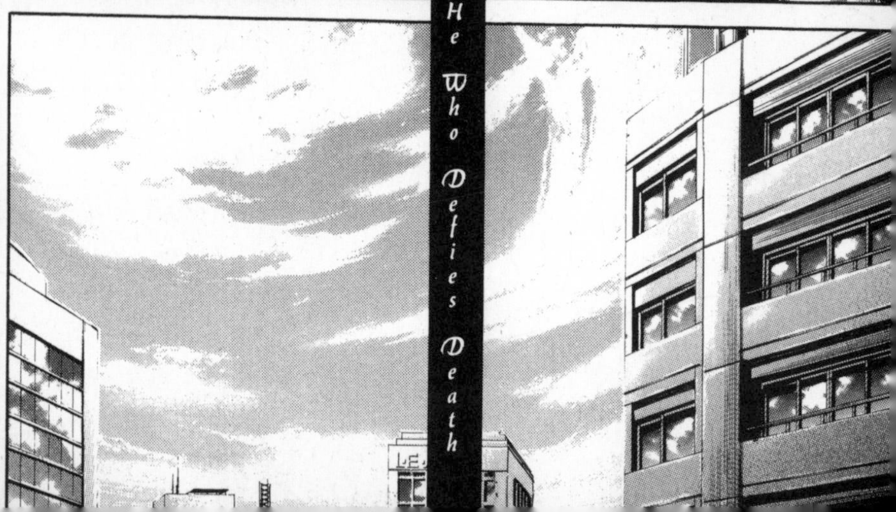

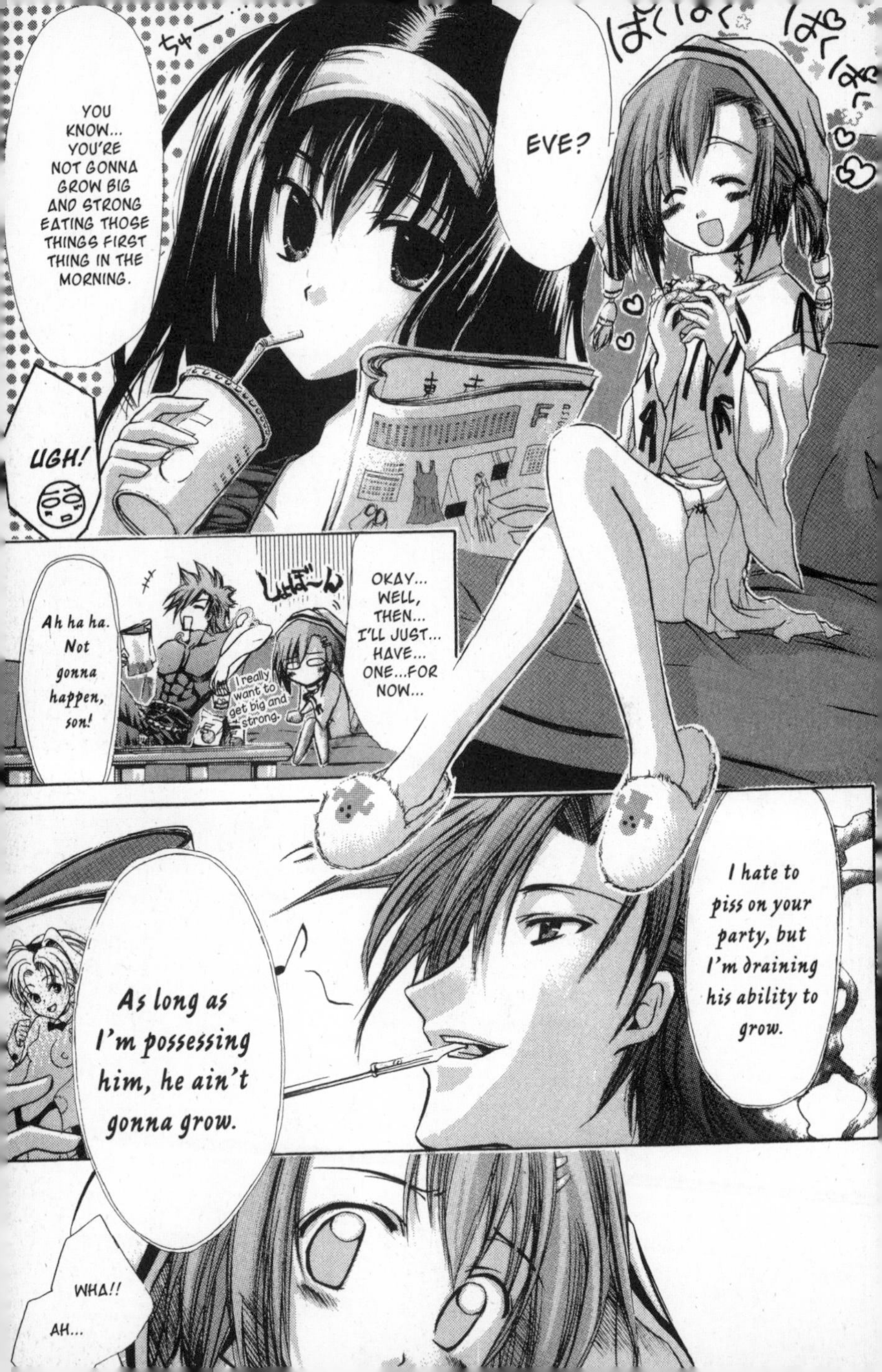
ぱくぱく ぱくぱく
EVE?
ちゃー…
YOU KNOW... YOU'RE NOT GONNA GROW BIG AND STRONG EATING THOSE THINGS FIRST THING IN THE MORNING.
UGH!
OKAY... WELL, THEN... I'LL JUST... HAVE... ONE...FOR NOW...
しょぼーん
I really want to get big and strong.
Ah ha ha. Not gonna happen, son!
I hate to piss on your party, but I'm draining his ability to grow.
As long as I'm possessing him, he ain't gonna grow.
WHA!!
AH...

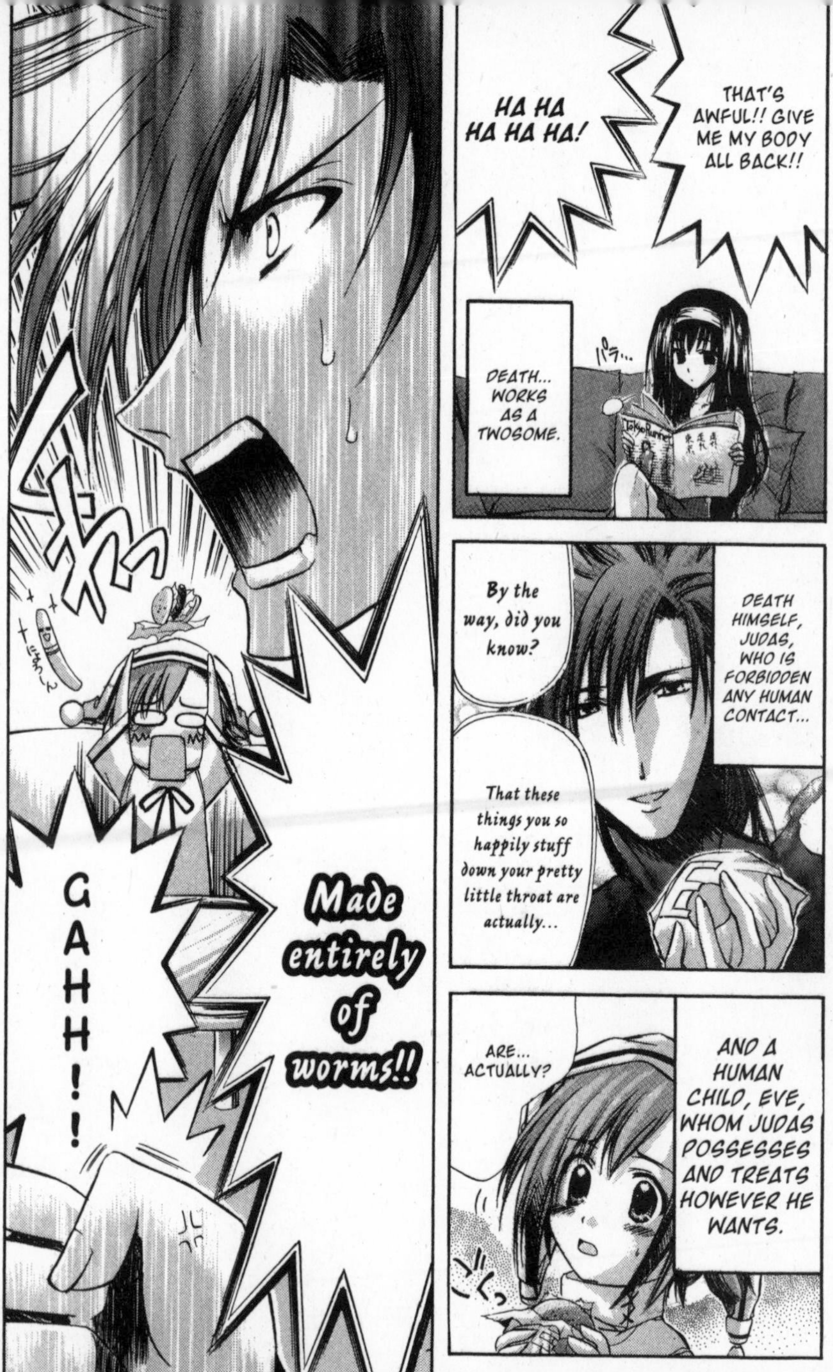
THAT'S AWFUL!! GIVE ME MY BODY ALL BACK!!
HA HA HA HA HA!
DEATH... WORKS AS A TWOSOME.
DEATH HIMSELF, JUDAS, WHO IS FORBIDDEN ANY HUMAN CONTACT...
By the way, did you know?
That these things you so happily stuff down your pretty little throat are actually...
AND A HUMAN CHILD, EVE, WHOM JUDAS POSSESSES AND TREATS HOWEVER HE WANTS.
ARE... ACTUALLY?
Made entirely of worms!!
GAHH!!

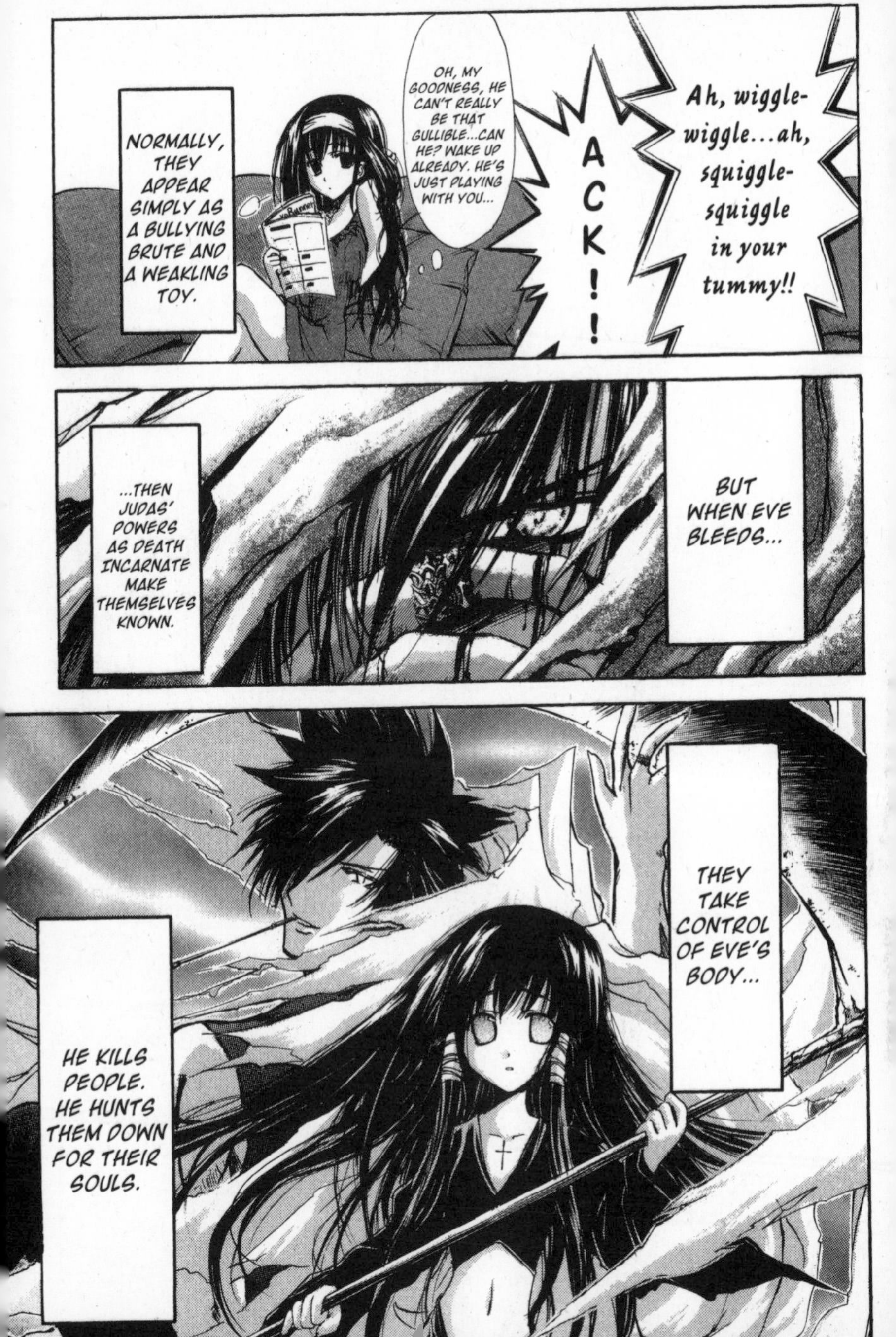

Ah, wiggle-wiggle...ah, squiggle-squiggle in your tummy!!
ACK!!
OH, MY GOODNESS, HE CAN'T REALLY BE THAT GULLIBLE...CAN HE? WAKE UP ALREADY. HE'S JUST PLAYING WITH YOU...
NORMALLY, THEY APPEAR SIMPLY AS A BULLYING BRUTE AND A WEAKLING TOY.
BUT WHEN EVE BLEEDS...
...THEN JUDAS' POWERS AS DEATH INCARNATE MAKE THEMSELVES KNOWN.
THEY TAKE CONTROL OF EVE'S BODY...
HE KILLS PEOPLE. HE HUNTS THEM DOWN FOR THEIR SOULS.

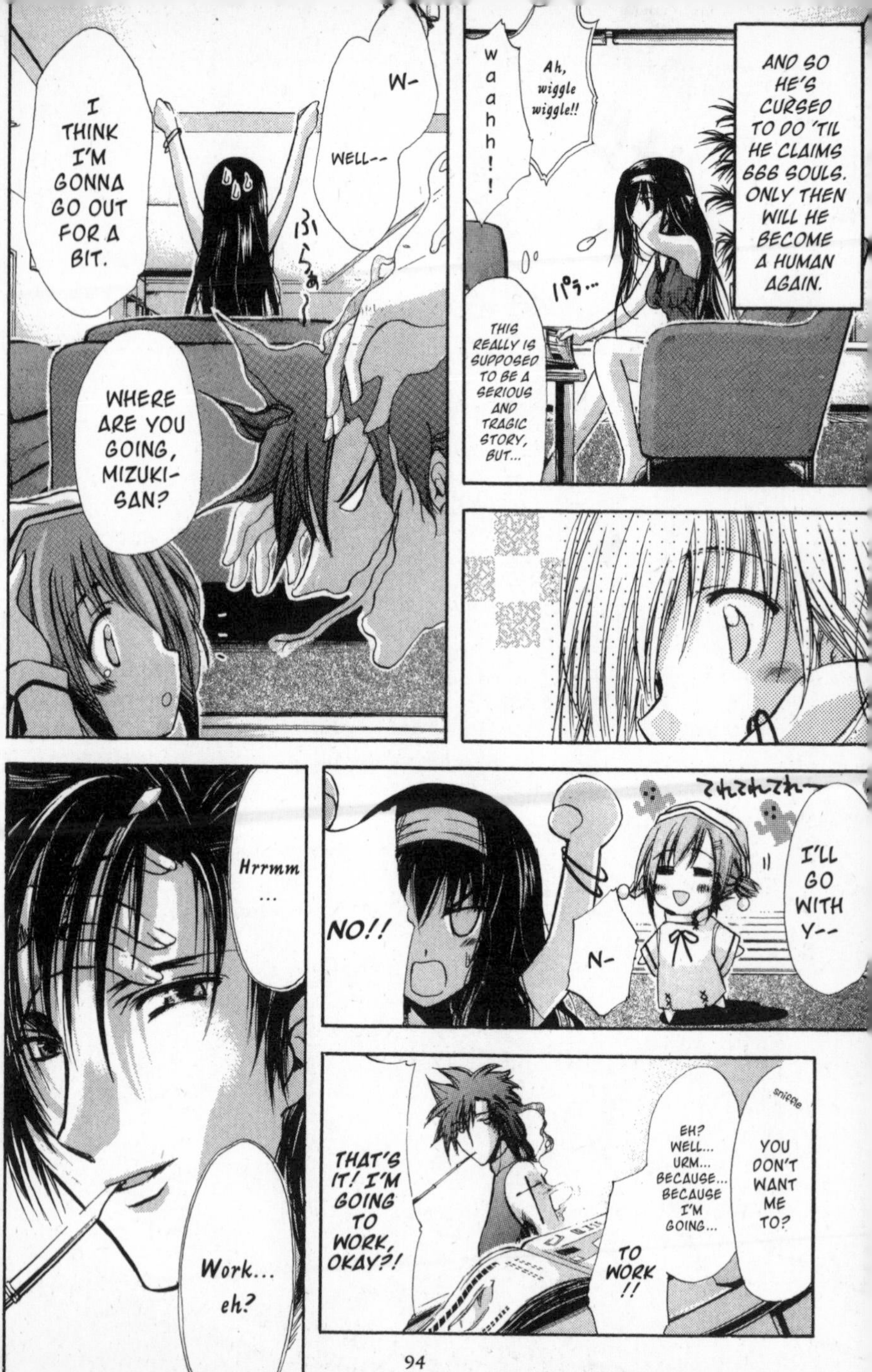
AND SO HE'S CURSED TO DO 'TIL HE CLAIMS 666 SOULS. ONLY THEN WILL HE BECOME A HUMAN AGAIN.
Ah, wiggle wiggle!!
waahh!!
パラ…
THIS REALLY IS SUPPOSED TO BE A SERIOUS AND TRAGIC STORY, BUT...
W-
WELL--
I THINK I'M GONNA GO OUT FOR A BIT.
ふらぁ~
WHERE ARE YOU GOING, MIZUKI-SAN?
てれてれてれ~
I'LL GO WITH Y--
N-
NO!!
sniffle
YOU DON'T WANT ME TO?
EH? WELL... URM... BECAUSE... BECAUSE I'M GOING...
TO WORK!!
THAT'S IT! I'M GOING TO WORK, OKAY?!
Hrrmm...
Work... eh?

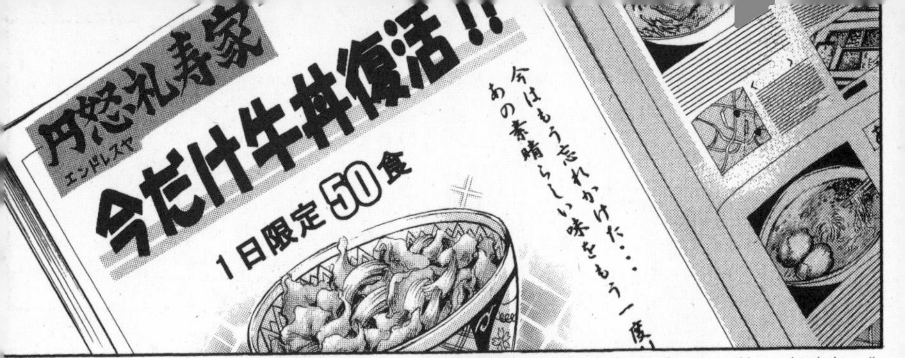
円怒礼寿家
エンドレスヤ
今だけ牛丼復活!!
1日限定50食
今はもう忘れかけた・・・
あの素晴らしい味をもう一度

Endless Restaurant. For a limited time only, the Beef Bowl is back!! Only 50 bowls to be served a day!! That taste you thought you'd forgotten...that scrumptious delicacy we bring back to you!!

JUDAS

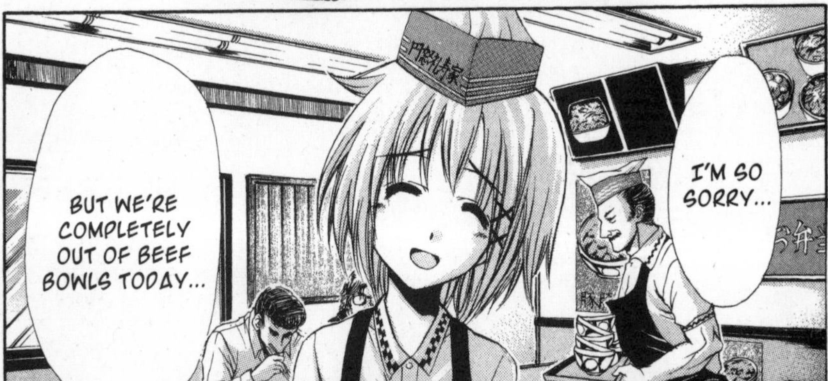
I'M SO SORRY...
BUT WE'RE COMPLETELY OUT OF BEEF BOWLS TODAY...

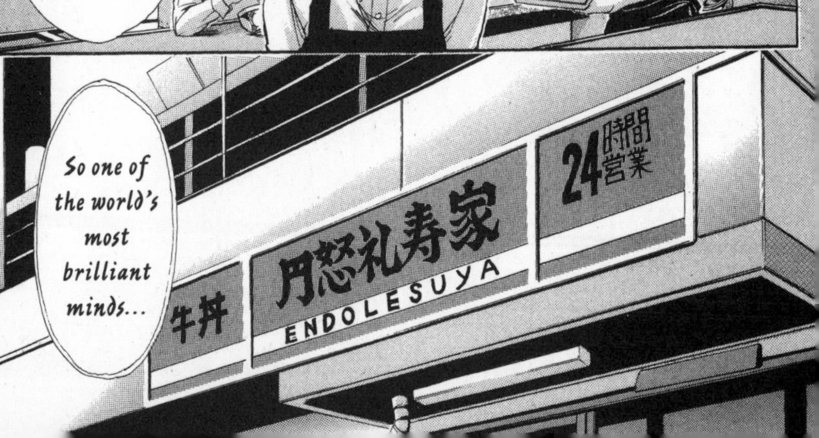
24時間営業
円怒礼寿家
ENDOLESUYA
牛丼
So one of the world's most brilliant minds...

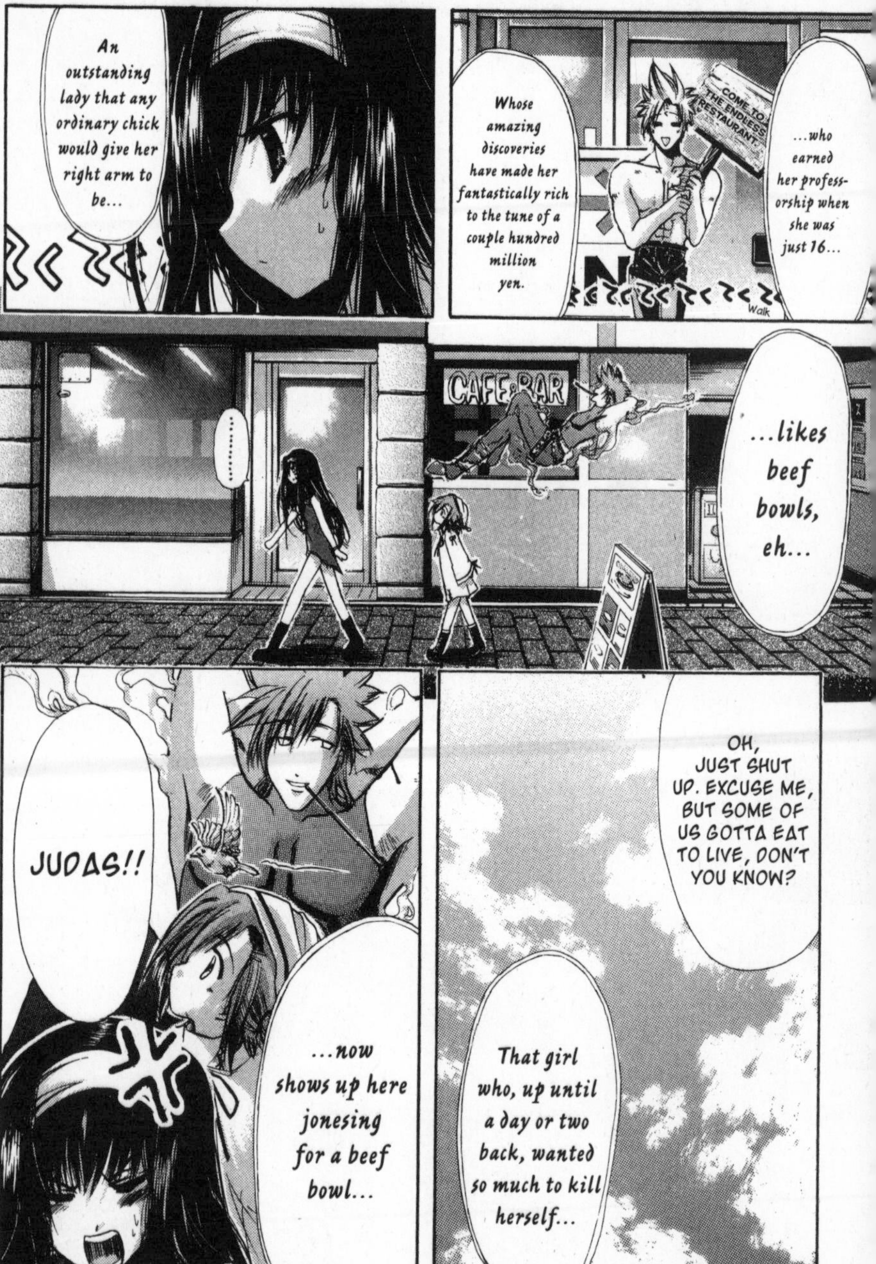

COME TO THE ENDLESS RESTAURANT.
...who earned her profess-orship when she was just 16...
Whose amazing discoveries have made her fantastically rich to the tune of a couple hundred million yen.
Walk
An outstanding lady that any ordinary chick would give her right arm to be...
...likes beef bowls, eh...
CAFE & BAR
......
OH, JUST SHUT UP. EXCUSE ME, BUT SOME OF US GOTTA EAT TO LIVE, DON'T YOU KNOW?
That girl who, up until a day or two back, wanted so much to kill herself...
...now shows up here jonesing for a beef bowl...
JUDAS!!

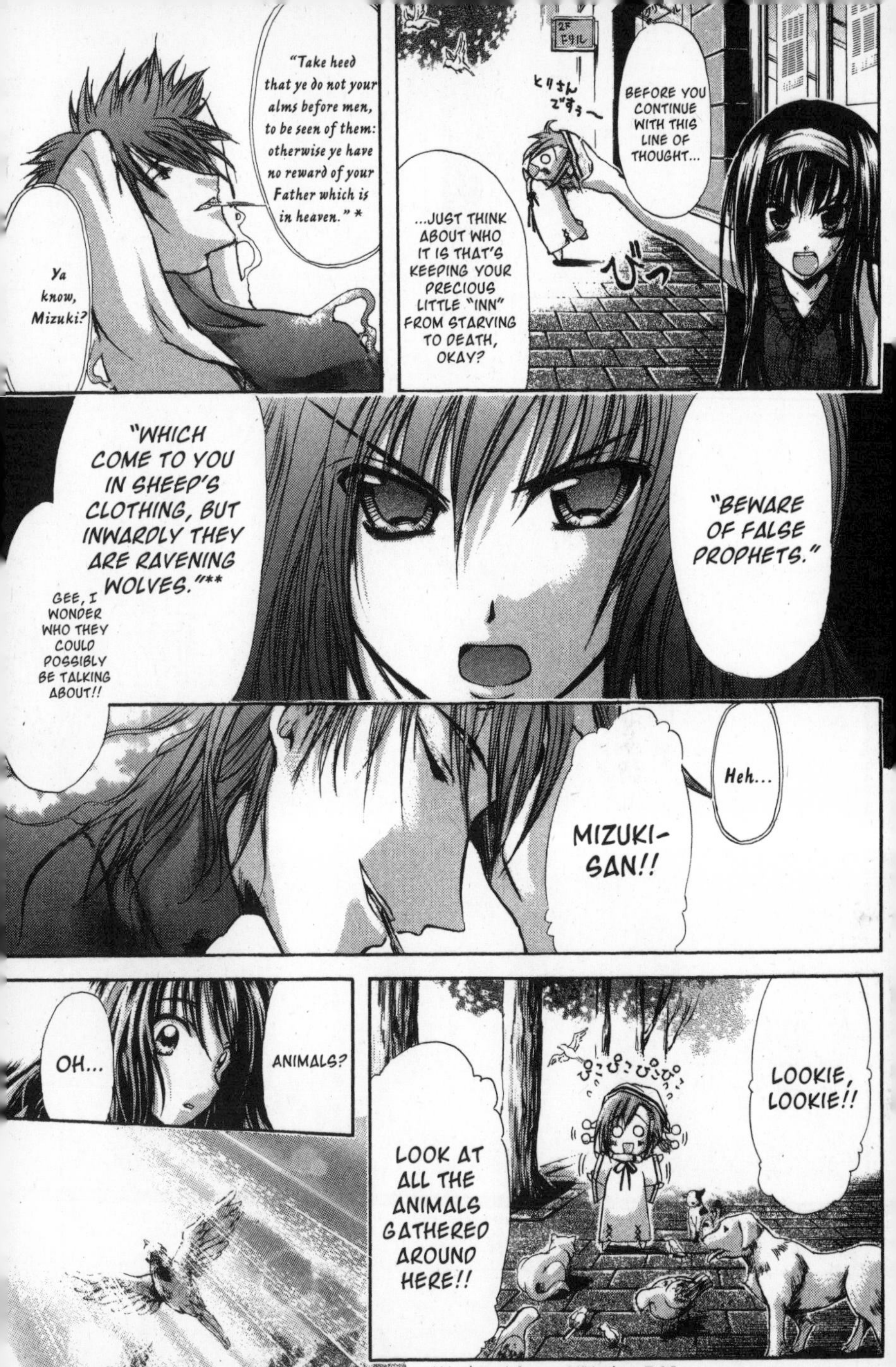
とりさんですぅ〜
BEFORE YOU CONTINUE WITH THIS LINE OF THOUGHT...
...JUST THINK ABOUT WHO IT IS THAT'S KEEPING YOUR PRECIOUS LITTLE "INN" FROM STARVING TO DEATH, OKAY?
びっ
"Take heed that ye do not your alms before men, to be seen of them: otherwise ye have no reward of your Father which is in heaven." *
Ya know, Mizuki?
"BEWARE OF FALSE PROPHETS."
"WHICH COME TO YOU IN SHEEP'S CLOTHING, BUT INWARDLY THEY ARE RAVENING WOLVES."**
GEE, I WONDER WHO THEY COULD POSSIBLY BE TALKING ABOUT!!
Heh...
MIZUKI-SAN!!
LOOKIE, LOOKIE!!
ぴこぴこぴこぴこ
LOOK AT ALL THE ANIMALS GATHERED AROUND HERE!!
ANIMALS?
OH...

*Matthew 6:1 **Matthew 7:15

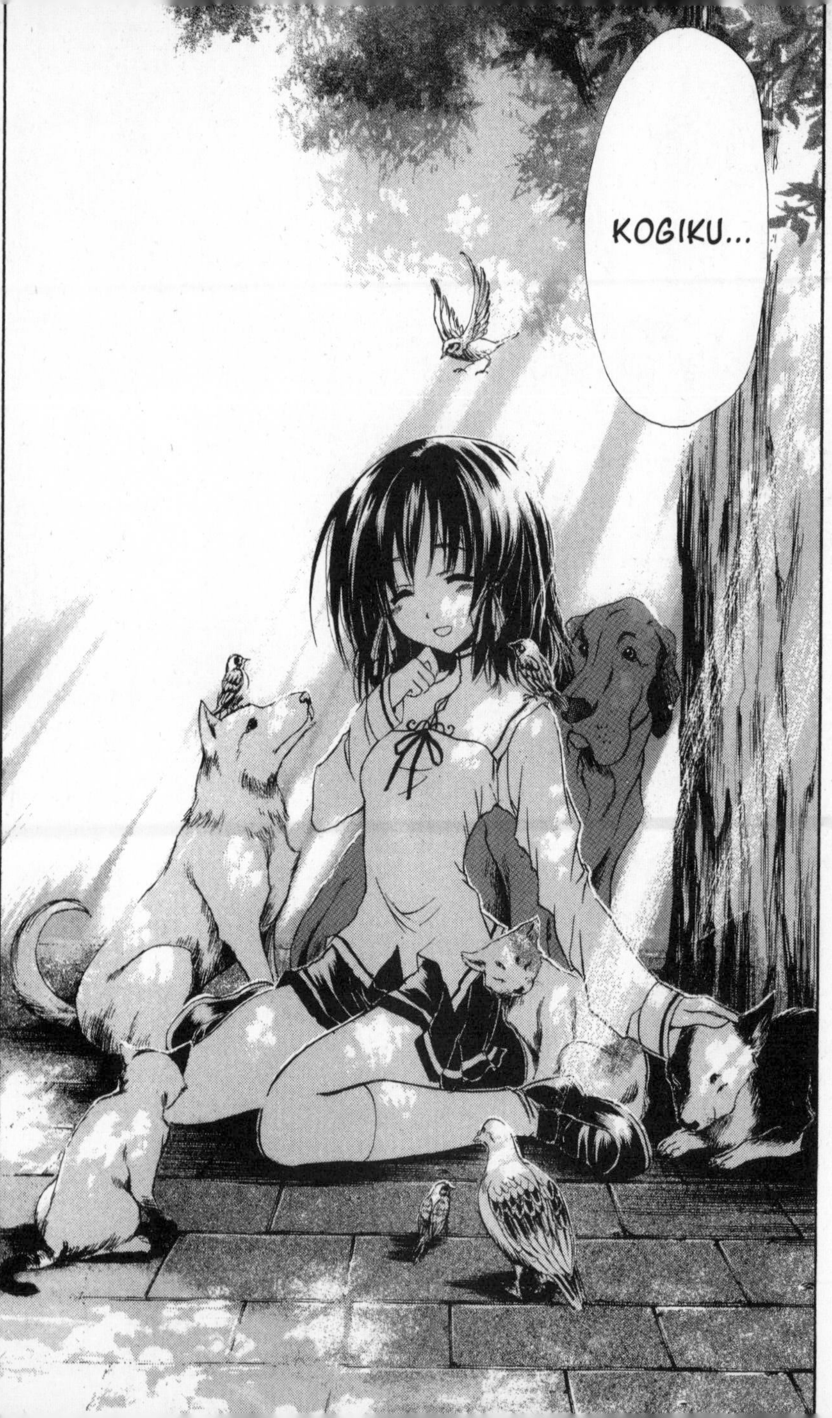
KOGIKU...

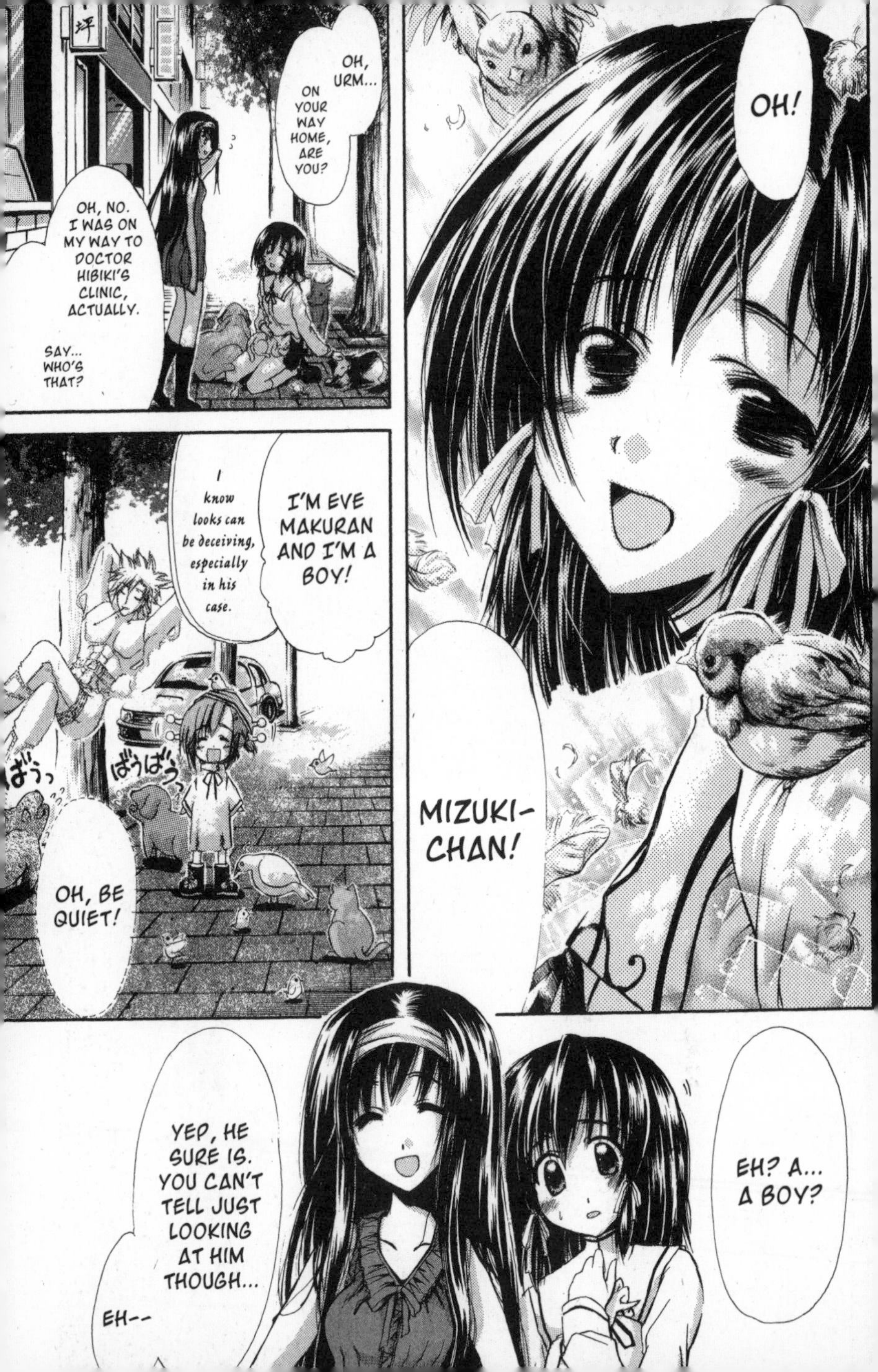
OH!
MIZUKI-CHAN!
OH, URM... ON YOUR WAY HOME, ARE YOU?
OH, NO. I WAS ON MY WAY TO DOCTOR HIBIKI'S CLINIC, ACTUALLY.
SAY... WHO'S THAT?
I'M EVE MAKURAN AND I'M A BOY!
I know looks can be deceiving, especially in his case.
ばうばうっ
ばうっ
OH, BE QUIET!
EH? A... A BOY?
YEP, HE SURE IS. YOU CAN'T TELL JUST LOOKING AT HIM THOUGH...
EH--

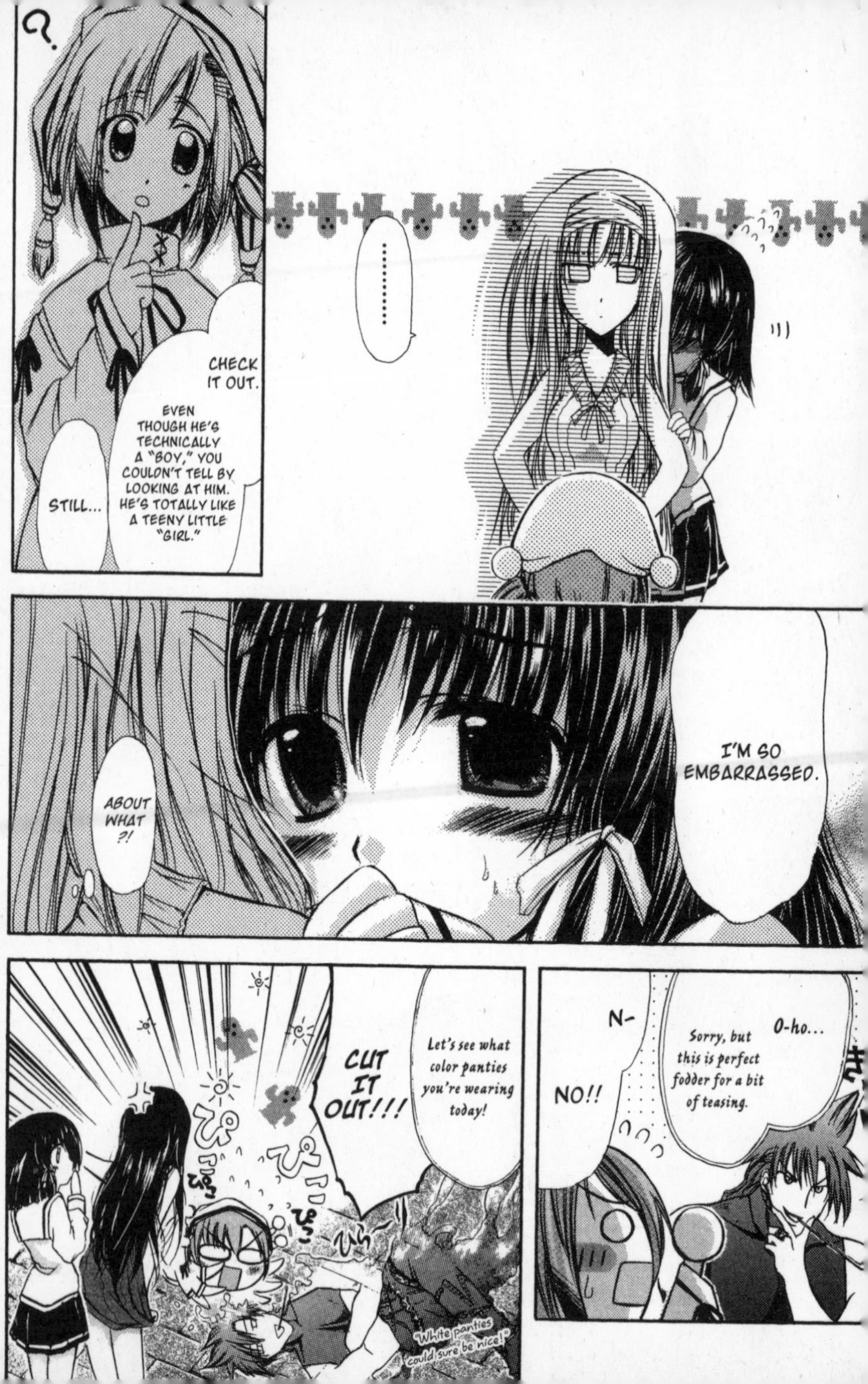
......
CHECK IT OUT.
EVEN THOUGH HE'S TECHNICALLY A "BOY," YOU COULDN'T TELL BY LOOKING AT HIM. HE'S TOTALLY LIKE A TEENY LITTLE "GIRL."
STILL...
I'M SO EMBARRASSED.
ABOUT WHAT?!
O-ho...
Sorry, but this is perfect fodder for a bit of teasing.
N-
NO!!
Let's see what color panties you're wearing today!
CUT IT OUT!!!
"White panties could sure be nice!"

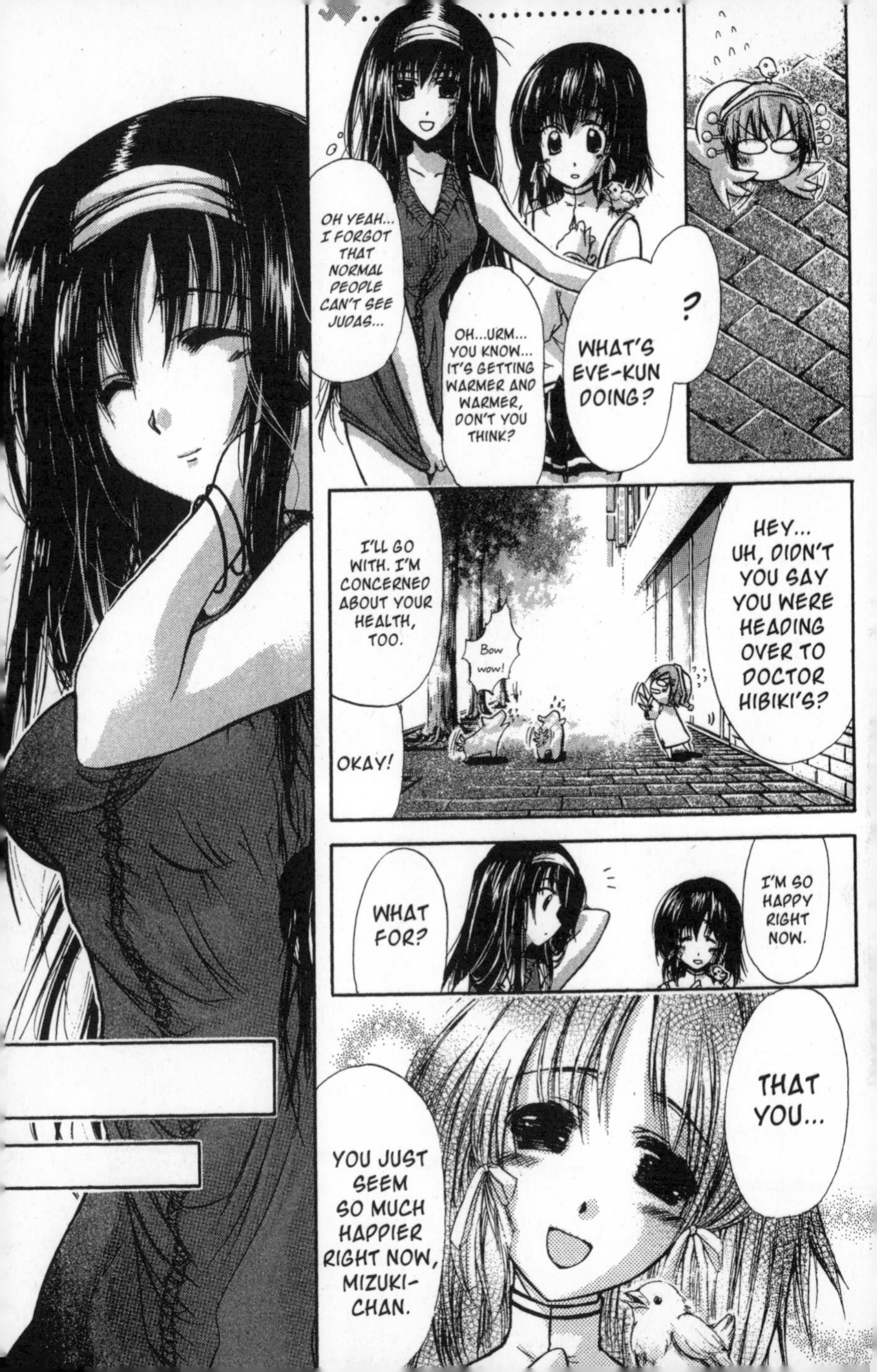
?
WHAT'S EVE-KUN DOING?
OH...URM... YOU KNOW... IT'S GETTING WARMER AND WARMER, DON'T YOU THINK?
OH YEAH... I FORGOT THAT NORMAL PEOPLE CAN'T SEE JUDAS...
HEY... UH, DIDN'T YOU SAY YOU WERE HEADING OVER TO DOCTOR HIBIKI'S?
Bow wow!
I'LL GO WITH. I'M CONCERNED ABOUT YOUR HEALTH, TOO.
OKAY!
I'M SO HAPPY RIGHT NOW.
WHAT FOR?
THAT YOU...
YOU JUST SEEM SO MUCH HAPPIER RIGHT NOW, MIZUKI-CHAN.

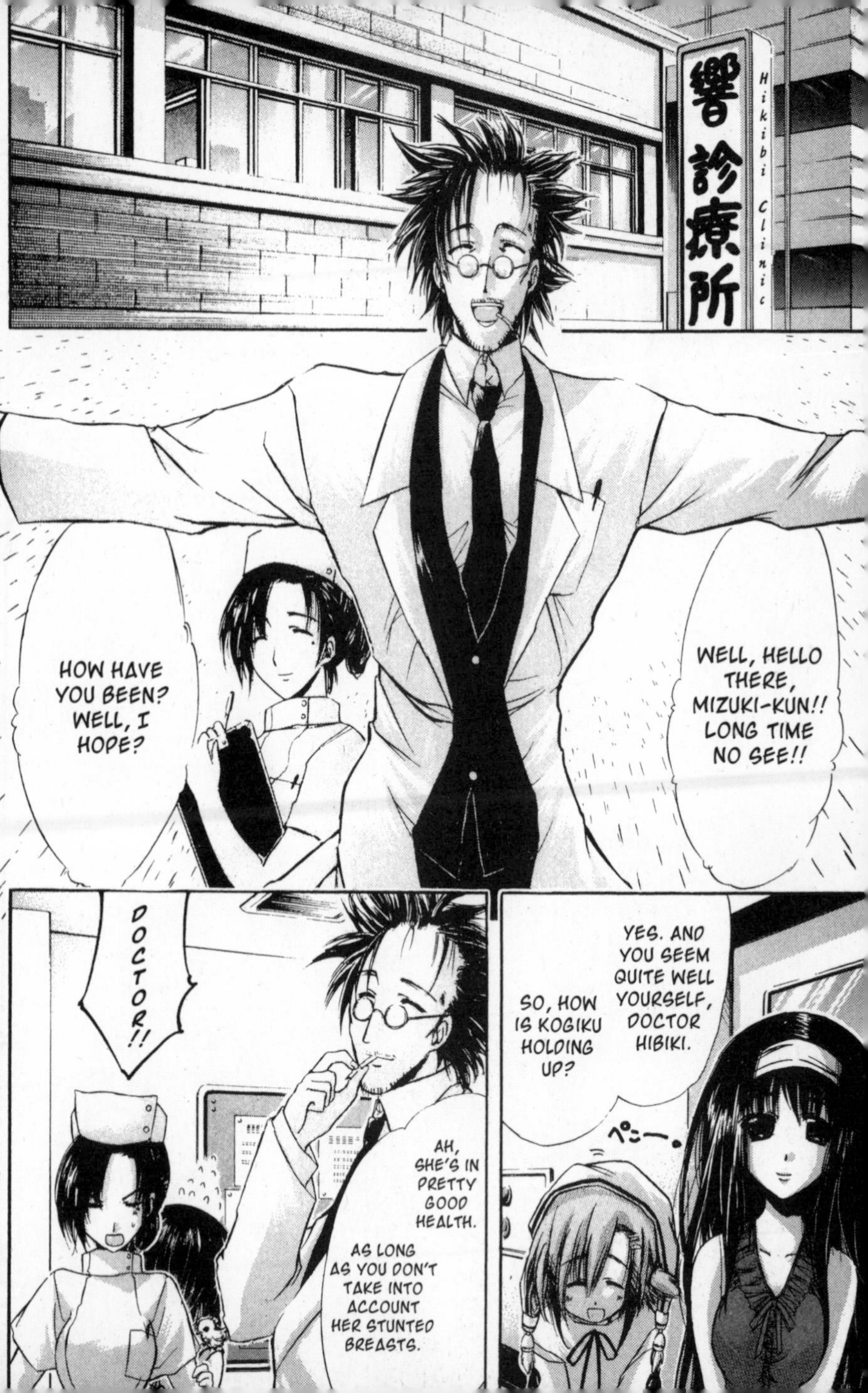
響診療所
Hikibi Clinic
WELL, HELLO THERE, MIZUKI-KUN!! LONG TIME NO SEE!!
HOW HAVE YOU BEEN? WELL, I HOPE?
YES. AND YOU SEEM QUITE WELL YOURSELF, DOCTOR HIBIKI.
SO, HOW IS KOGIKU HOLDING UP?
ぺこー
AH, SHE'S IN PRETTY GOOD HEALTH.
AS LONG AS YOU DON'T TAKE INTO ACCOUNT HER STUNTED BREASTS.
DOCTOR!!

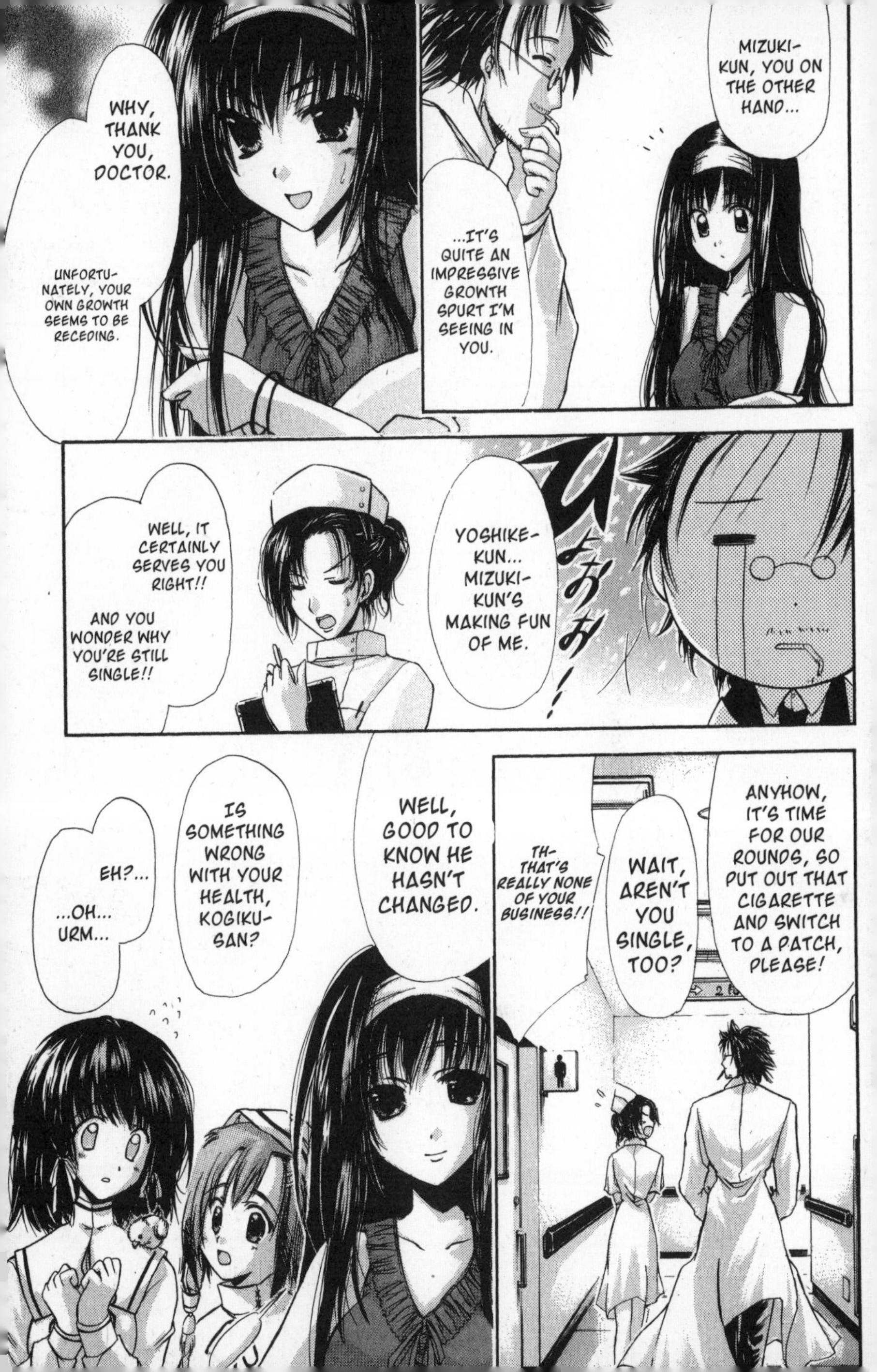
MIZUKI-KUN, YOU ON THE OTHER HAND...
...IT'S QUITE AN IMPRESSIVE GROWTH SPURT I'M SEEING IN YOU.
WHY, THANK YOU, DOCTOR.
UNFORTUNATELY, YOUR OWN GROWTH SEEMS TO BE RECEDING.
YOSHIKE-KUN... MIZUKI-KUN'S MAKING FUN OF ME.
WELL, IT CERTAINLY SERVES YOU RIGHT!!
AND YOU WONDER WHY YOU'RE STILL SINGLE!!
ANYHOW, IT'S TIME FOR OUR ROUNDS, SO PUT OUT THAT CIGARETTE AND SWITCH TO A PATCH, PLEASE!
WAIT, AREN'T YOU SINGLE, TOO?
TH-THAT'S REALLY NONE OF YOUR BUSINESS!!
WELL, GOOD TO KNOW HE HASN'T CHANGED.
IS SOMETHING WRONG WITH YOUR HEALTH, KOGIKU-SAN?
EH?... ...OH... URM...

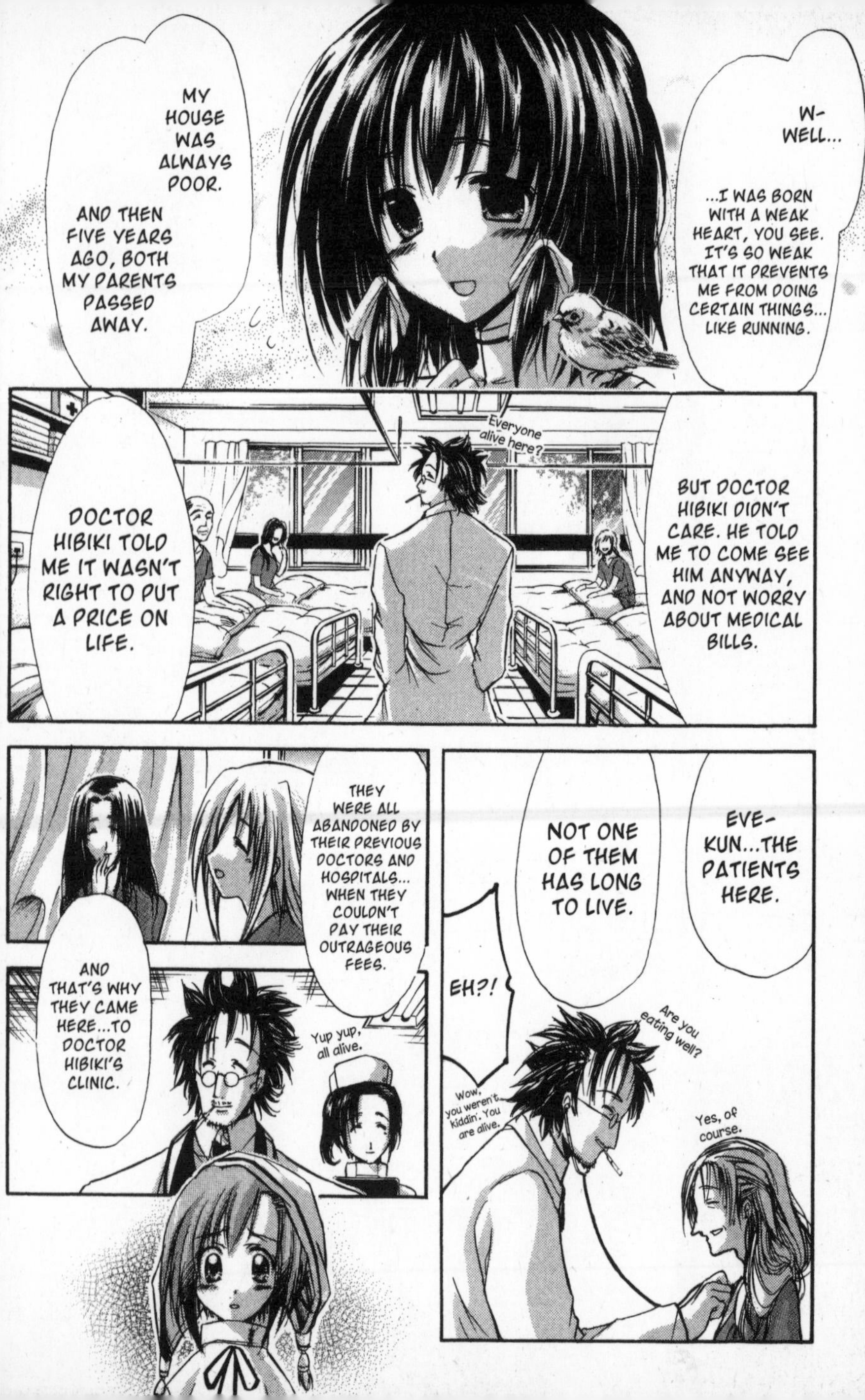
W-
WELL...
...I WAS BORN WITH A WEAK HEART, YOU SEE. IT'S SO WEAK THAT IT PREVENTS ME FROM DOING CERTAIN THINGS... LIKE RUNNING.
MY HOUSE WAS ALWAYS POOR.
AND THEN FIVE YEARS AGO, BOTH MY PARENTS PASSED AWAY.
BUT DOCTOR HIBIKI DIDN'T CARE. HE TOLD ME TO COME SEE HIM ANYWAY, AND NOT WORRY ABOUT MEDICAL BILLS.
Everyone alive here?
DOCTOR HIBIKI TOLD ME IT WASN'T RIGHT TO PUT A PRICE ON LIFE.
EVE-KUN...THE PATIENTS HERE.
NOT ONE OF THEM HAS LONG TO LIVE.
EH?!
Are you eating well?
Yes, of course.
Wow, you weren't kiddin'. You are alive.
THEY WERE ALL ABANDONED BY THEIR PREVIOUS DOCTORS AND HOSPITALS... WHEN THEY COULDN'T PAY THEIR OUTRAGEOUS FEES.
AND THAT'S WHY THEY CAME HERE...TO DOCTOR HIBIKI'S CLINIC.
Yup yup, all alive.

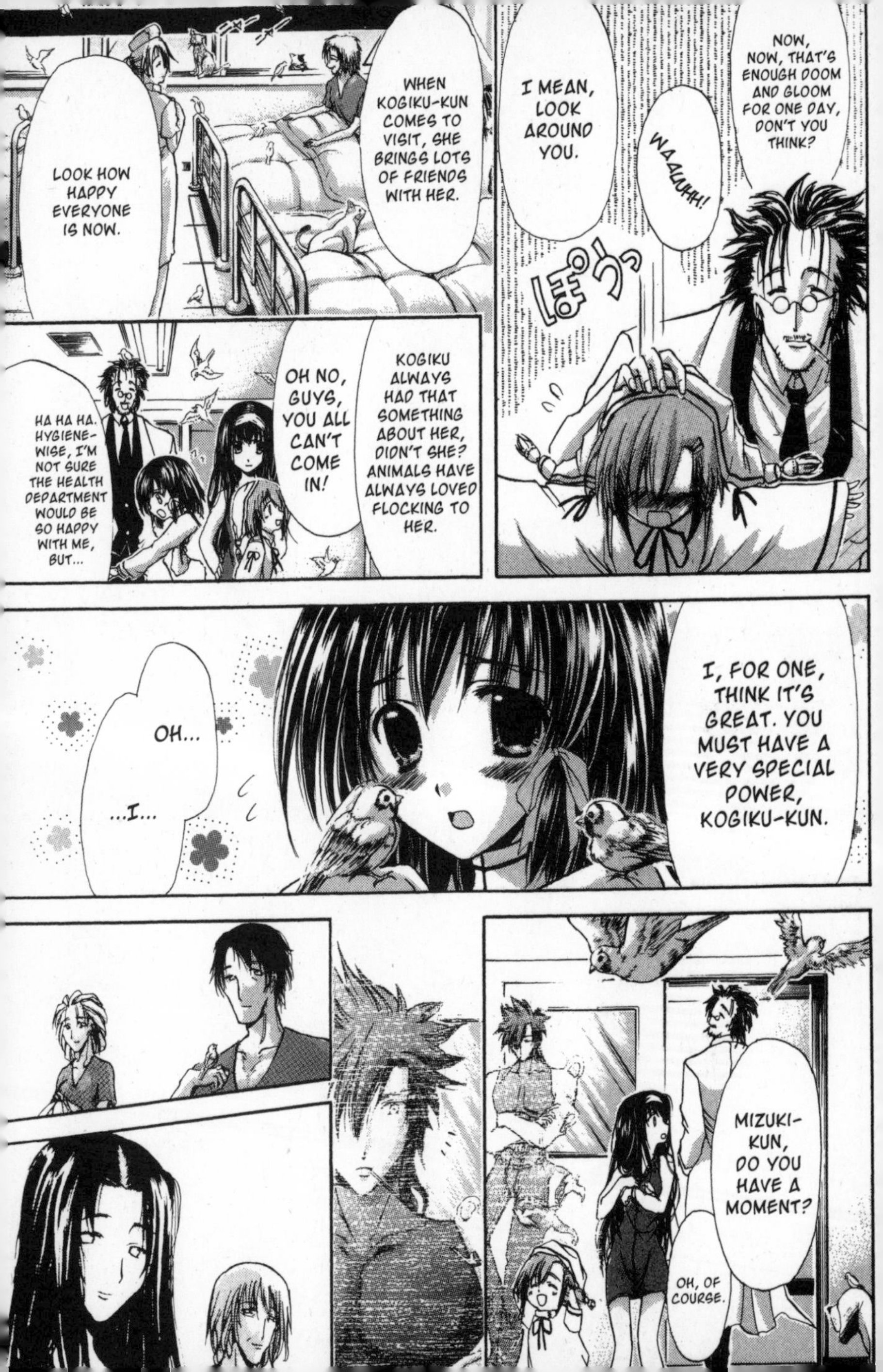
NOW, NOW, THAT'S ENOUGH DOOM AND GLOOM FOR ONE DAY, DON'T YOU THINK?
I MEAN, LOOK AROUND YOU.
WAAUHH!
ぽうっ
WHEN KOGIKU-KUN COMES TO VISIT, SHE BRINGS LOTS OF FRIENDS WITH HER.
LOOK HOW HAPPY EVERYONE IS NOW.
KOGIKU ALWAYS HAD THAT SOMETHING ABOUT HER, DIDN'T SHE? ANIMALS HAVE ALWAYS LOVED FLOCKING TO HER.
OH NO, GUYS, YOU ALL CAN'T COME IN!
HA HA HA. HYGIENE-WISE, I'M NOT SURE THE HEALTH DEPARTMENT WOULD BE SO HAPPY WITH ME, BUT...
I, FOR ONE, THINK IT'S GREAT. YOU MUST HAVE A VERY SPECIAL POWER, KOGIKU-KUN.
OH...
...I...
MIZUKI-KUN, DO YOU HAVE A MOMENT?
OH, OF COURSE.

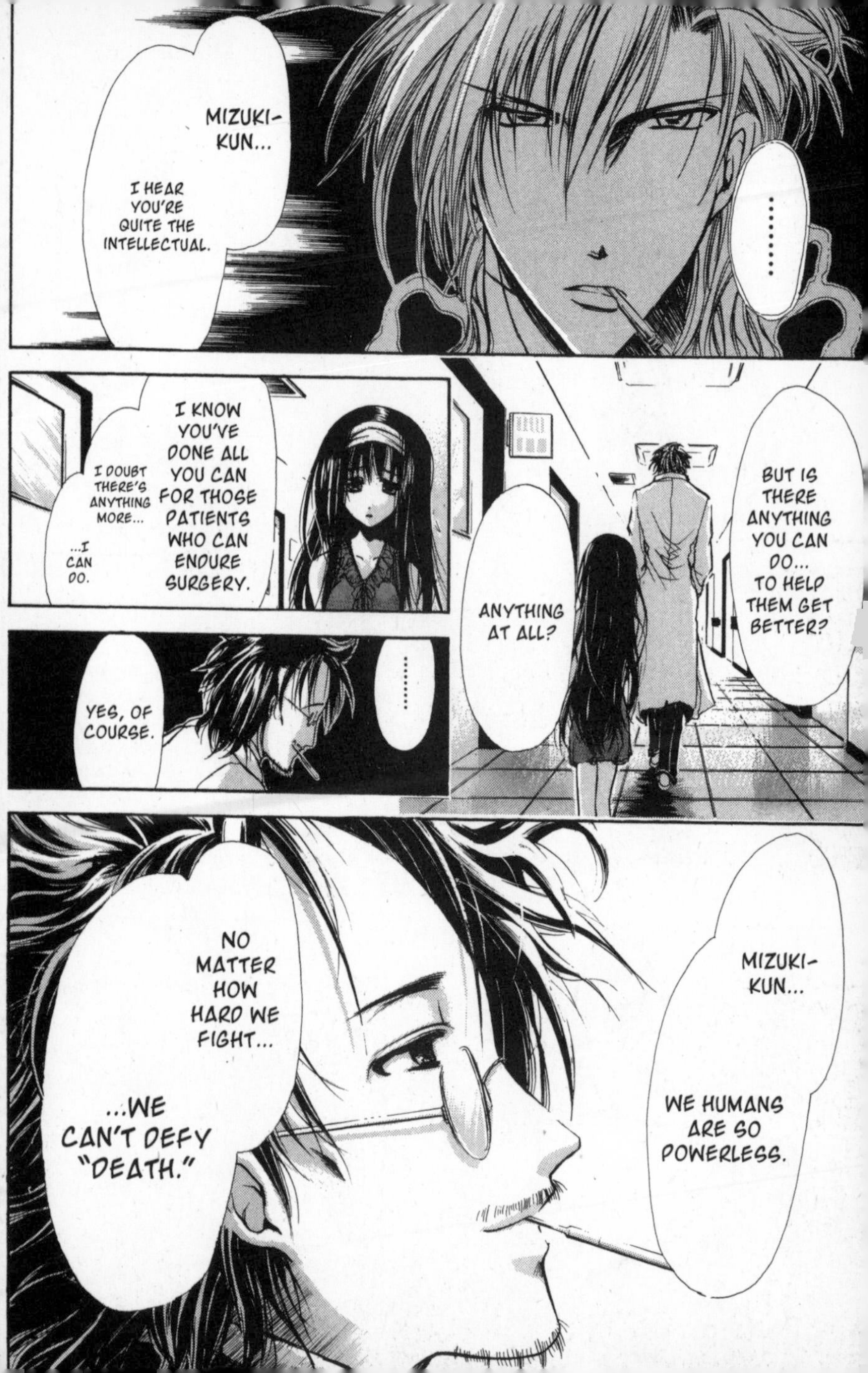
MIZUKI-KUN...
I HEAR YOU'RE QUITE THE INTELLECTUAL.
......
BUT IS THERE ANYTHING YOU CAN DO... TO HELP THEM GET BETTER?
ANYTHING AT ALL?
I KNOW YOU'VE DONE ALL YOU CAN FOR THOSE PATIENTS WHO CAN ENDURE SURGERY.
I DOUBT THERE'S ANYTHING MORE...
...I CAN DO.
......
YES, OF COURSE.
MIZUKI-KUN...
WE HUMANS ARE SO POWERLESS.
NO MATTER HOW HARD WE FIGHT...
...WE CAN'T DEFY "DEATH."

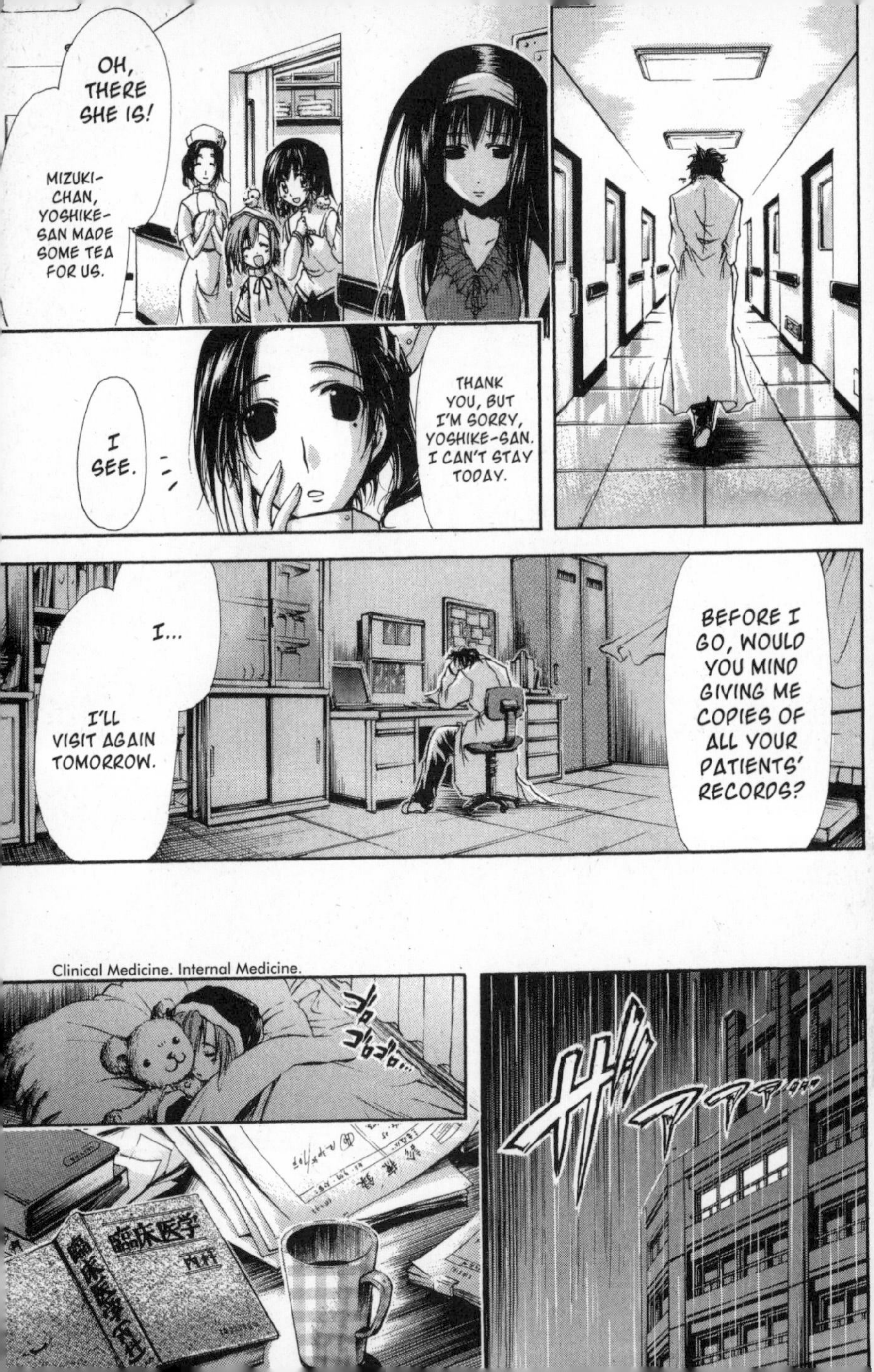
OH, THERE SHE IS!
MIZUKI-CHAN, YOSHIKE-SAN MADE SOME TEA FOR US.
THANK YOU, BUT I'M SORRY, YOSHIKE-SAN. I CAN'T STAY TODAY.
I SEE.
BEFORE I GO, WOULD YOU MIND GIVING ME COPIES OF ALL YOUR PATIENTS' RECORDS?
I...
I'LL VISIT AGAIN TOMORROW.
Clinical Medicine. Internal Medicine.
臨床医学
内科

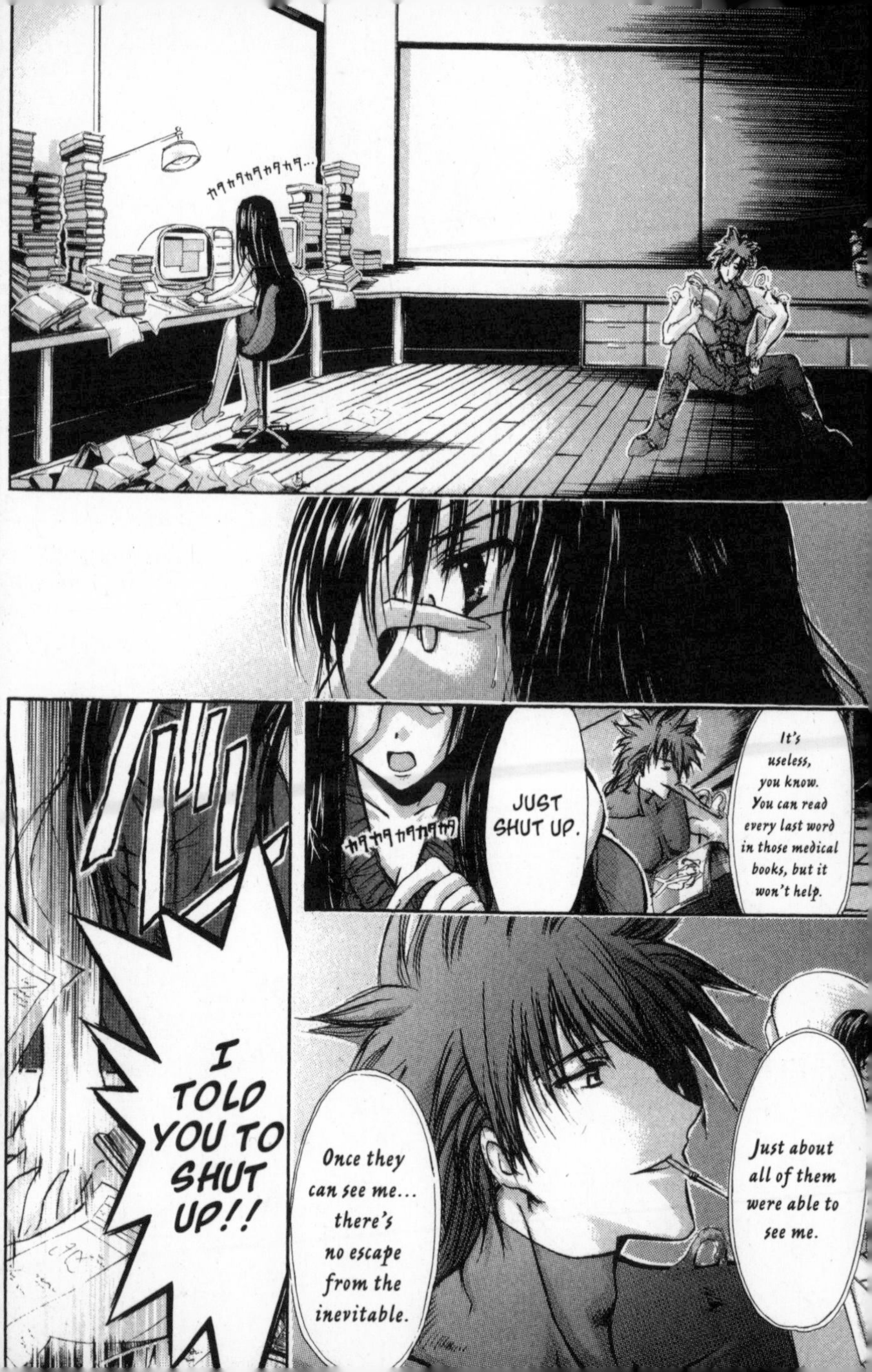
カタカタカタカタカタ…
It's useless, you know. You can read every last word in those medical books, but it won't help.
JUST SHUT UP.
カタカタカタカタカタ
Just about all of them were able to see me.
Once they can see me... there's no escape from the inevitable.
I TOLD YOU TO SHUT UP!!

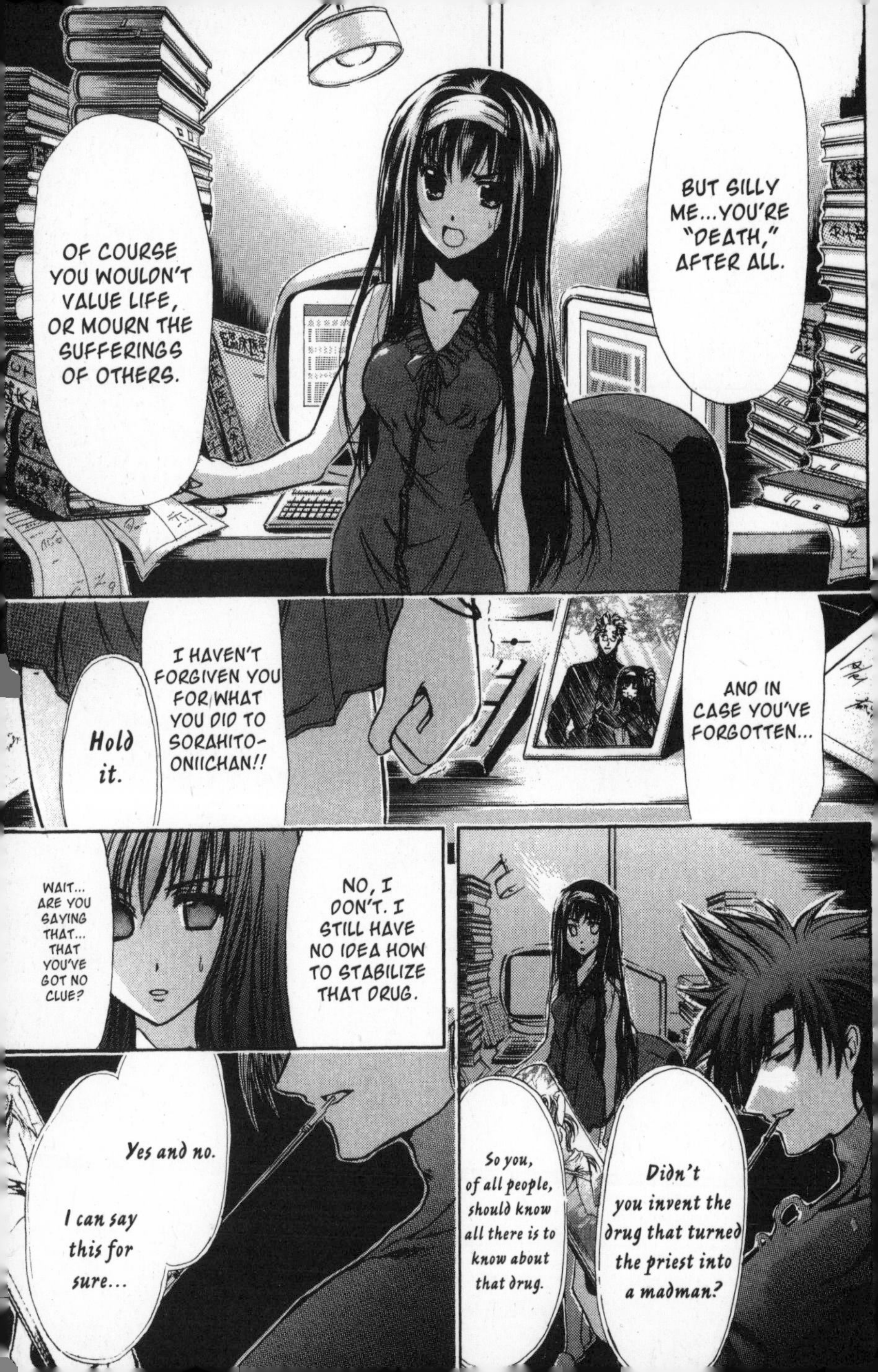
BUT SILLY ME...YOU'RE "DEATH," AFTER ALL.
OF COURSE YOU WOULDN'T VALUE LIFE, OR MOURN THE SUFFERINGS OF OTHERS.
AND IN CASE YOU'VE FORGOTTEN...
I HAVEN'T FORGIVEN YOU FOR WHAT YOU DID TO SORAHITO-ONIICHAN!!
Hold it.
Didn't you invent the drug that turned the priest into a madman?
So you, of all people, should know all there is to know about that drug.
NO, I DON'T. I STILL HAVE NO IDEA HOW TO STABILIZE THAT DRUG.
WAIT... ARE YOU SAYING THAT... THAT YOU'VE GOT NO CLUE?
Yes and no.
I can say this for sure...

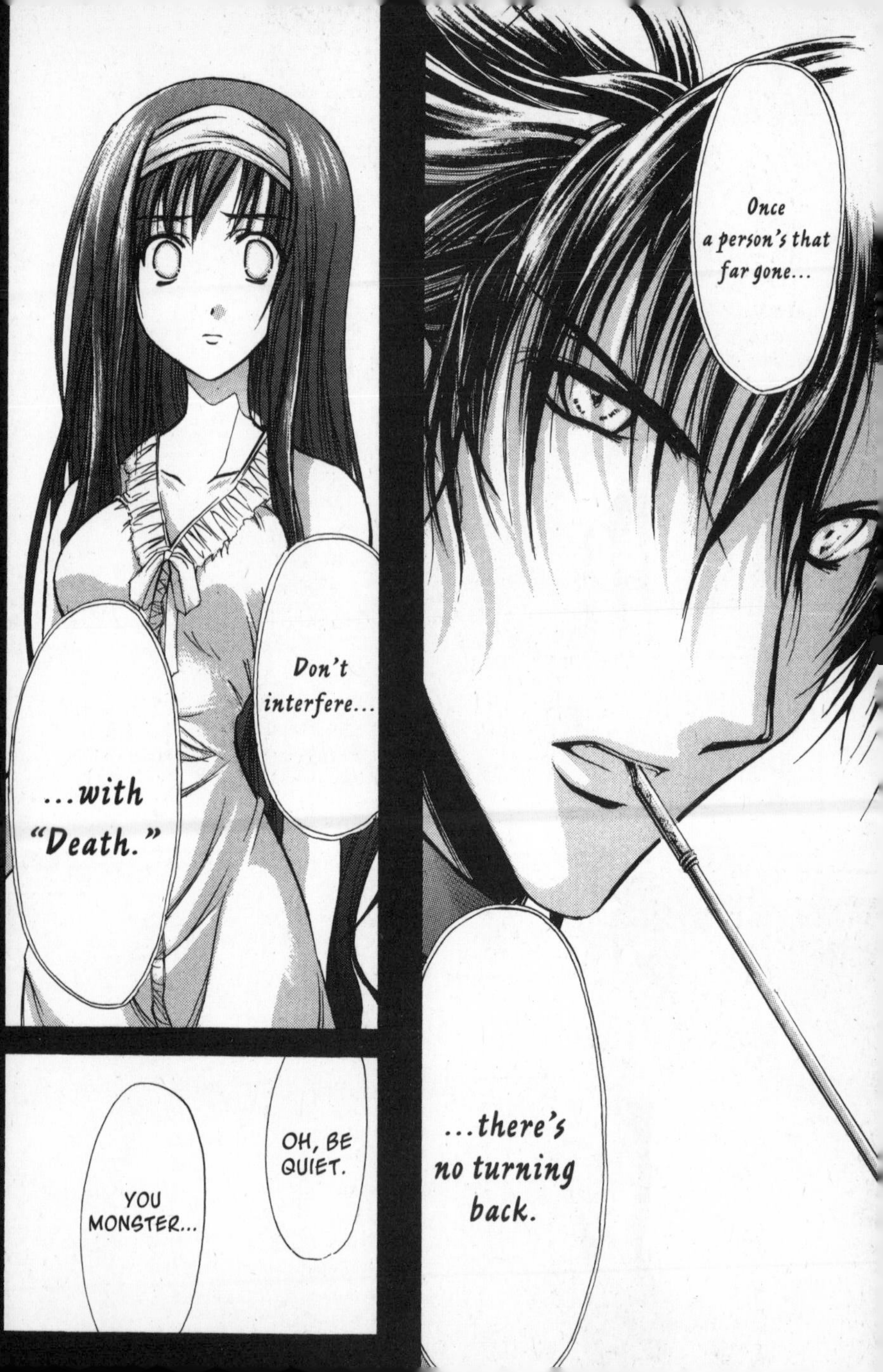
Once a person's that far gone...
...there's no turning back.
Don't interfere...
...with "Death."
OH, BE QUIET.
YOU MONSTER...

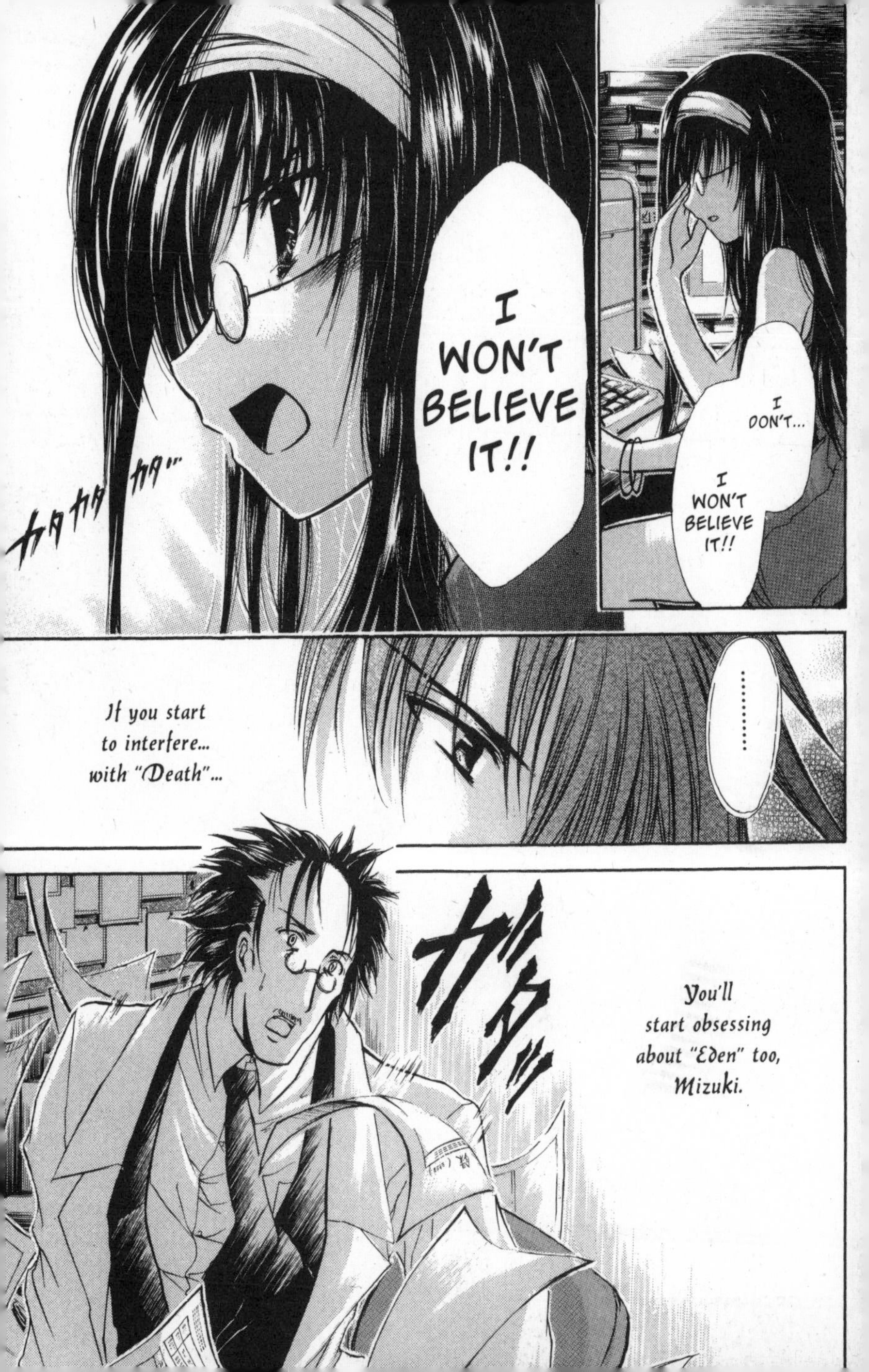
I DON'T...
I WON'T BELIEVE IT!!
I WON'T BELIEVE IT!!
カタカタ カタ
......
If you start to interfere... with "Death"...
You'll start obsessing about "Eden" too, Mizuki.
ガタッ

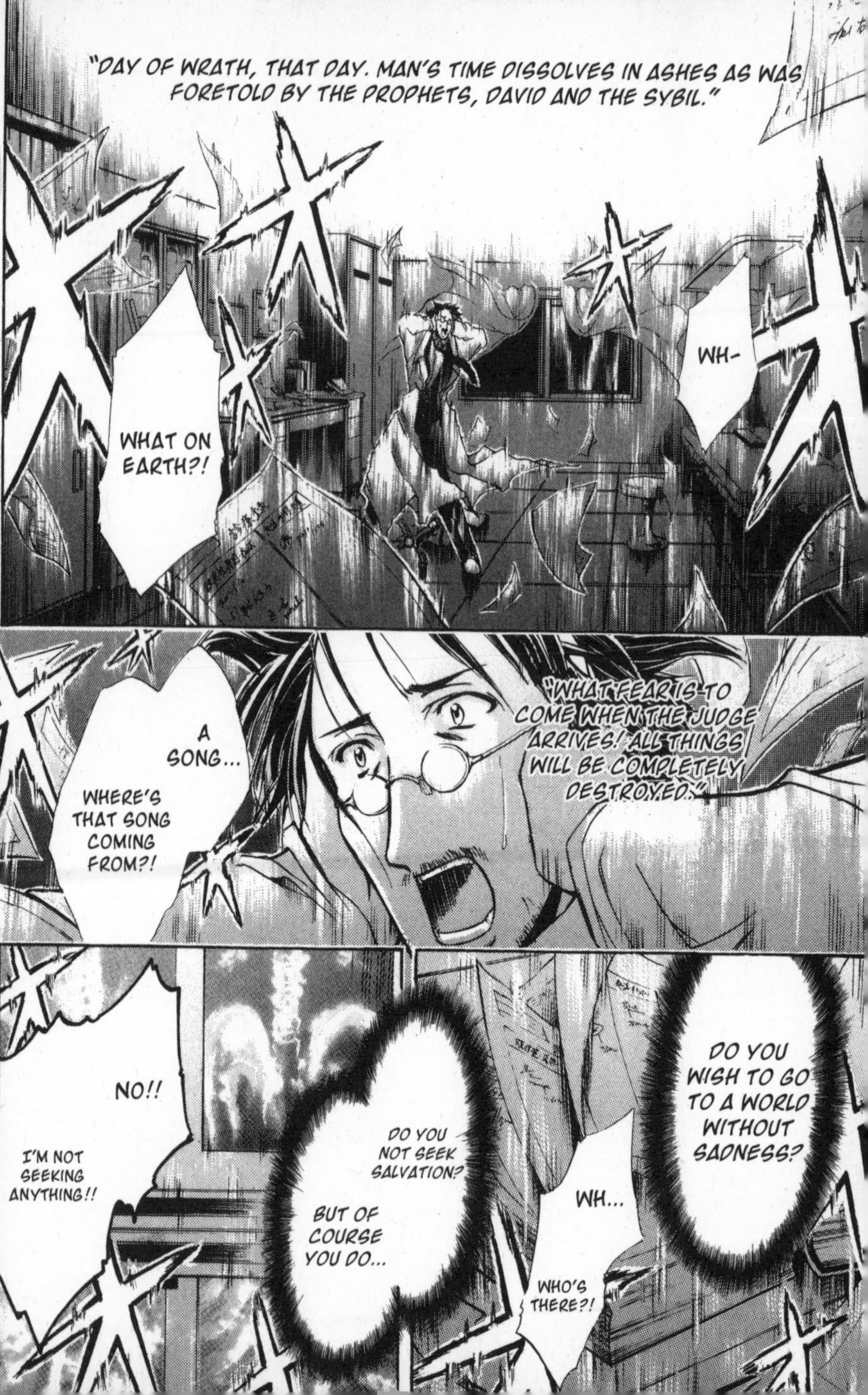
"DAY OF WRATH, THAT DAY. MAN'S TIME DISSOLVES IN ASHES AS WAS FORETOLD BY THE PROPHETS, DAVID AND THE SYBIL."
WH-
WHAT ON EARTH?!
"WHAT FEAR IS TO COME WHEN THE JUDGE ARRIVES! ALL THINGS WILL BE COMPLETELY DESTROYED."
A SONG...
WHERE'S THAT SONG COMING FROM?!
DO YOU WISH TO GO TO A WORLD WITHOUT SADNESS?
WH...
WHO'S THERE?!
DO YOU NOT SEEK SALVATION?
BUT OF COURSE YOU DO...
NO!!
I'M NOT SEEKING ANYTHING!!

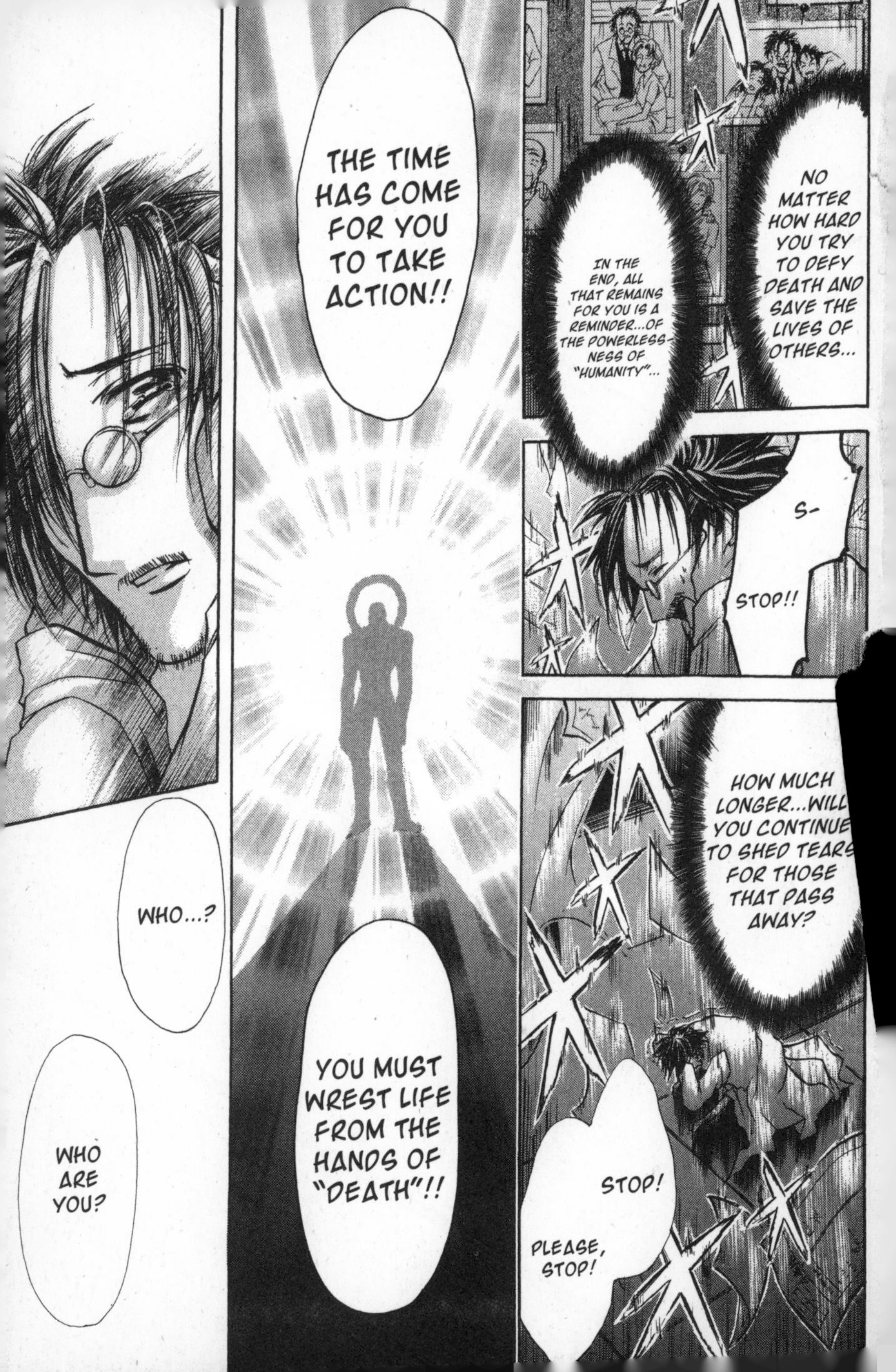
NO MATTER HOW HARD YOU TRY TO DEFY DEATH AND SAVE THE LIVES OF OTHERS...
IN THE END, ALL THAT REMAINS FOR YOU IS A REMINDER...OF THE POWERLESS-NESS OF "HUMANITY"...
S-
STOP!!
HOW MUCH LONGER...WILL YOU CONTINUE TO SHED TEARS FOR THOSE THAT PASS AWAY?
STOP!
PLEASE, STOP!
THE TIME HAS COME FOR YOU TO TAKE ACTION!!
YOU MUST WREST LIFE FROM THE HANDS OF "DEATH"!!
WHO...?
WHO ARE YOU?

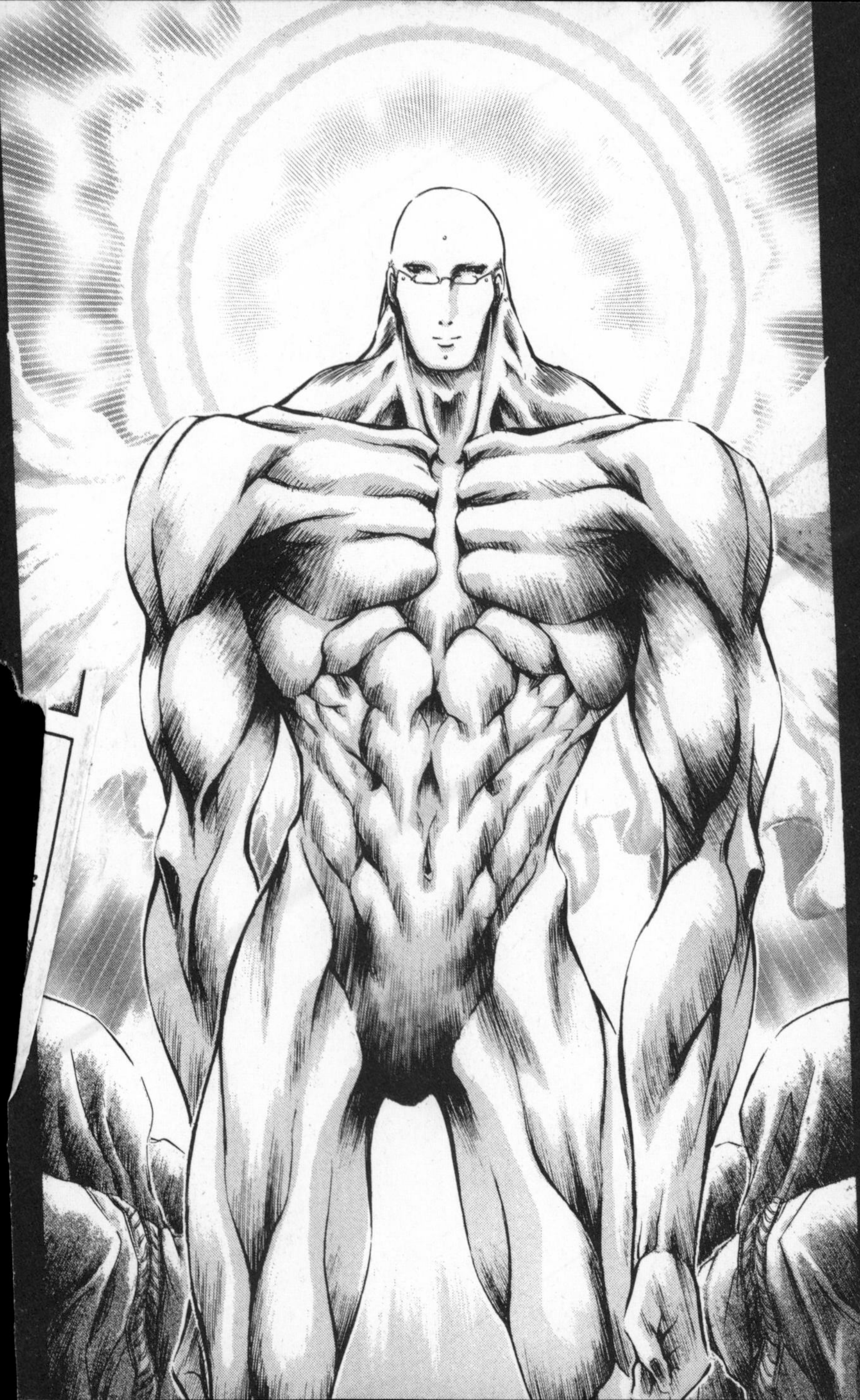

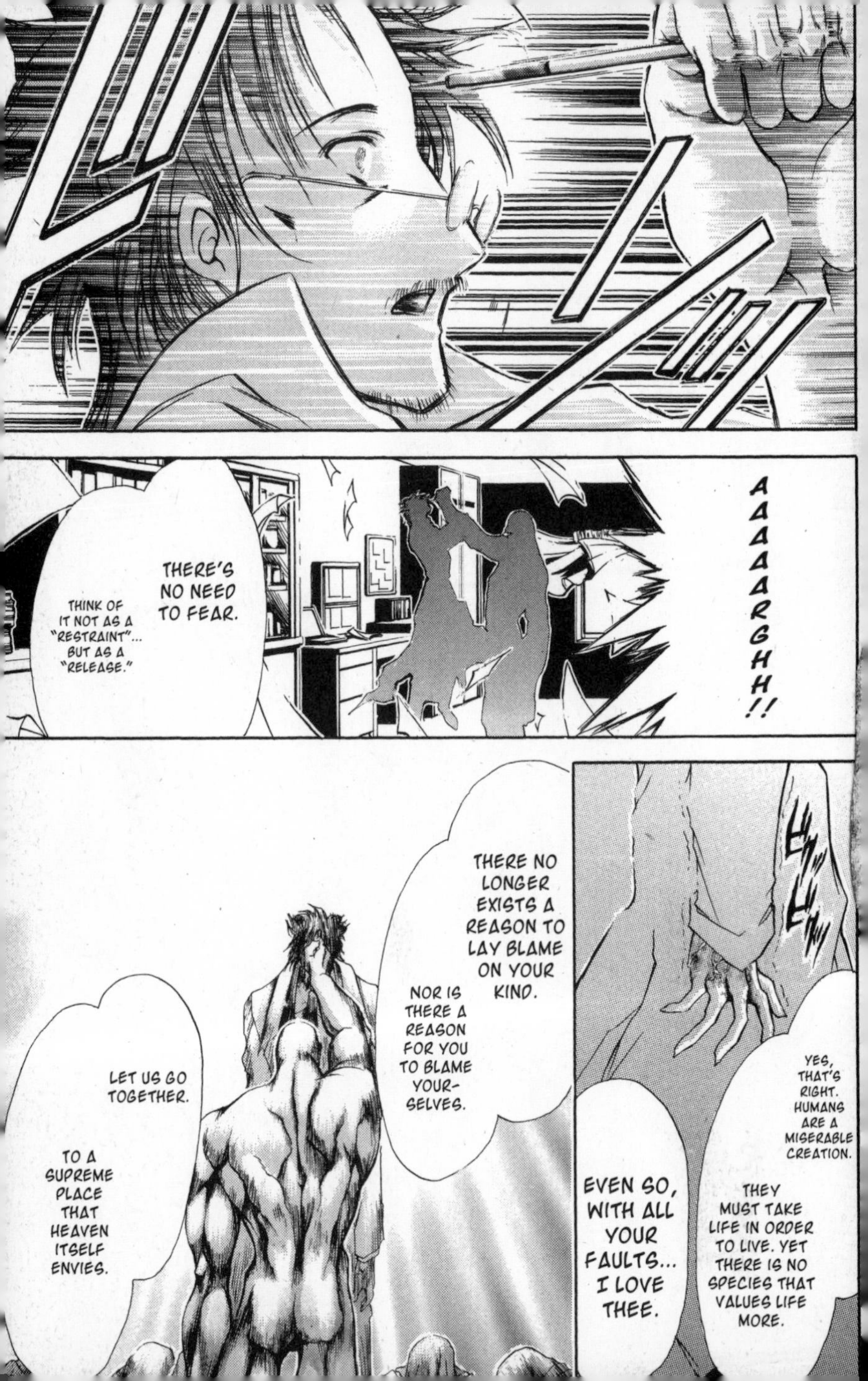
AAAAARGHH!!
THERE'S NO NEED TO FEAR.
THINK OF IT NOT AS A "RESTRAINT"... BUT AS A "RELEASE."
YES, THAT'S RIGHT. HUMANS ARE A MISERABLE CREATION.
THEY MUST TAKE LIFE IN ORDER TO LIVE. YET THERE IS NO SPECIES THAT VALUES LIFE MORE.
EVEN SO, WITH ALL YOUR FAULTS... I LOVE THEE.
THERE NO LONGER EXISTS A REASON TO LAY BLAME ON YOUR KIND.
NOR IS THERE A REASON FOR YOU TO BLAME YOUR-SELVES.
LET US GO TOGETHER.
TO A SUPREME PLACE THAT HEAVEN ITSELF ENVIES.

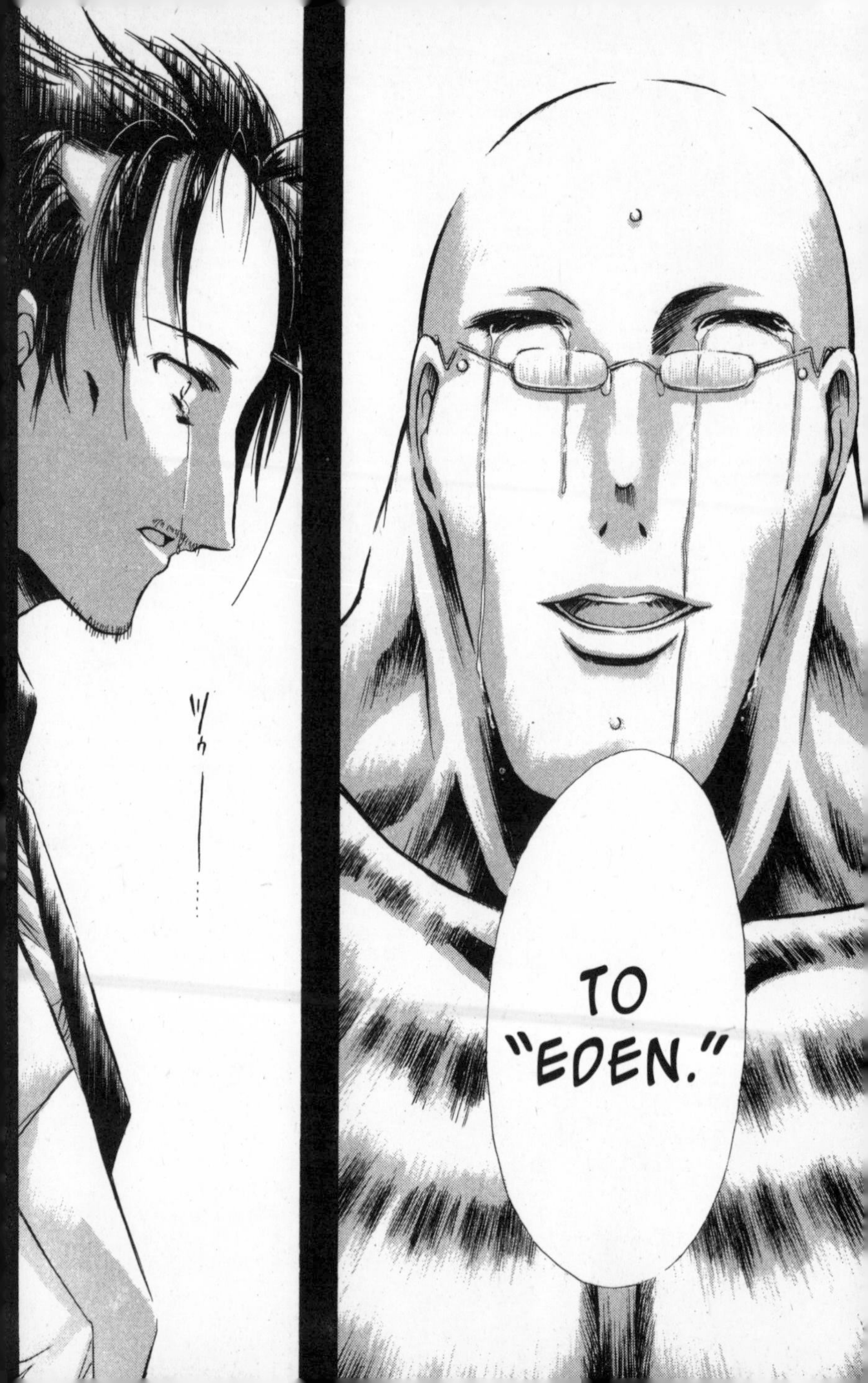
TO "EDEN."
ツゥー……

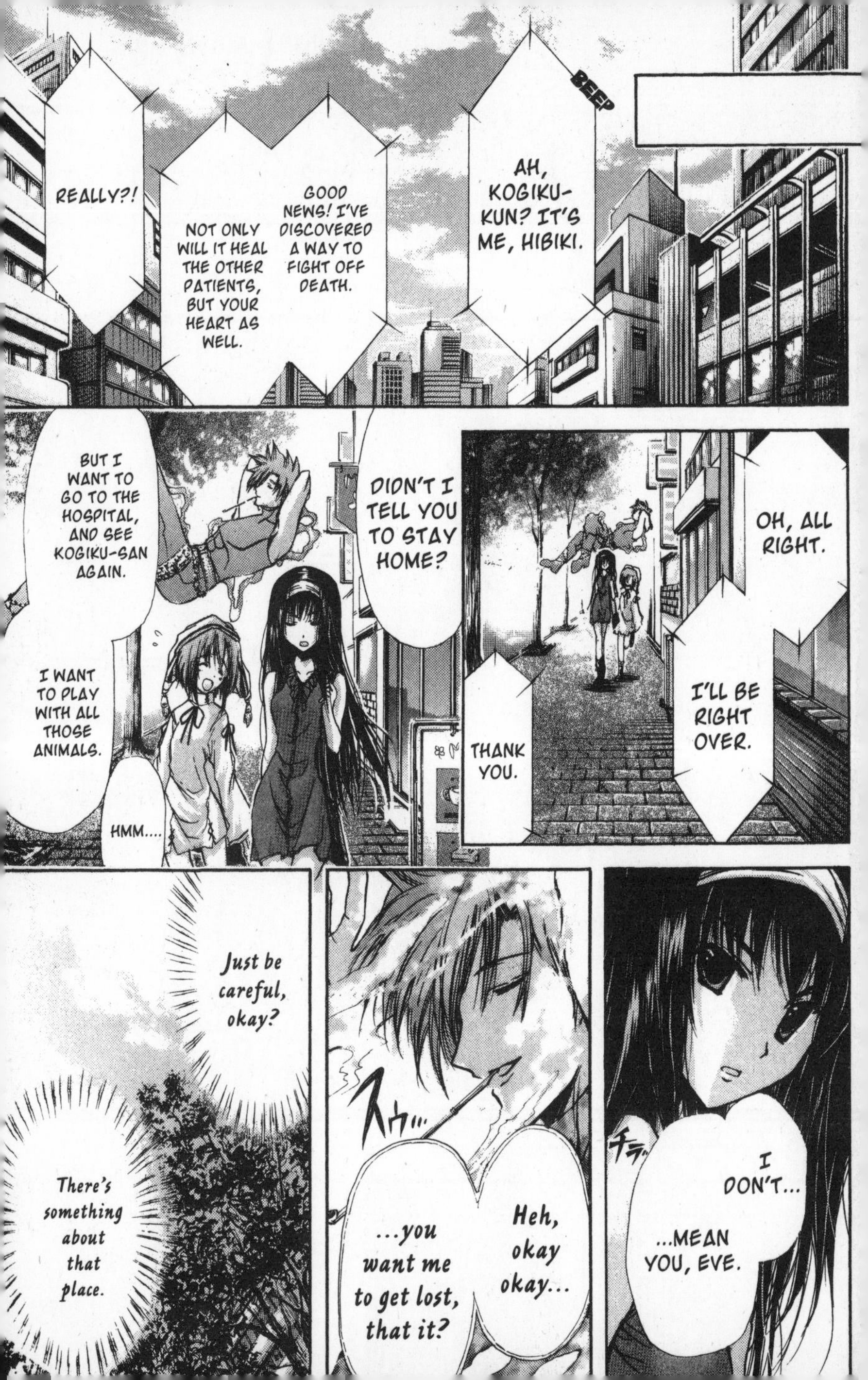
BEEP
AH, KOGIKU-KUN? IT'S ME, HIBIKI.
GOOD NEWS! I'VE DISCOVERED A WAY TO FIGHT OFF DEATH.
NOT ONLY WILL IT HEAL THE OTHER PATIENTS, BUT YOUR HEART AS WELL.
REALLY?!
OH, ALL RIGHT.
I'LL BE RIGHT OVER.
THANK YOU.
DIDN'T I TELL YOU TO STAY HOME?
BUT I WANT TO GO TO THE HOSPITAL, AND SEE KOGIKU-SAN AGAIN.
I WANT TO PLAY WITH ALL THOSE ANIMALS.
HMM....
チラ
I DON'T...
...MEAN YOU, EVE.
スゥ…
Heh, okay okay...
...you want me to get lost, that it?
Just be careful, okay?
There's something about that place.

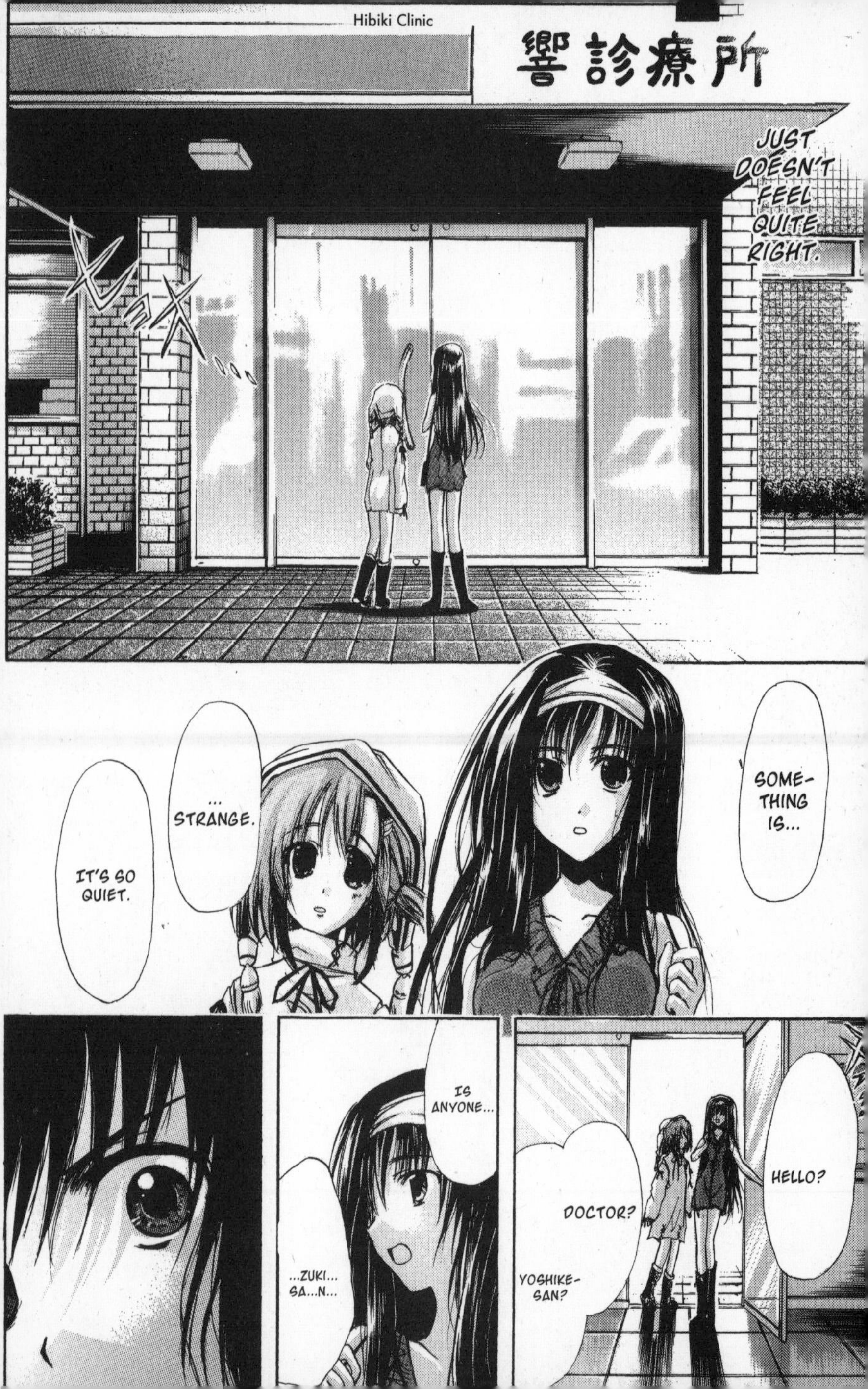
Hibiki Clinic
響診療所
JUST DOESN'T FEEL QUITE RIGHT.
SOME-THING IS...
...STRANGE.
IT'S SO QUIET.
HELLO?
DOCTOR?
YOSHIKE-SAN?
IS ANYONE...
...ZUKI... SA...N...

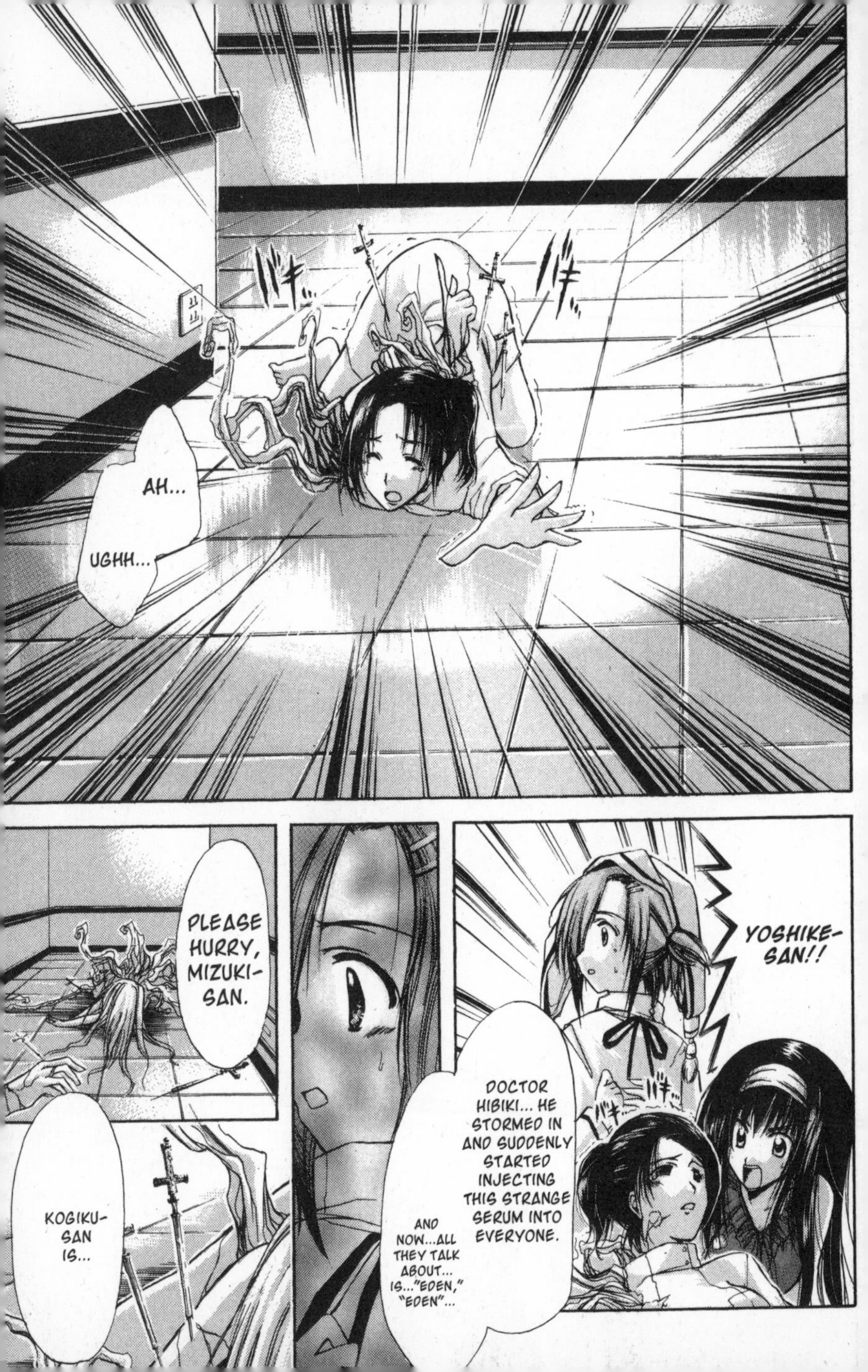
AH...
UGHH...
YOSHIKE-SAN!!
DOCTOR HIBIKI... HE STORMED IN AND SUDDENLY STARTED INJECTING THIS STRANGE SERUM INTO EVERYONE.
AND NOW...ALL THEY TALK ABOUT... IS..."EDEN," "EDEN"...
PLEASE HURRY, MIZUKI-SAN.
KOGIKU-SAN IS...

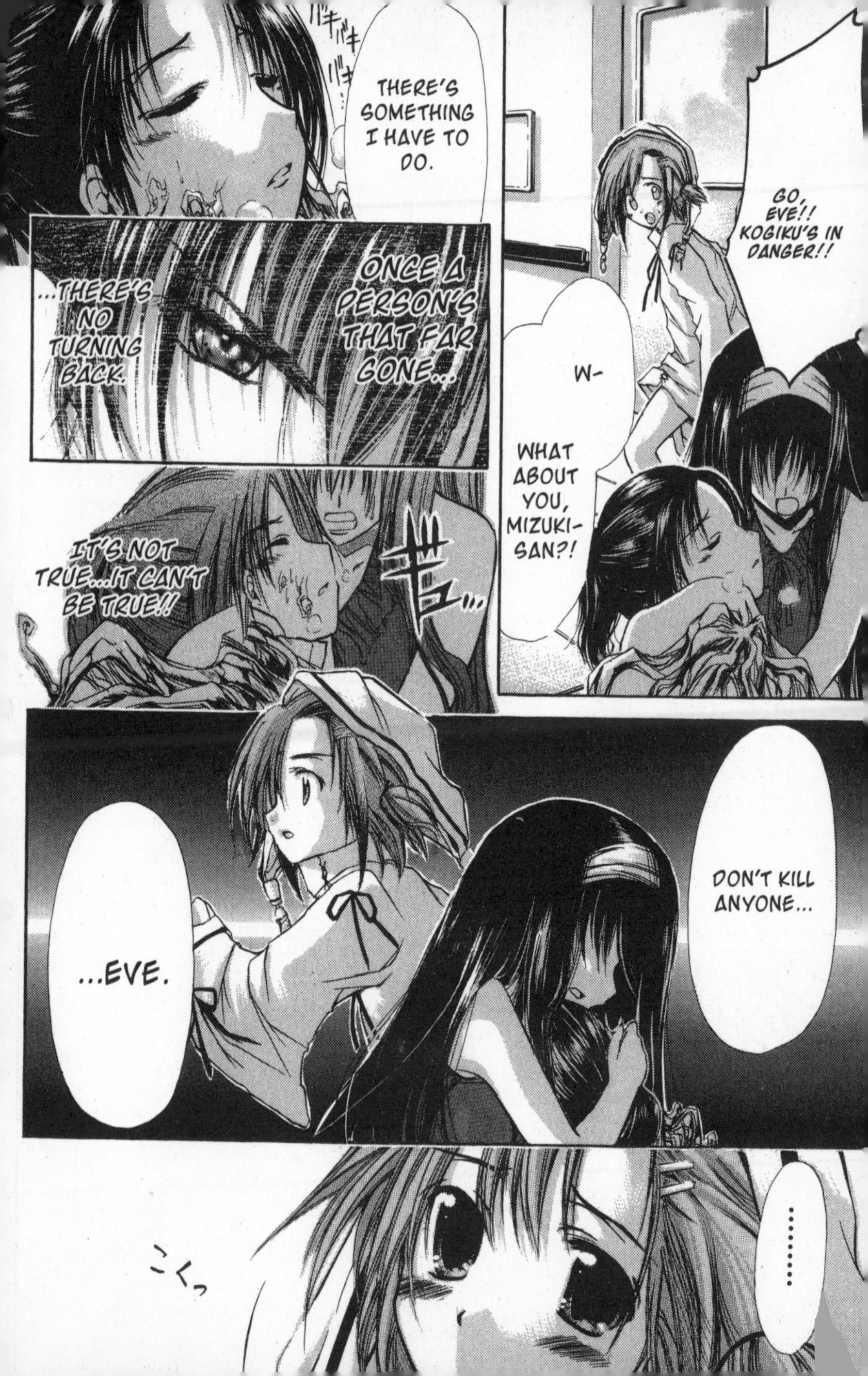
GO, EVE!! KOGIKU'S IN DANGER!!
W-
WHAT ABOUT YOU, MIZUKI-SAN?!
THERE'S SOMETHING I HAVE TO DO.
ONCE A PERSON'S THAT FAR GONE...
...THERE'S NO TURNING BACK.
IT'S NOT TRUE...IT CAN'T BE TRUE!!
DON'T KILL ANYONE...
...EVE.
......
こくっ

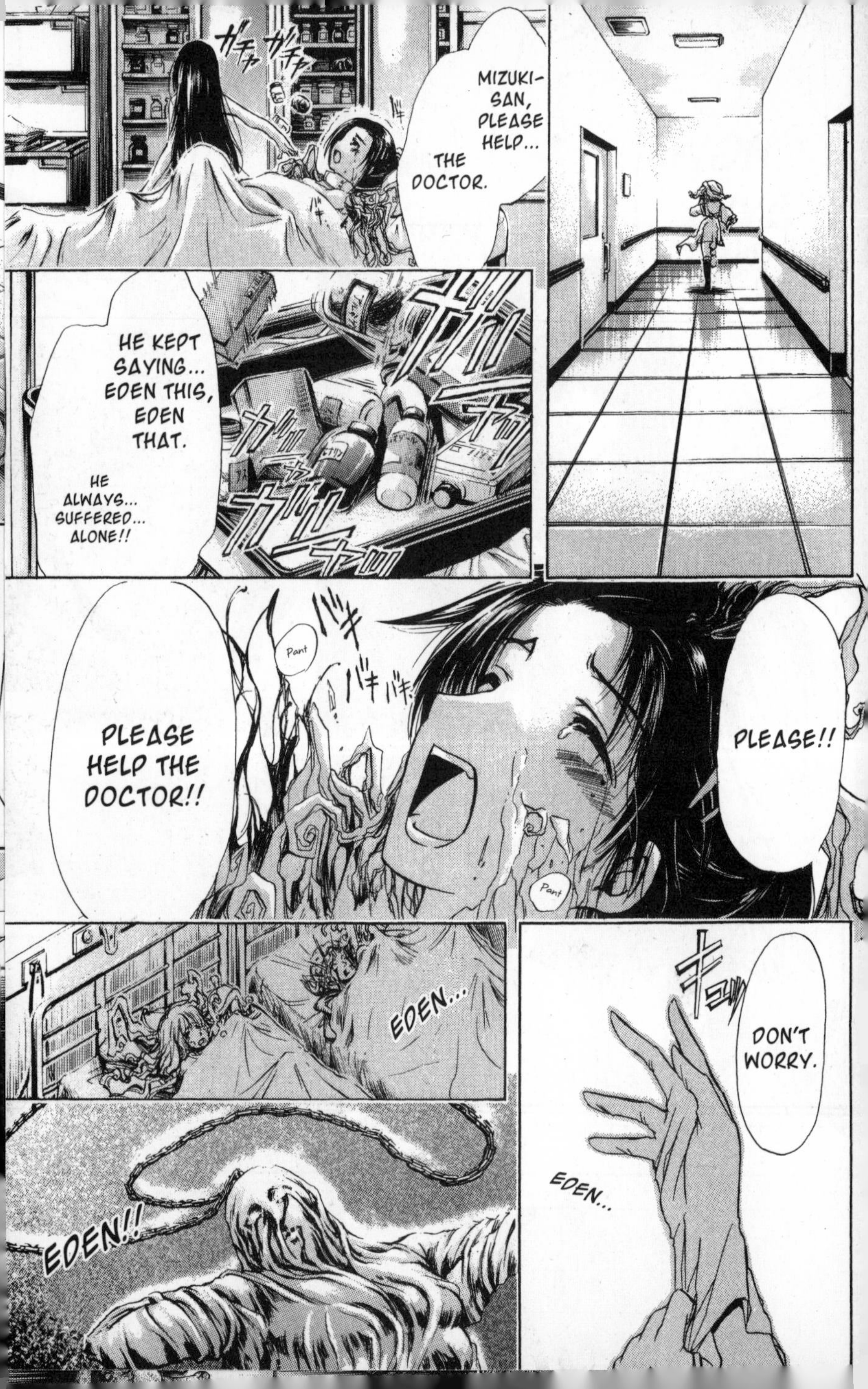

ガチャ ガチャ
MIZUKI-SAN, PLEASE HELP... THE DOCTOR.
HE KEPT SAYING... EDEN THIS, EDEN THAT.
HE ALWAYS... SUFFERED... ALONE!!
PLEASE!!
PLEASE HELP THE DOCTOR!!
Pant
Pant
DON'T WORRY.
EDEN...
EDEN...
EDEN!!

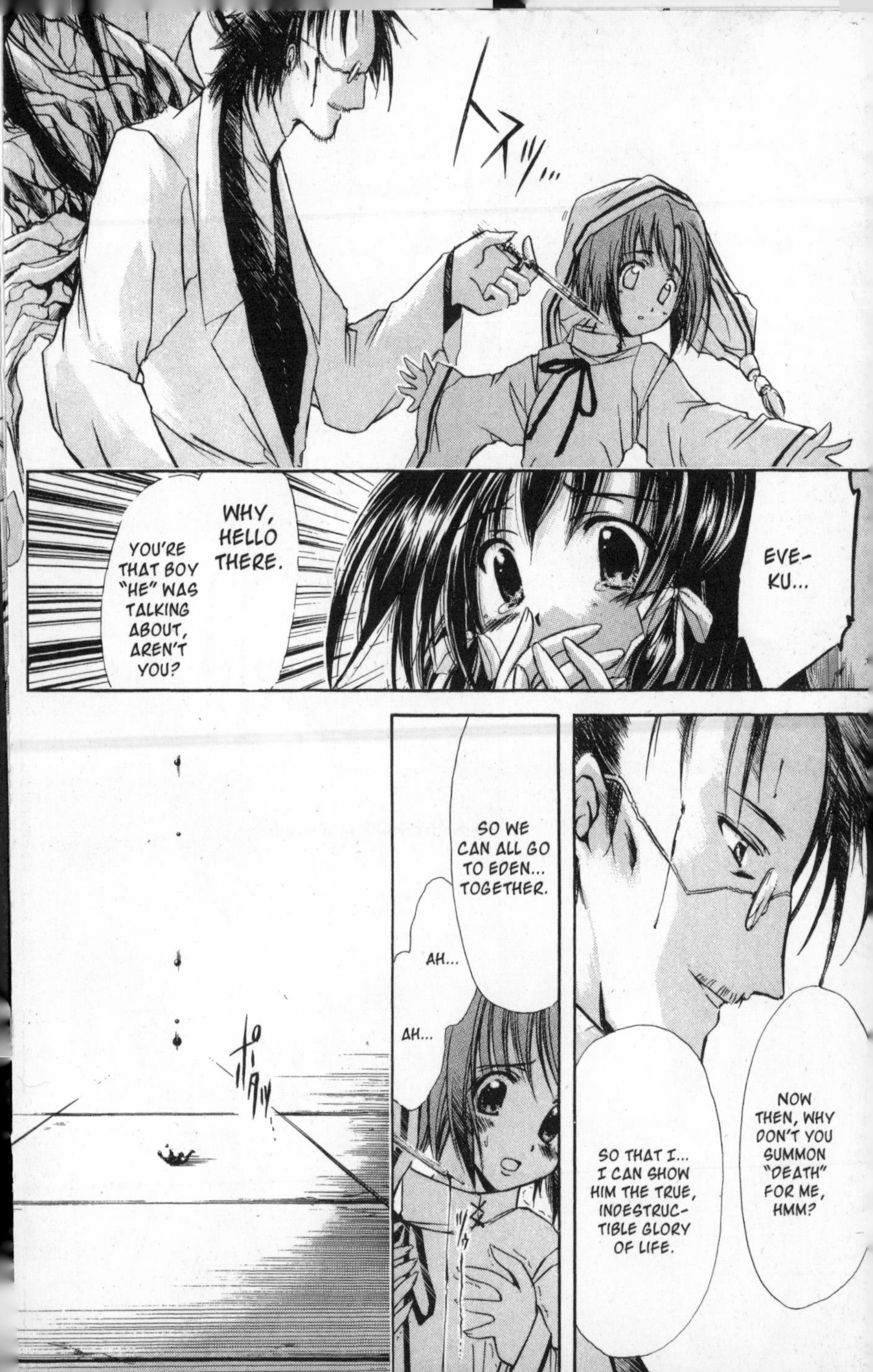
トスッ…
EVE-KU...
WHY, HELLO THERE.
YOU'RE THAT BOY "HE" WAS TALKING ABOUT, AREN'T YOU?
NOW THEN, WHY DON'T YOU SUMMON "DEATH" FOR ME, HMM?
SO THAT I... I CAN SHOW HIM THE TRUE, INDESTRUC-TIBLE GLORY OF LIFE.
SO WE CAN ALL GO TO EDEN... TOGETHER.
AH...
AH...

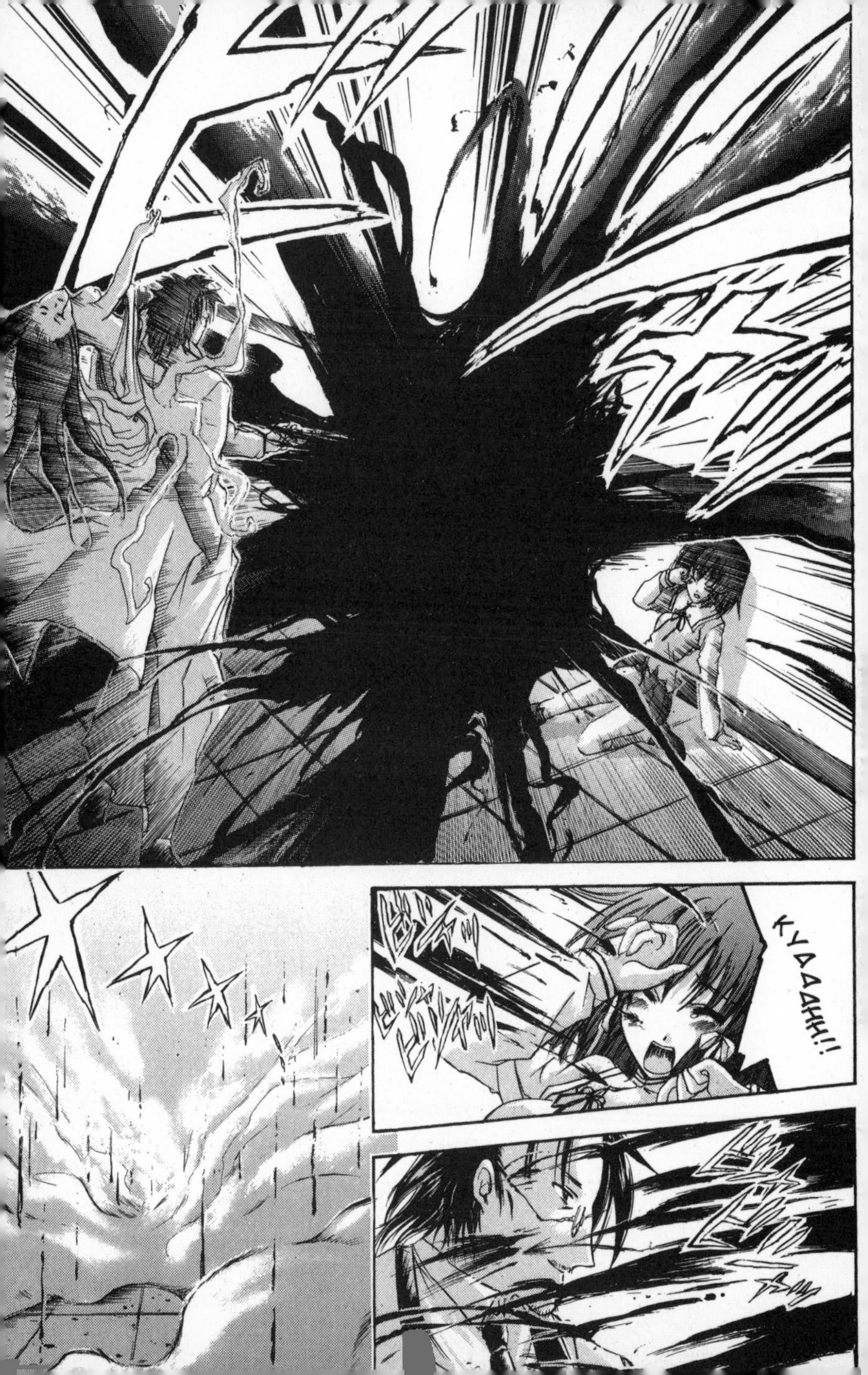
KYAAAHH!!

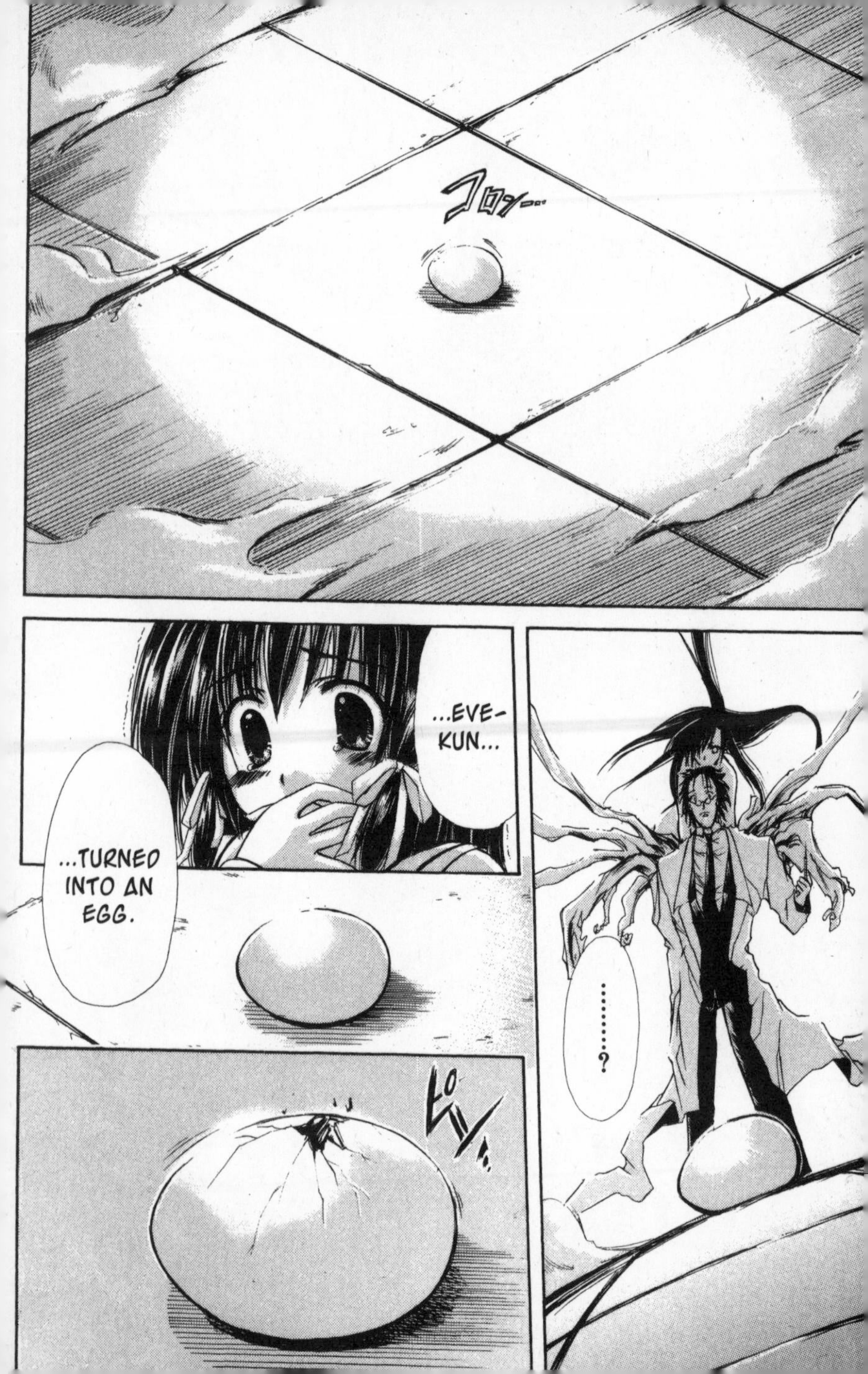

コロン…
......?
...EVE-KUN...
...TURNED INTO AN EGG.

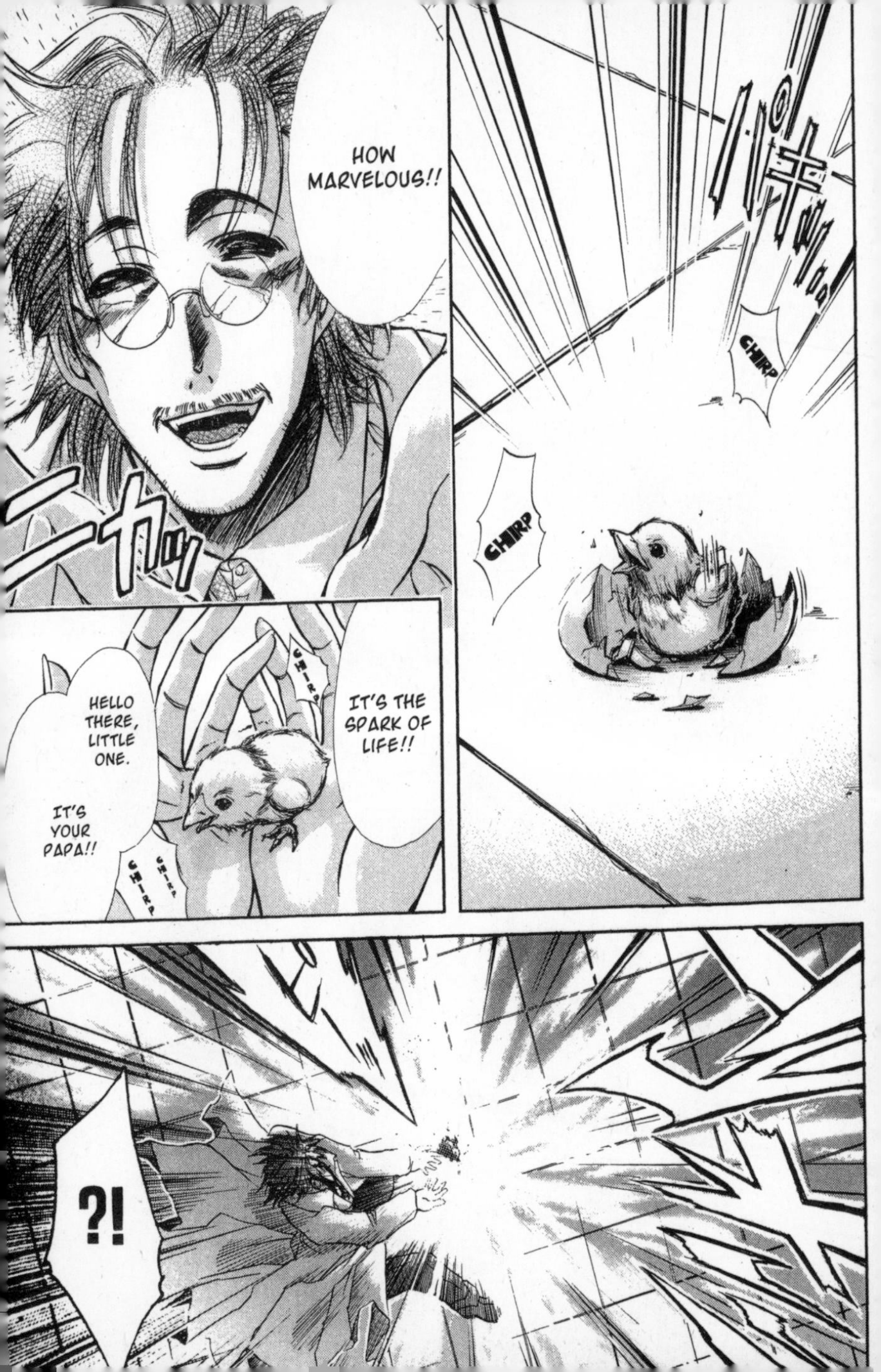
CHIRP
CHIRP
HOW MARVELOUS!!
ニカッ
IT'S THE SPARK OF LIFE!!
CHIRP
HELLO THERE, LITTLE ONE.
IT'S YOUR PAPA!!
CHIRP
CHIRP
?!

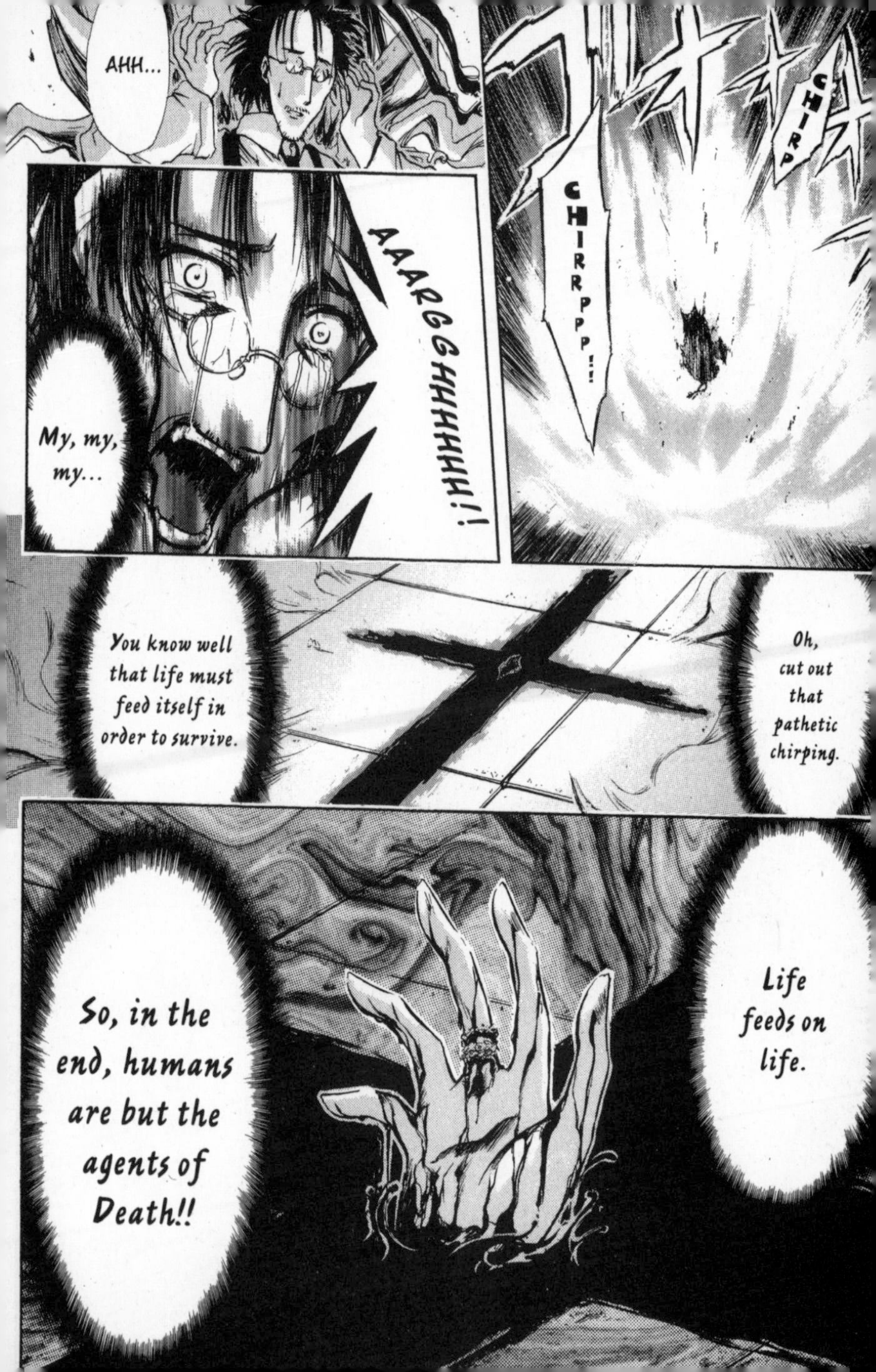

CHIRP
CHIRRPPP!!
AHH...
AAARGGHHHHHH!!
My, my, my...
Oh, cut out that pathetic chirping.
You know well that life must feed itself in order to survive.
Life feeds on life.
So, in the end, humans are but the agents of Death!!

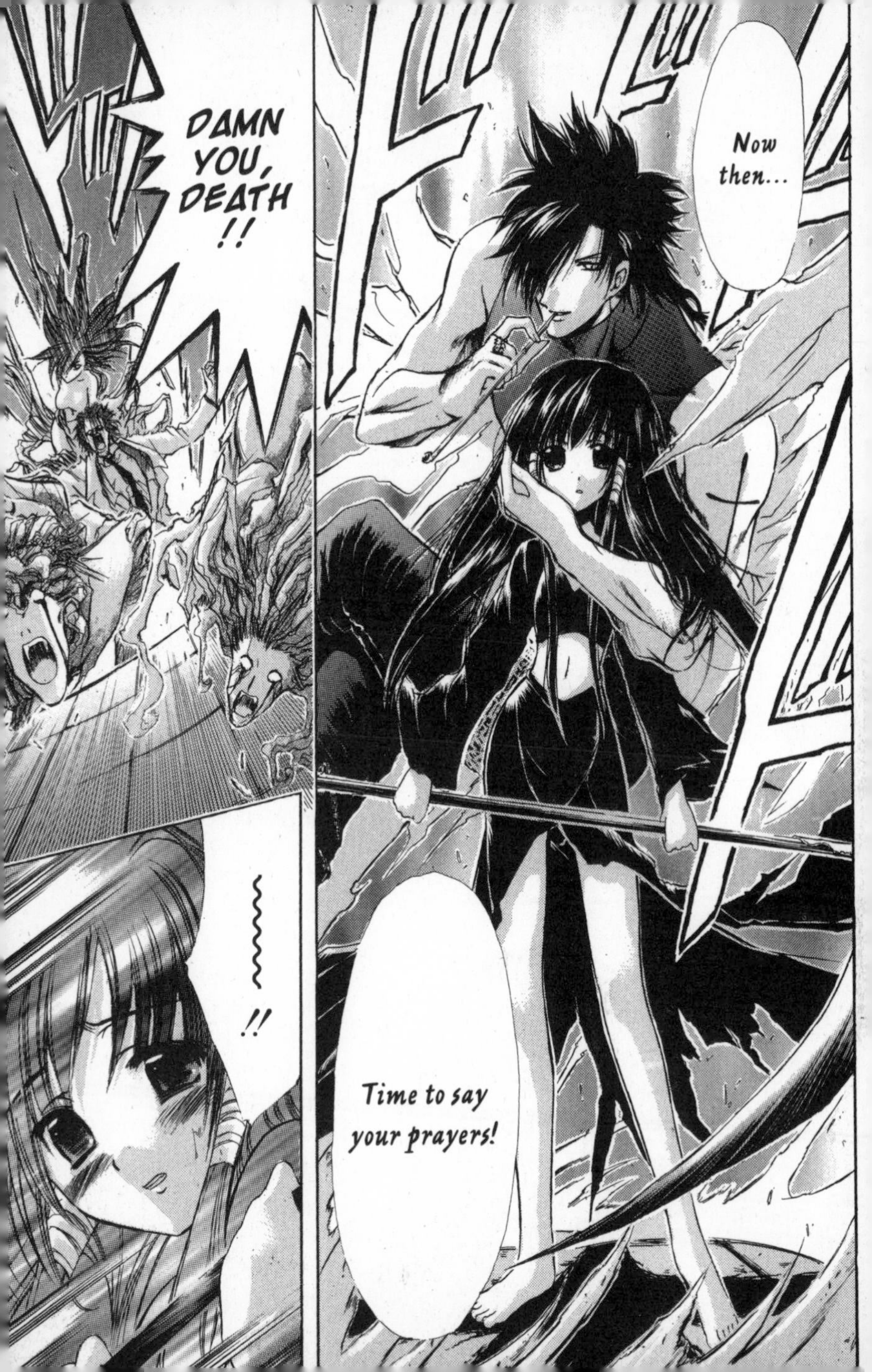
Now then...
Time to say your prayers!
DAMN YOU, DEATH!!
!!

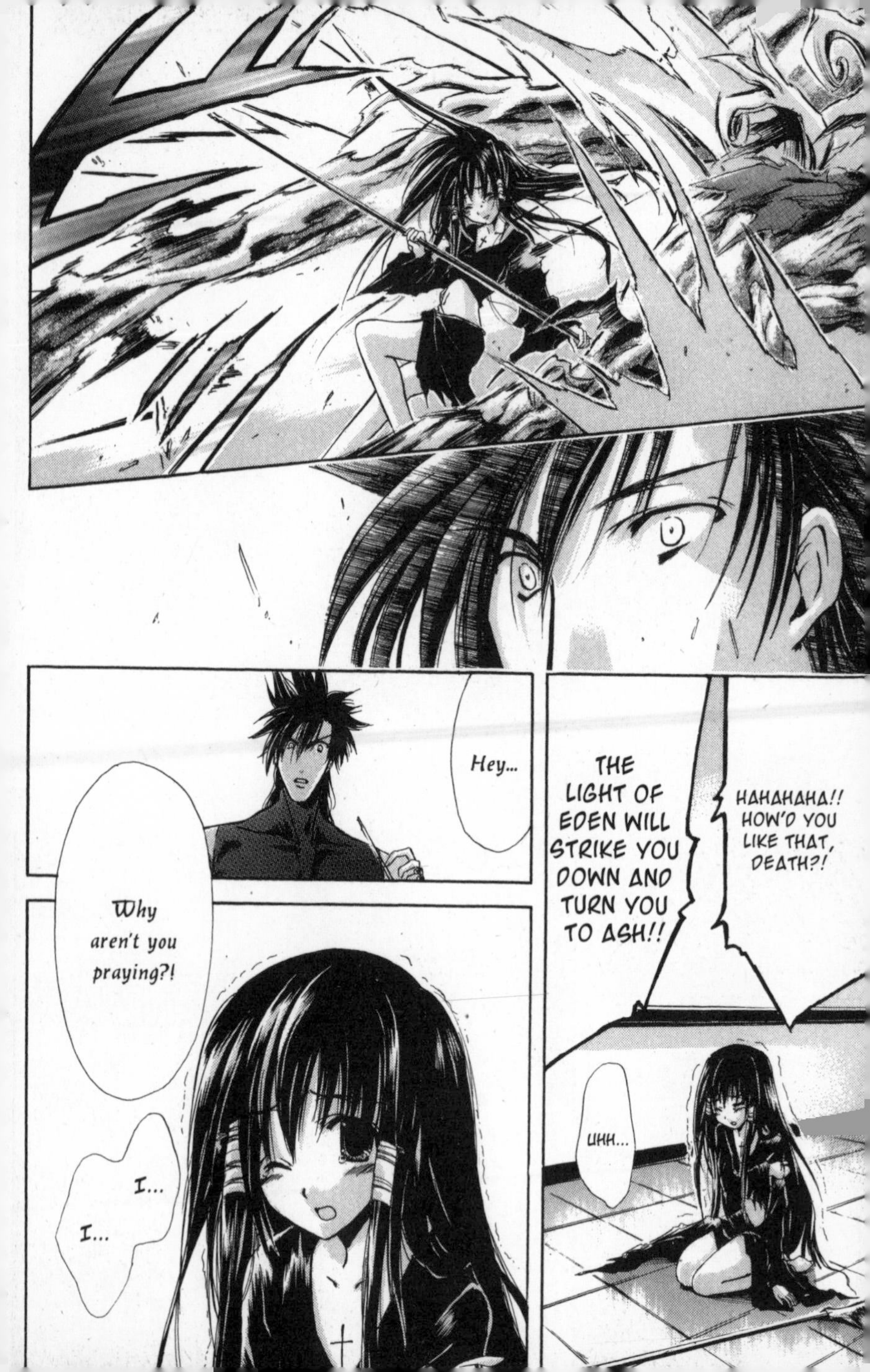
HAHAHAHA!! HOW'D YOU LIKE THAT, DEATH?!
THE LIGHT OF EDEN WILL STRIKE YOU DOWN AND TURN YOU TO ASH!!
UHH...
Hey...
Why aren't you praying?!
I...
I...

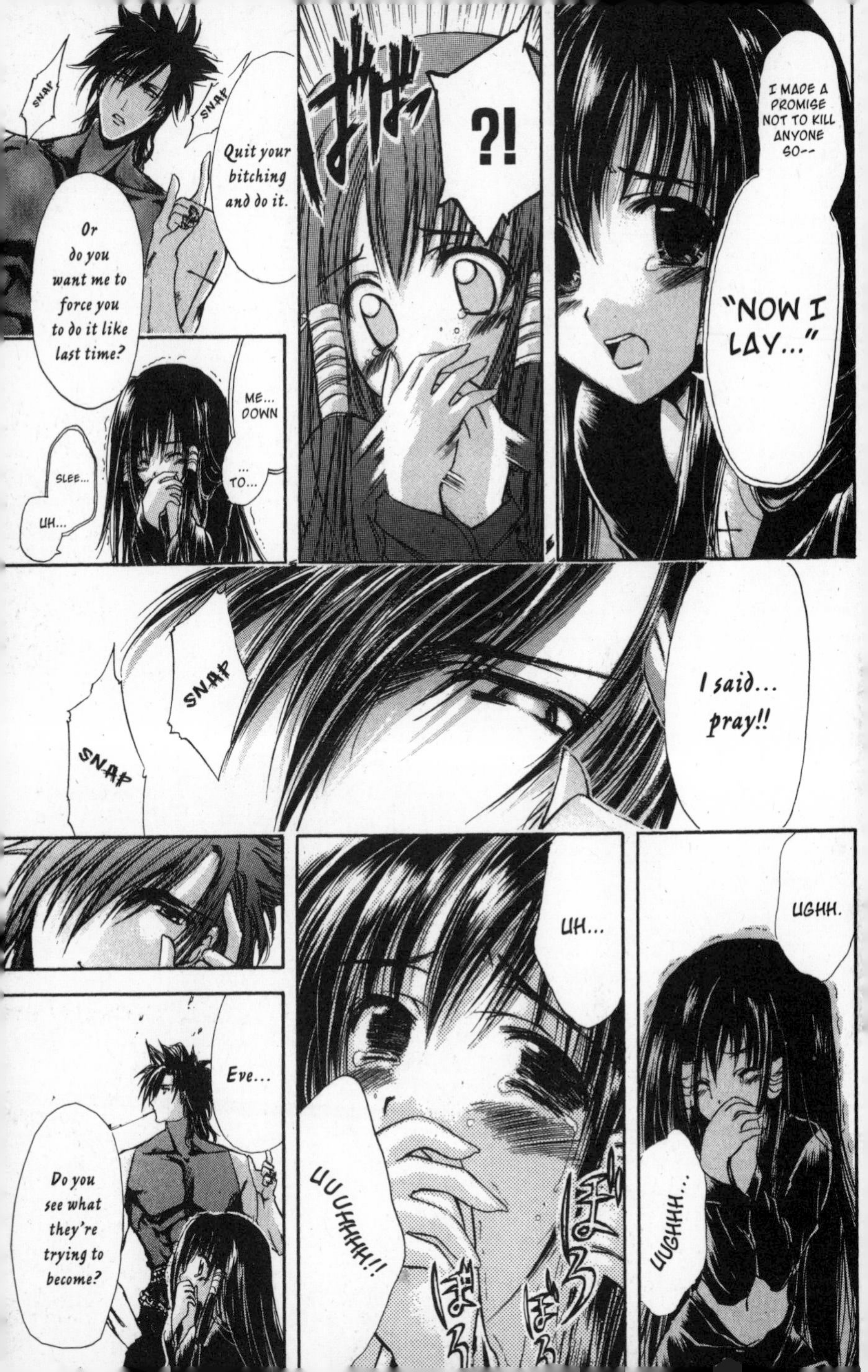
I MADE A PROMISE NOT TO KILL ANYONE SO--
"NOW I LAY..."
?!
SNAP
SNAP
Quit your bitching and do it.
Or do you want me to force you to do it like last time?
ME... DOWN
... TO...
SLEE...
UH...
I said... pray!!
SNAP
SNAP
UGHH.
UUGHHH...
UH...
UUUHHHH!!
Eve...
Do you see what they're trying to become?

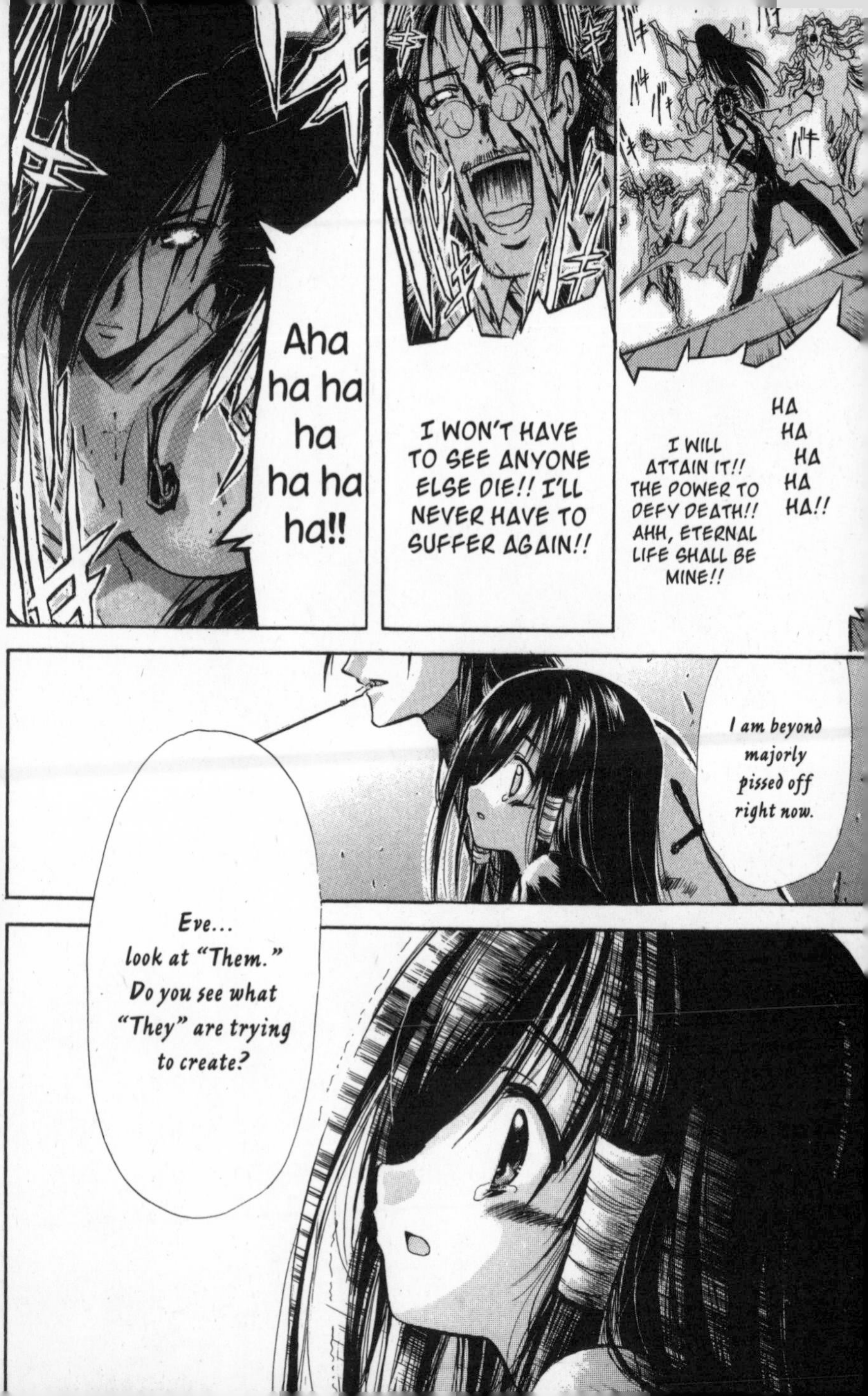
HA HA HA HA HA!!
I WILL ATTAIN IT!! THE POWER TO DEFY DEATH!! AHH, ETERNAL LIFE SHALL BE MINE!!
I WON'T HAVE TO SEE ANYONE ELSE DIE!! I'LL NEVER HAVE TO SUFFER AGAIN!!
Aha ha ha ha ha ha ha!!
I am beyond majorly pissed off right now.
Eve... look at "Them." Do you see what "They" are trying to create?

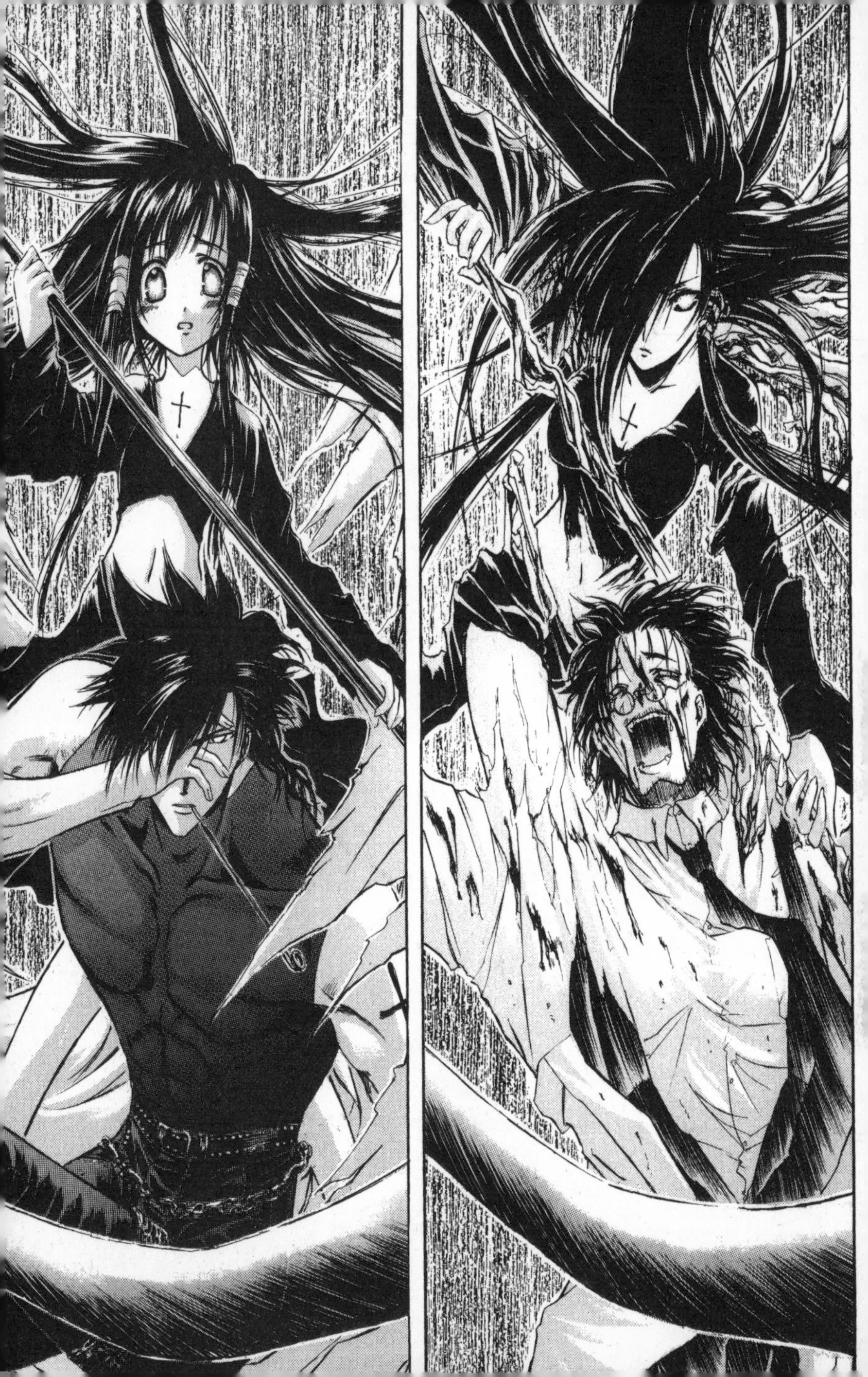

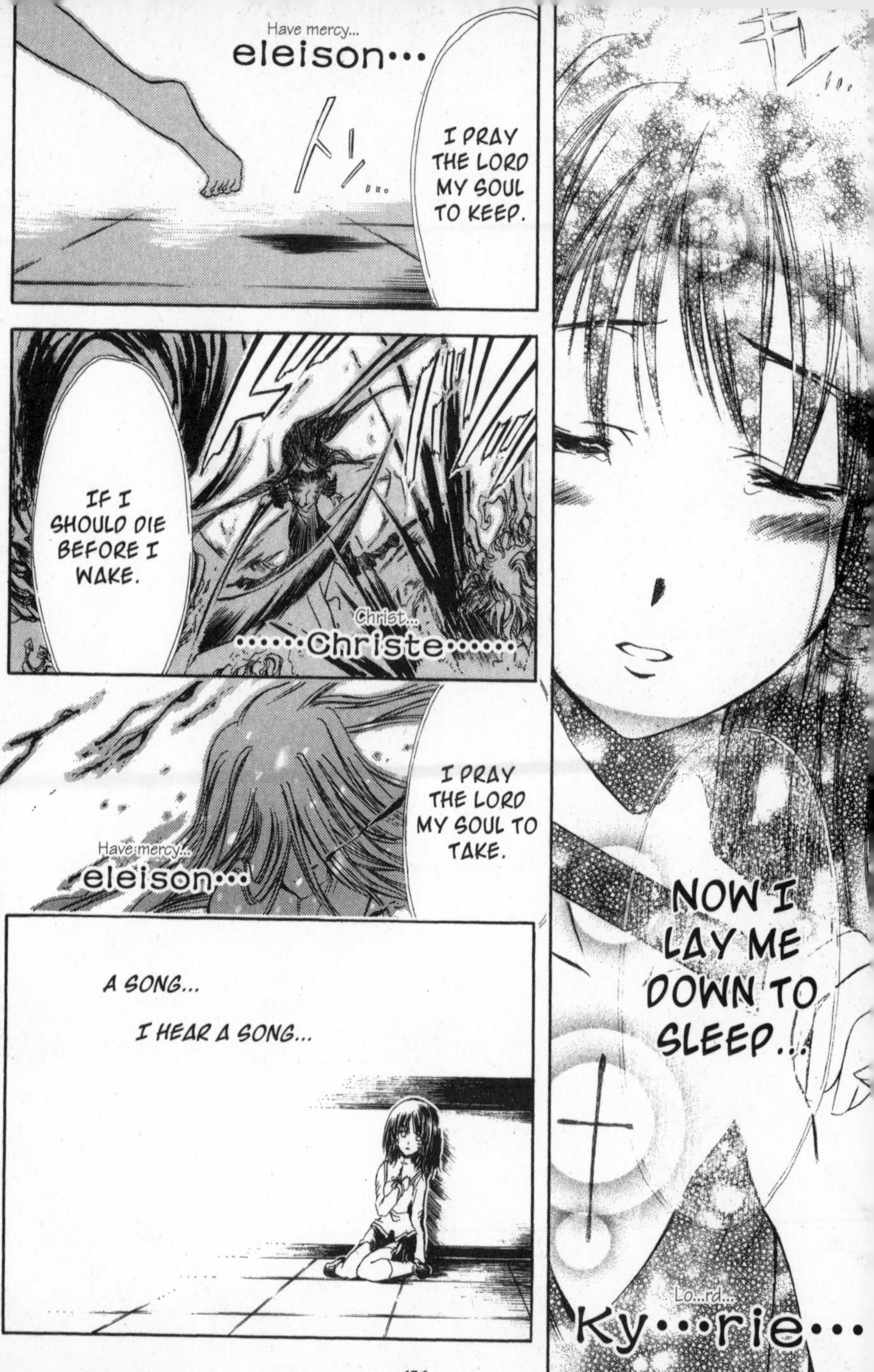
NOW I LAY ME DOWN TO SLEEP...
Lo...rd...
Ky···rie···
Have mercy...
eleison···
I PRAY THE LORD MY SOUL TO KEEP.
IF I SHOULD DIE BEFORE I WAKE.
Christ...
······Christe······
I PRAY THE LORD MY SOUL TO TAKE.
Have mercy...
eleison···
A SONG...
I HEAR A SONG...

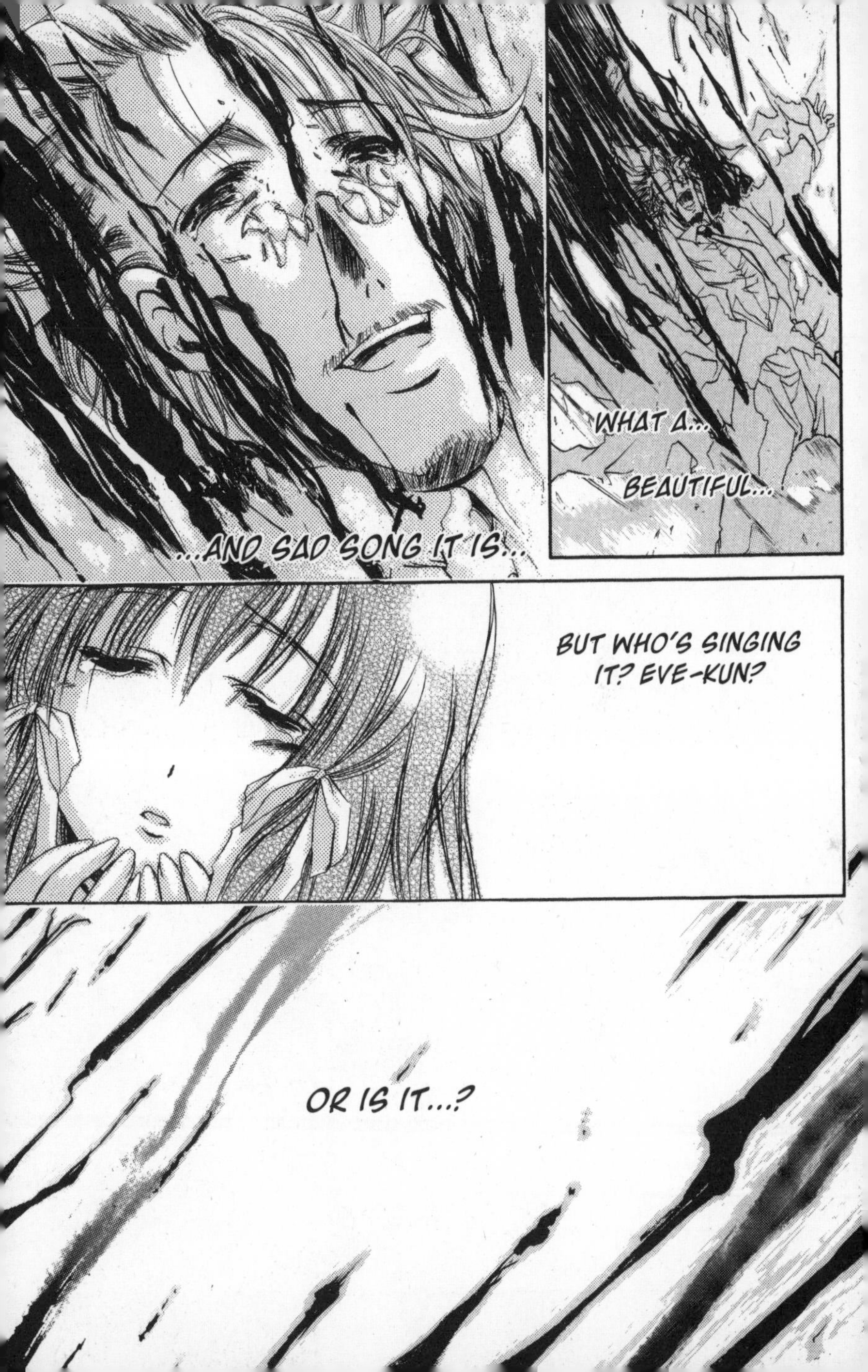
WHAT A...
BEAUTIFUL...
...AND SAD SONG IT IS...
BUT WHO'S SINGING IT? EVE-KUN?
OR IS IT...?

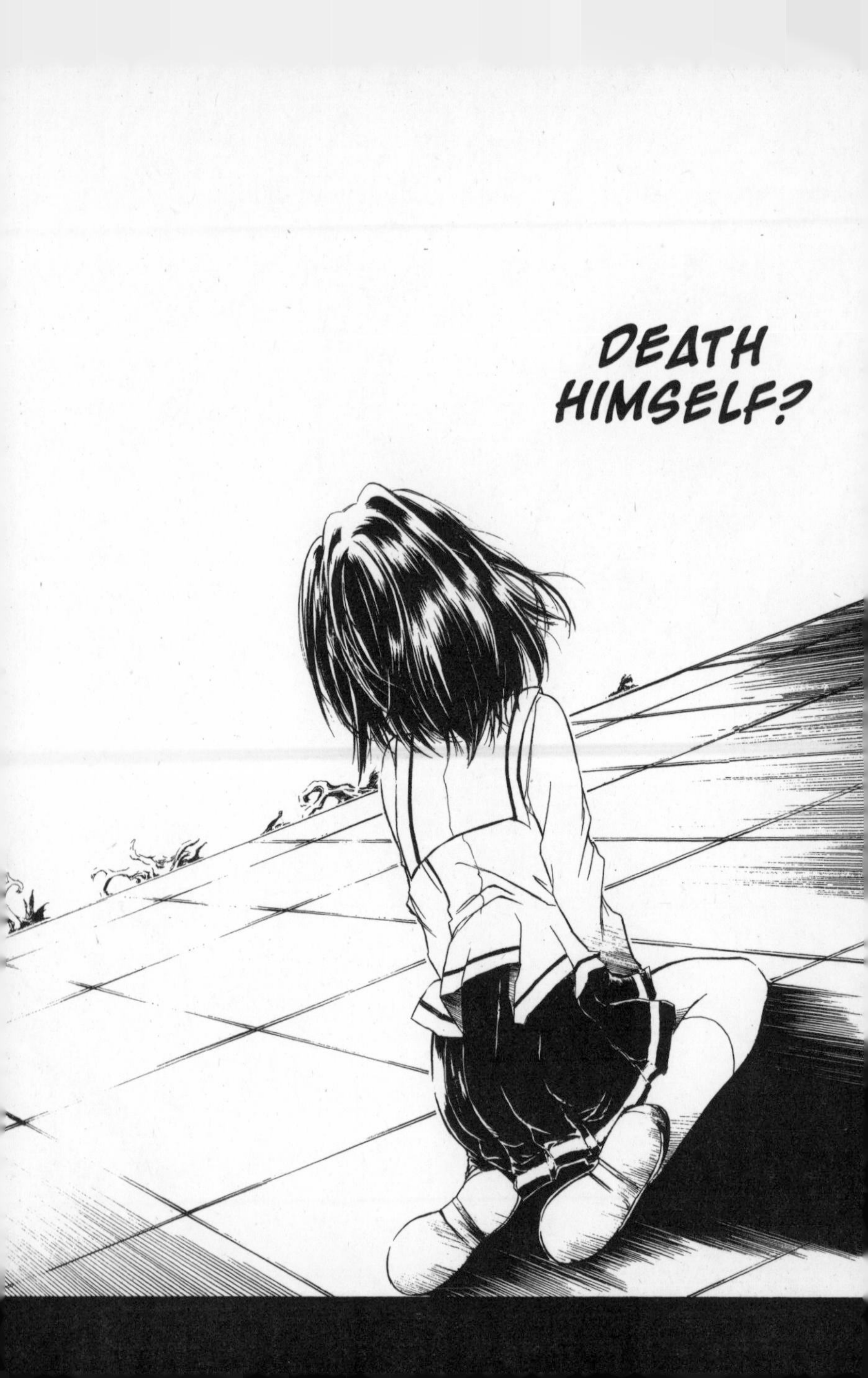
DEATH HIMSELF?

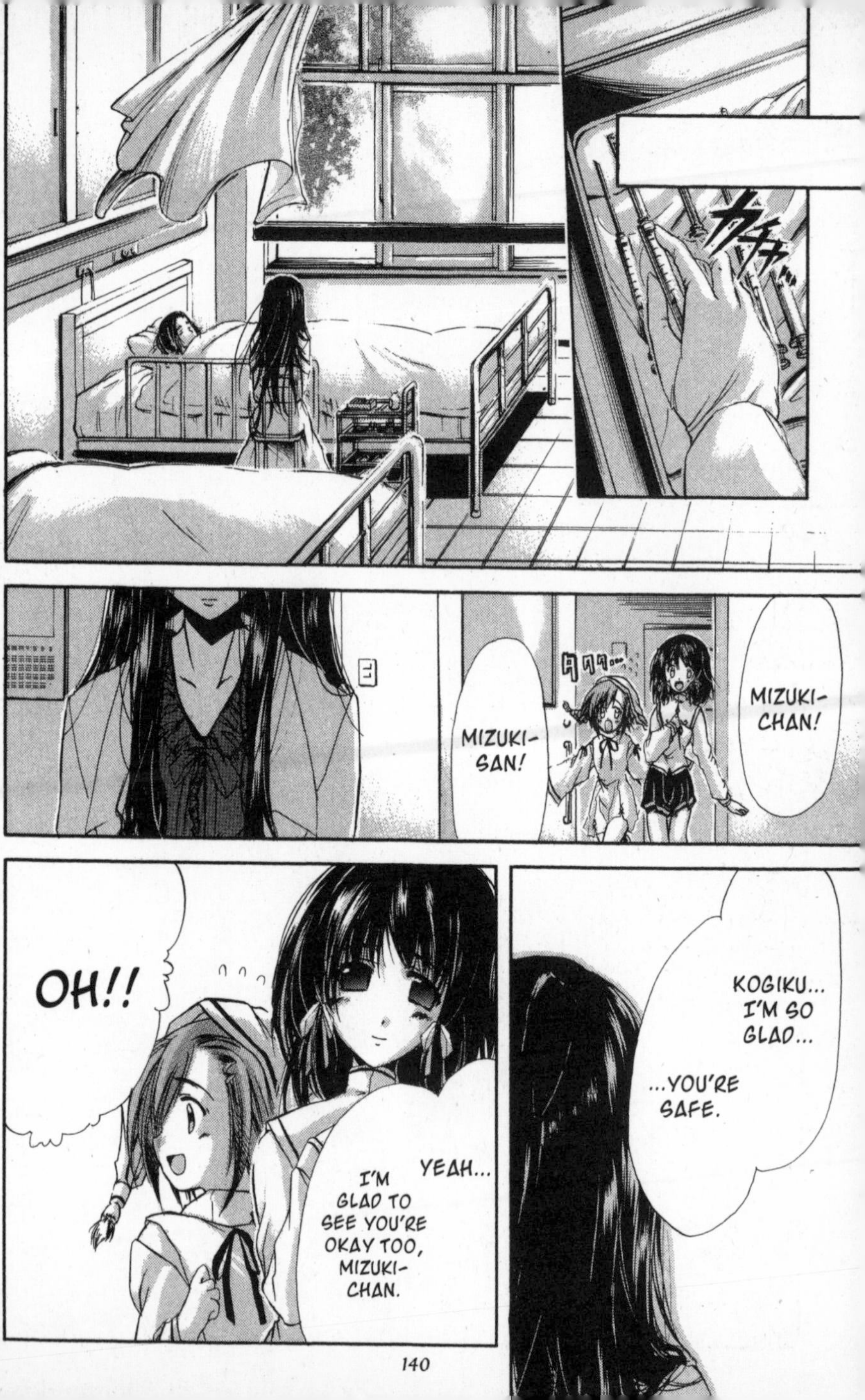

MIZUKI-CHAN!
MIZUKI-SAN!
KOGIKU... I'M SO GLAD...
...YOU'RE SAFE.
OH!!
YEAH...
I'M GLAD TO SEE YOU'RE OKAY TOO, MIZUKI-CHAN.

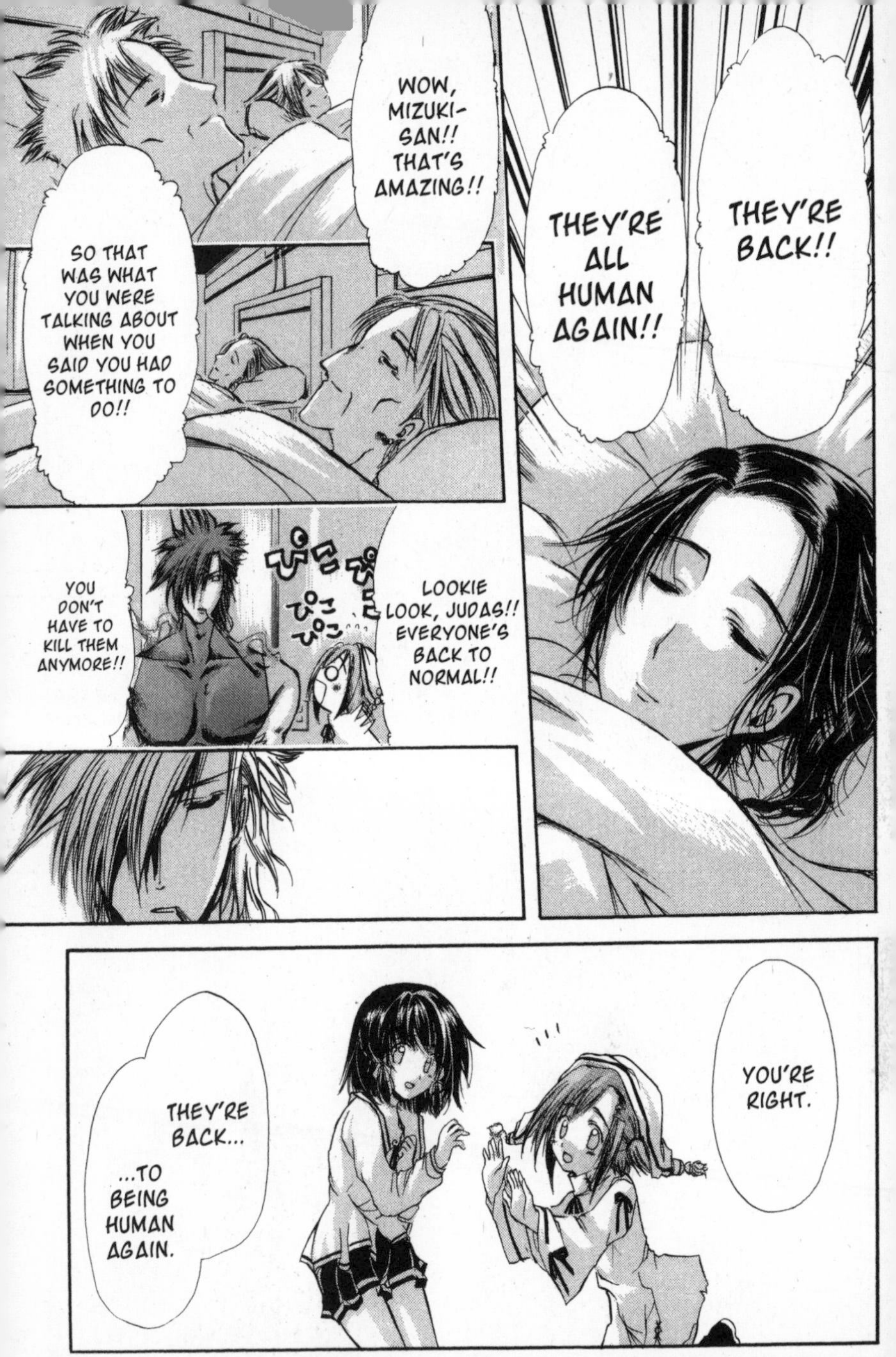
THEY'RE BACK!!
THEY'RE ALL HUMAN AGAIN!!
WOW, MIZUKI-SAN!! THAT'S AMAZING!!
SO THAT WAS WHAT YOU WERE TALKING ABOUT WHEN YOU SAID YOU HAD SOMETHING TO DO!!
LOOKIE LOOK, JUDAS!! EVERYONE'S BACK TO NORMAL!!
YOU DON'T HAVE TO KILL THEM ANYMORE!!
YOU'RE RIGHT.
THEY'RE BACK...
...TO BEING HUMAN AGAIN.

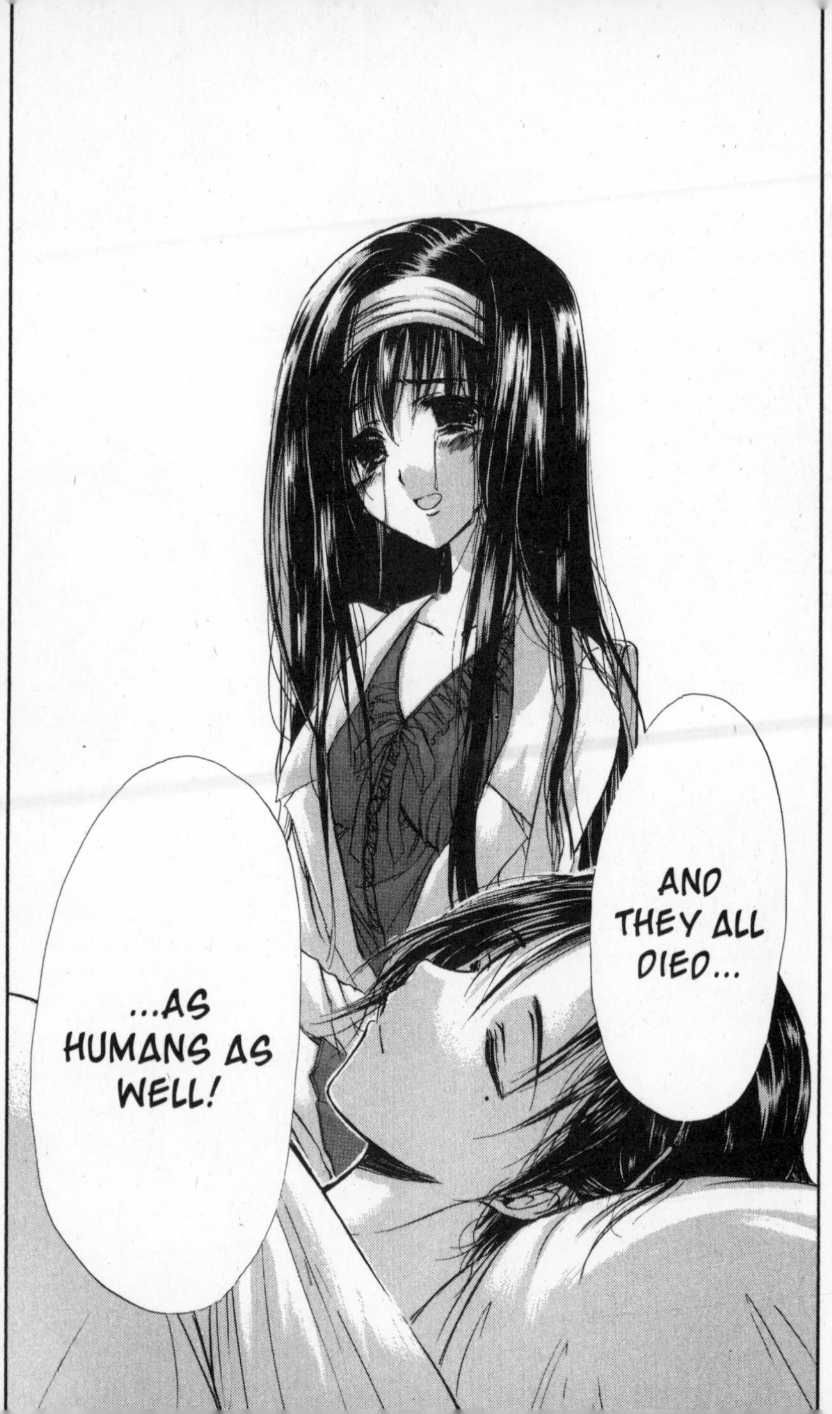
AND THEY ALL DIED...
...AS HUMANS AS WELL!

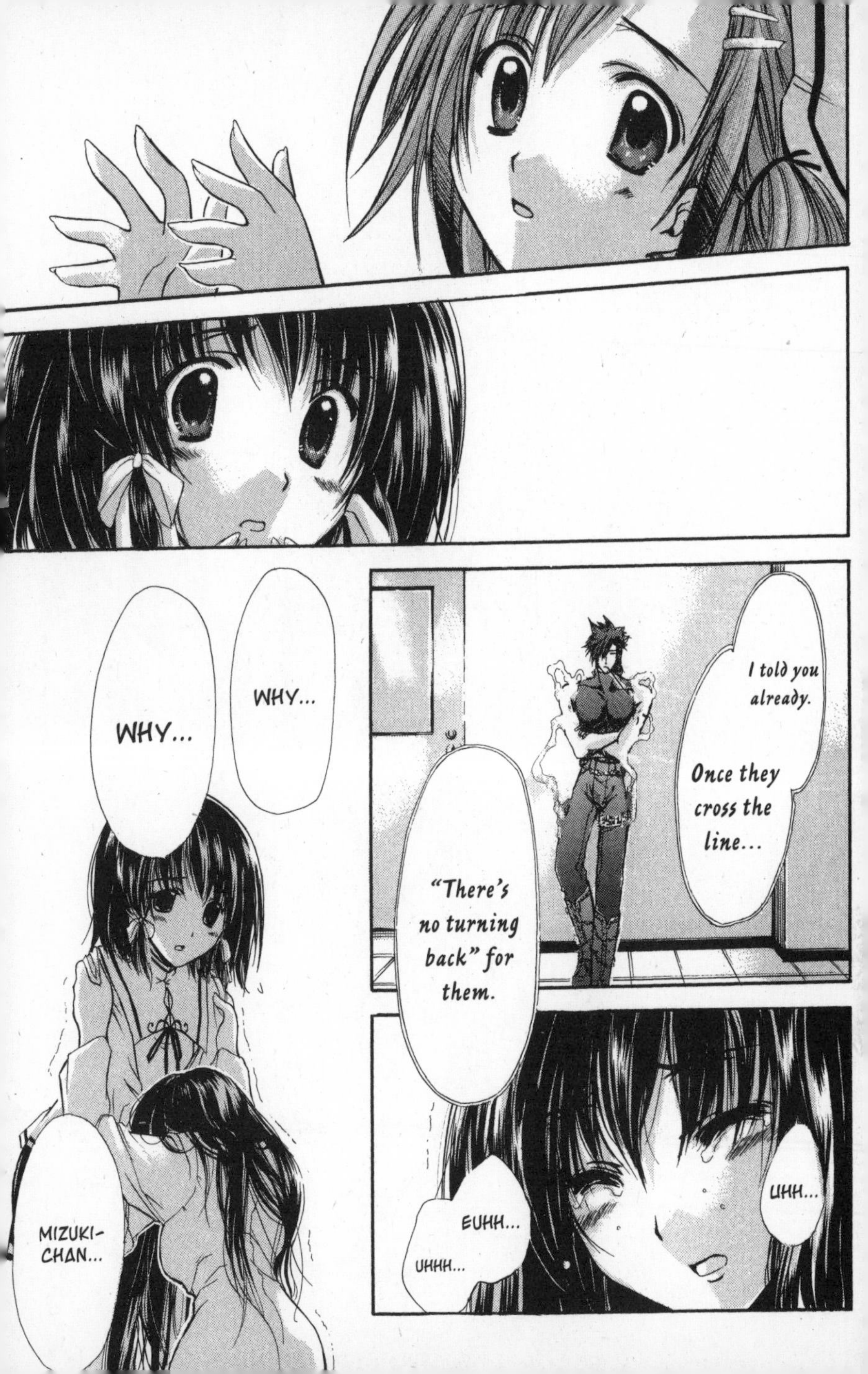
I told you already.
Once they cross the line...
"There's no turning back" for them.
UHH...
EUHH...
UHHH...
WHY...
WHY...
MIZUKI-CHAN...

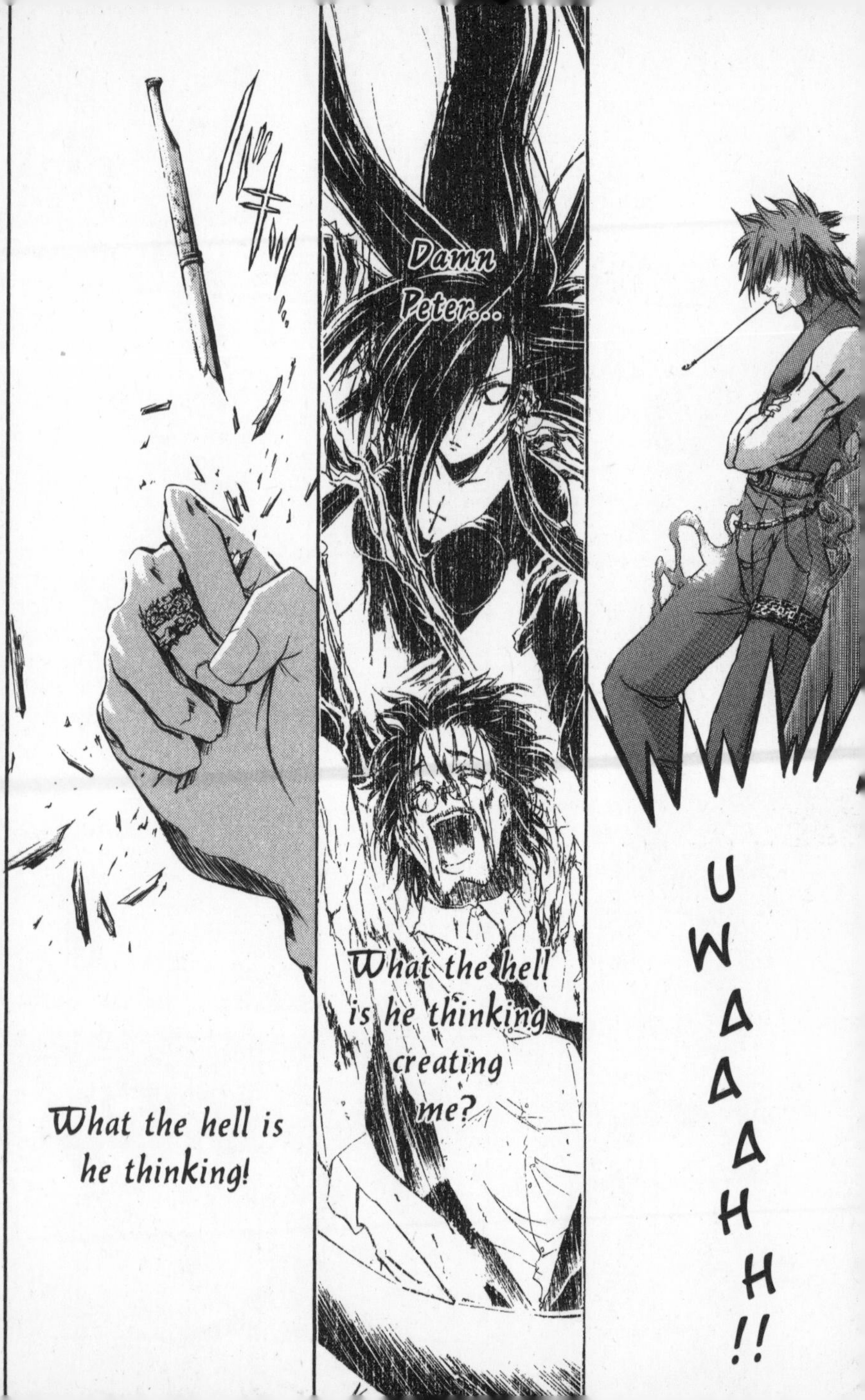
UWAAAHH!!
Damn Peter...
What the hell is he thinking creating me?
What the hell is he thinking!

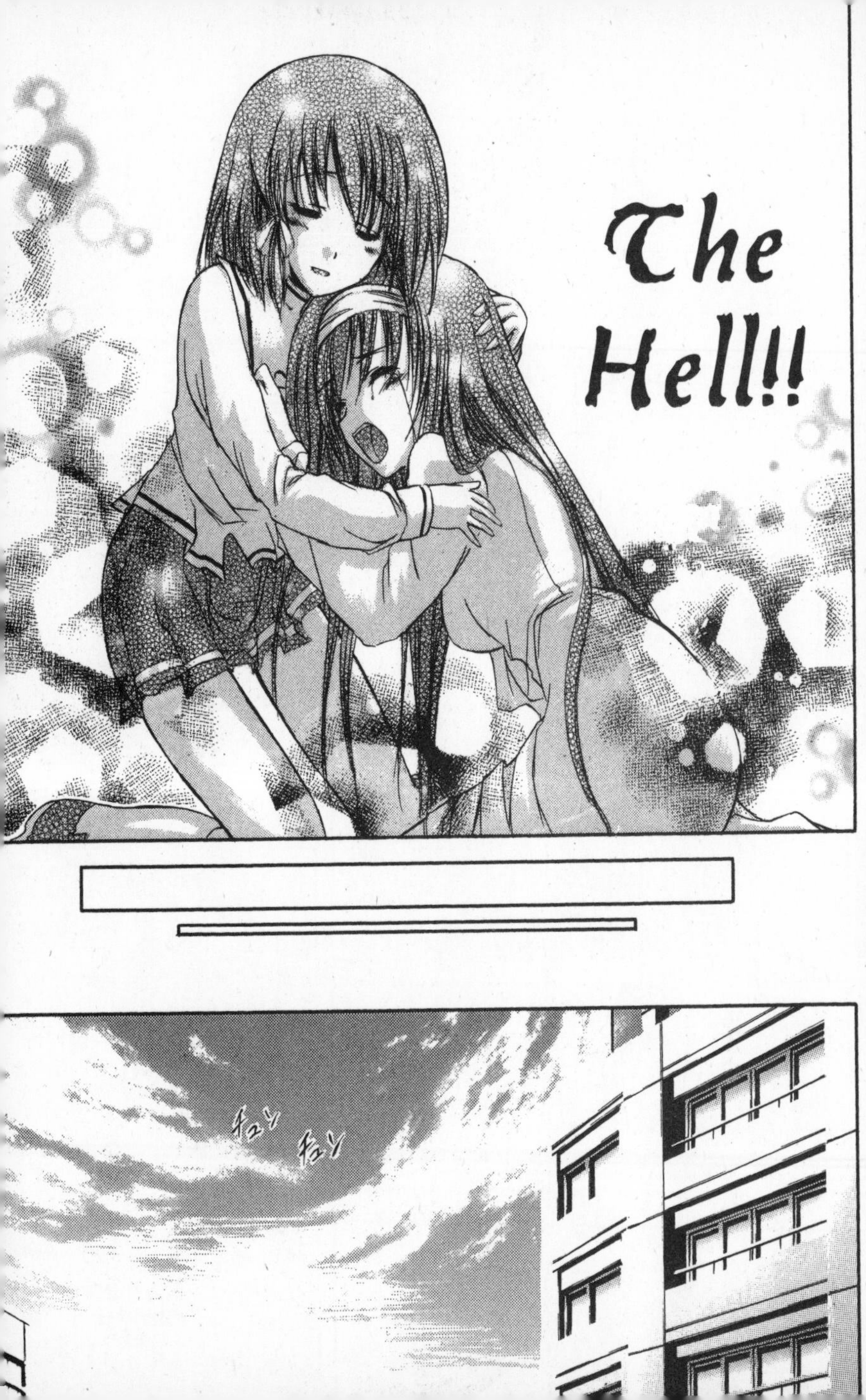
The Hell!!
チュン チュン

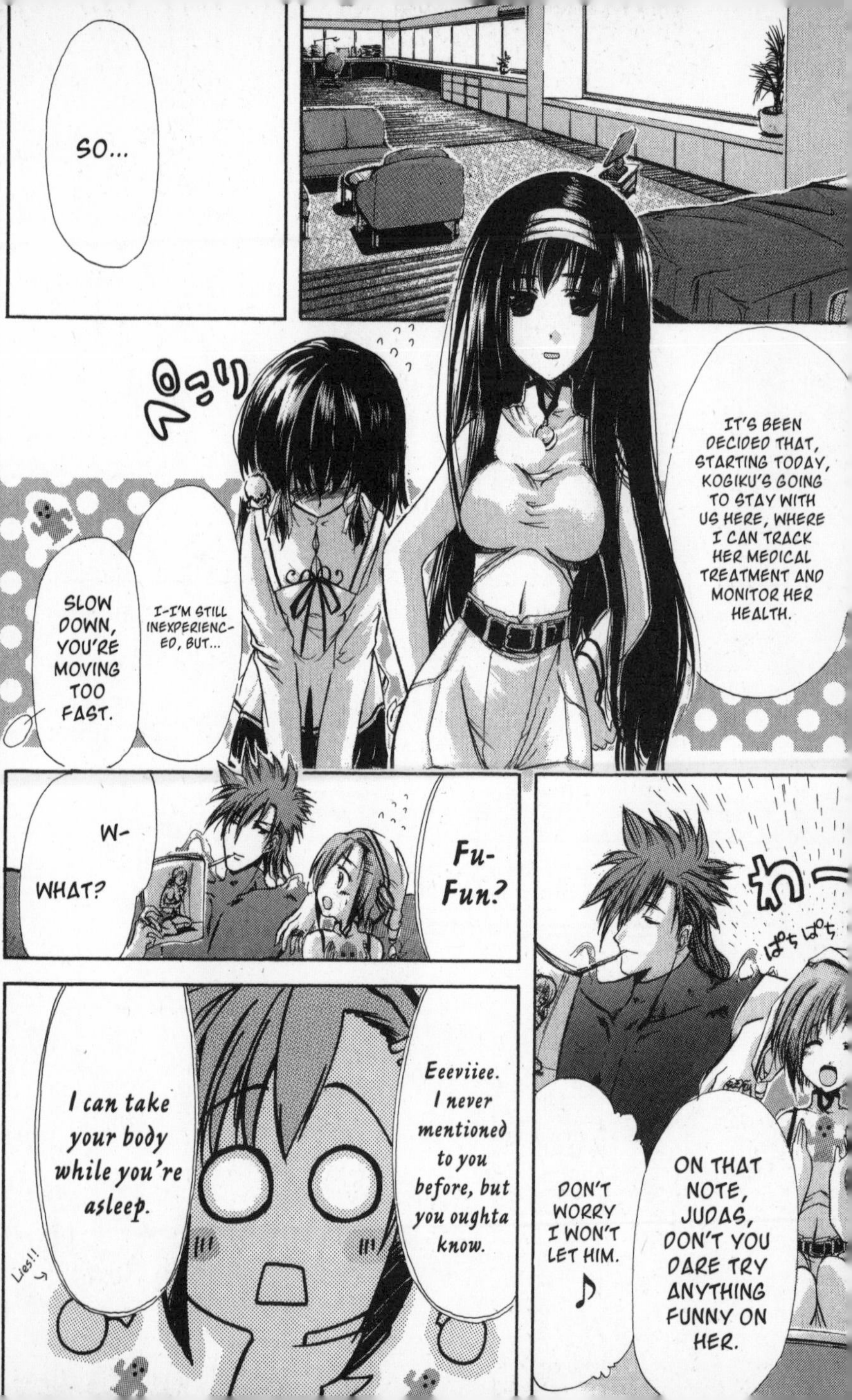
SO...
IT'S BEEN DECIDED THAT, STARTING TODAY, KOGIKU'S GOING TO STAY WITH US HERE, WHERE I CAN TRACK HER MEDICAL TREATMENT AND MONITOR HER HEALTH.
I-I'M STILL INEXPERIENCED, BUT...
SLOW DOWN, YOU'RE MOVING TOO FAST.
わー
ぱちぱち
ON THAT NOTE, JUDAS, DON'T YOU DARE TRY ANYTHING FUNNY ON HER.
DON'T WORRY I WON'T LET HIM. ♪
Fu-Fun?
W- WHAT?
Eeeviiee. I never mentioned to you before, but you oughta know.
I can take your body while you're asleep.
Lies!!

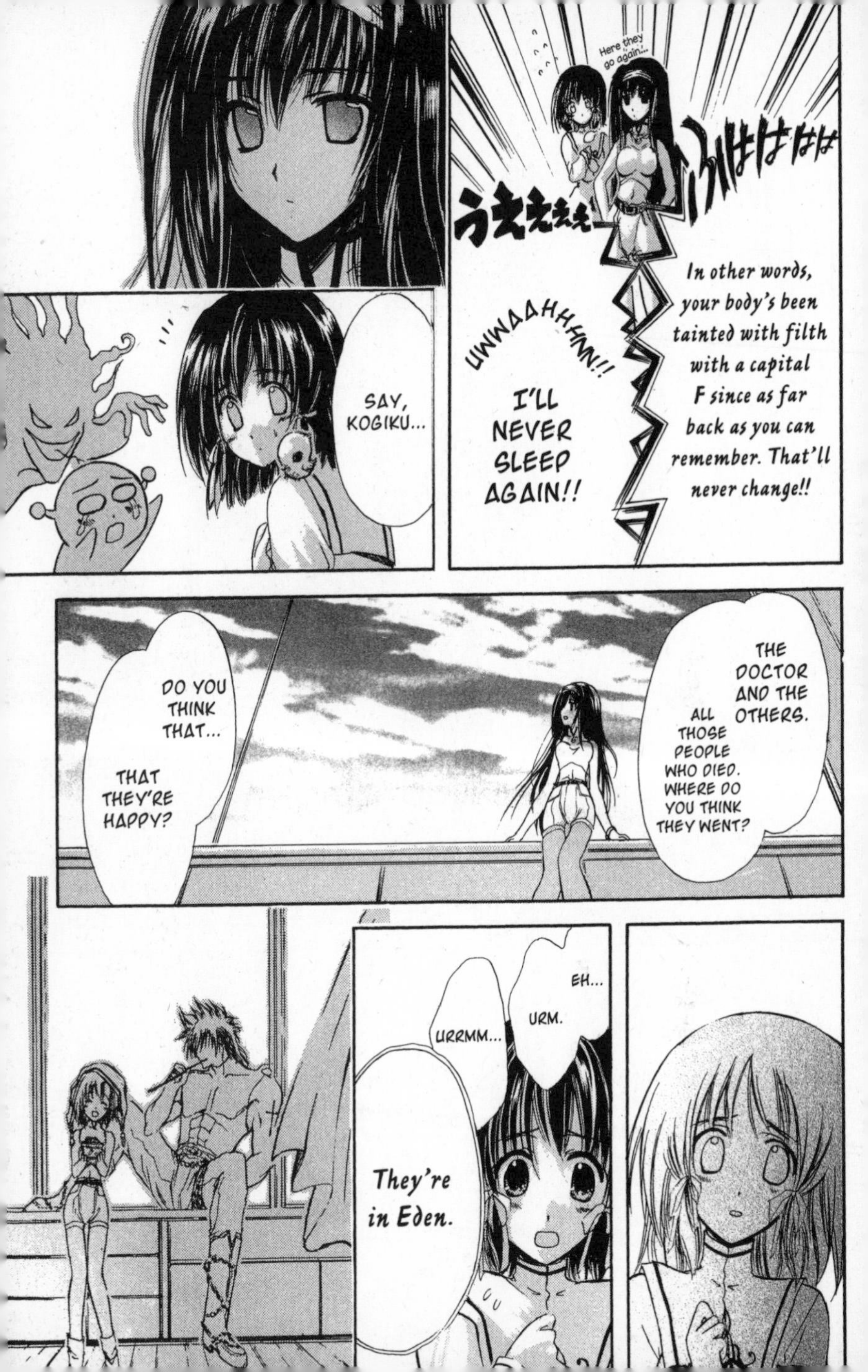

Here they go again...
ふはははは
In other words, your body's been tainted with filth with a capital F since as far back as you can remember. That'll never change!!
うええええ
UWWAAHHHNN!!
I'LL NEVER SLEEP AGAIN!!
SAY, KOGIKU...
THE DOCTOR AND THE OTHERS.
ALL THOSE PEOPLE WHO DIED. WHERE DO YOU THINK THEY WENT?
DO YOU THINK THAT...
THAT THEY'RE HAPPY?
EH...
URM.
URRMM...
They're in Eden.

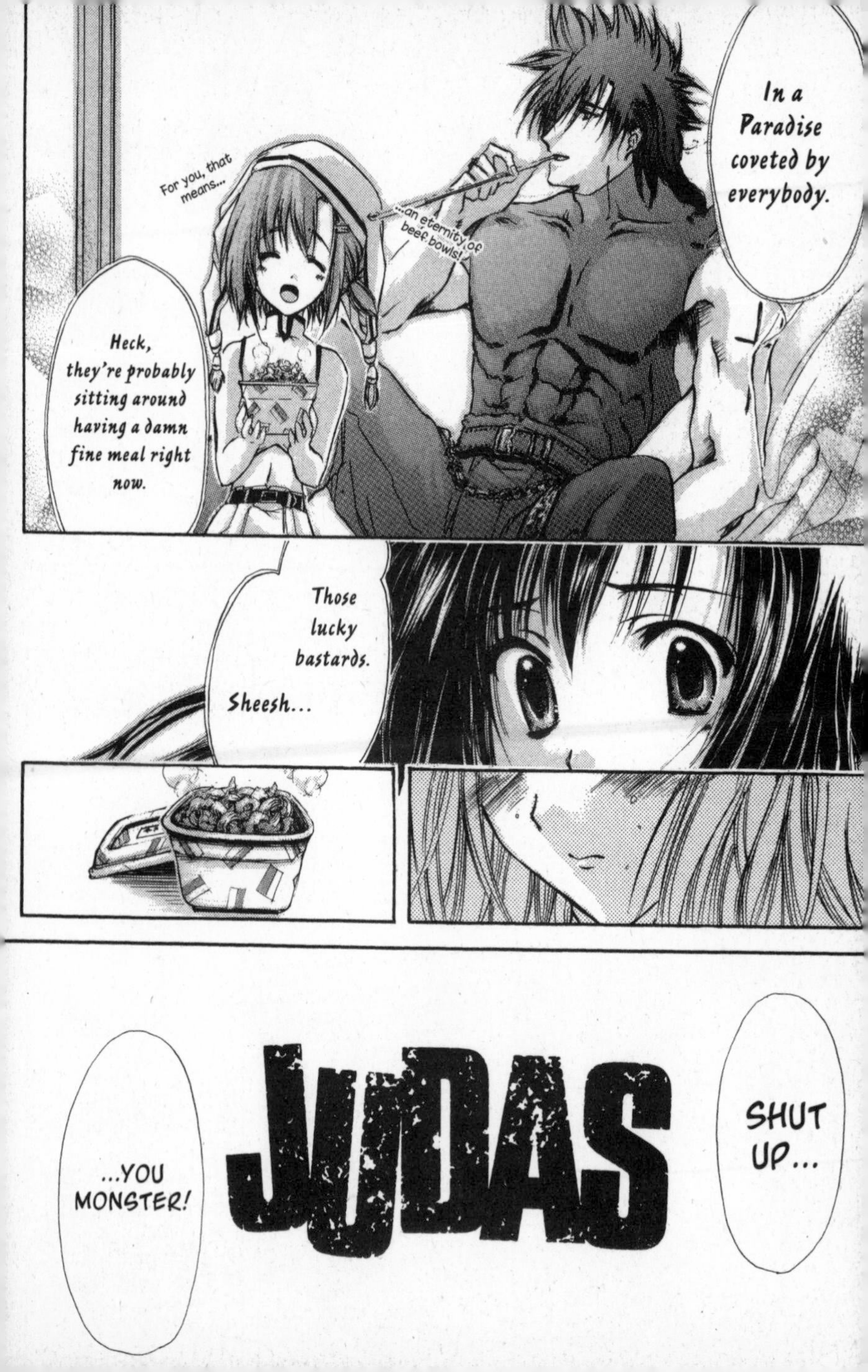
In a Paradise coveted by everybody.
For you, that means...
...an eternity of beef bowls!
Heck, they're probably sitting around having a damn fine meal right now.
Those lucky bastards.
Sheesh...
SHUT UP...
JUDAS
...YOU MONSTER!

JUDAS

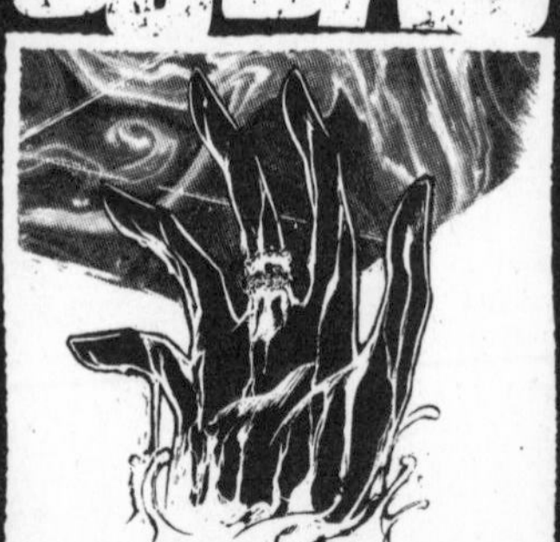

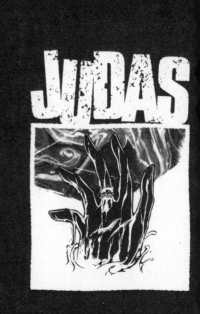

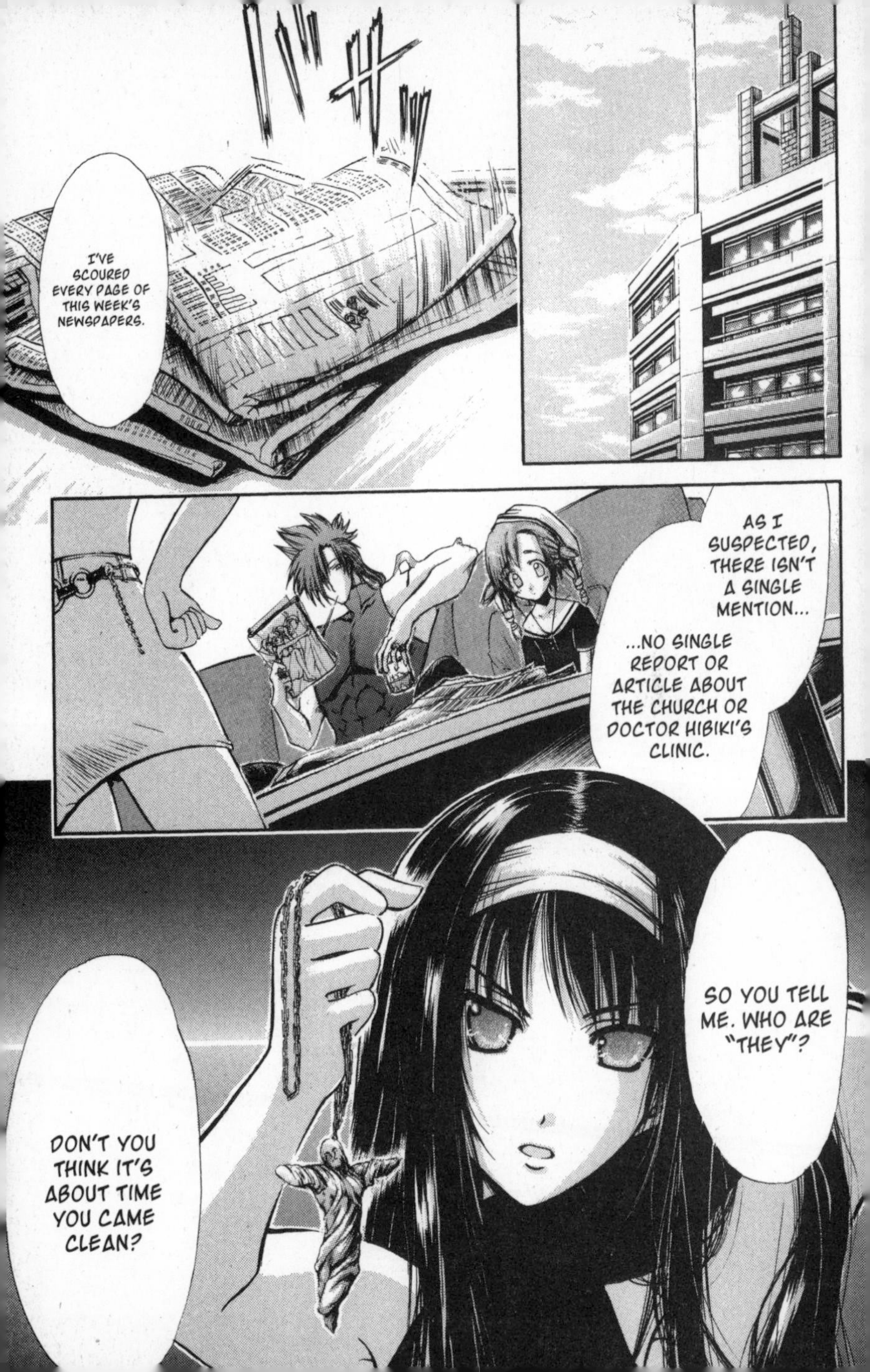
I'VE SCOURED EVERY PAGE OF THIS WEEK'S NEWSPAPERS.
AS I SUSPECTED, THERE ISN'T A SINGLE MENTION...
...NO SINGLE REPORT OR ARTICLE ABOUT THE CHURCH OR DOCTOR HIBIKI'S CLINIC.
SO YOU TELL ME. WHO ARE "THEY"?
DON'T YOU THINK IT'S ABOUT TIME YOU CAME CLEAN?

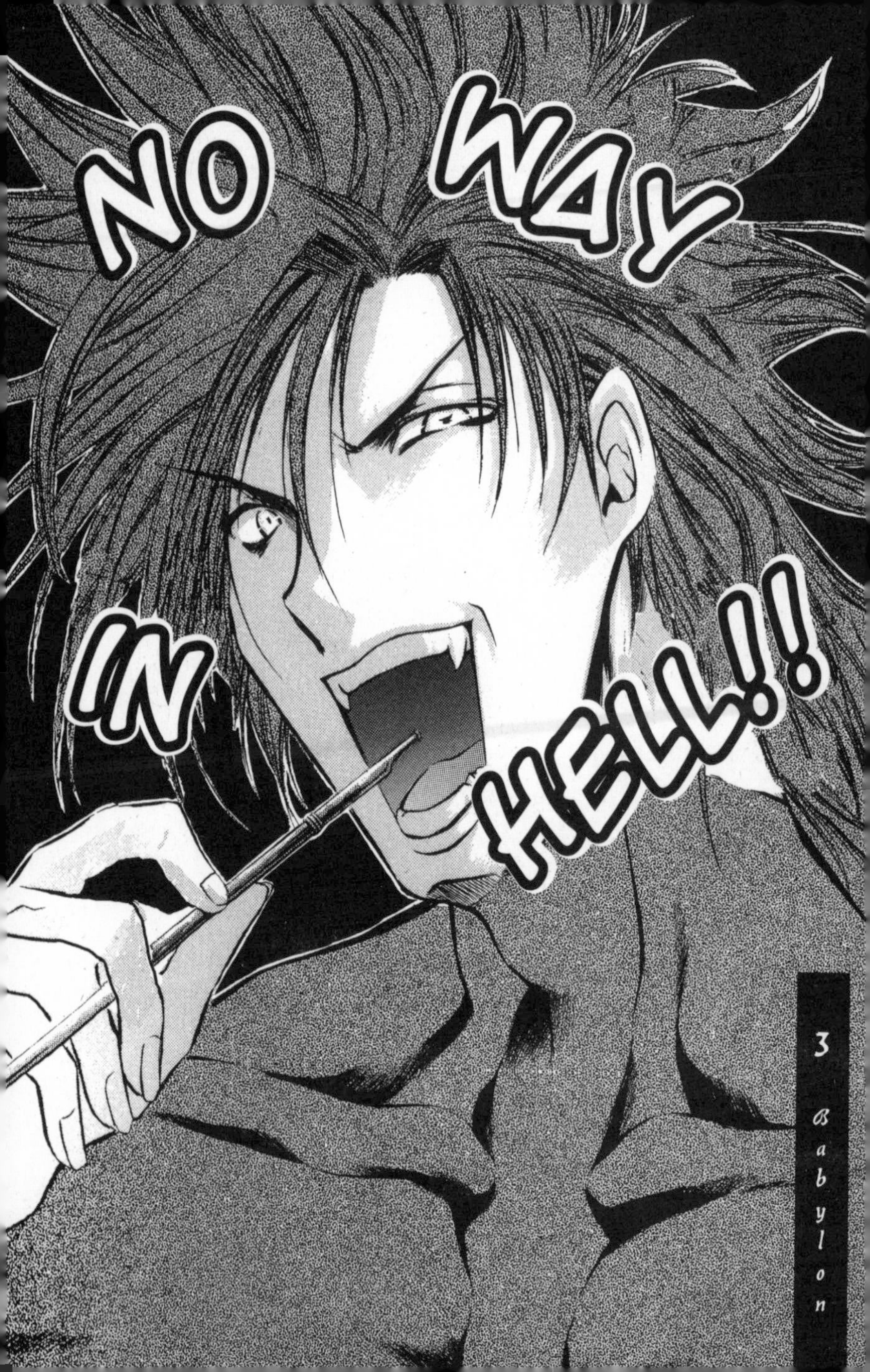
NO WAY IN HELL!!
3 Babylon

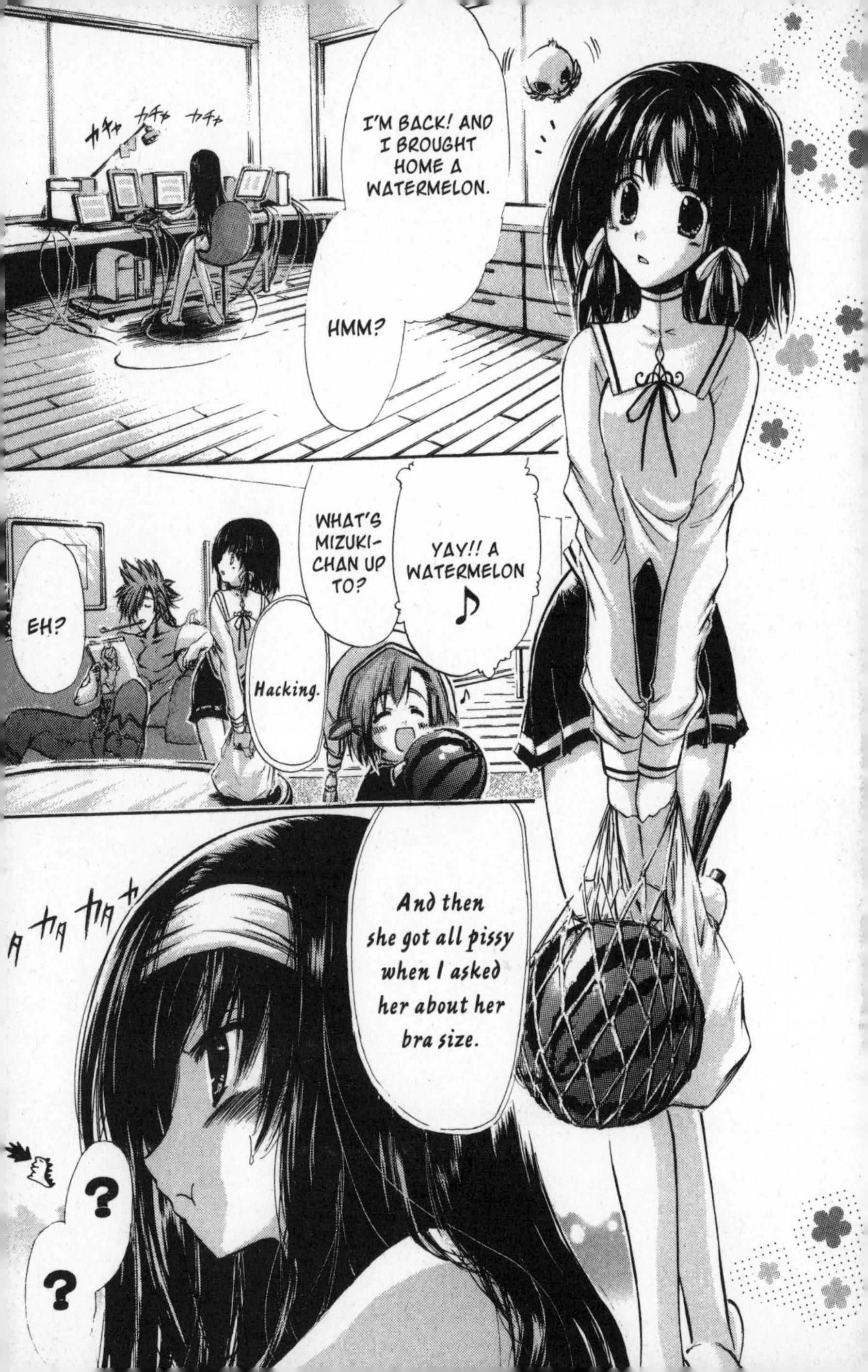
I'M BACK! AND I BROUGHT HOME A WATERMELON.
HMM?
YAY!! A WATERMELON ♪
WHAT'S MIZUKI-CHAN UP TO?
Hacking.
EH?
And then she got all pissy when I asked her about her bra size.
?
?

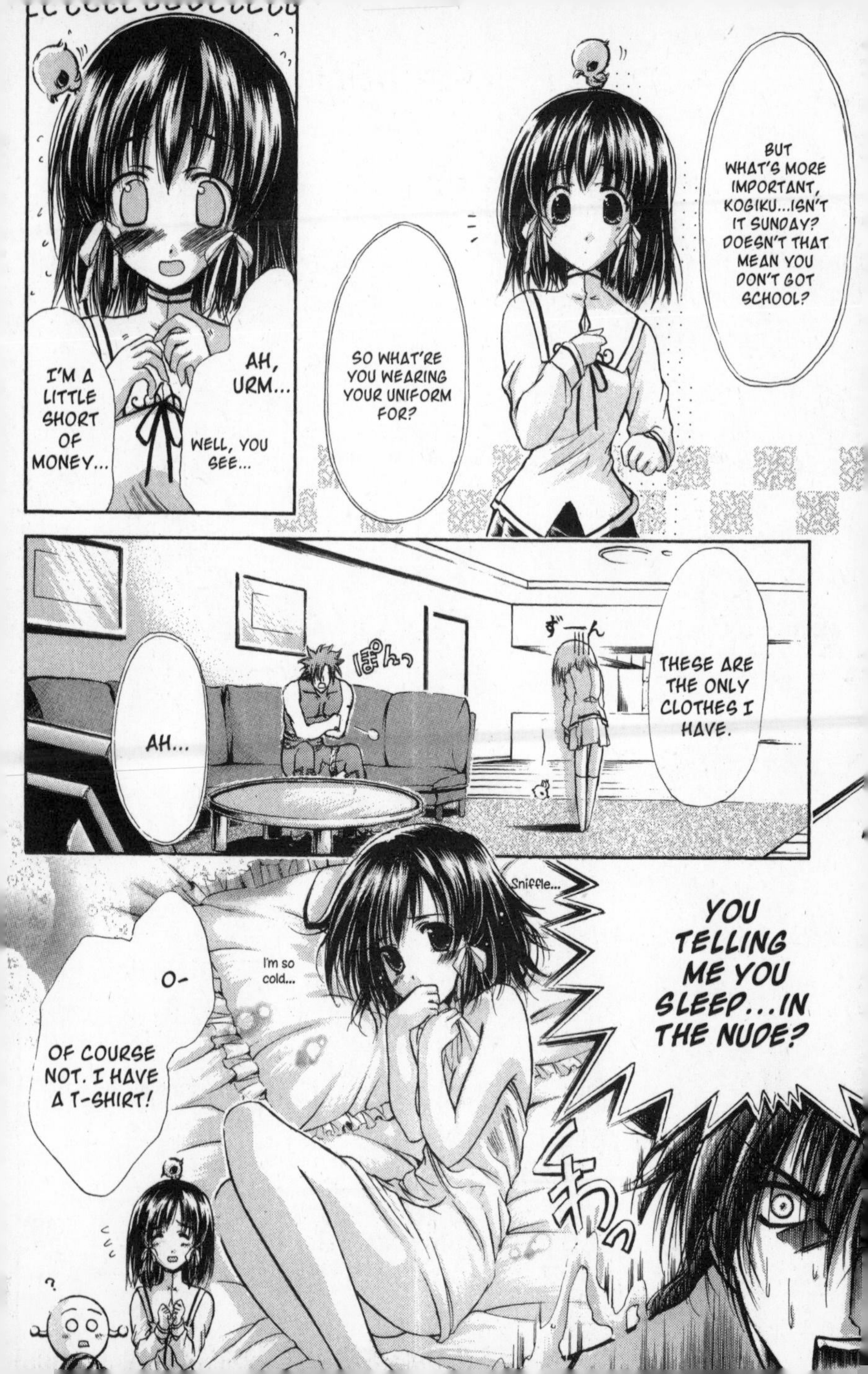
BUT WHAT'S MORE IMPORTANT, KOGIKU...ISN'T IT SUNDAY? DOESN'T THAT MEAN YOU DON'T GOT SCHOOL?
SO WHAT'RE YOU WEARING YOUR UNIFORM FOR?
AH, URM...
WELL, YOU SEE...
I'M A LITTLE SHORT OF MONEY...
THESE ARE THE ONLY CLOTHES I HAVE.
ずーん
ぽんっ
AH...
YOU TELLING ME YOU SLEEP...IN THE NUDE?
Sniffle...
I'm so cold...
O-
OF COURSE NOT. I HAVE A T-SHIRT!
わっ

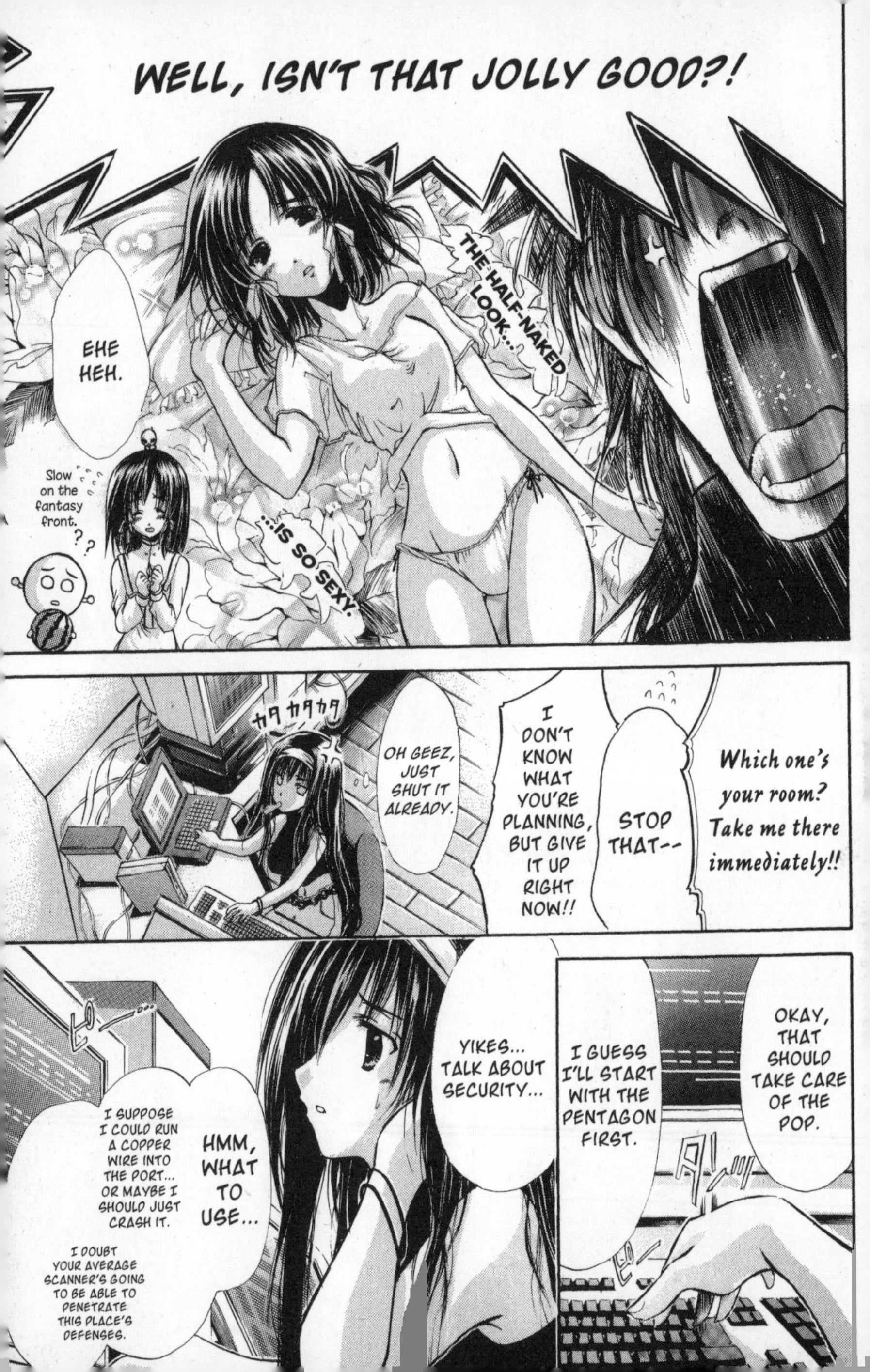
WELL, ISN'T THAT JOLLY GOOD?!
THE HALF-NAKED LOOK...
...IS SO SEXY.
EHE HEH.
Slow on the fantasy front.
Which one's your room? Take me there immediately!!
STOP THAT--
I DON'T KNOW WHAT YOU'RE PLANNING, BUT GIVE IT UP RIGHT NOW!!
OH GEEZ, JUST SHUT IT ALREADY.
カタカタカタ
OKAY, THAT SHOULD TAKE CARE OF THE POP.
I GUESS I'LL START WITH THE PENTAGON FIRST.
YIKES... TALK ABOUT SECURITY...
HMM, WHAT TO USE...
I SUPPOSE I COULD RUN A COPPER WIRE INTO THE PORT... OR MAYBE I SHOULD JUST CRASH IT.
I DOUBT YOUR AVERAGE SCANNER'S GOING TO BE ABLE TO PENETRATE THIS PLACE'S DEFENSES.

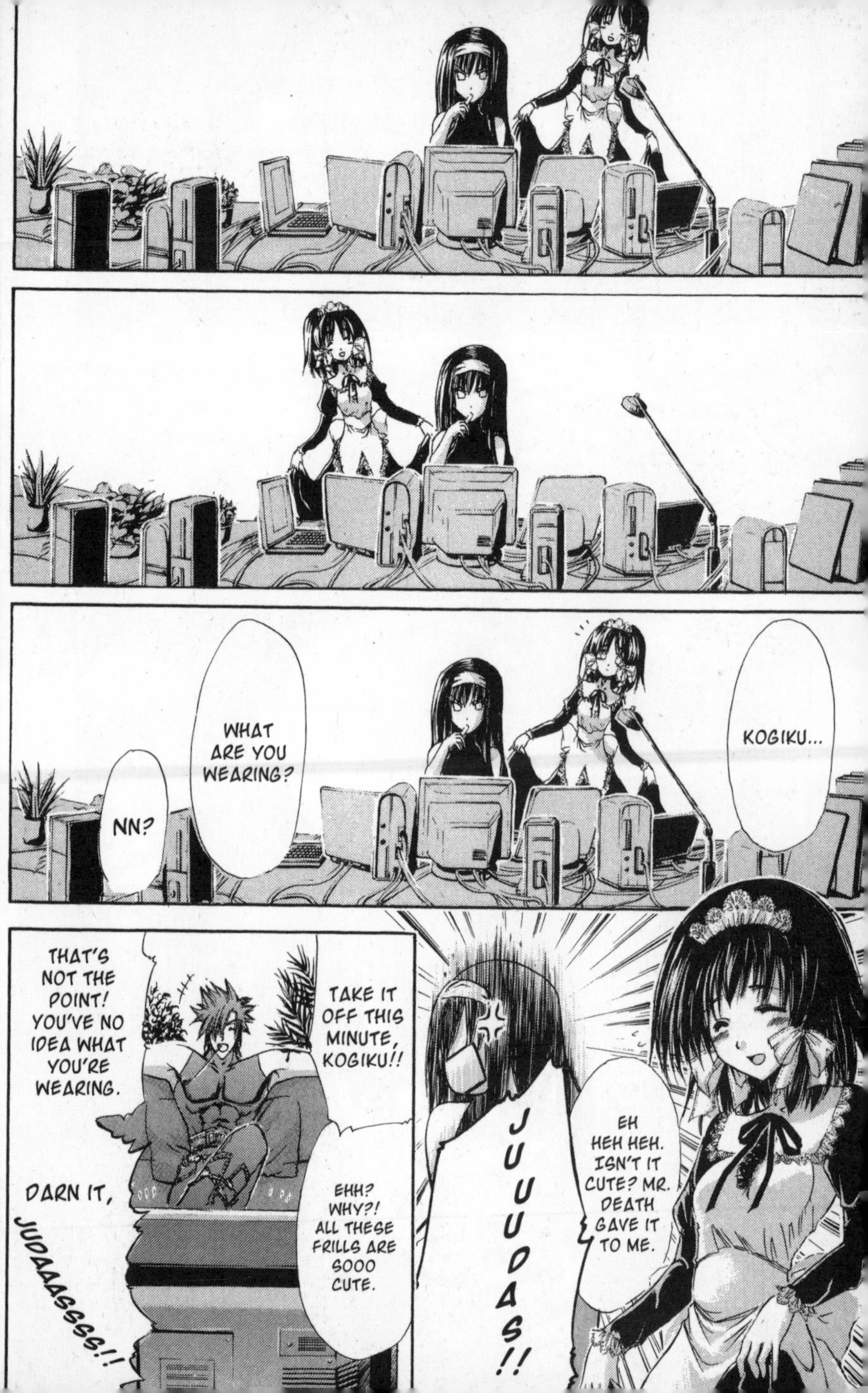
KOGIKU...
WHAT ARE YOU WEARING?
NN?
EH HEH HEH. ISN'T IT CUTE? MR. DEATH GAVE IT TO ME.
JUUUDAS!!
TAKE IT OFF THIS MINUTE, KOGIKU!!
EHH? WHY?! ALL THESE FRILLS ARE SOOO CUTE.
THAT'S NOT THE POINT! YOU'VE NO IDEA WHAT YOU'RE WEARING.
DARN IT, JUDAAASSSS!!

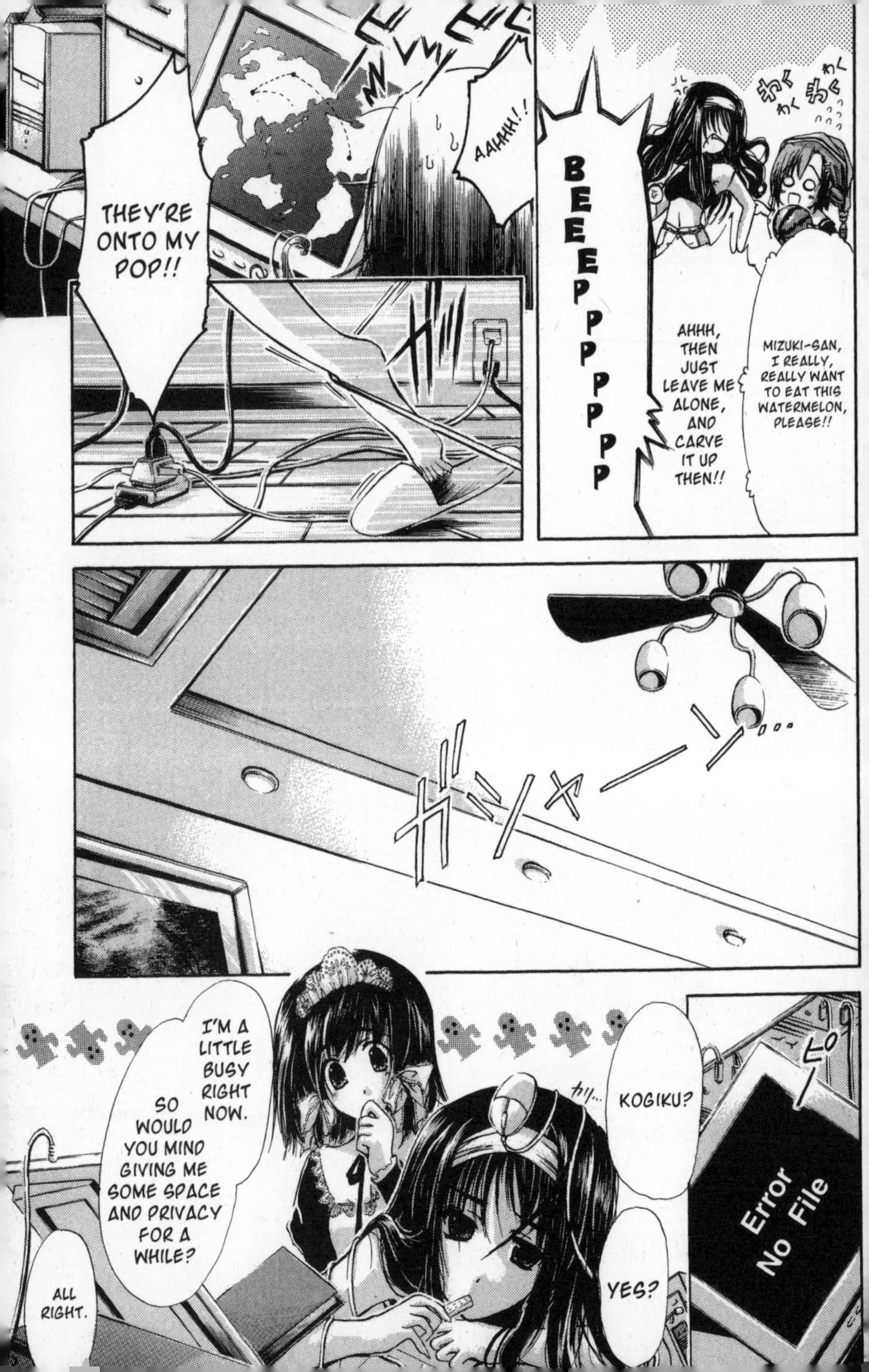
MIZUKI-SAN, I REALLY, REALLY WANT TO EAT THIS WATERMELON, PLEASE!!
AHHH, THEN JUST LEAVE ME ALONE, AND CARVE IT UP THEN!!
BEEEEPPPPPPP
AAHHH!!
THEY'RE ONTO MY POP!!
Error No File
KOGIKU?
YES?
I'M A LITTLE BUSY RIGHT NOW.
SO WOULD YOU MIND GIVING ME SOME SPACE AND PRIVACY FOR A WHILE?
ALL RIGHT.

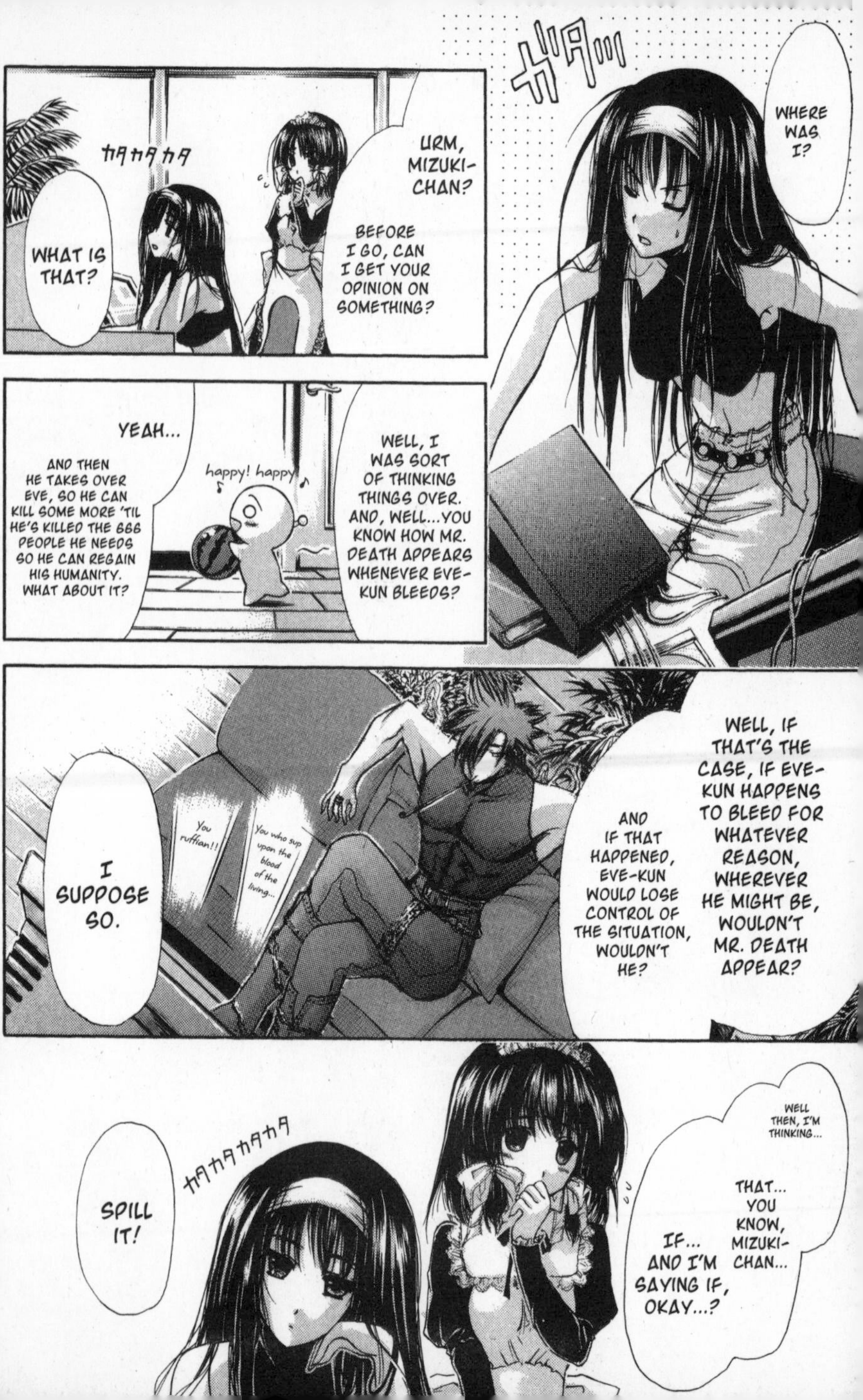
ガタッ
WHERE WAS I?
URM, MIZUKI-CHAN?
BEFORE I GO, CAN I GET YOUR OPINION ON SOMETHING?
カタカタカタ
WHAT IS THAT?
WELL, I WAS SORT OF THINKING THINGS OVER. AND, WELL...YOU KNOW HOW MR. DEATH APPEARS WHENEVER EVE-KUN BLEEDS?
happy! happy
YEAH...
AND THEN HE TAKES OVER EVE, SO HE CAN KILL SOME MORE 'TIL HE'S KILLED THE 666 PEOPLE HE NEEDS SO HE CAN REGAIN HIS HUMANITY. WHAT ABOUT IT?
WELL, IF THAT'S THE CASE, IF EVE-KUN HAPPENS TO BLEED FOR WHATEVER REASON, WHEREVER HE MIGHT BE, WOULDN'T MR. DEATH APPEAR?
AND IF THAT HAPPENED, EVE-KUN WOULD LOSE CONTROL OF THE SITUATION, WOULDN'T HE?
You who sup upon the blood of the living...
You ruffian!!
I SUPPOSE SO.
WELL THEN, I'M THINKING...
THAT... YOU KNOW, MIZUKI-CHAN...
IF... AND I'M SAYING IF, OKAY...?
カタカタカタカタ
SPILL IT!

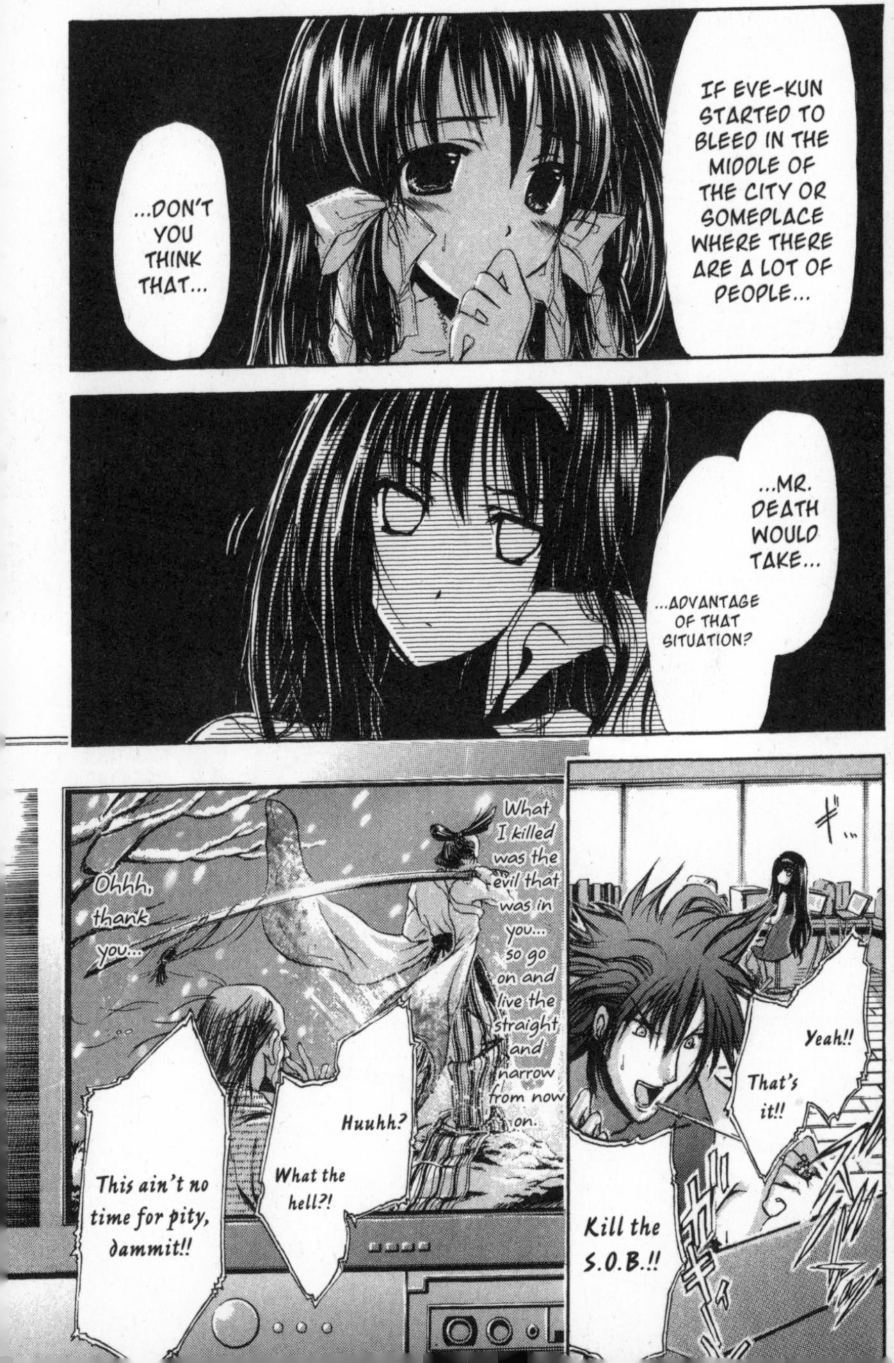
IF EVE-KUN STARTED TO BLEED IN THE MIDDLE OF THE CITY OR SOMEPLACE WHERE THERE ARE A LOT OF PEOPLE...
...DON'T YOU THINK THAT...
...MR. DEATH WOULD TAKE...
...ADVANTAGE OF THAT SITUATION?
ギ‥
Yeah!!
That's it!!
Kill the S.O.B.!!
What I killed was the evil that was in you... so go on and live the straight and narrow from now on.
Ohhh, thank you...
Huuhh?
What the hell?!
This ain't no time for pity, dammit!!

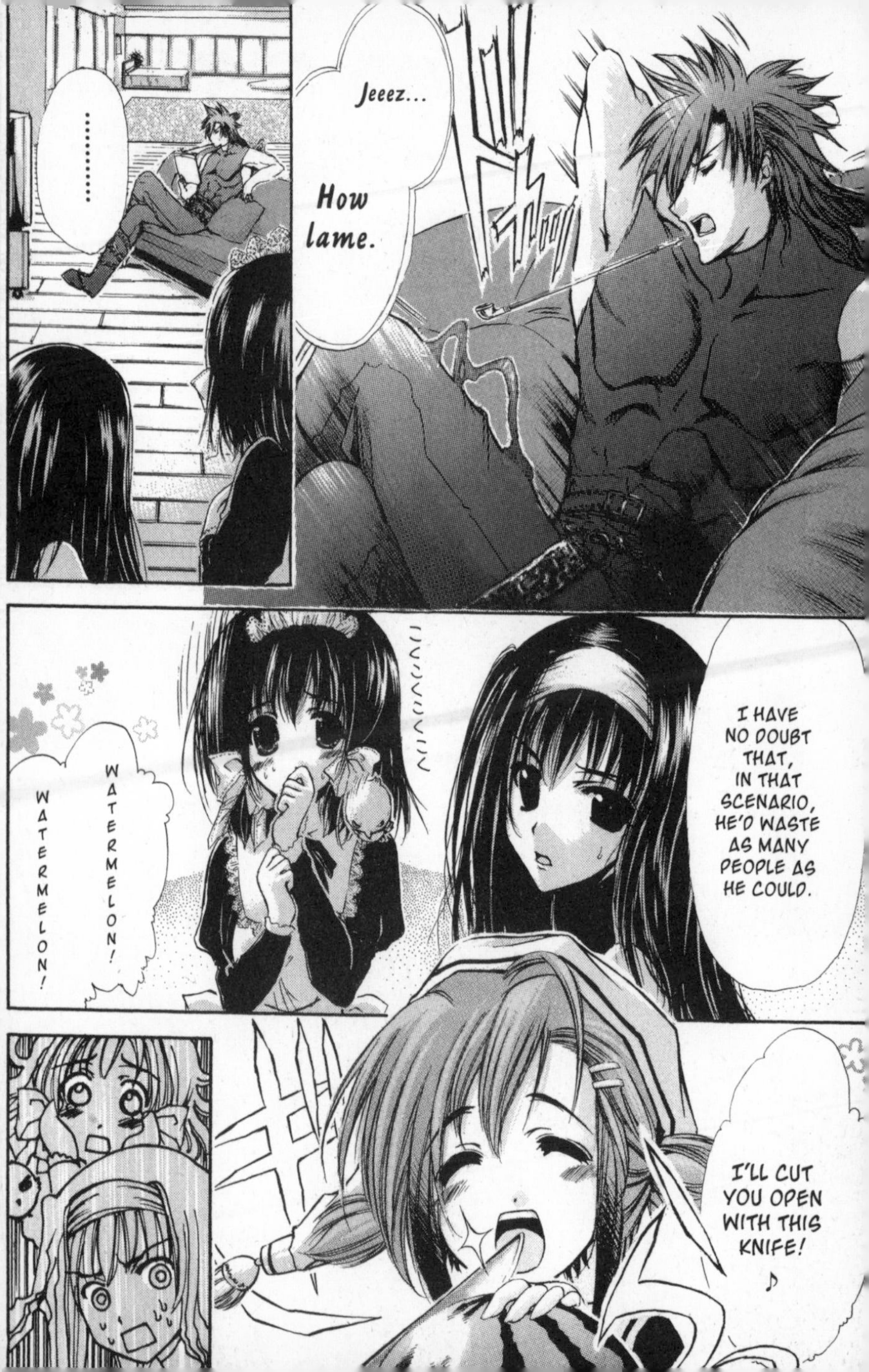
Jeeez...
How lame.
......
I HAVE NO DOUBT THAT, IN THAT SCENARIO, HE'D WASTE AS MANY PEOPLE AS HE COULD.
WATERMELON! WATERMELON!
I'LL CUT YOU OPEN WITH THIS KNIFE! ♪

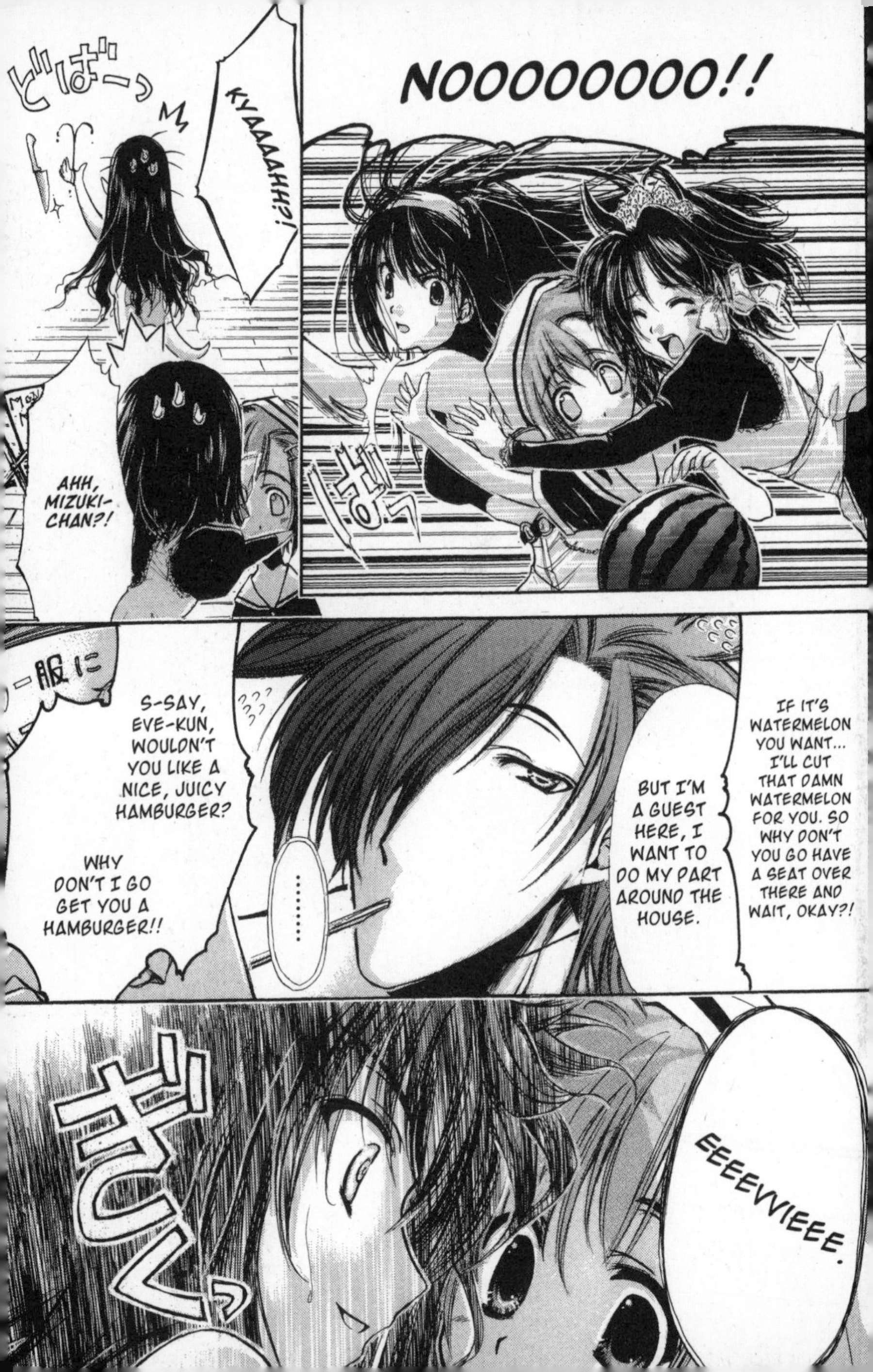
NOOOOOOOO!!
どばーっ
KYAAAAAHH?!
AHH, MIZUKI-CHAN?!
IF IT'S WATERMELON YOU WANT... I'LL CUT THAT DAMN WATERMELON FOR YOU. SO WHY DON'T YOU GO HAVE A SEAT OVER THERE AND WAIT, OKAY?!
BUT I'M A GUEST HERE, I WANT TO DO MY PART AROUND THE HOUSE.
....
S-SAY, EVE-KUN, WOULDN'T YOU LIKE A NICE, JUICY HAMBURGER?
WHY DON'T I GO GET YOU A HAMBURGER!!
EEEEVVIEEEE.
ぎくっ

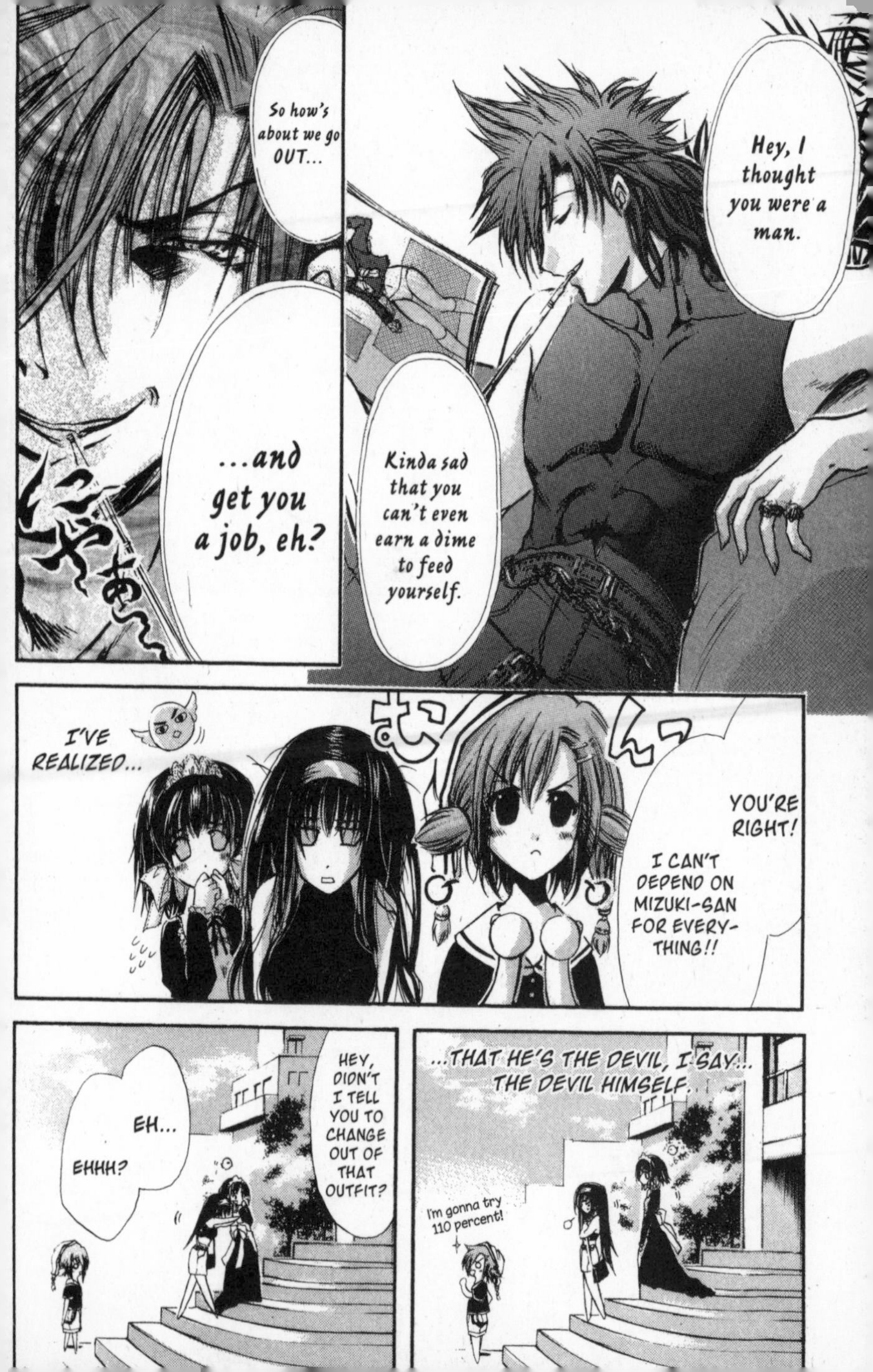

Hey, I thought you were a man.
Kinda sad that you can't even earn a dime to feed yourself.
So how's about we go OUT...
...and get you a job, eh?
YOU'RE RIGHT!
I CAN'T DEPEND ON MIZUKI-SAN FOR EVERY-THING!!
I'VE REALIZED...
...THAT HE'S THE DEVIL, I SAY... THE DEVIL HIMSELF.
I'm gonna try 110 percent!
HEY, DIDN'T I TELL YOU TO CHANGE OUT OF THAT OUTFIT?
EH...
EHHH?

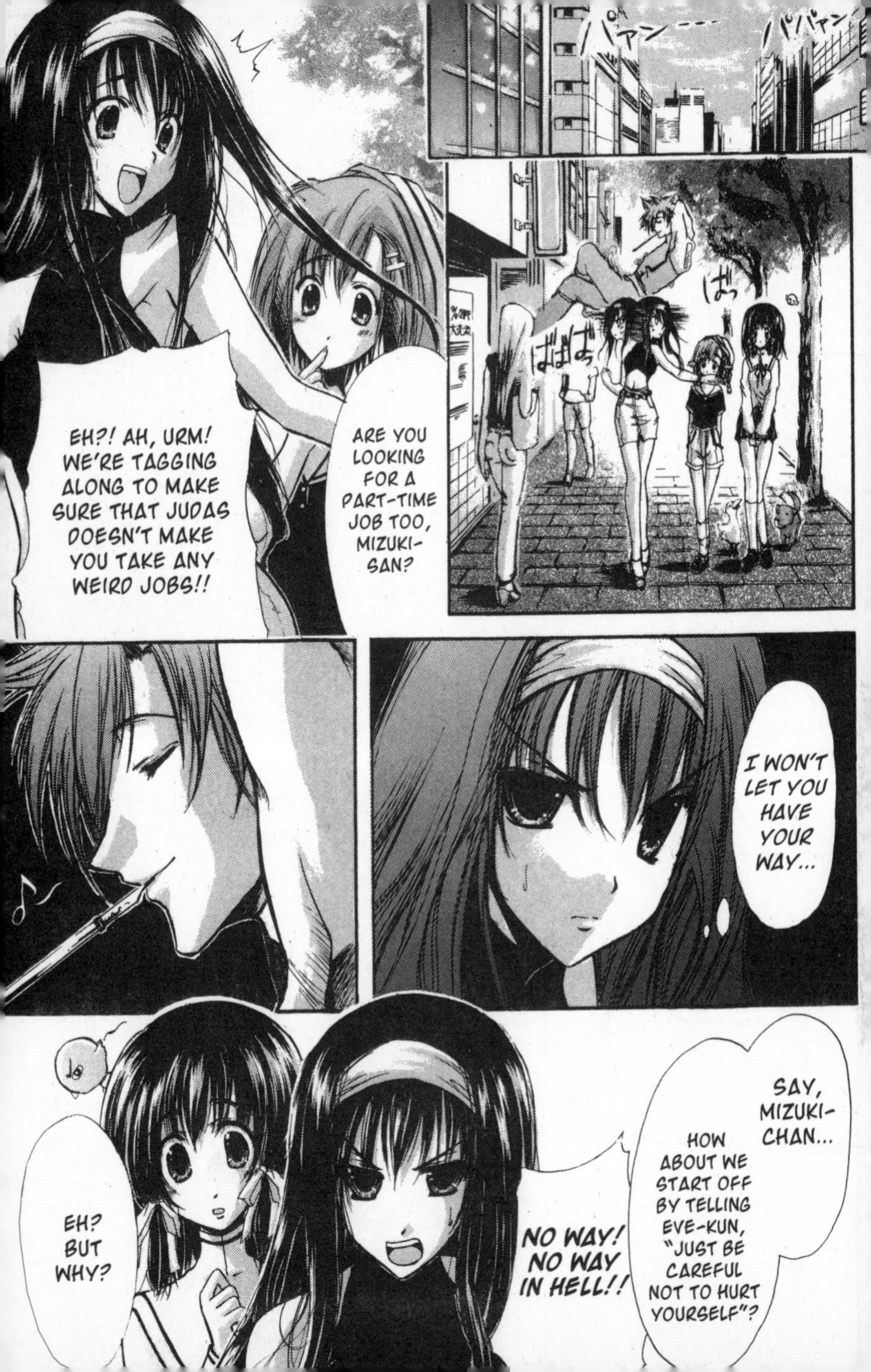

パァン―――
パパァン
ばっ
ばばばっ
ARE YOU LOOKING FOR A PART-TIME JOB TOO, MIZUKI-SAN?
EH?! AH, URM! WE'RE TAGGING ALONG TO MAKE SURE THAT JUDAS DOESN'T MAKE YOU TAKE ANY WEIRD JOBS!!
I WON'T LET YOU HAVE YOUR WAY...
SAY, MIZUKI-CHAN...
HOW ABOUT WE START OFF BY TELLING EVE-KUN, "JUST BE CAREFUL NOT TO HURT YOURSELF"?
NO WAY! NO WAY IN HELL!!
EH? BUT WHY?

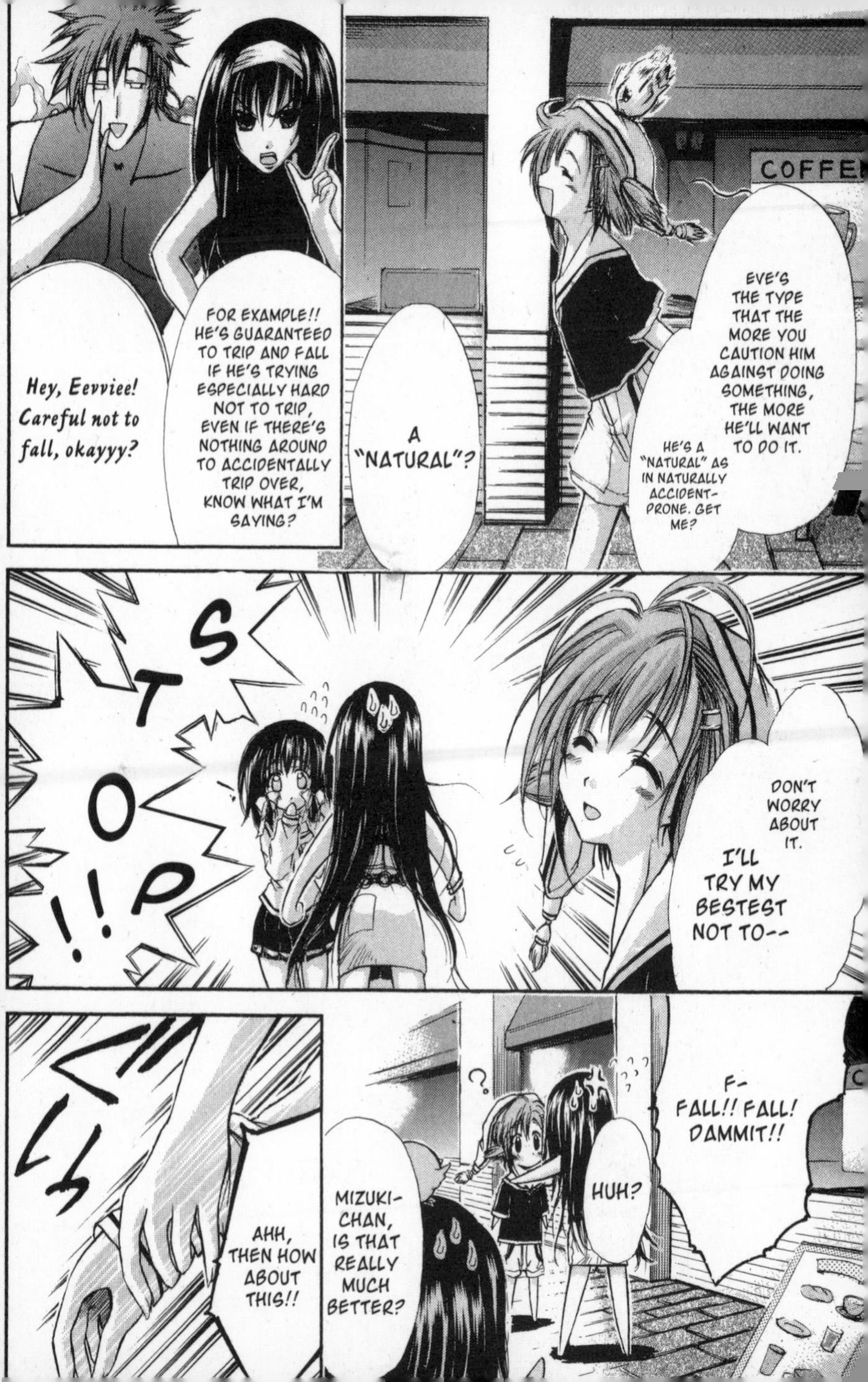
COFFE
EVE'S THE TYPE THAT THE MORE YOU CAUTION HIM AGAINST DOING SOMETHING, THE MORE HE'LL WANT TO DO IT.
A "NATURAL"?
HE'S A "NATURAL" AS IN NATURALLY ACCIDENT-PRONE. GET ME?
FOR EXAMPLE!! HE'S GUARANTEED TO TRIP AND FALL IF HE'S TRYING ESPECIALLY HARD NOT TO TRIP, EVEN IF THERE'S NOTHING AROUND TO ACCIDENTALLY TRIP OVER, KNOW WHAT I'M SAYING?
Hey, Eevviee! Careful not to fall, okayyy?
DON'T WORRY ABOUT IT.
I'LL TRY MY BESTEST NOT TO--
STOP!!
F- FALL!! FALL! DAMMIT!!
HUH?
MIZUKI-CHAN, IS THAT REALLY MUCH BETTER?
AHH, THEN HOW ABOUT THIS!!

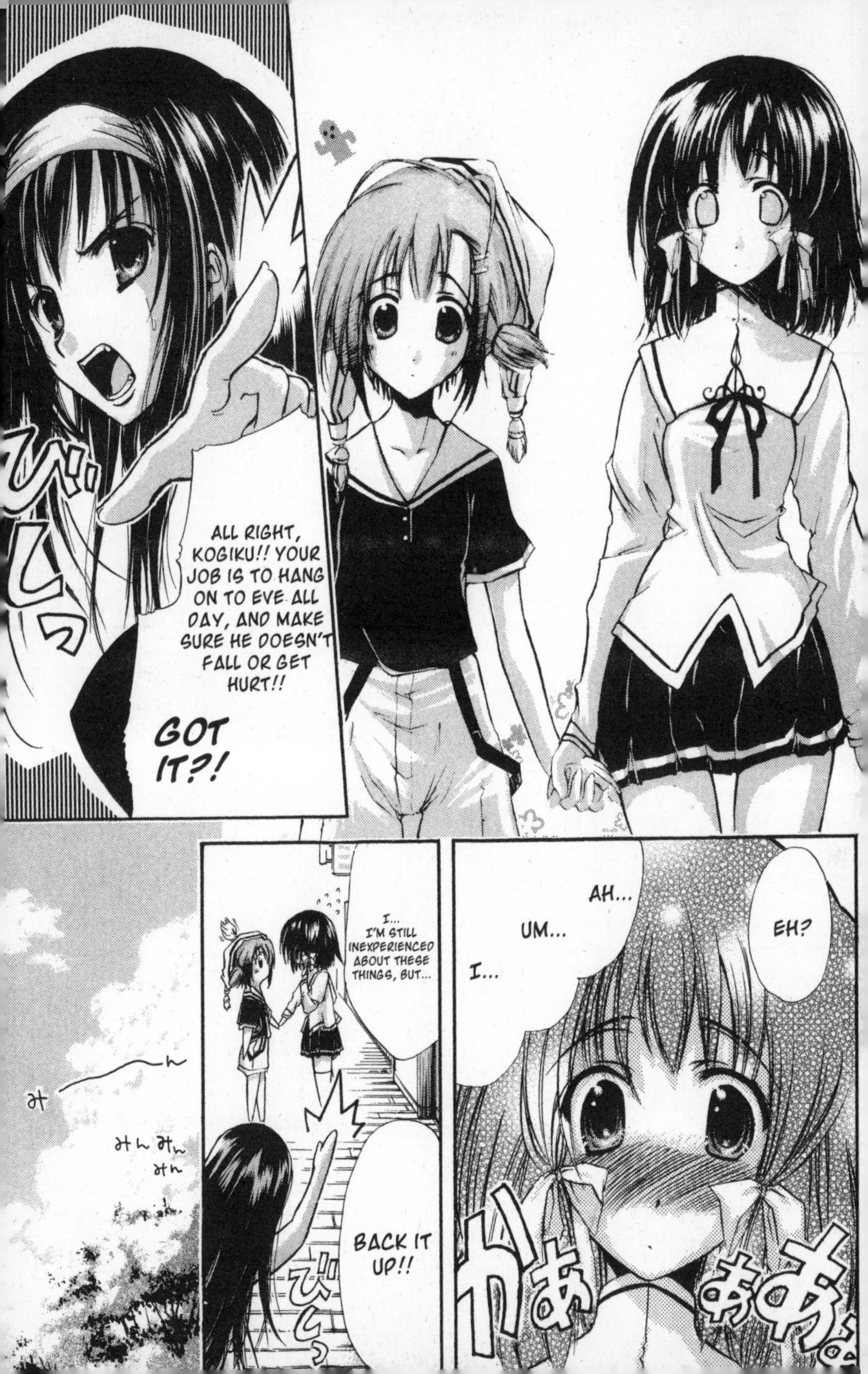
ALL RIGHT, KOGIKU!! YOUR JOB IS TO HANG ON TO EVE ALL DAY, AND MAKE SURE HE DOESN'T FALL OR GET HURT!!
GOT IT?!
EH?
AH...
UM...
I...
I... I'M STILL INEXPERIENCED ABOUT THESE THINGS, BUT...
BACK IT UP!!

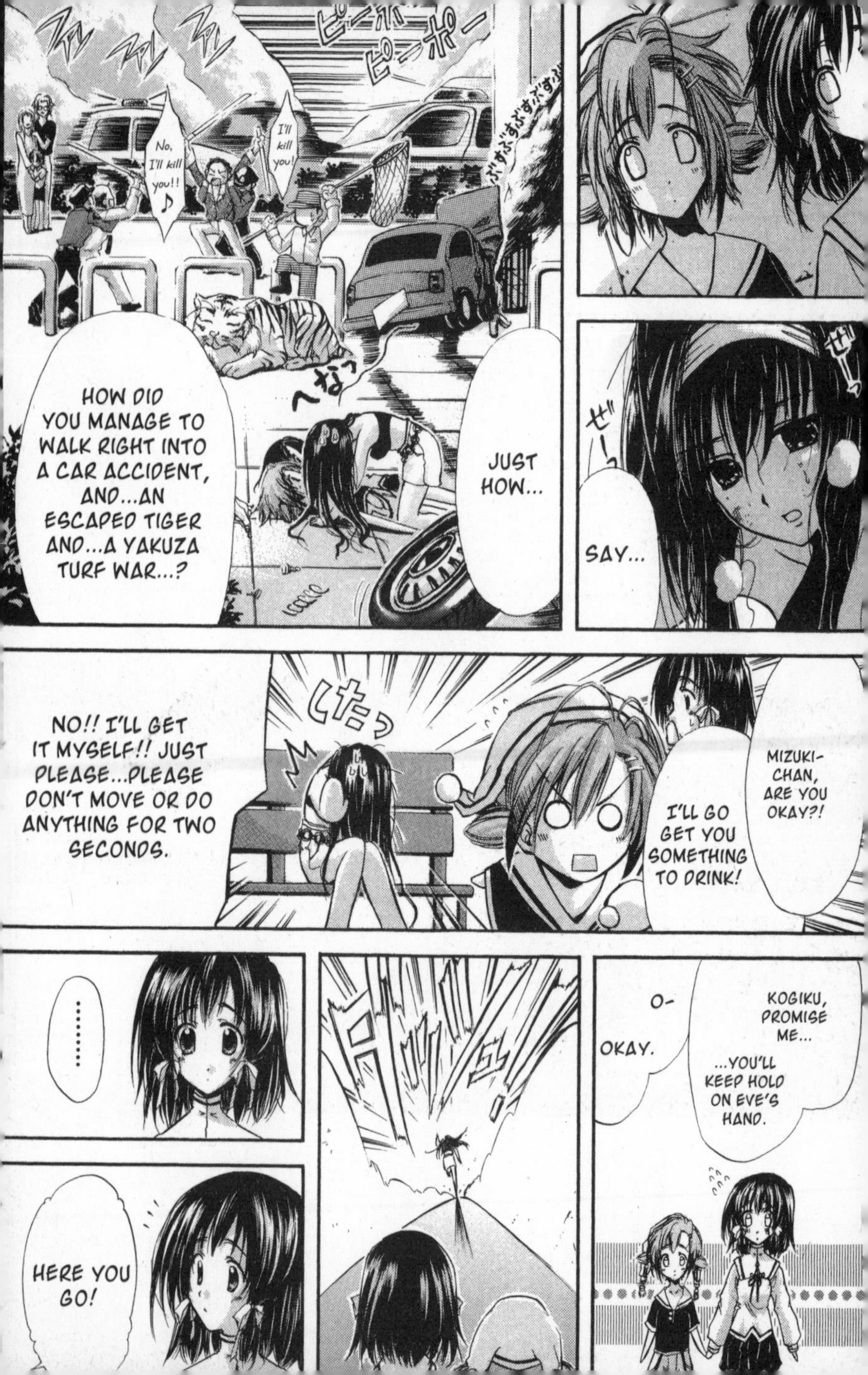
SAY...
I'll kill you!
No, I'll kill you!! ♪
JUST HOW...
HOW DID YOU MANAGE TO WALK RIGHT INTO A CAR ACCIDENT, AND...AN ESCAPED TIGER AND...A YAKUZA TURF WAR...?
MIZUKI-CHAN, ARE YOU OKAY?!
I'LL GO GET YOU SOMETHING TO DRINK!
NO!! I'LL GET IT MYSELF!! JUST PLEASE...PLEASE DON'T MOVE OR DO ANYTHING FOR TWO SECONDS.
KOGIKU, PROMISE ME...
...YOU'LL KEEP HOLD ON EVE'S HAND.
O-OKAY.
....
HERE YOU GO!

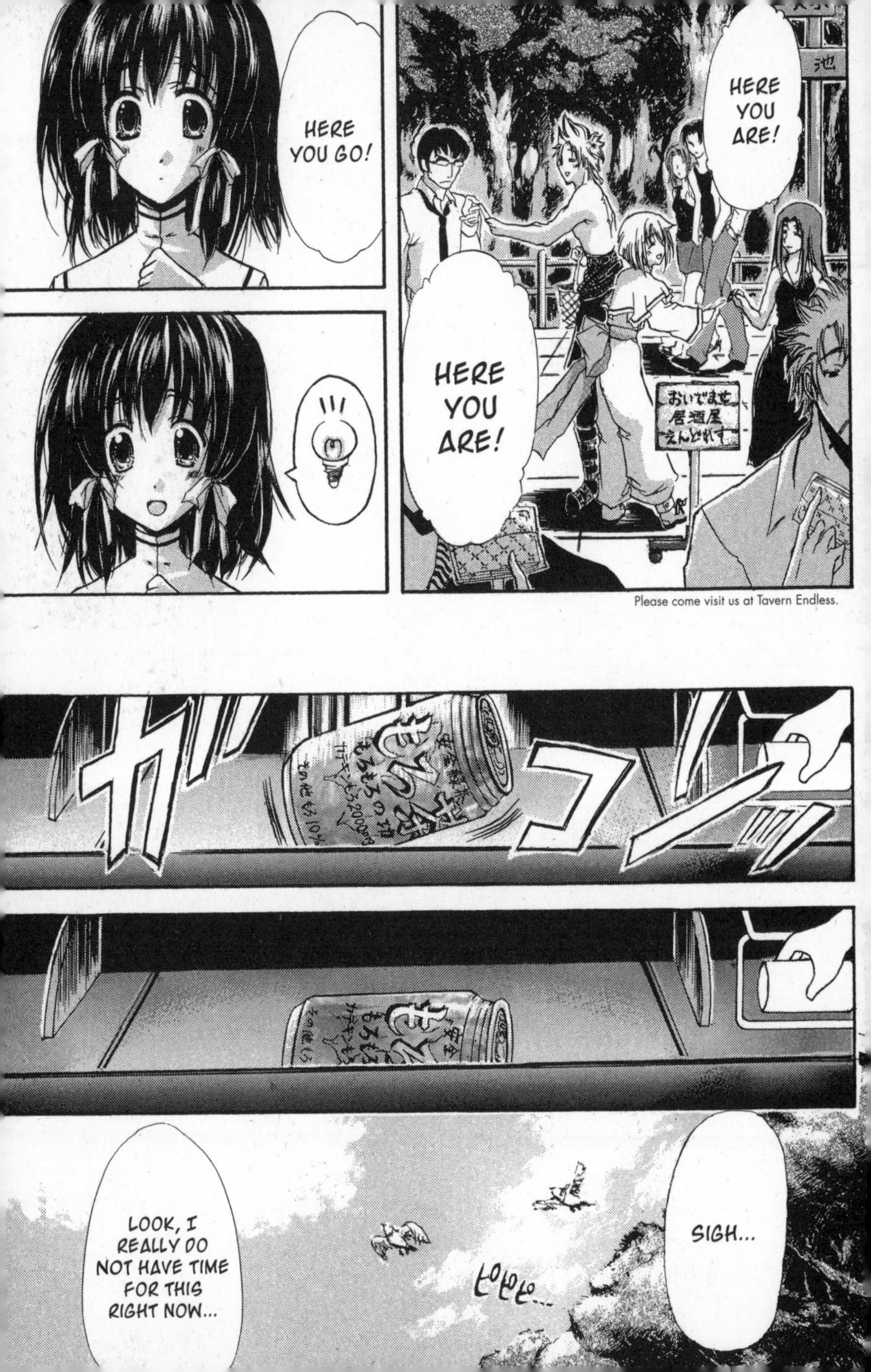
池
HERE YOU ARE!
おいでませ 居酒屋 えんどれす
HERE YOU ARE!
HERE YOU GO!
ガコン
SIGH...
ピピピ...
LOOK, I REALLY DO NOT HAVE TIME FOR THIS RIGHT NOW...
Please come visit us at Tavern Endless.

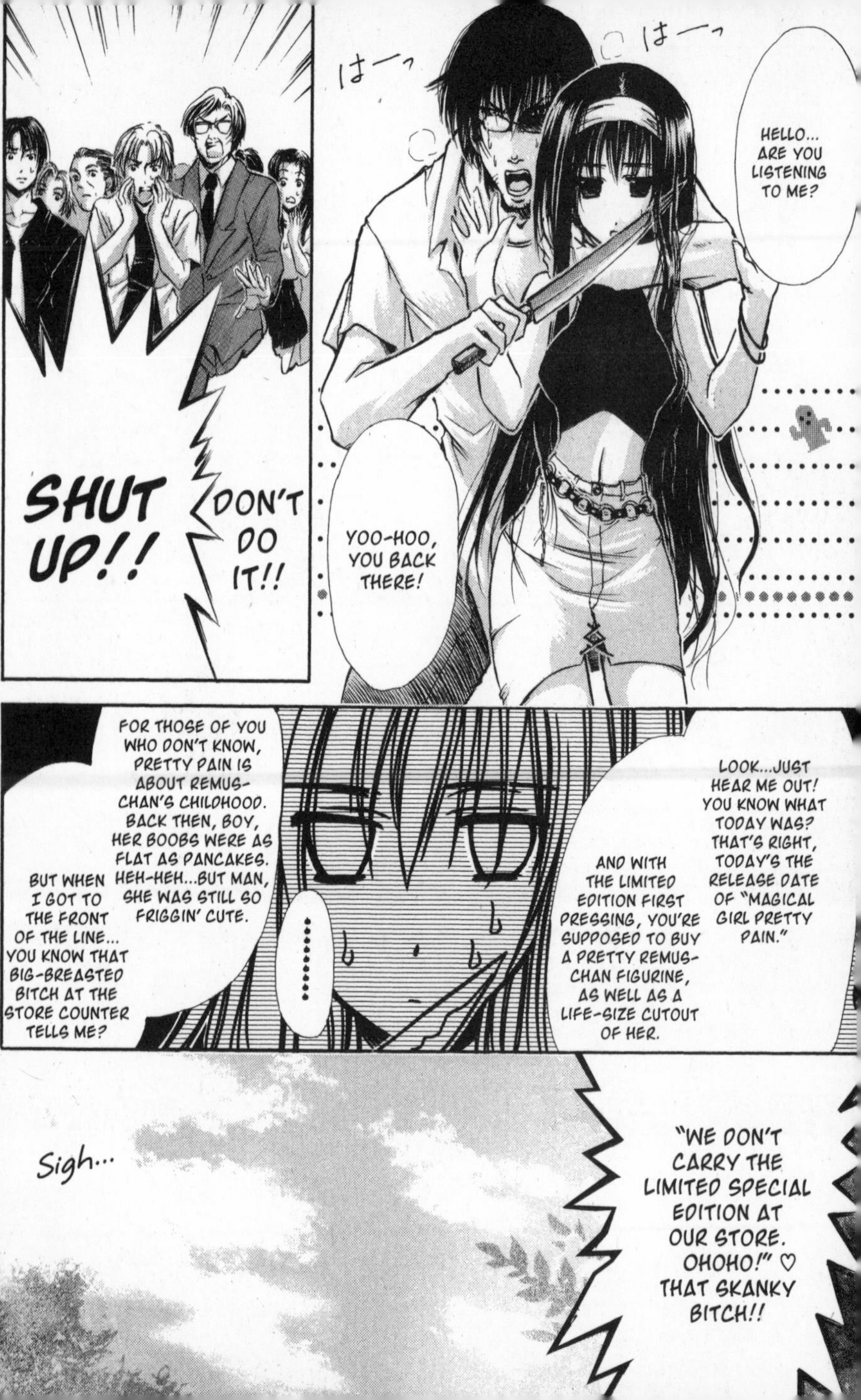
はーっ
はーっ
HELLO... ARE YOU LISTENING TO ME?
YOO-HOO, YOU BACK THERE!
DON'T DO IT!!
SHUT UP!!
LOOK...JUST HEAR ME OUT! YOU KNOW WHAT TODAY WAS? THAT'S RIGHT, TODAY'S THE RELEASE DATE OF "MAGICAL GIRL PRETTY PAIN."
AND WITH THE LIMITED EDITION FIRST PRESSING, YOU'RE SUPPOSED TO BUY A PRETTY REMUS-CHAN FIGURINE, AS WELL AS A LIFE-SIZE CUTOUT OF HER.
FOR THOSE OF YOU WHO DON'T KNOW, PRETTY PAIN IS ABOUT REMUS-CHAN'S CHILDHOOD. BACK THEN, BOY, HER BOOBS WERE AS FLAT AS PANCAKES. HEH-HEH...BUT MAN, SHE WAS STILL SO FRIGGIN' CUTE.
BUT WHEN I GOT TO THE FRONT OF THE LINE... YOU KNOW THAT BIG-BREASTED BITCH AT THE STORE COUNTER TELLS ME?
"WE DON'T CARRY THE LIMITED SPECIAL EDITION AT OUR STORE. OHOHO!" ♡ THAT SKANKY BITCH!!
Sigh...

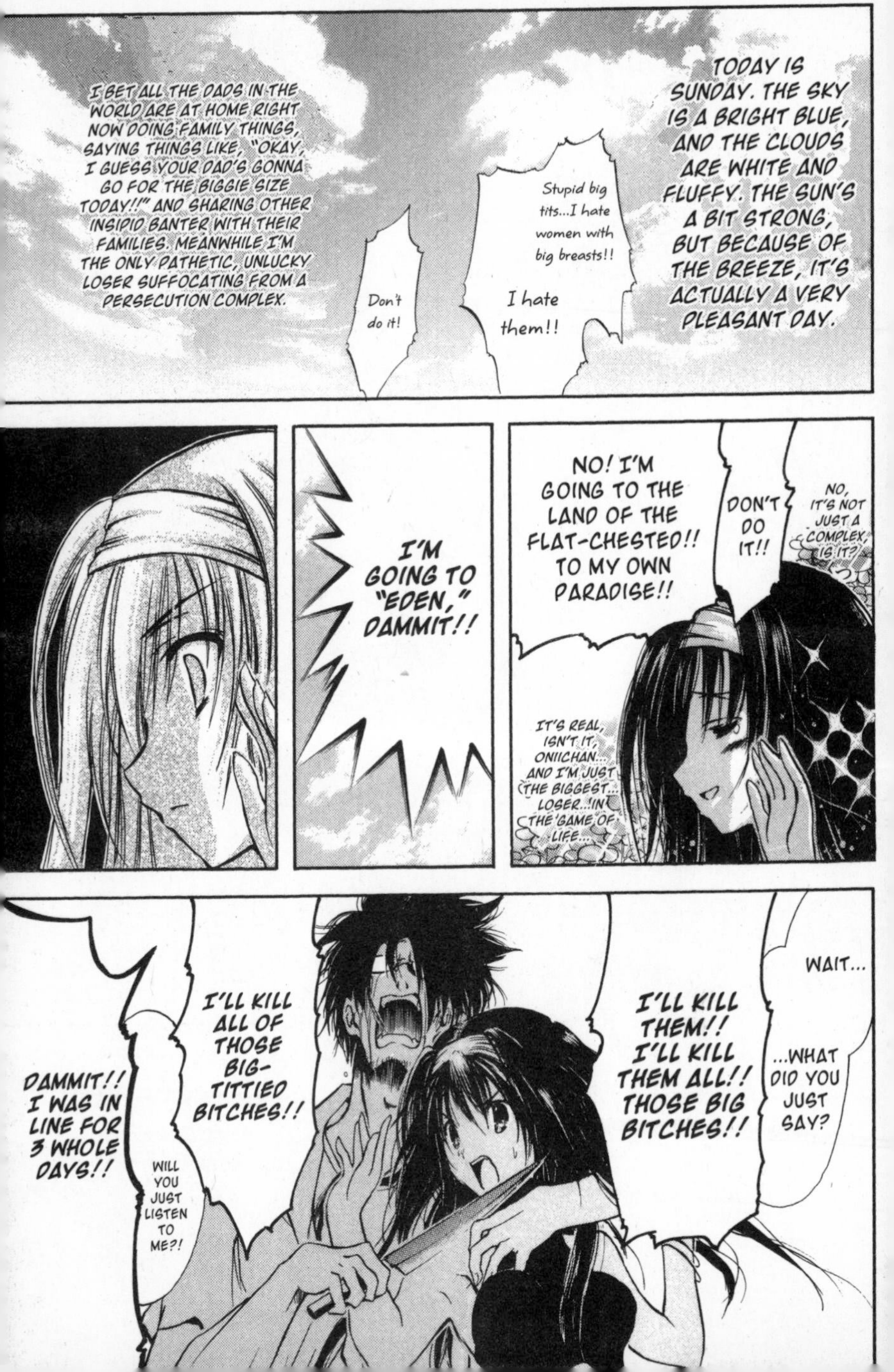
TODAY IS SUNDAY. THE SKY IS A BRIGHT BLUE, AND THE CLOUDS ARE WHITE AND FLUFFY. THE SUN'S A BIT STRONG, BUT BECAUSE OF THE BREEZE, IT'S ACTUALLY A VERY PLEASANT DAY.
Stupid big tits...I hate women with big breasts!!
I hate them!!
Don't do it!
I BET ALL THE DADS IN THE WORLD ARE AT HOME RIGHT NOW DOING FAMILY THINGS, SAYING THINGS LIKE, "OKAY, I GUESS YOUR DAD'S GONNA GO FOR THE BIGGIE SIZE TODAY!!" AND SHARING OTHER INSIPID BANTER WITH THEIR FAMILIES. MEANWHILE I'M THE ONLY PATHETIC, UNLUCKY LOSER SUFFOCATING FROM A PERSECUTION COMPLEX.
NO, IT'S NOT JUST A COMPLEX, IS IT?
DON'T DO IT!!
NO! I'M GOING TO THE LAND OF THE FLAT-CHESTED!! TO MY OWN PARADISE!!
IT'S REAL, ISN'T IT, ONIICHAN... AND I'M JUST THE BIGGEST LOSER...IN THE GAME OF LIFE...
I'M GOING TO "EDEN," DAMMIT!!
WAIT...
...WHAT DID YOU JUST SAY?
I'LL KILL THEM!! I'LL KILL THEM ALL!! THOSE BIG BITCHES!!
I'LL KILL ALL OF THOSE BIG-TITTIED BITCHES!!
DAMMIT!! I WAS IN LINE FOR 3 WHOLE DAYS!!
WILL YOU JUST LISTEN TO ME?!

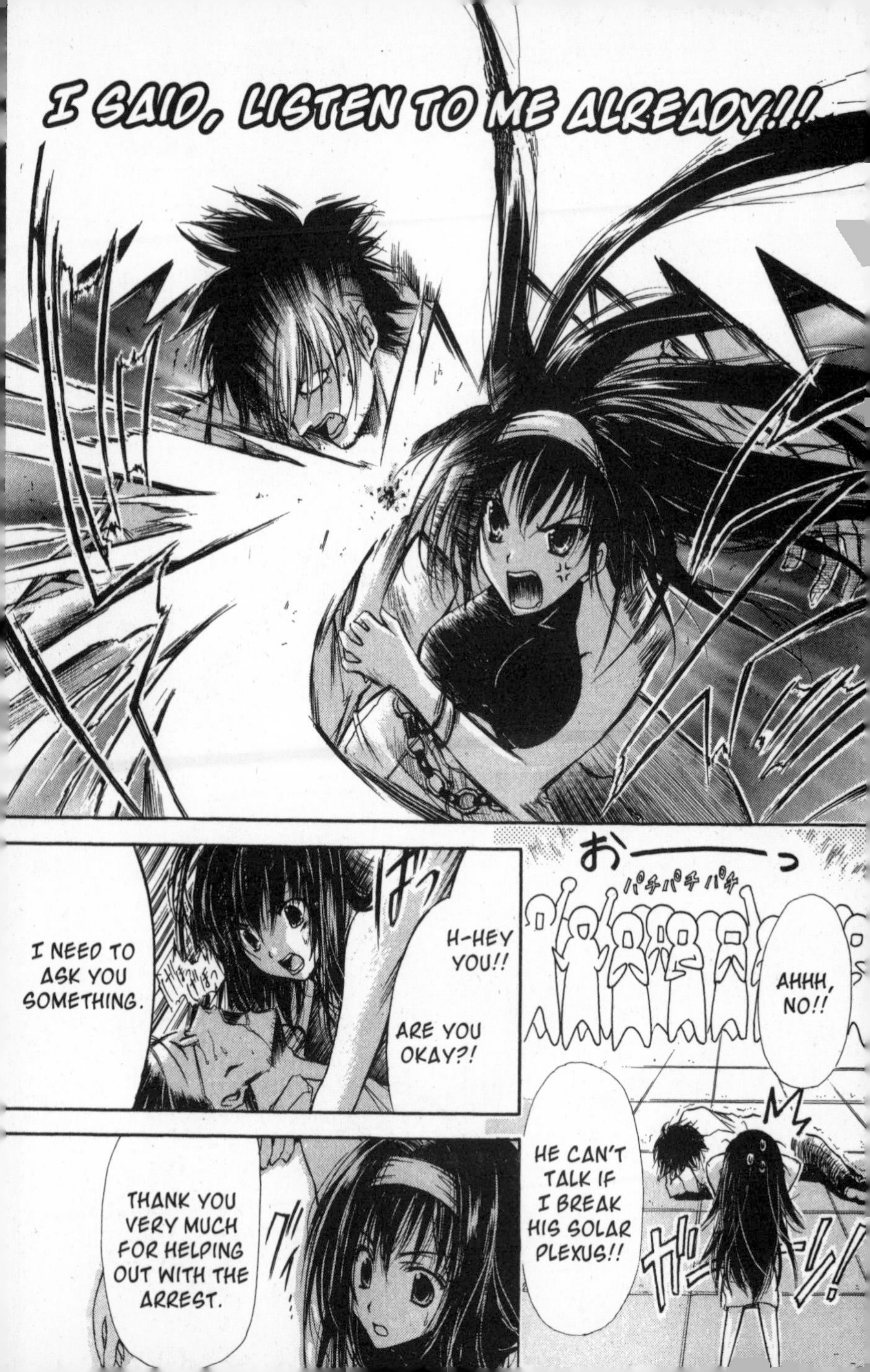
I SAID, LISTEN TO ME ALREADY!!!
お――っ
パチパチパチ
AHHH, NO!!
HE CAN'T TALK IF I BREAK HIS SOLAR PLEXUS!!
H-HEY YOU!!
ARE YOU OKAY?!
I NEED TO ASK YOU SOMETHING.
THANK YOU VERY MUCH FOR HELPING OUT WITH THE ARREST.

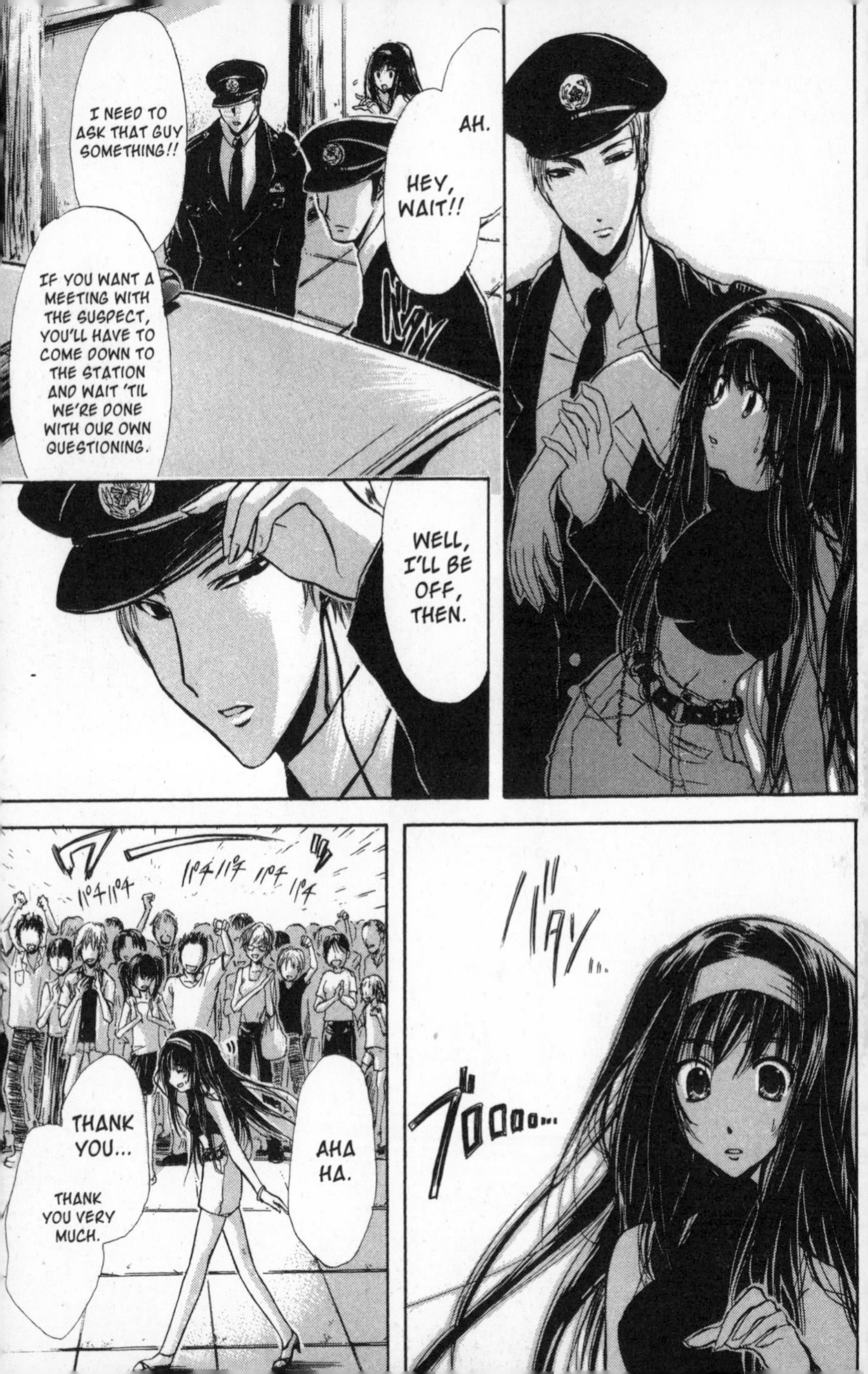
AH.
HEY, WAIT!!
I NEED TO ASK THAT GUY SOMETHING!!
IF YOU WANT A MEETING WITH THE SUSPECT, YOU'LL HAVE TO COME DOWN TO THE STATION AND WAIT 'TIL WE'RE DONE WITH OUR OWN QUESTIONING.
WELL, I'LL BE OFF, THEN.
バタン…
ブロロロロ…
パチパチ パチ パチ
パチパチ
AHA HA.
THANK YOU...
THANK YOU VERY MUCH.

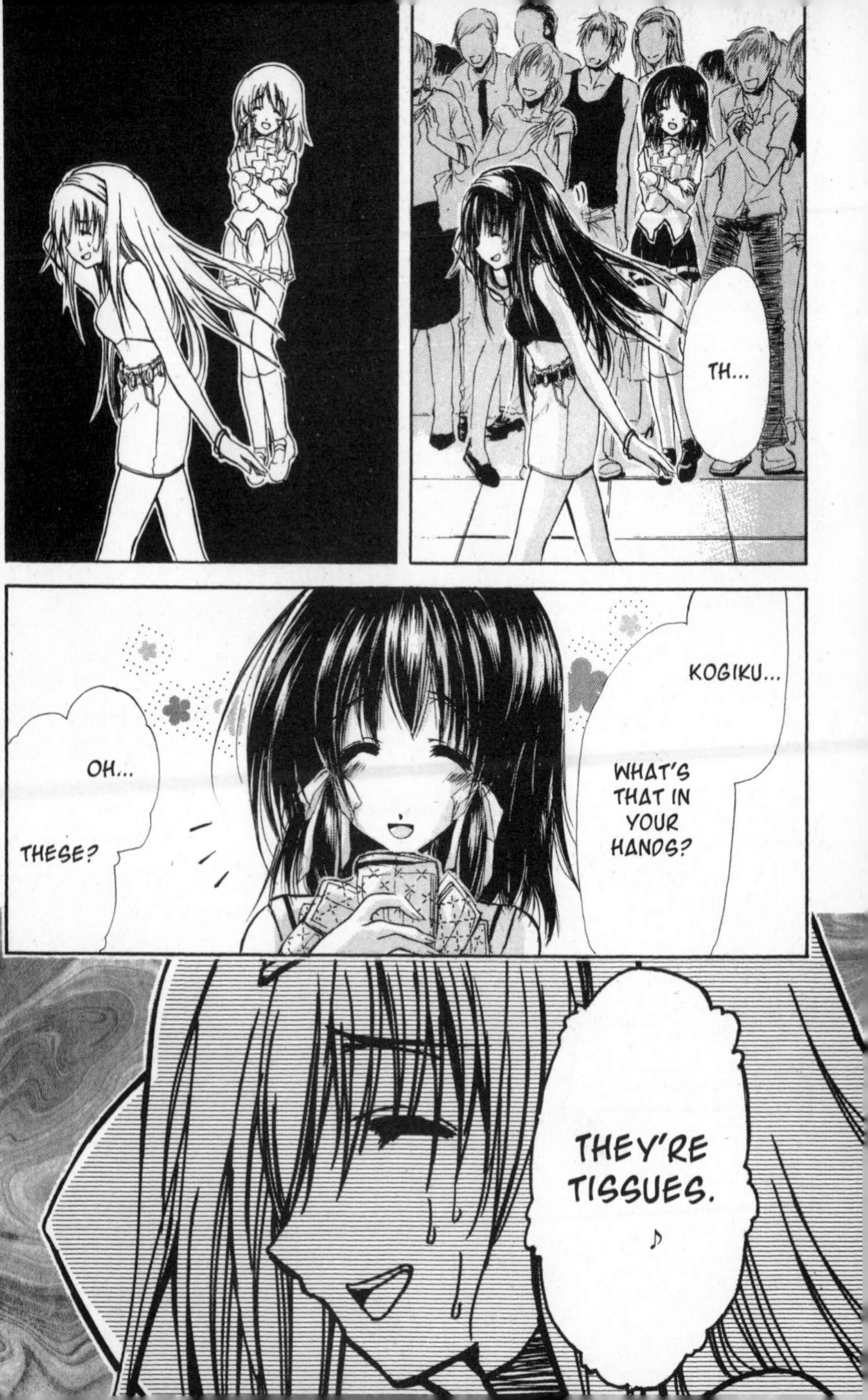
TH...
KOGIKU...
WHAT'S THAT IN YOUR HANDS?
OH...
THESE?
THEY'RE TISSUES. ♪

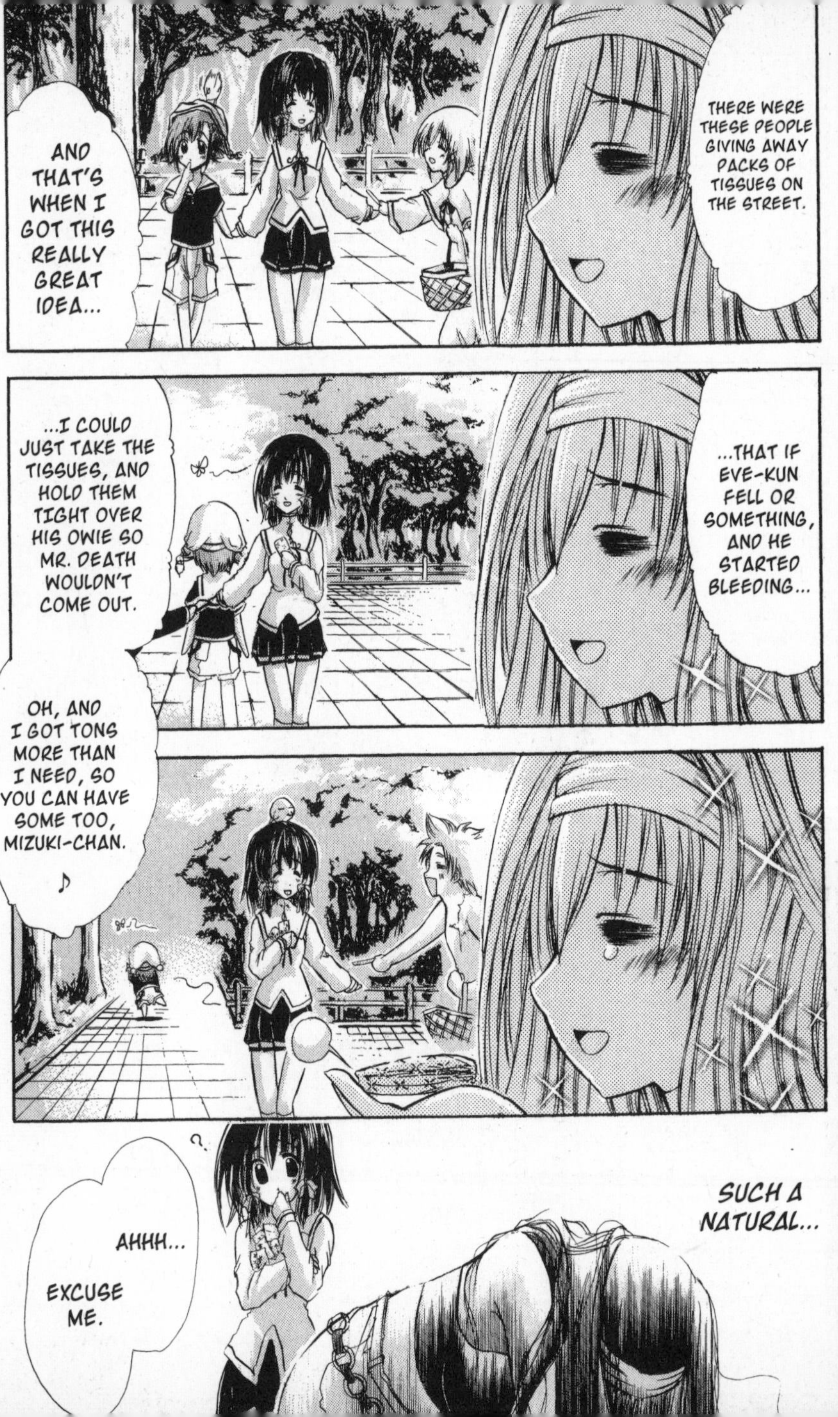
THERE WERE THESE PEOPLE GIVING AWAY PACKS OF TISSUES ON THE STREET.
AND THAT'S WHEN I GOT THIS REALLY GREAT IDEA...
...THAT IF EVE-KUN FELL OR SOMETHING, AND HE STARTED BLEEDING...
...I COULD JUST TAKE THE TISSUES, AND HOLD THEM TIGHT OVER HIS OWIE SO MR. DEATH WOULDN'T COME OUT.
OH, AND I GOT TONS MORE THAN I NEED, SO YOU CAN HAVE SOME TOO, MIZUKI-CHAN. ♪
SUCH A NATURAL...
AHHH...
EXCUSE ME.

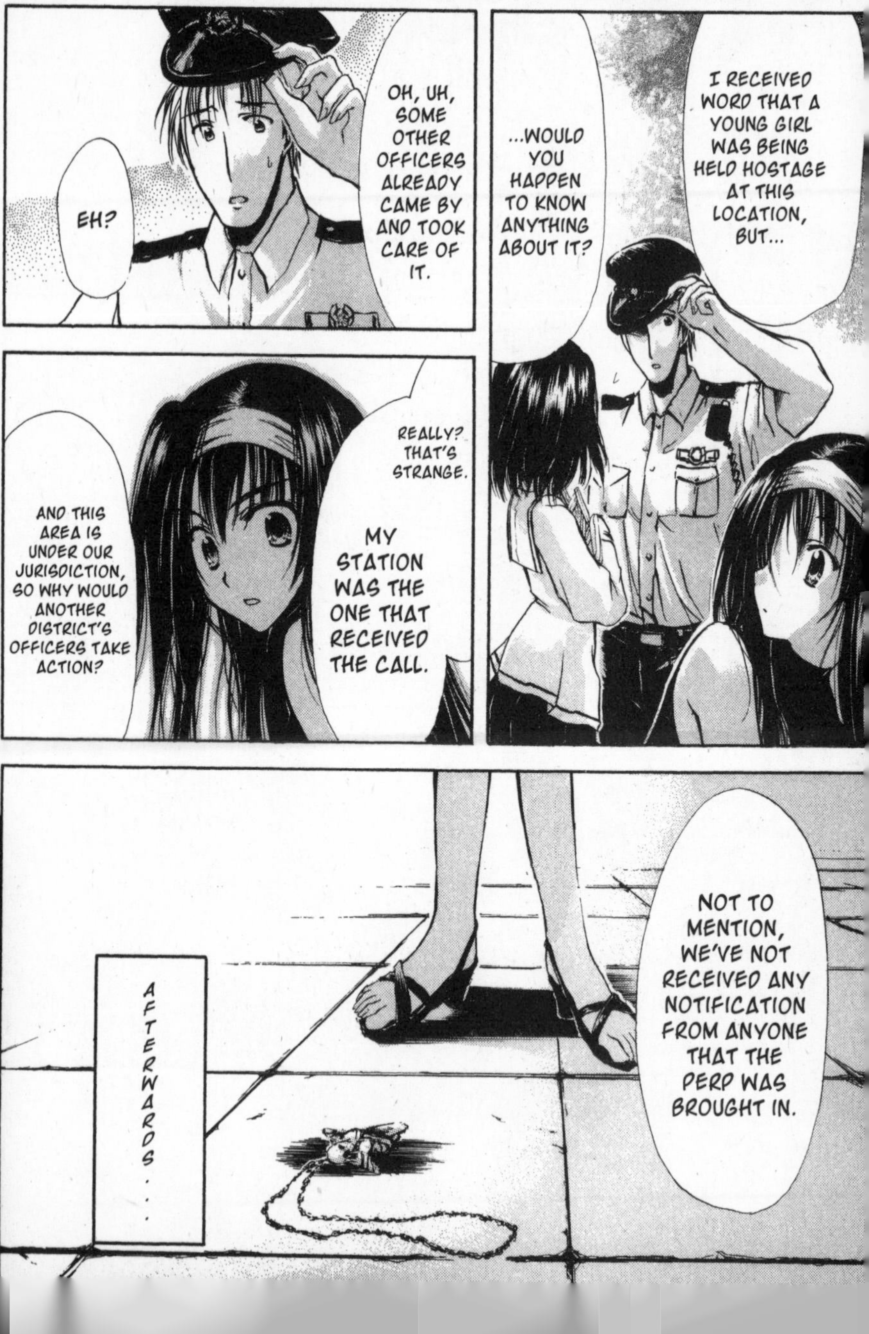
I RECEIVED WORD THAT A YOUNG GIRL WAS BEING HELD HOSTAGE AT THIS LOCATION, BUT...
...WOULD YOU HAPPEN TO KNOW ANYTHING ABOUT IT?
OH, UH, SOME OTHER OFFICERS ALREADY CAME BY AND TOOK CARE OF IT.
EH?
REALLY? THAT'S STRANGE.
MY STATION WAS THE ONE THAT RECEIVED THE CALL.
AND THIS AREA IS UNDER OUR JURISDICTION, SO WHY WOULD ANOTHER DISTRICT'S OFFICERS TAKE ACTION?
NOT TO MENTION, WE'VE NOT RECEIVED ANY NOTIFICATION FROM ANYONE THAT THE PERP WAS BROUGHT IN.
AFTERWARDS...

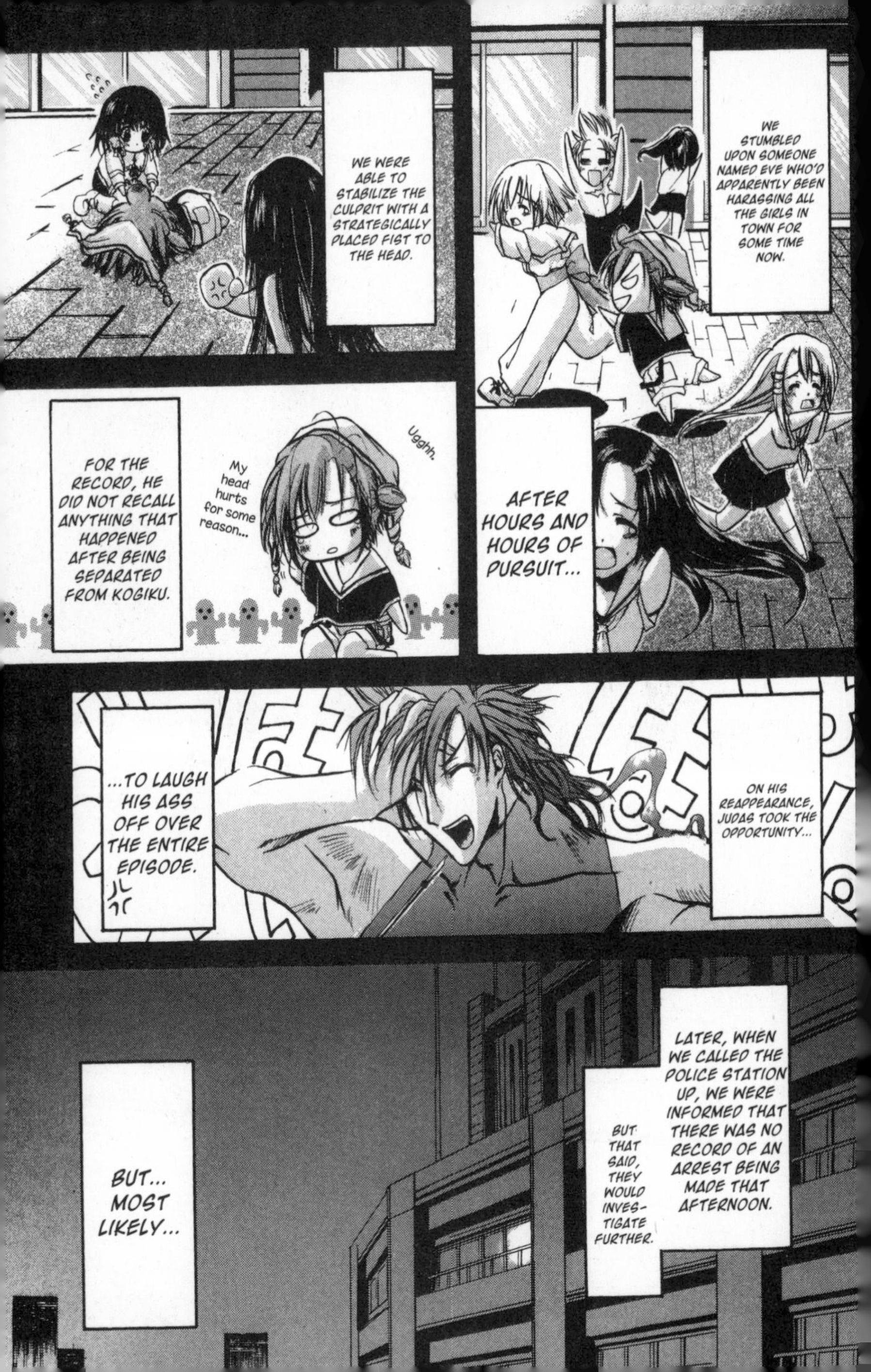
WE STUMBLED UPON SOMEONE NAMED EVE WHO'D APPARENTLY BEEN HARASSING ALL THE GIRLS IN TOWN FOR SOME TIME NOW.
AFTER HOURS AND HOURS OF PURSUIT...
WE WERE ABLE TO STABILIZE THE CULPRIT WITH A STRATEGICALLY PLACED FIST TO THE HEAD.
Ugghh.
My head hurts for some reason...
FOR THE RECORD, HE DID NOT RECALL ANYTHING THAT HAPPENED AFTER BEING SEPARATED FROM KOGIKU.
ON HIS REAPPEARANCE, JUDAS TOOK THE OPPORTUNITY...
...TO LAUGH HIS ASS OFF OVER THE ENTIRE EPISODE.
LATER, WHEN WE CALLED THE POLICE STATION UP, WE WERE INFORMED THAT THERE WAS NO RECORD OF AN ARREST BEING MADE THAT AFTERNOON.
BUT THAT SAID, THEY WOULD INVESTIGATE FURTHER.
BUT... MOST LIKELY...

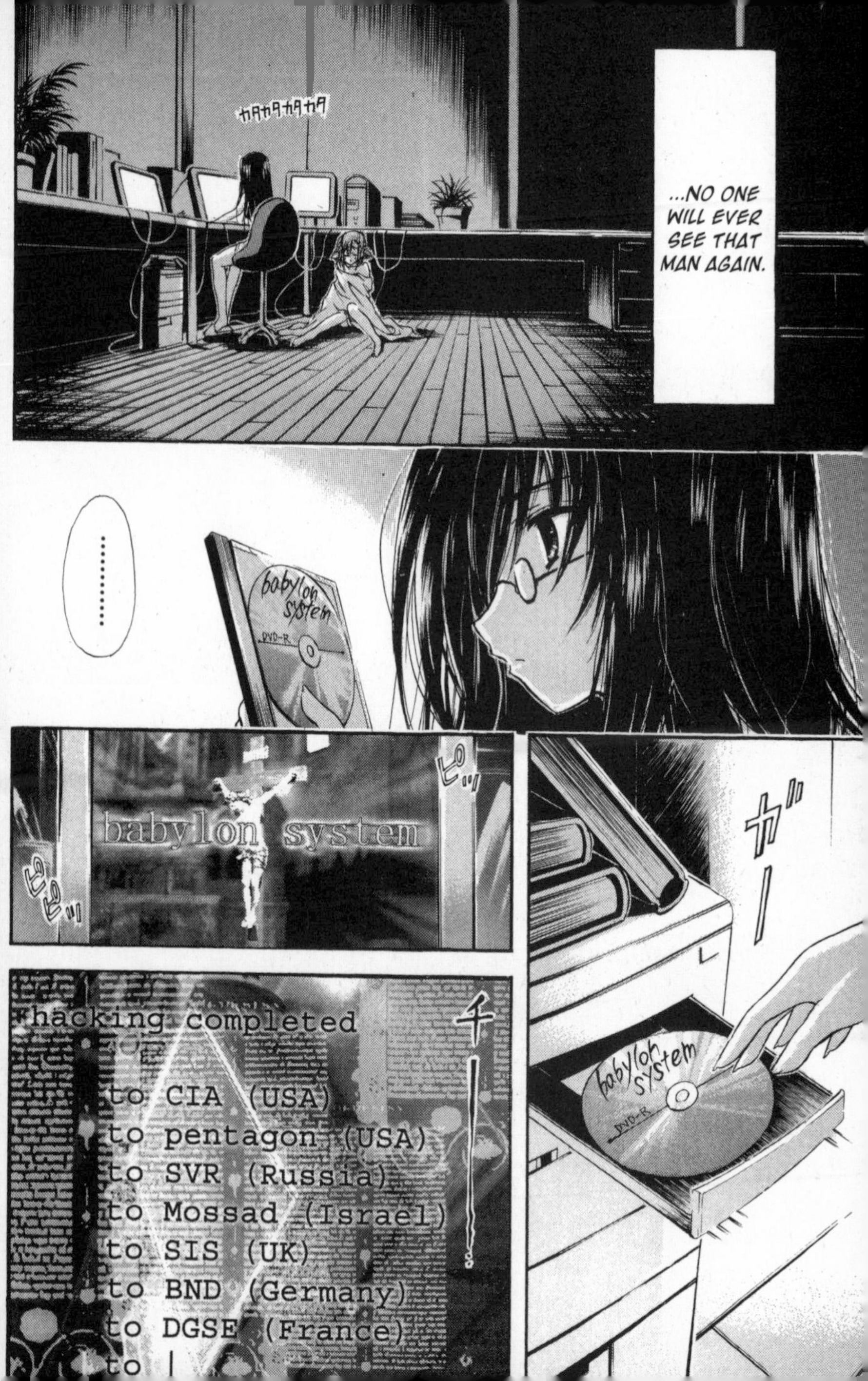
...NO ONE WILL EVER SEE THAT MAN AGAIN.
カタカタカタカタ
......
babylon system
DVD-R
ガー
babylon system
DVD-R
ピッ
babylon system
ピピッ
チー
hacking completed
to CIA (USA)
to pentagon (USA)
to SVR (Russia)
to Mossad (Israel)
to SIS (UK)
to BND (Germany)
to DGSE (France)
to

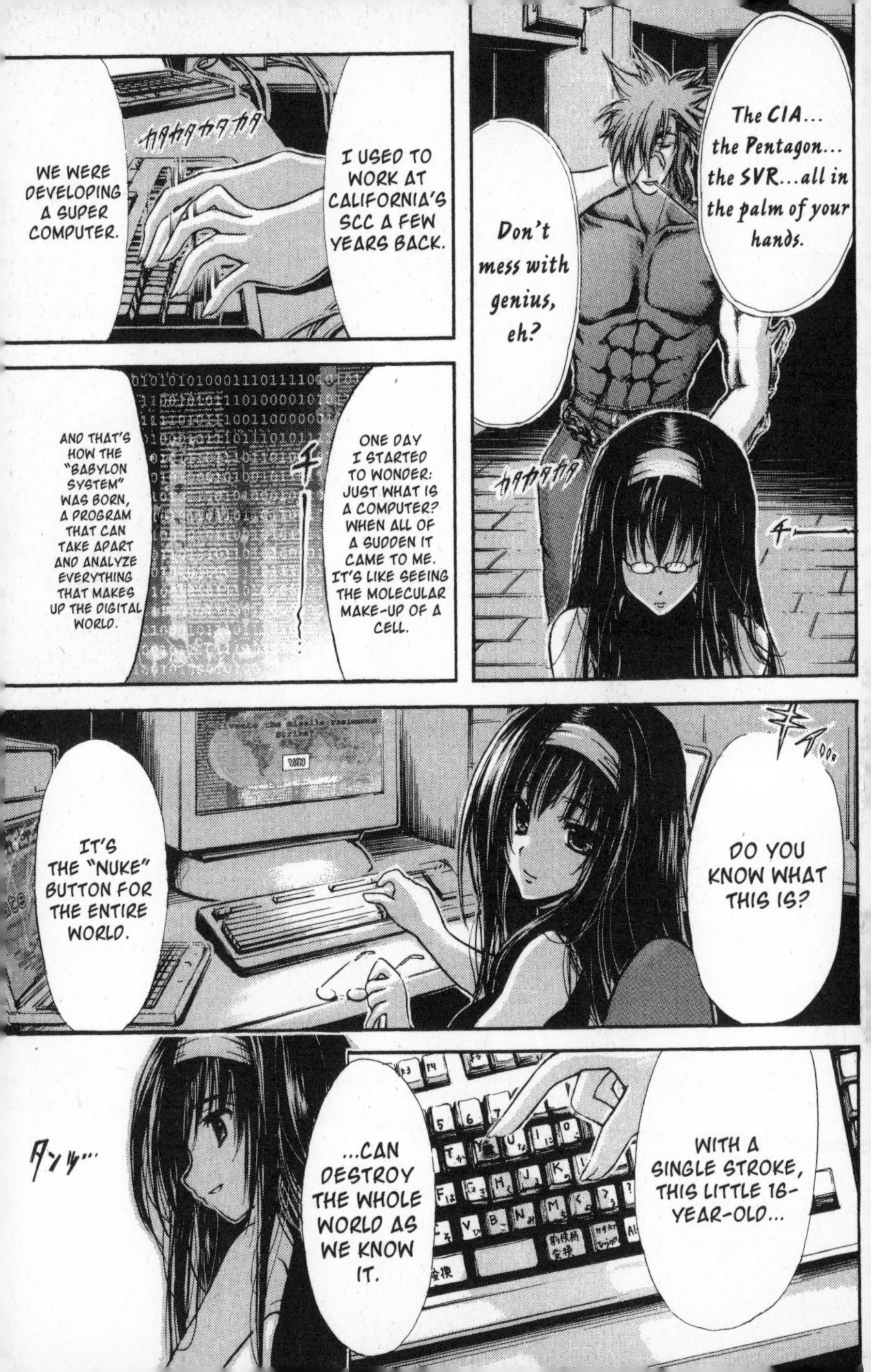
The CIA... the Pentagon... the SVR...all in the palm of your hands.
Don't mess with genius, eh?
I USED TO WORK AT CALIFORNIA'S SCC A FEW YEARS BACK.
カタカタカタカタ
WE WERE DEVELOPING A SUPER COMPUTER.
ONE DAY I STARTED TO WONDER: JUST WHAT IS A COMPUTER? WHEN ALL OF A SUDDEN IT CAME TO ME. IT'S LIKE SEEING THE MOLECULAR MAKE-UP OF A CELL.
AND THAT'S HOW THE "BABYLON SYSTEM" WAS BORN, A PROGRAM THAT CAN TAKE APART AND ANALYZE EVERYTHING THAT MAKES UP THE DIGITAL WORLD.
DO YOU KNOW WHAT THIS IS?
IT'S THE "NUKE" BUTTON FOR THE ENTIRE WORLD.
WITH A SINGLE STROKE, THIS LITTLE 16-YEAR-OLD...
...CAN DESTROY THE WHOLE WORLD AS WE KNOW IT.
ダンッ…

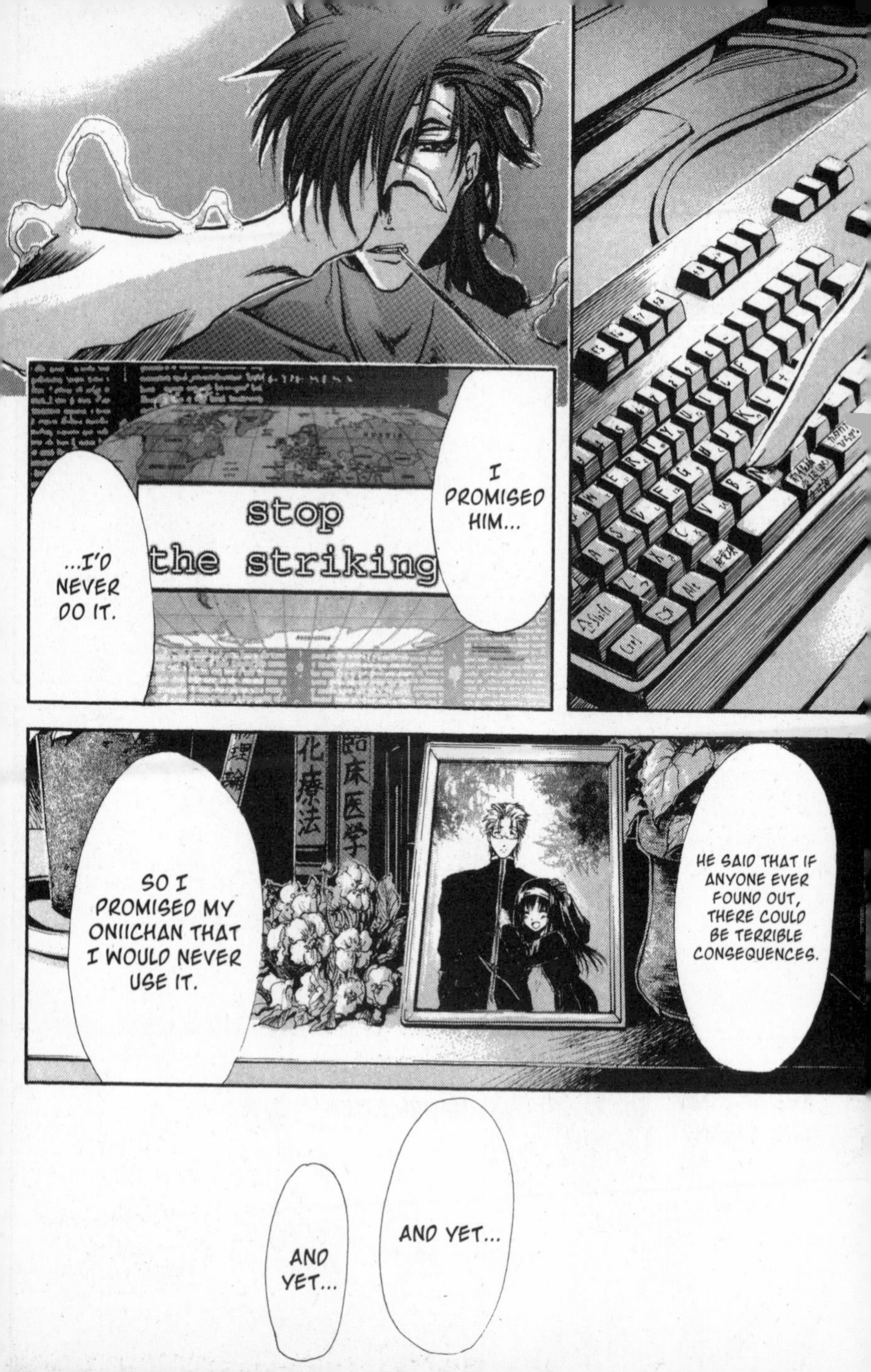
I PROMISED HIM...
stop the striking
...I'D NEVER DO IT.
HE SAID THAT IF ANYONE EVER FOUND OUT, THERE COULD BE TERRIBLE CONSEQUENCES.
SO I PROMISED MY ONIICHAN THAT I WOULD NEVER USE IT.
AND YET...
AND YET...

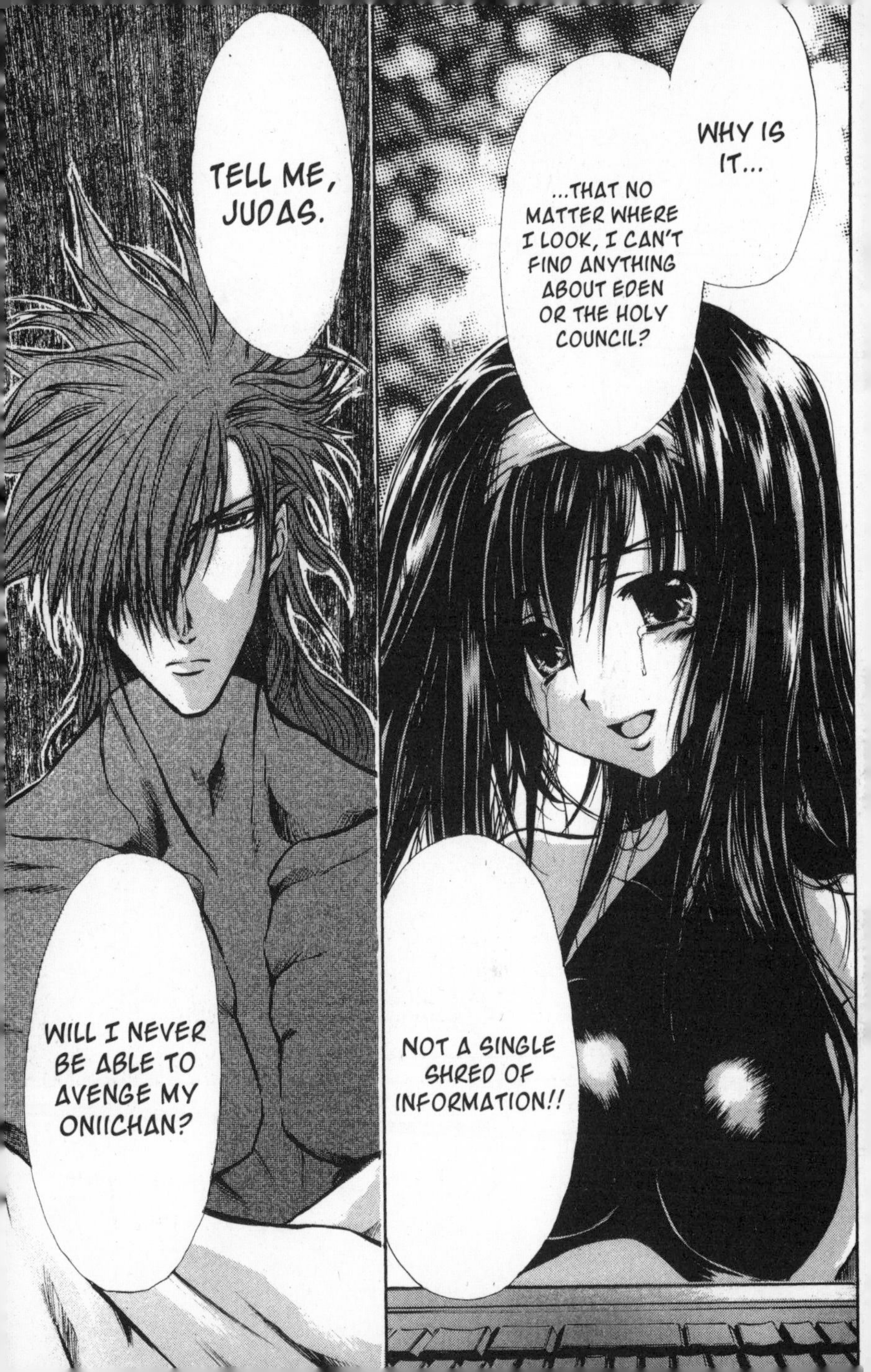
WHY IS IT...
...THAT NO MATTER WHERE I LOOK, I CAN'T FIND ANYTHING ABOUT EDEN OR THE HOLY COUNCIL?
NOT A SINGLE SHRED OF INFORMATION!!
TELL ME, JUDAS.
WILL I NEVER BE ABLE TO AVENGE MY ONIICHAN?

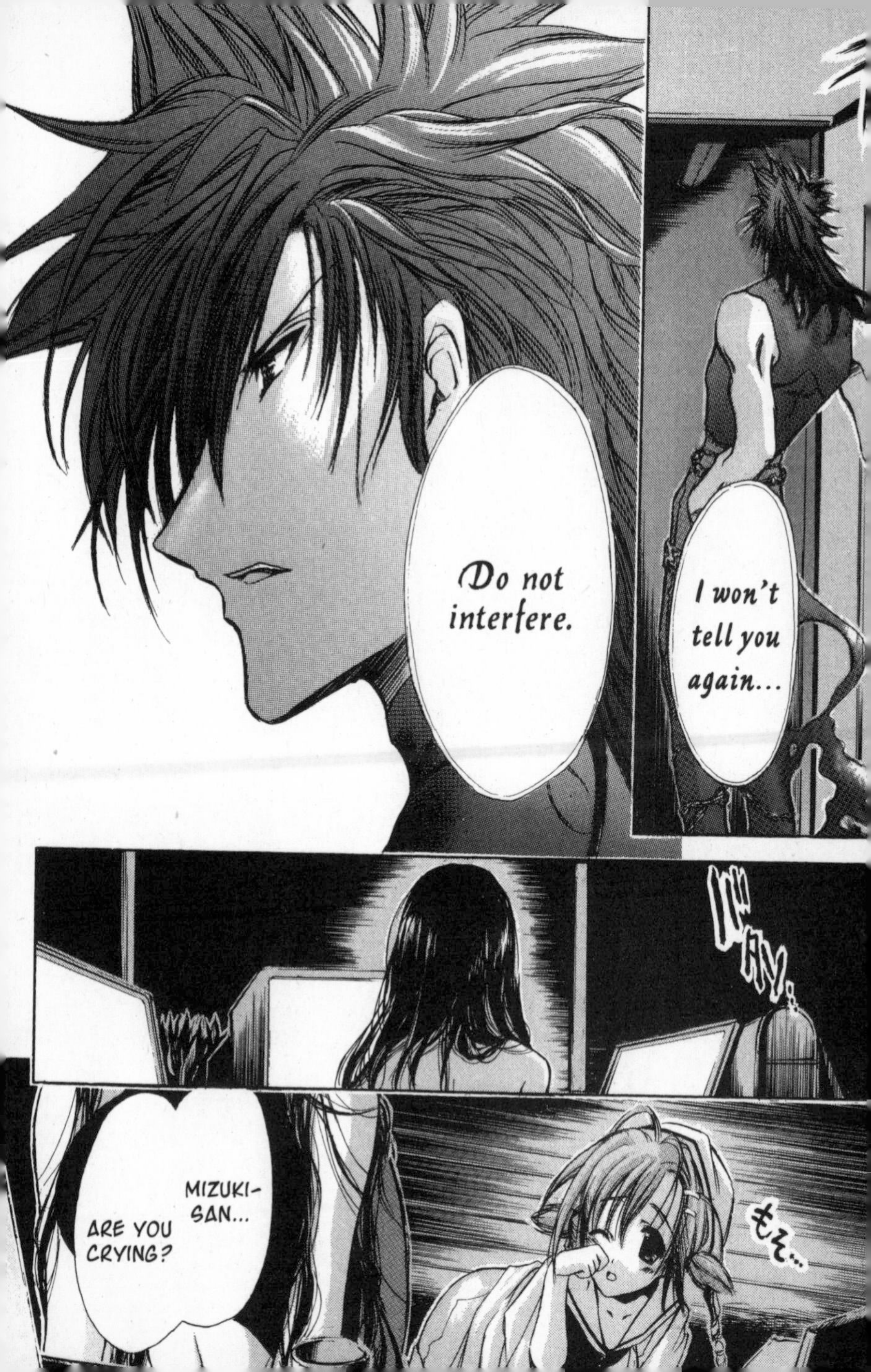
I won't tell you again...
Do not interfere.
もそ...
MIZUKI-SAN... ARE YOU CRYING?

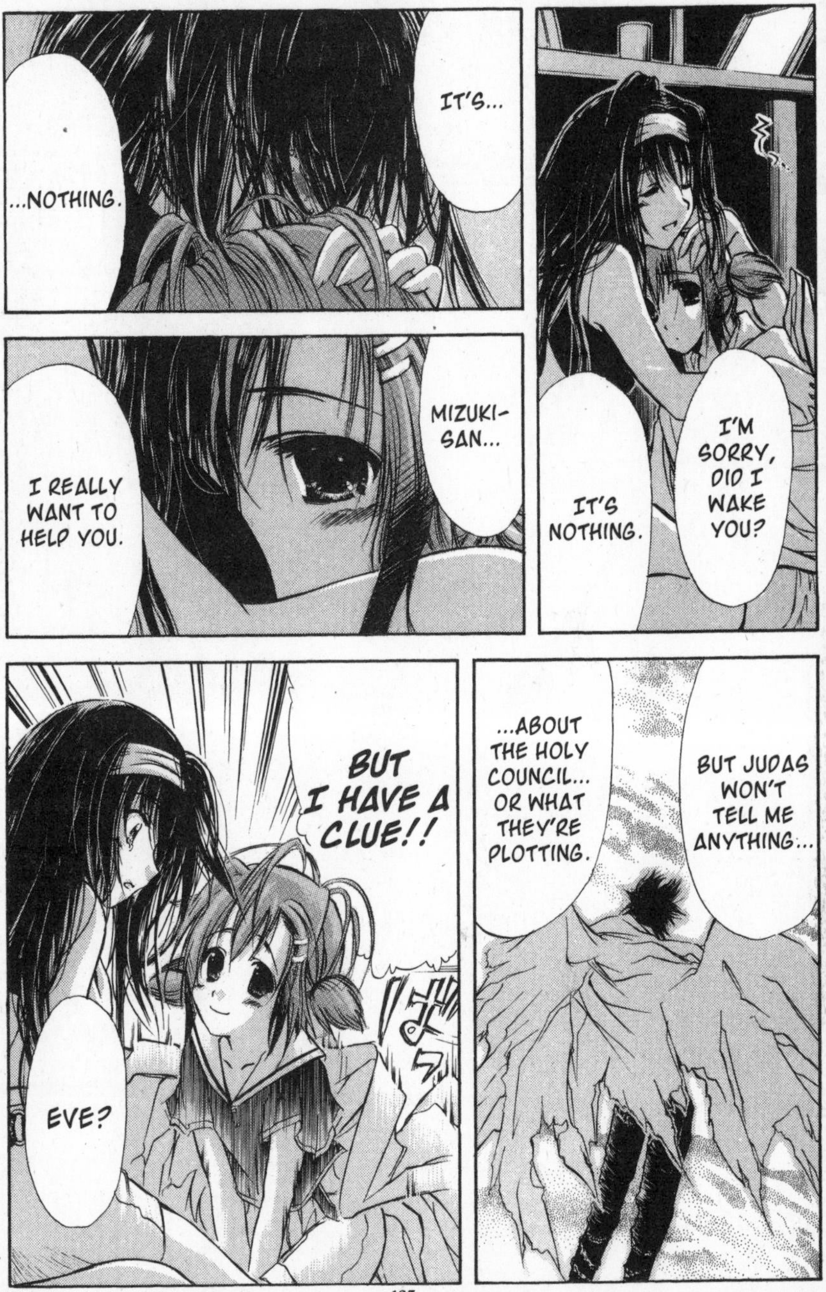
I'M SORRY, DID I WAKE YOU?
IT'S NOTHING.
IT'S...
...NOTHING.
MIZUKI-SAN...
I REALLY WANT TO HELP YOU.
BUT JUDAS WON'T TELL ME ANYTHING...
...ABOUT THE HOLY COUNCIL... OR WHAT THEY'RE PLOTTING.
BUT I HAVE A CLUE!!
EVE?

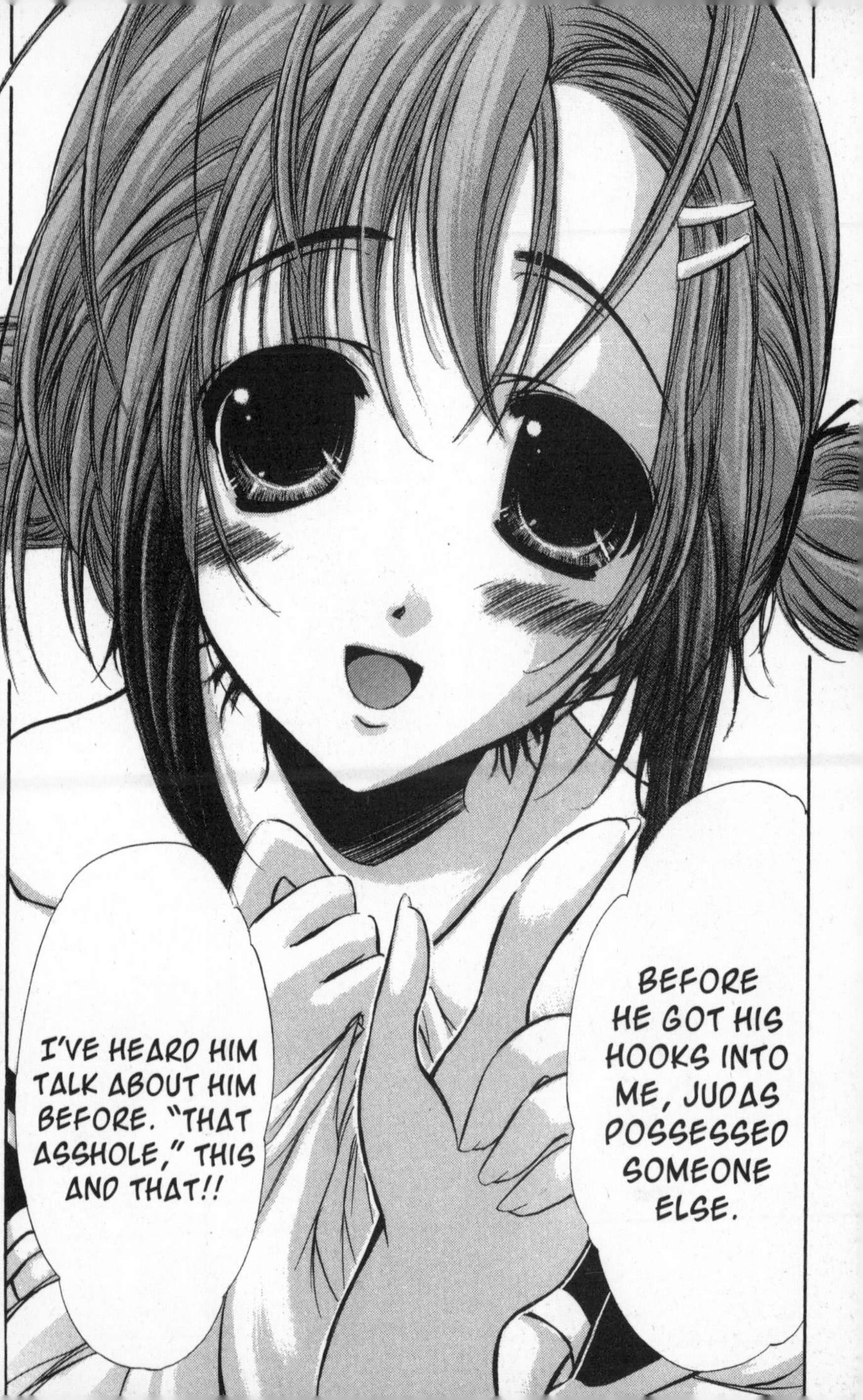
BEFORE HE GOT HIS HOOKS INTO ME, JUDAS POSSESSED SOMEONE ELSE.
I'VE HEARD HIM TALK ABOUT HIM BEFORE. "THAT ASSHOLE," THIS AND THAT!!

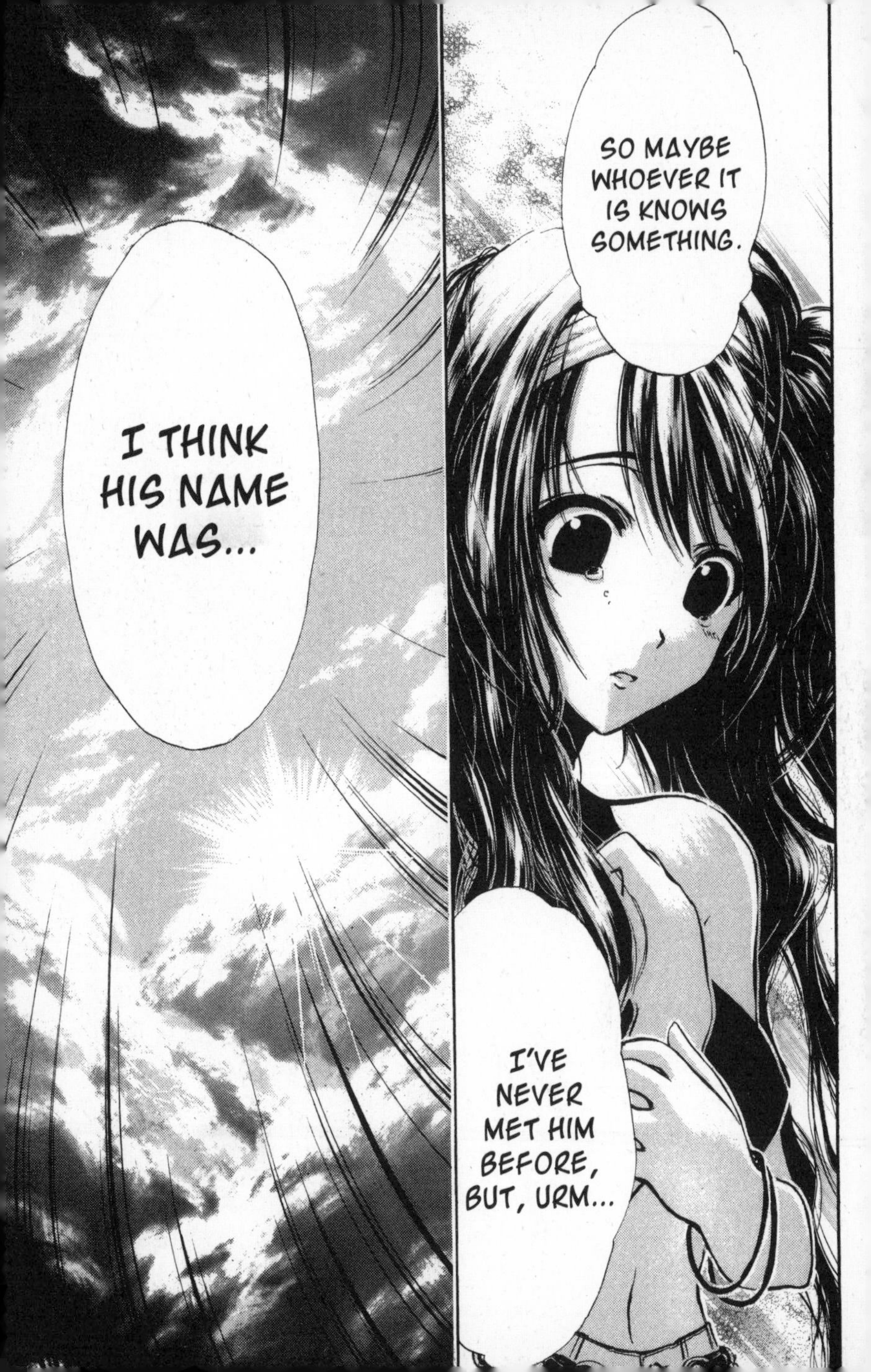
SO MAYBE WHOEVER IT IS KNOWS SOMETHING.
I'VE NEVER MET HIM BEFORE, BUT, URM...
I THINK HIS NAME WAS...

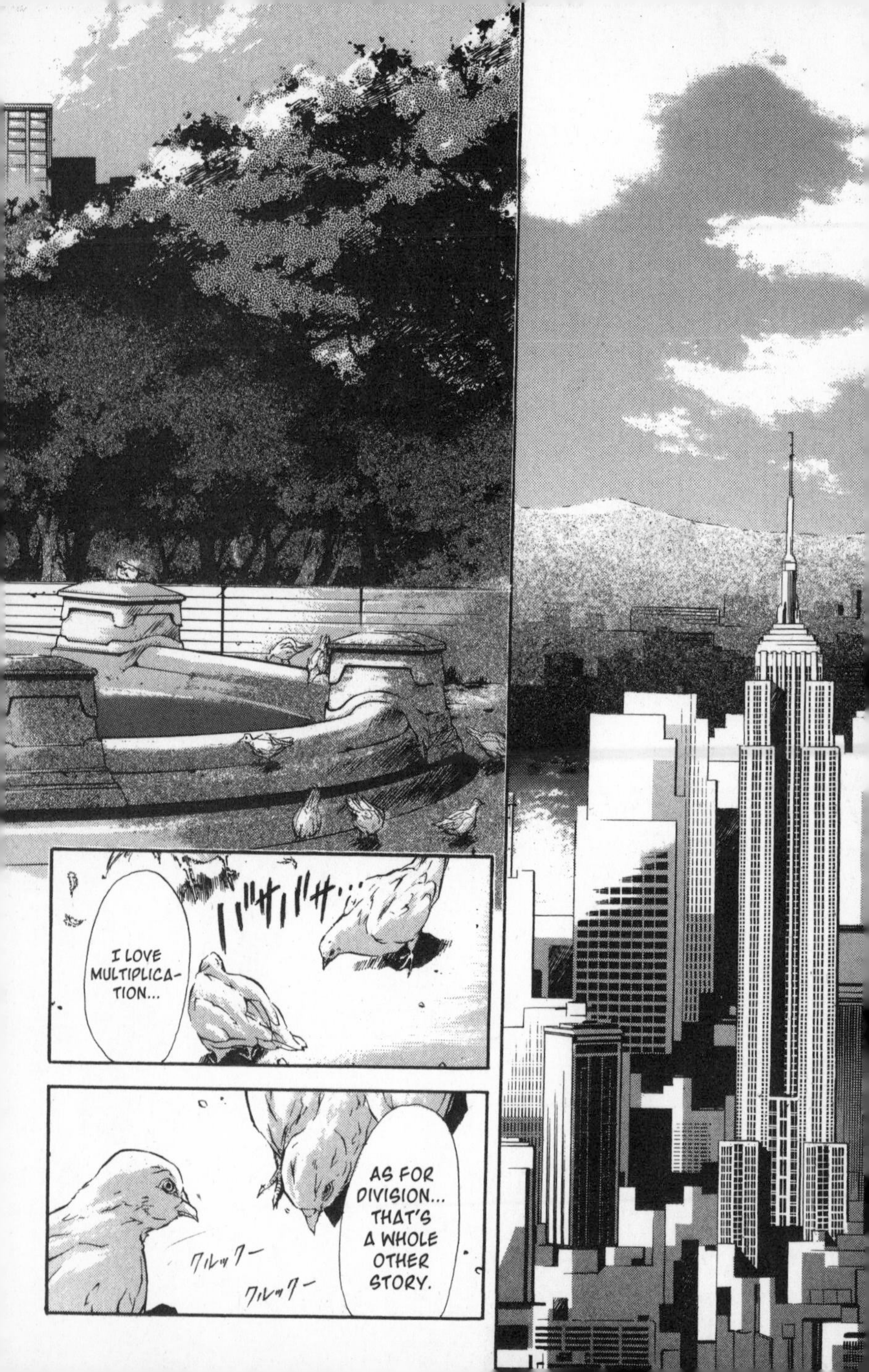
バサバサ…
I LOVE MULTIPLICA-
TION…
AS FOR
DIVISION…
THAT'S
A WHOLE
OTHER
STORY.
クルックー
クルックー

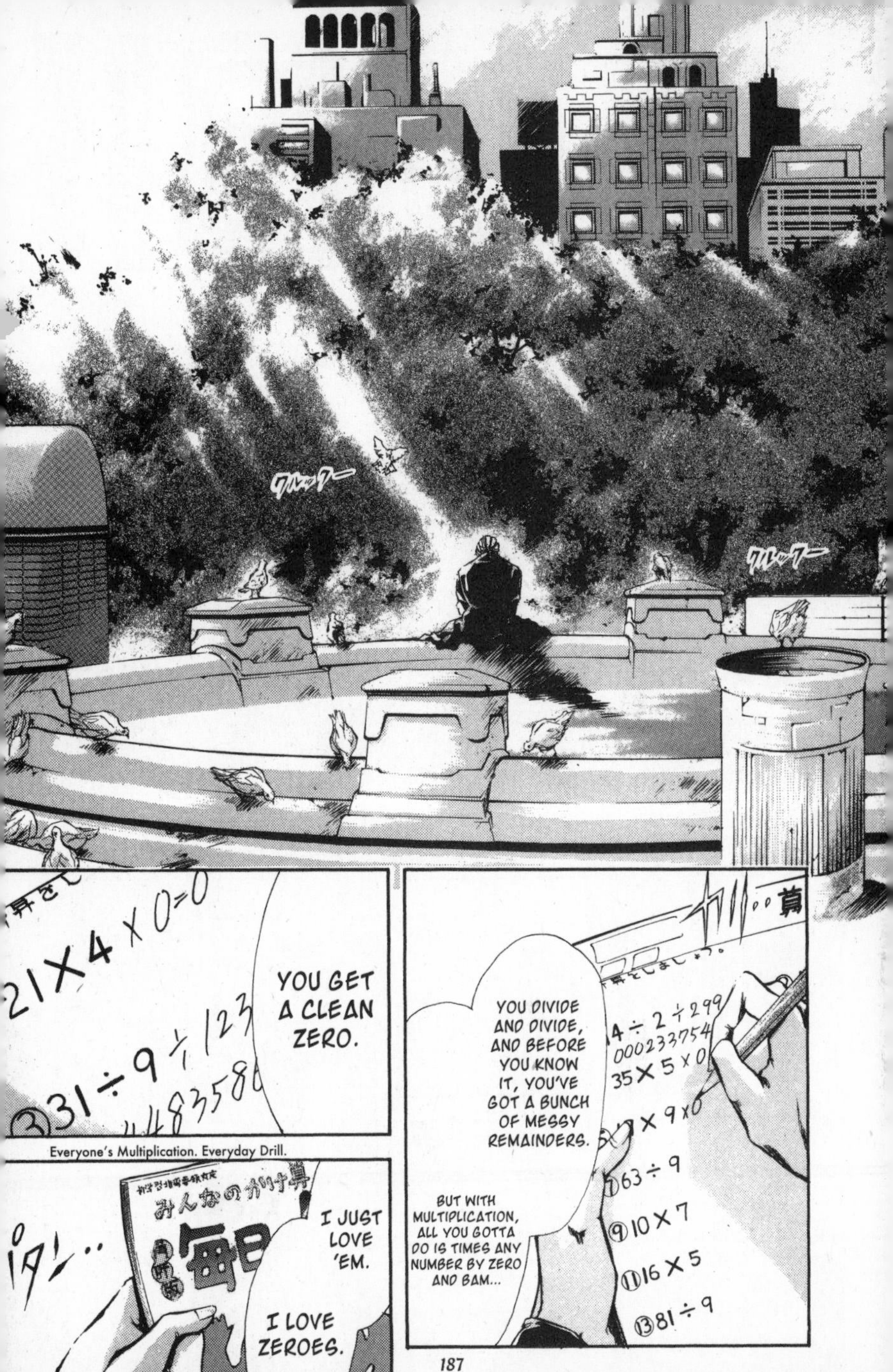

クルックー
クルックー
YOU DIVIDE AND DIVIDE, AND BEFORE YOU KNOW IT, YOU'VE GOT A BUNCH OF MESSY REMAINDERS.
BUT WITH MULTIPLICATION, ALL YOU GOTTA DO IS TIMES ANY NUMBER BY ZERO AND BAM...
YOU GET A CLEAN ZERO.
Everyone's Multiplication. Everyday Drill.
みんなのかけ算
毎日
I JUST LOVE 'EM.
I LOVE ZEROES.

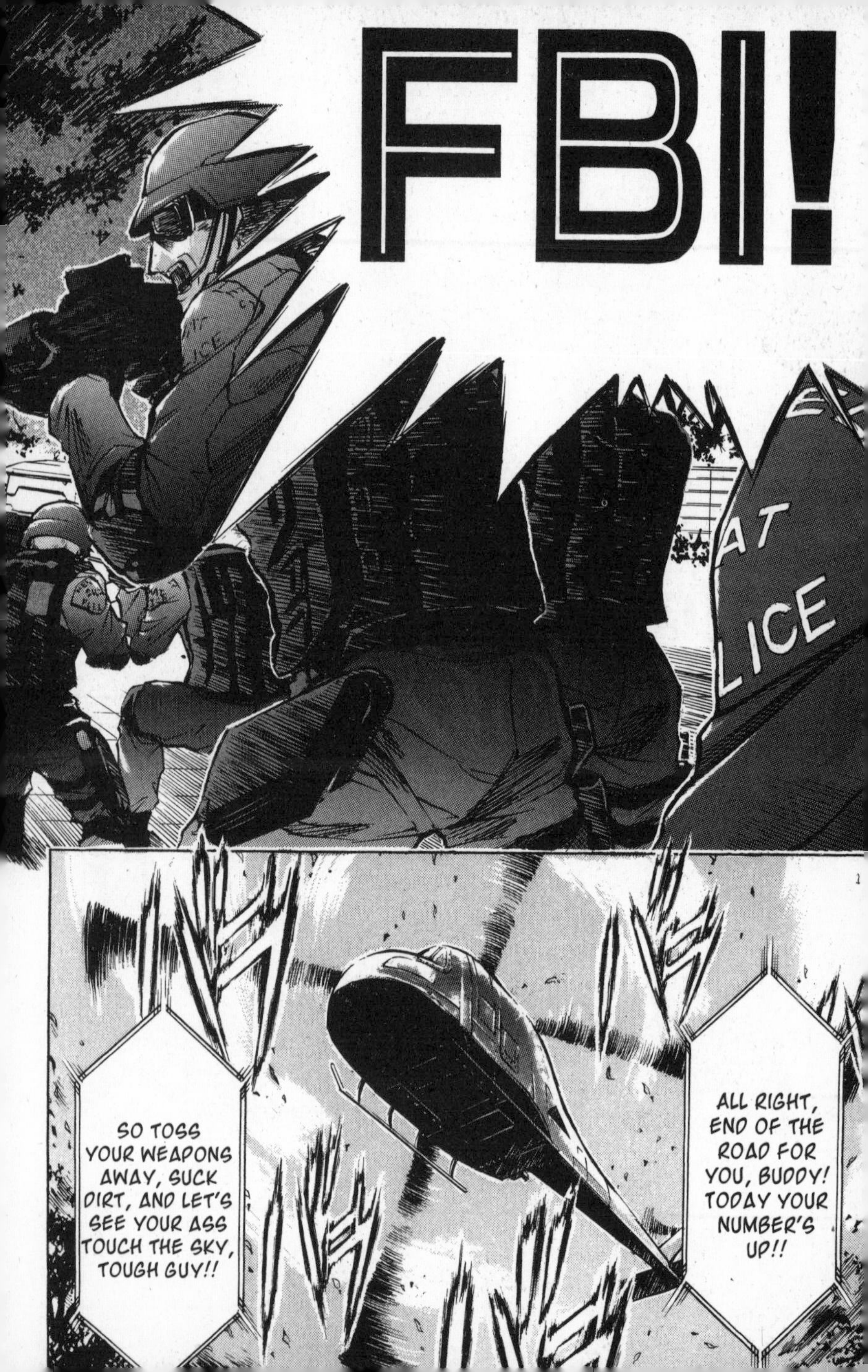
FBI!
AT
LICE
ALL RIGHT, END OF THE ROAD FOR YOU, BUDDY! TODAY YOUR NUMBER'S UP!!
SO TOSS YOUR WEAPONS AWAY, SUCK DIRT, AND LET'S SEE YOUR ASS TOUCH THE SKY, TOUGH GUY!!

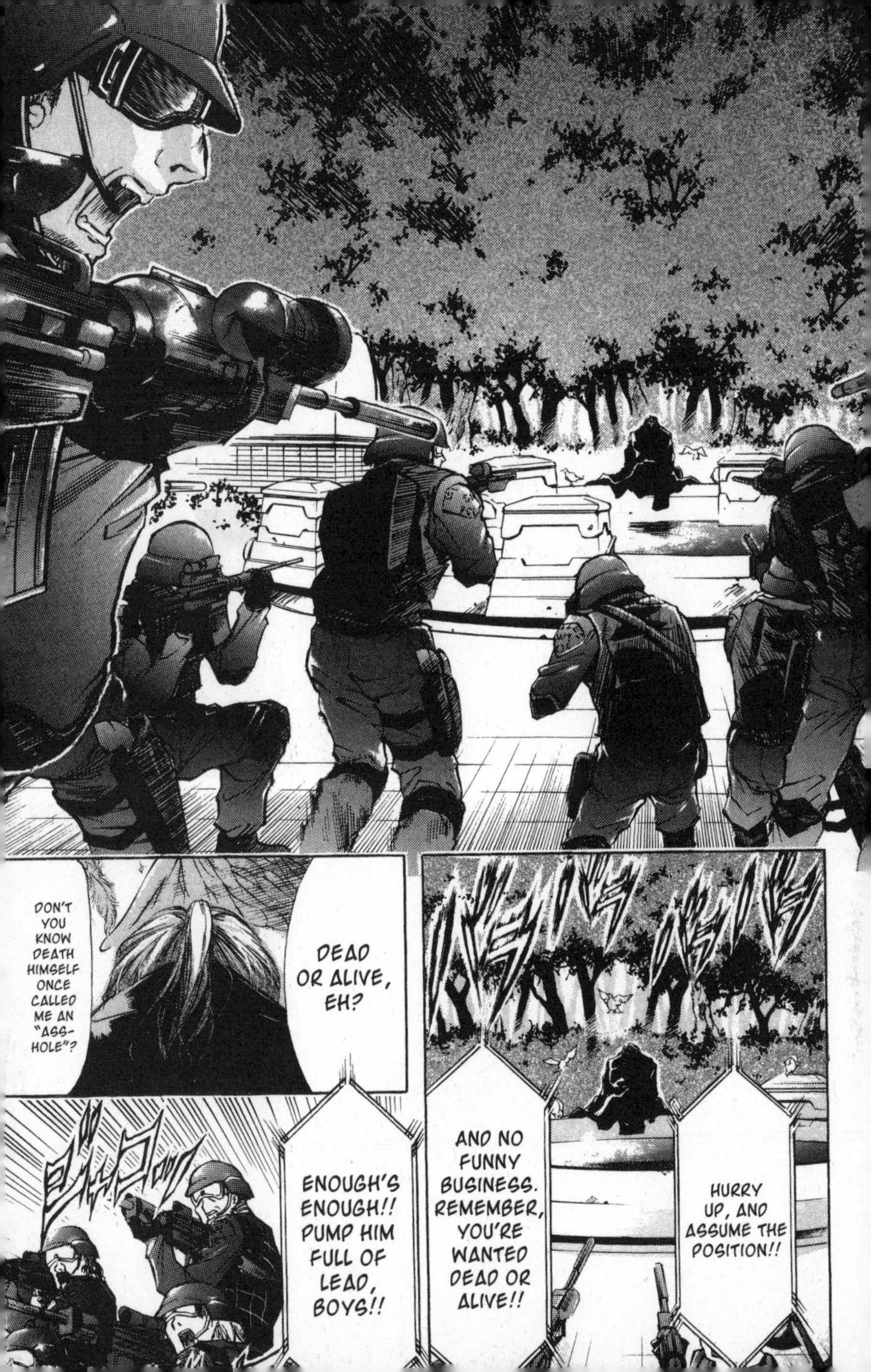
DEAD OR ALIVE, EH?
DON'T YOU KNOW DEATH HIMSELF ONCE CALLED ME AN "ASS-HOLE"?
HURRY UP, AND ASSUME THE POSITION!!
AND NO FUNNY BUSINESS. REMEMBER, YOU'RE WANTED DEAD OR ALIVE!!
ENOUGH'S ENOUGH!! PUMP HIM FULL OF LEAD, BOYS!!

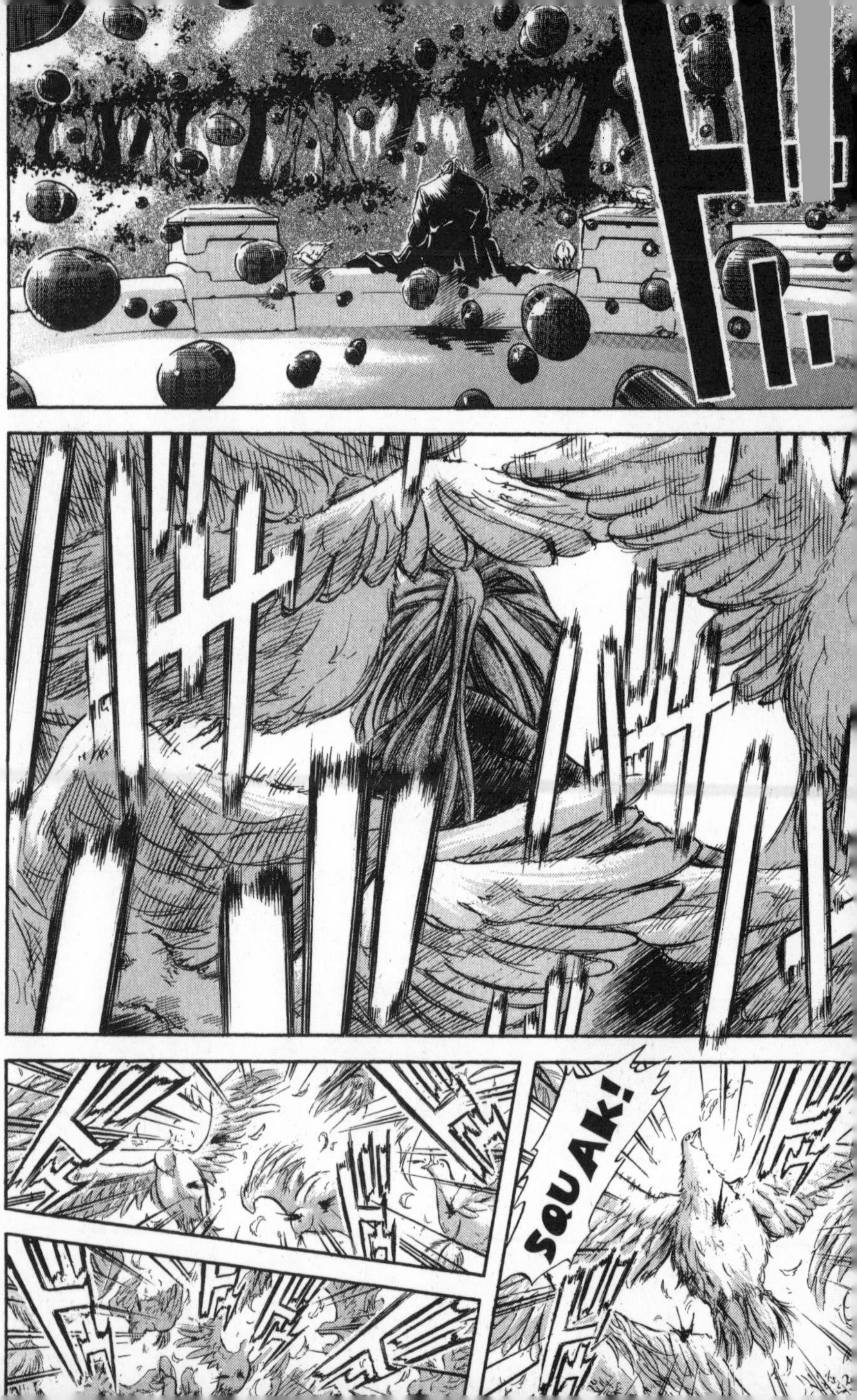
SQUAK!

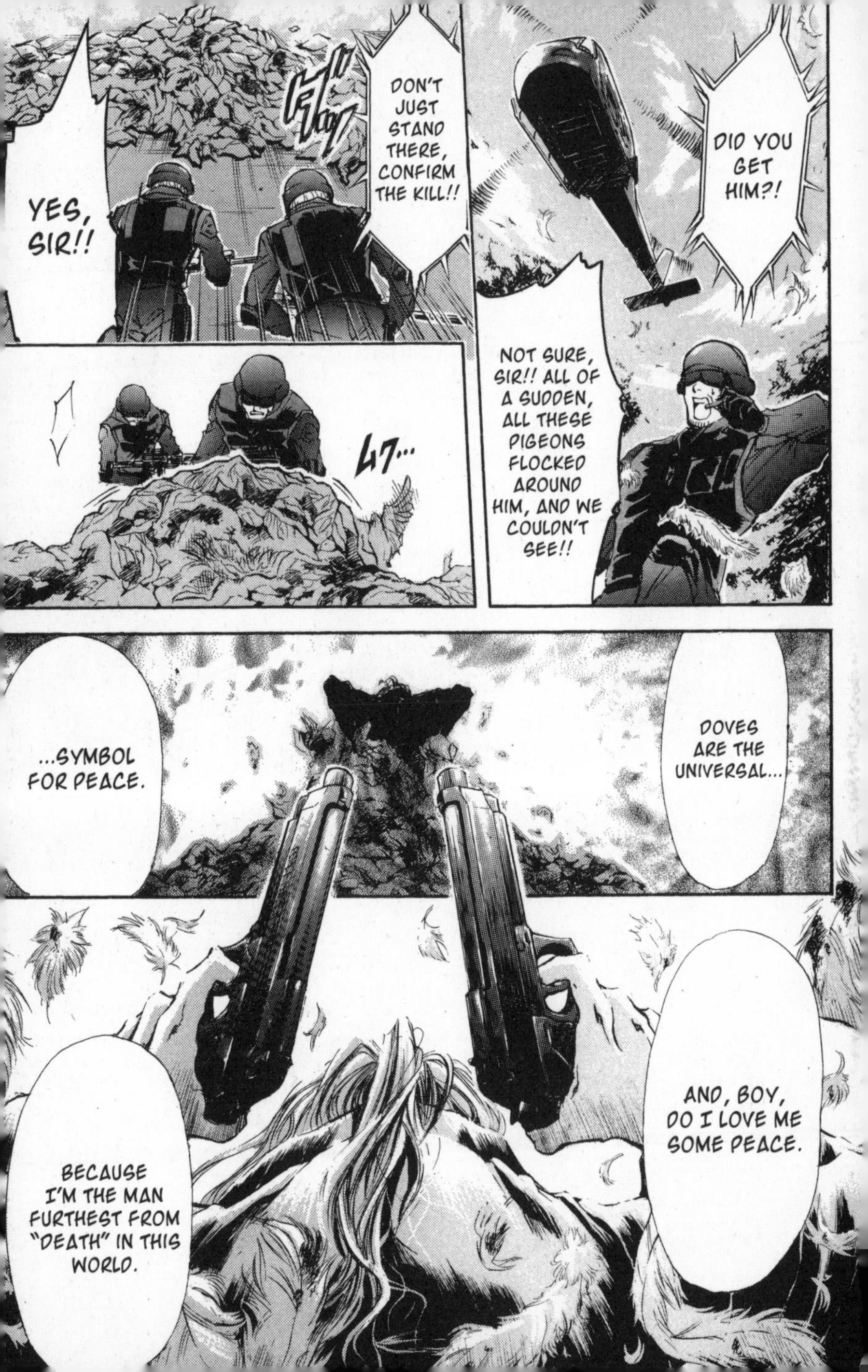
DID YOU GET HIM?!
DON'T JUST STAND THERE, CONFIRM THE KILL!!
YES, SIR!!
NOT SURE, SIR!! ALL OF A SUDDEN, ALL THESE PIGEONS FLOCKED AROUND HIM, AND WE COULDN'T SEE!!
DOVES ARE THE UNIVERSAL...
...SYMBOL FOR PEACE.
AND, BOY, DO I LOVE ME SOME PEACE.
BECAUSE I'M THE MAN FURTHEST FROM "DEATH" IN THIS WORLD.

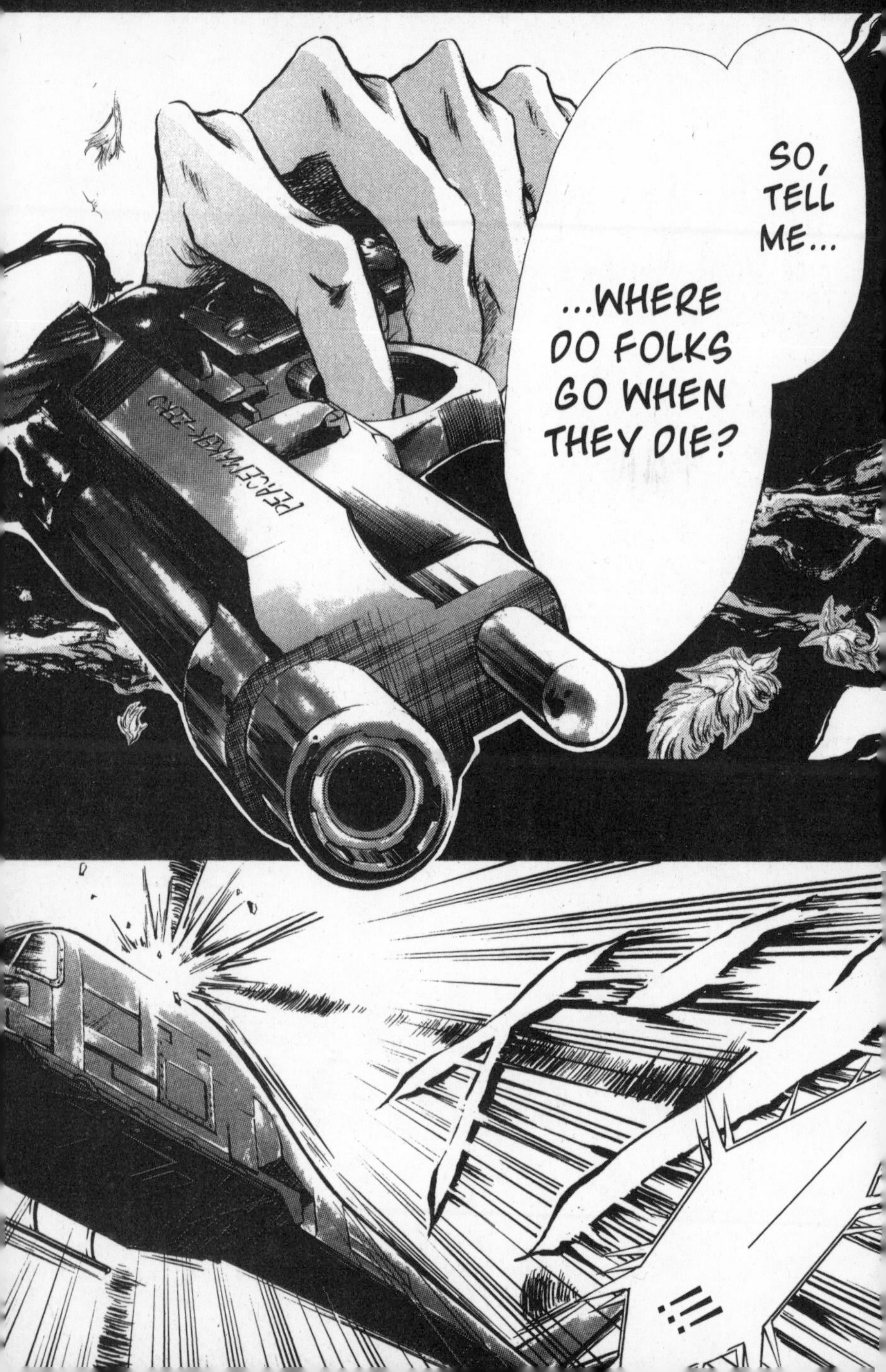
SO, TELL ME...
...WHERE DO FOLKS GO WHEN THEY DIE?
PEACEMAKER-ZERO

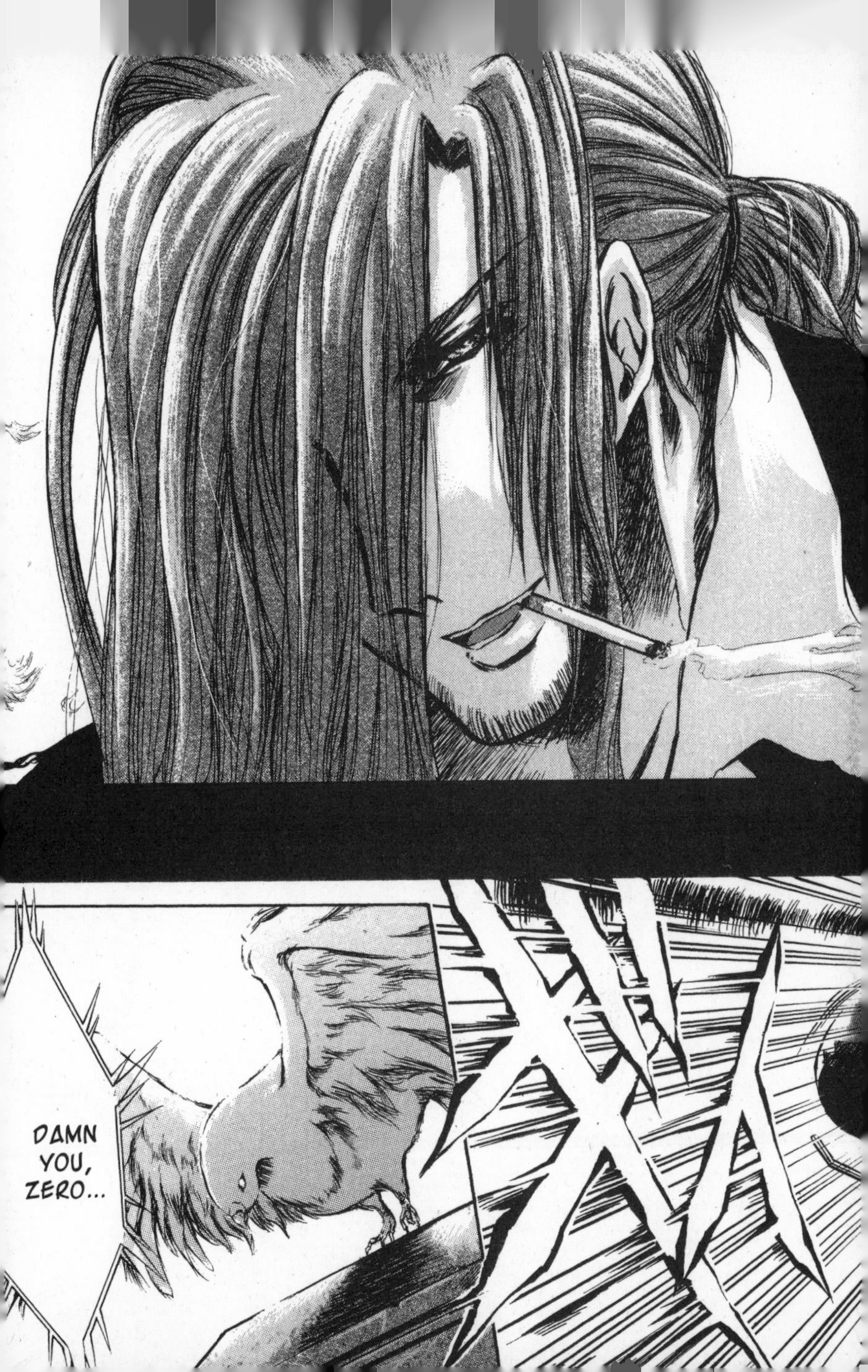
DAMN YOU, ZERO...

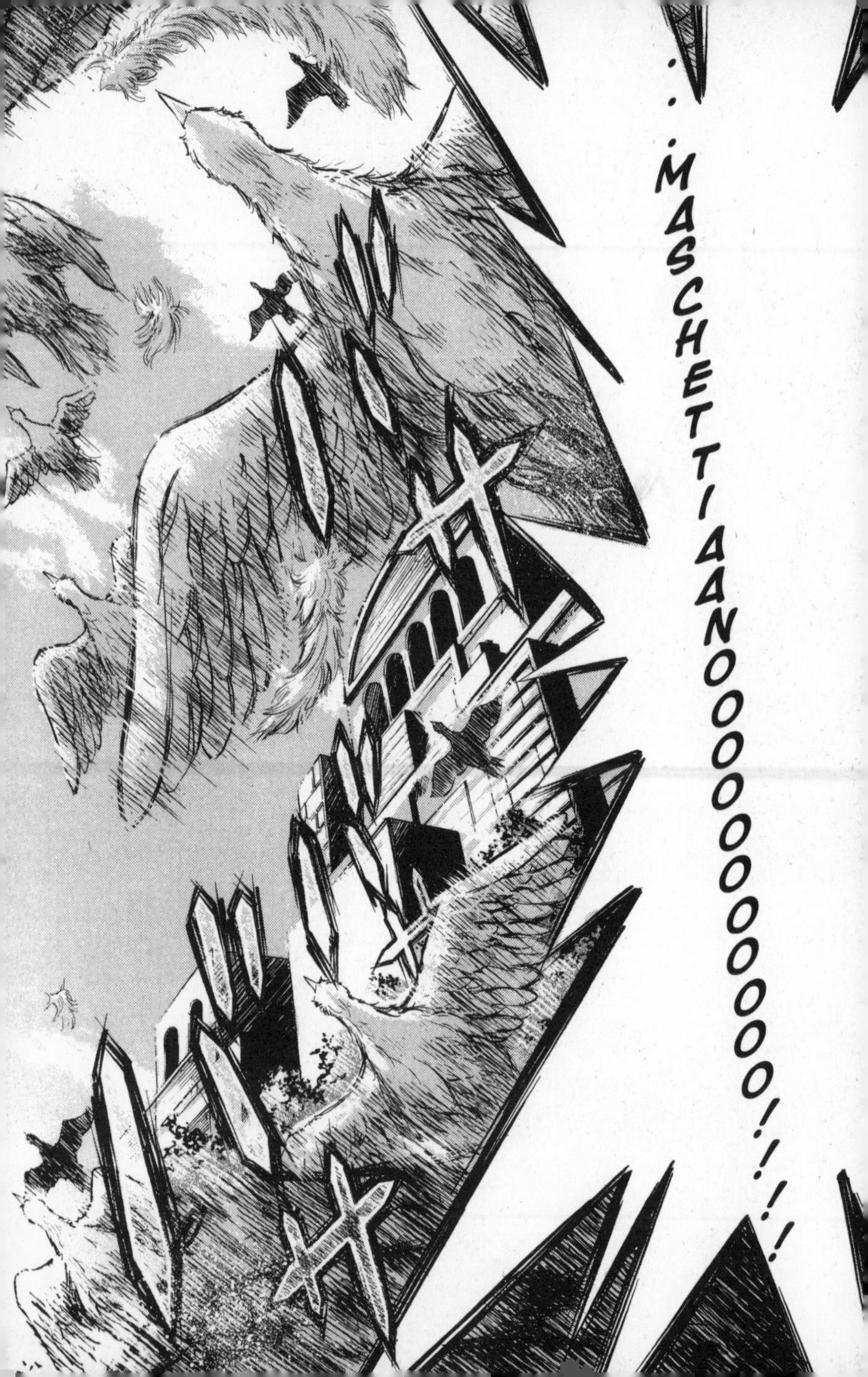
...MASCHETTIAANOOOOOOOOOO!!!!

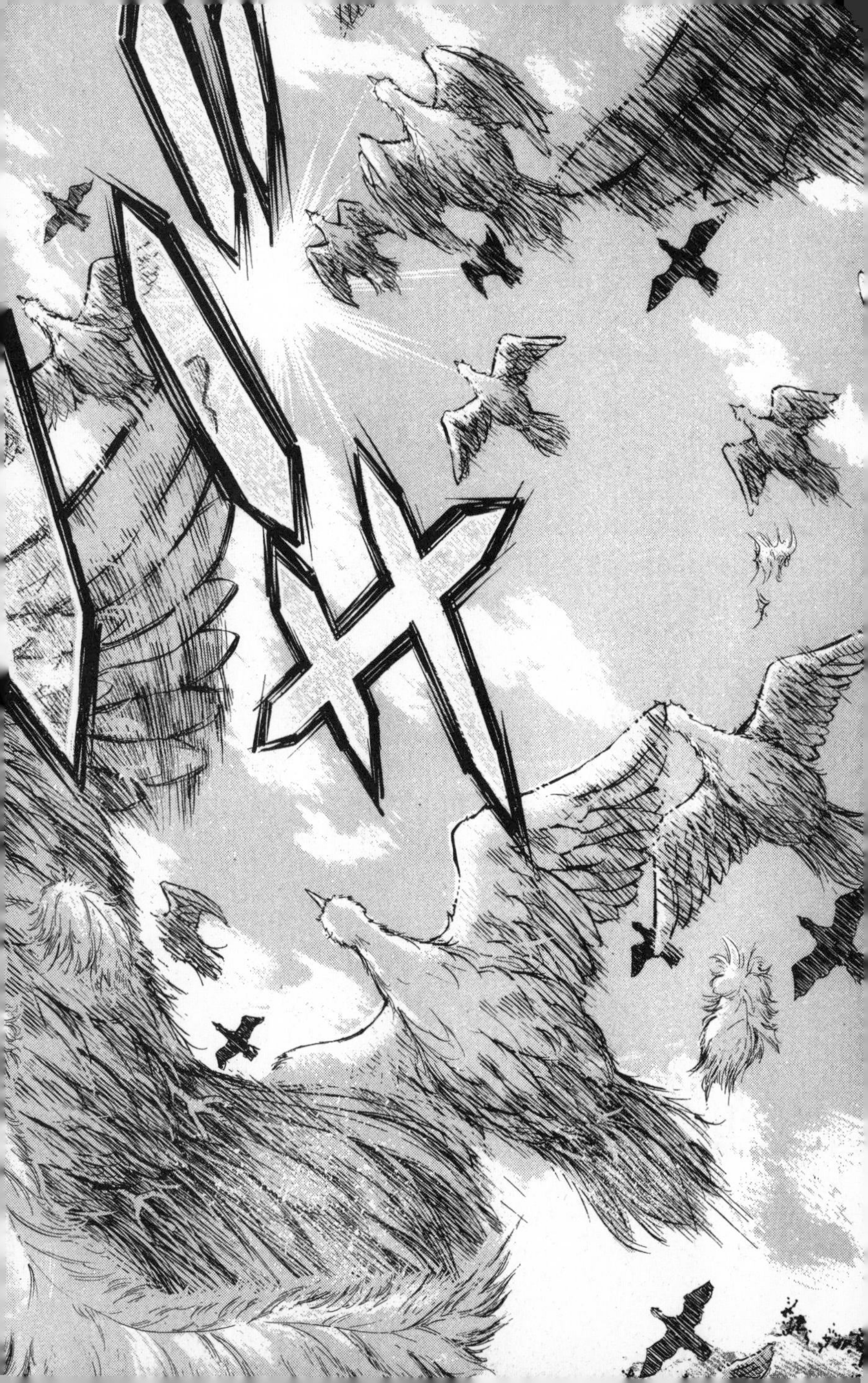

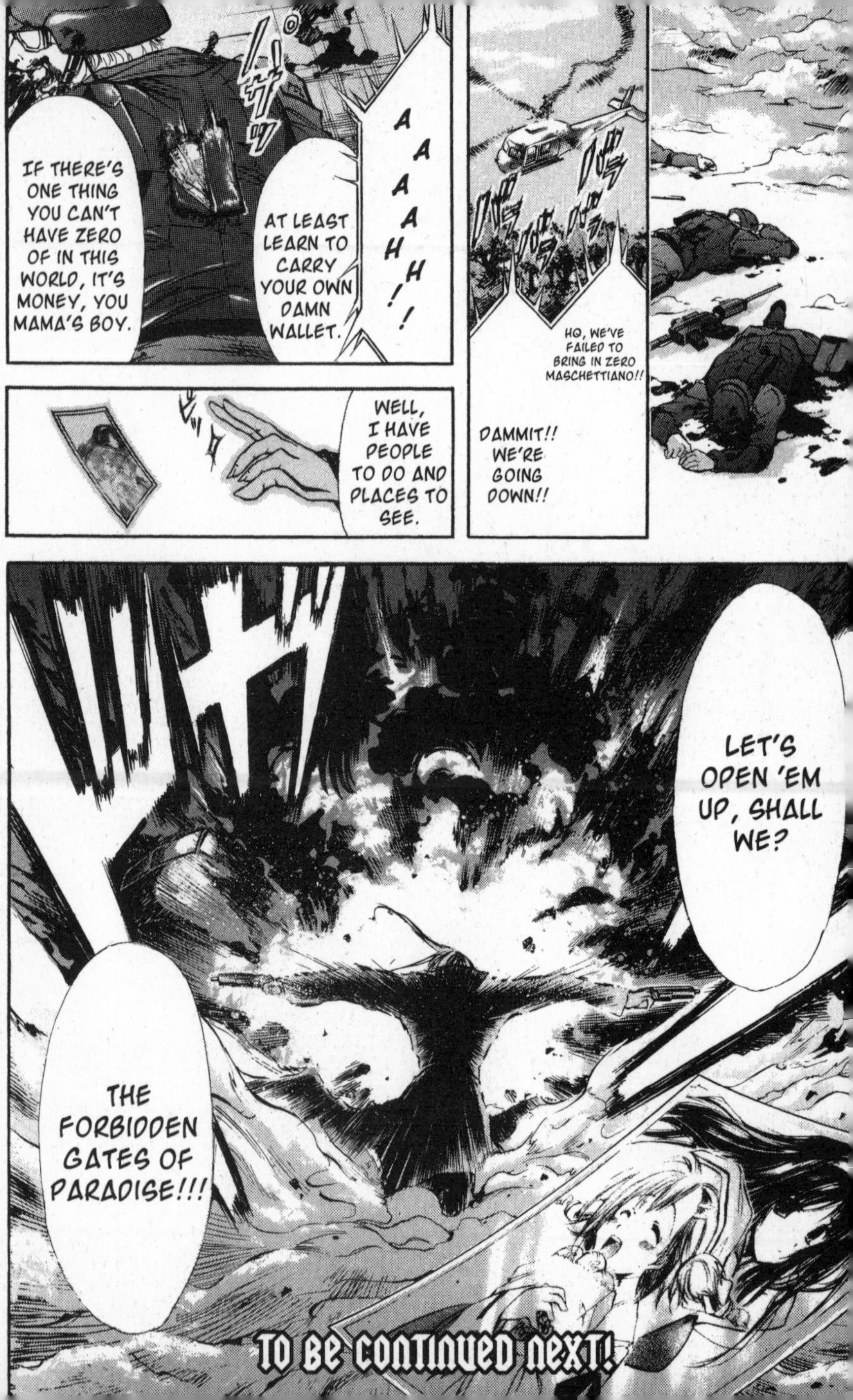
HQ, WE'VE FAILED TO BRING IN ZERO MASCHETTIANO!!
DAMMIT!! WE'RE GOING DOWN!!
AAAAH!!
AT LEAST LEARN TO CARRY YOUR OWN DAMN WALLET.
IF THERE'S ONE THING YOU CAN'T HAVE ZERO OF IN THIS WORLD, IT'S MONEY, YOU MAMA'S BOY.
WELL, I HAVE PEOPLE TO DO AND PLACES TO SEE.
LET'S OPEN 'EM UP, SHALL WE?
THE FORBIDDEN GATES OF PARADISE!!!
TO BE CONTINUED NEXT!

JUDAS

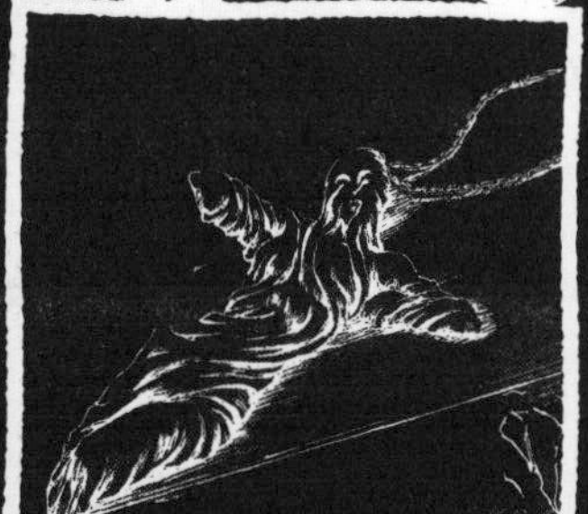

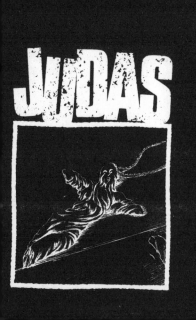

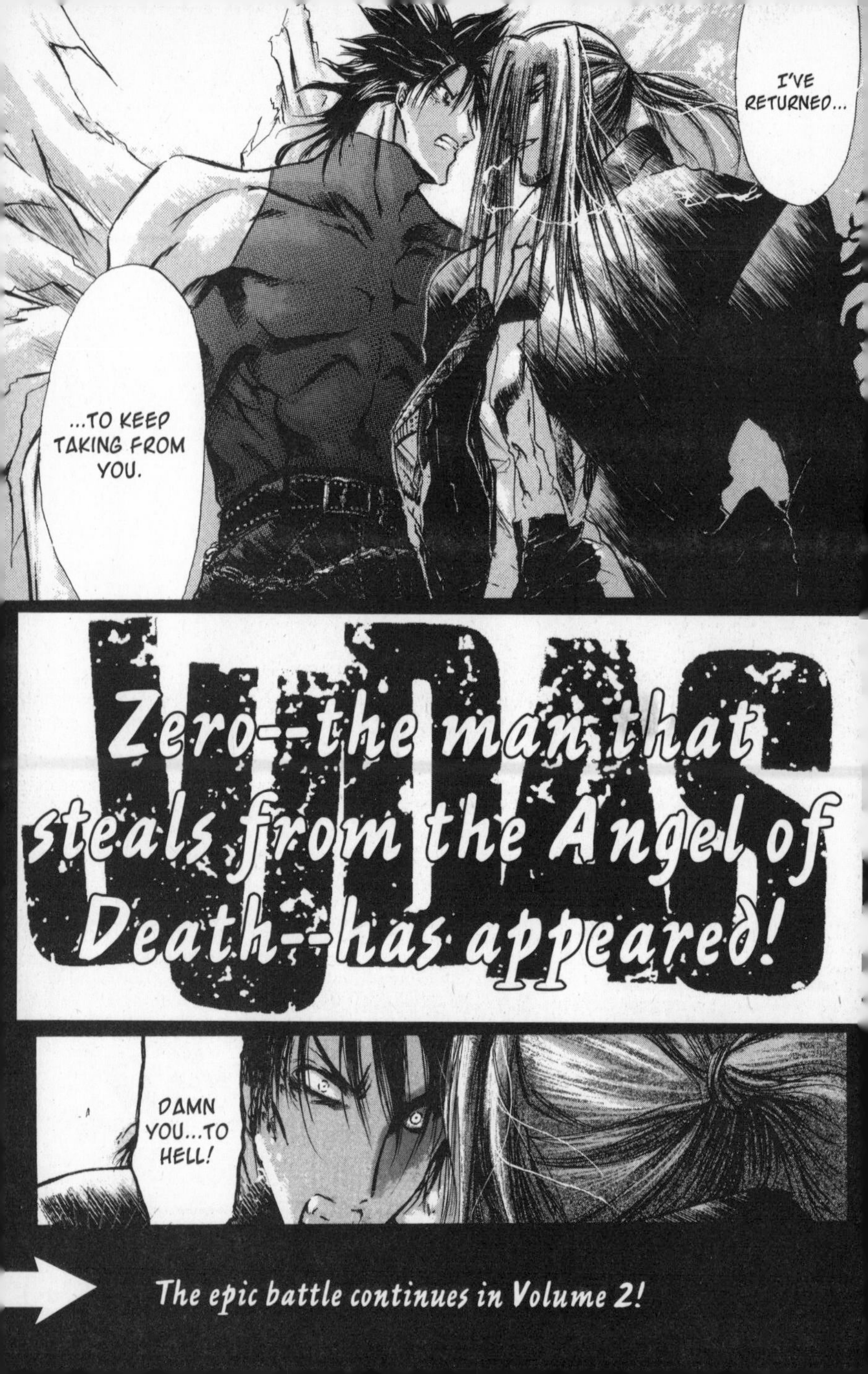
I'VE RETURNED...
...TO KEEP TAKING FROM YOU.
Zero--the man that steals from the Angel of Death--has appeared!
DAMN YOU...TO HELL!
The epic battle continues in Volume 2!

YOU HAVEN'T CHANGED A BIT, MAMA'S BOY.

HEH HEH HEH...

Say what?

NOW THEN...

...TAKE BACK YOUR "SIN."

Zero, the man that Judas was attached to before Eve... What does this man, who returns everything to Nothingness, steal from the Angel of Death? What is Peter's true goal? And what role does the Holy Council play? The chains of the past that envelop Judas are revealed in volume 2!

The Angel of Death versus Nothingness!

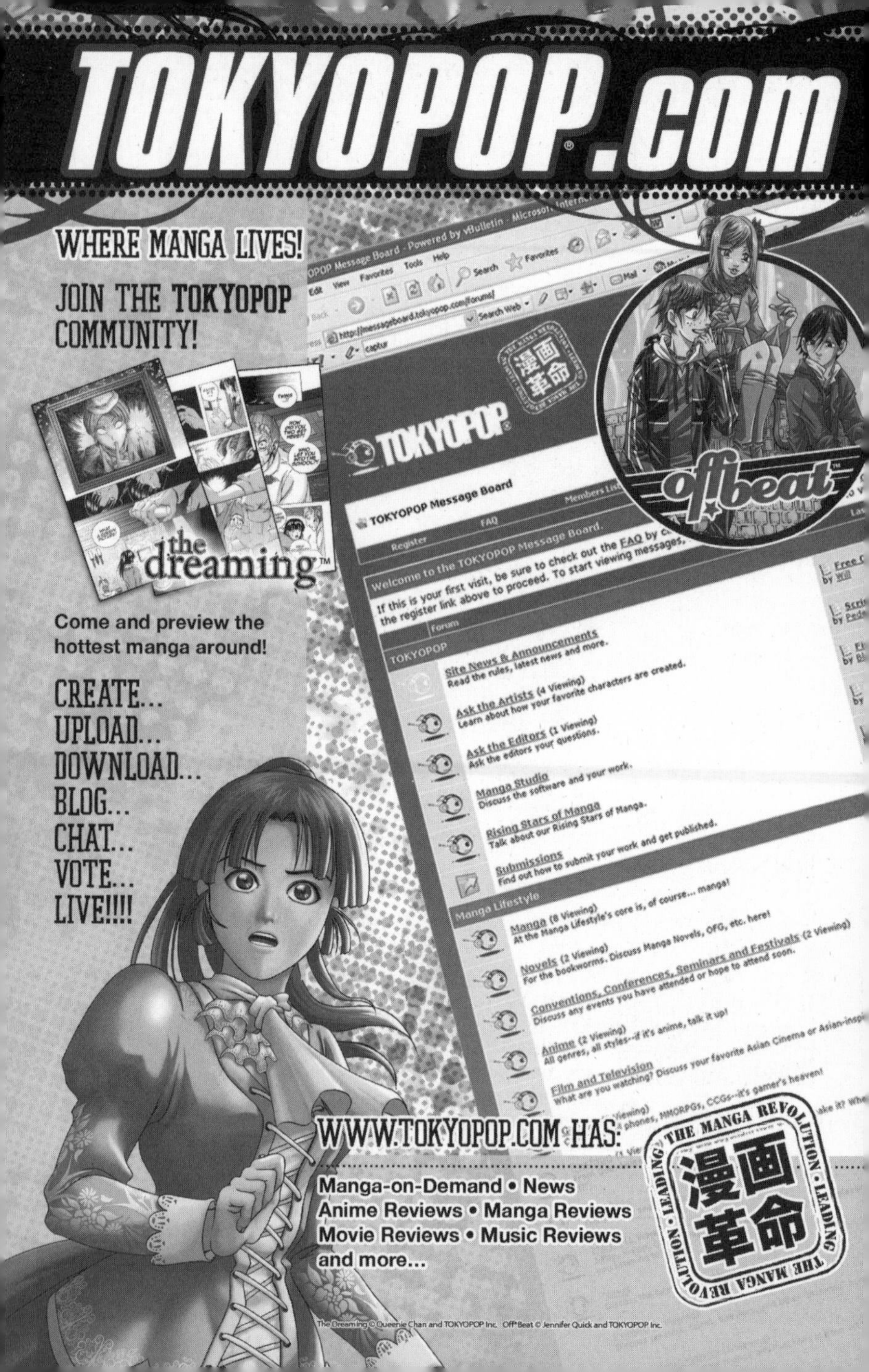
TOKYOPOP.com
WHERE MANGA LIVES!
JOIN THE TOKYOPOP COMMUNITY!
the dreaming
Come and preview the hottest manga around!
CREATE...
UPLOAD...
DOWNLOAD...
BLOG...
CHAT...
VOTE...
LIVE!!!!
offbeat
TOKYOPOP Message Board
Welcome to the TOKYOPOP Message Board.
Site News & Announcements
Read the rules, latest news and more.
Ask the Artists
Learn about how your favorite characters are created.
Ask the Editors
Ask the editors your questions.
Manga Studio
Discuss the software and your work.
Rising Stars of Manga
Talk about our Rising Stars of Manga.
Submissions
Find out how to submit your work and get published.
Manga Lifestyle
WWW.TOKYOPOP.COM HAS:
Manga-on-Demand • News
Anime Reviews • Manga Reviews
Movie Reviews • Music Reviews
and more...
THE MANGA REVOLUTION • LEADING
漫画革命
The Dreaming © Queenie Chan and TOKYOPOP Inc. Off*Beat © Jennifer Quick and TOKYOPOP Inc.

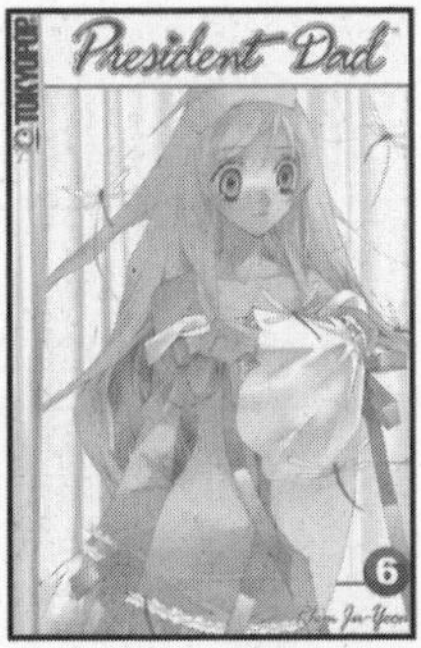
President Dad
TOKYOPOP
6

PRESIDENT DAD

BY JU-YEON RHIM

In spite of the kind of dorky title, this book is tremendously fun and stylish. The mix of romance and truly bizarre comedy won me over in a heartbeat. When young Ami's father becomes the new president of South Korea, suddenly she is forced into a limelight that she never looked for and isn't particularly excited about. She's got your typical teenage crushes on pop idols (and a mysterious boy from her past who may be a North Korean spy! Who'd have thought there'd be global politics thrown into a shojo series?!), and more than her fair share of crazy relatives, but now she's also got a super-tough bodyguard who can disguise himself as anyone you can possibly imagine, and the eyes of the nation are upon her! This underrated manhwa totally deserves a second look!

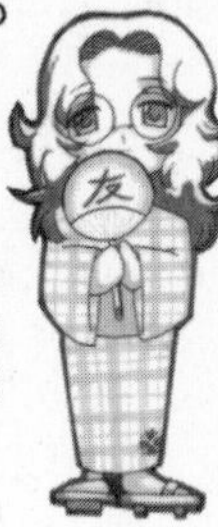

~Lillian Diaz-Pryzbyl, Editor

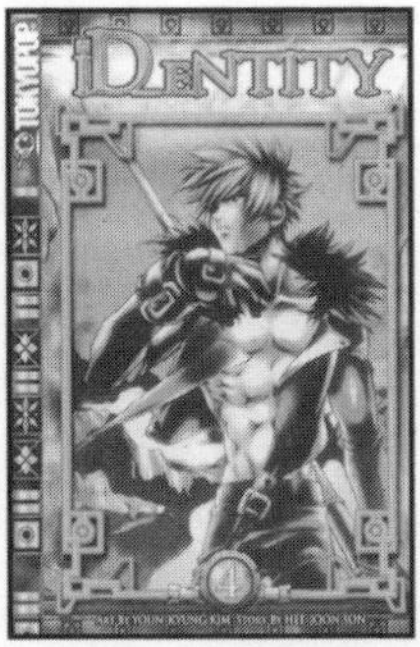
iDENTITY
TOKYOPOP
4

ID_ENTITY

BY HEE-JOON SON AND YOUN-KYUNG KIM

As a fan of online gaming, I've really been enjoying *iD_eNTITY.* Packed with action, intrigue and loads of laughs, *iD_eNTITY* is a raucous romp through a virtual world that's obviously written and illustrated by fellow gamers. Hee-Joon Son and Youn-Kyung Kim utilize gaming's terms and conventions while keeping the story simple and entertaining enough for noobs (a glossary of gaming terms is included in the back). Anyone else out there who has already absorbed *.hack* and is looking for a new gaming adventure to go on would do well to start here.

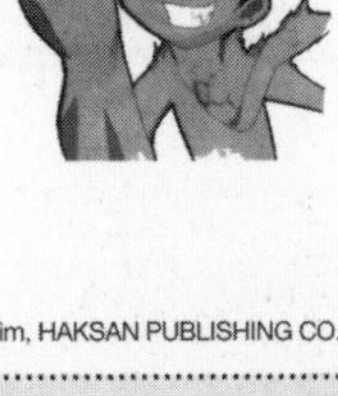

~Tim Beedle, Editor

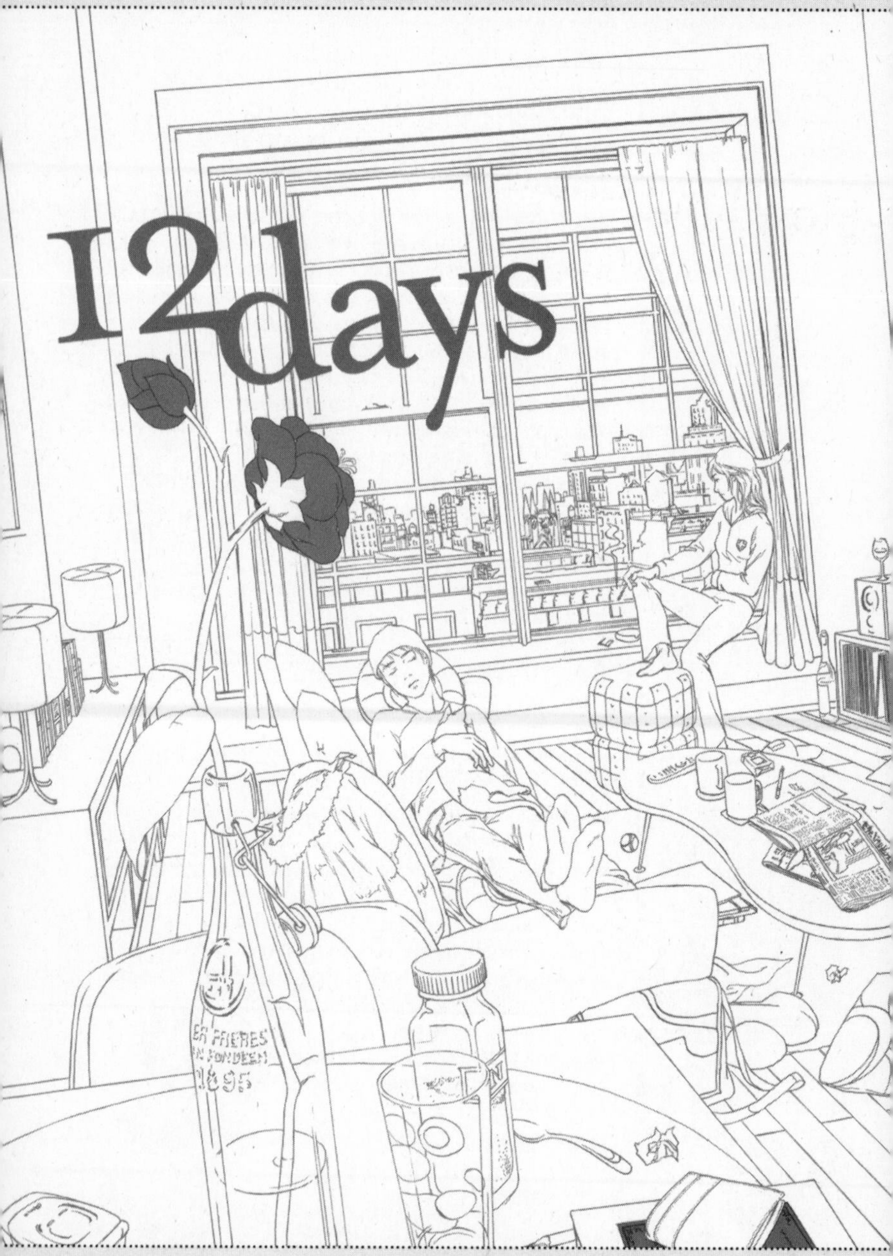
12days
ER FRERES
EN FONDEEN
1895

How long would it take to get over...
losing the love of your life?

When Jackie's ex-lover Noah dies, she decides the quickest way to get over her is to hold a personal ritual with Noah's ashes. Jackie consumes the ashes in the form of smoothies for 12 days, hoping the pain will subside. But will that be enough?

From the internationally published illustrator June Kim.

DRAMA

OT OLDER TEEN AGE 16+

© June Kim and TOKYOPOP Inc.

FOR MORE INFORMATION VISIT:

ELEMENTAL GELADE

A SKY PIRATE MANGA BOUND TO HOOK YOU!

Rookie sky pirate Coud Van Giruet discovers a most unusual bounty: a young girl named Ren who is an "Edel Raid"—a living weapon that lends extraordinary powers to humans. But just as he realizes Ren is a very valuable treasure, she is captured! Can Coud and Arc Aile join forces and rescue her without killing themselves...or each other?

THE MANGA THAT SPARKED THE HIT ANIME!!

ACTION

T
TEEN
AGE 13+

© MAYUMI AZUMA

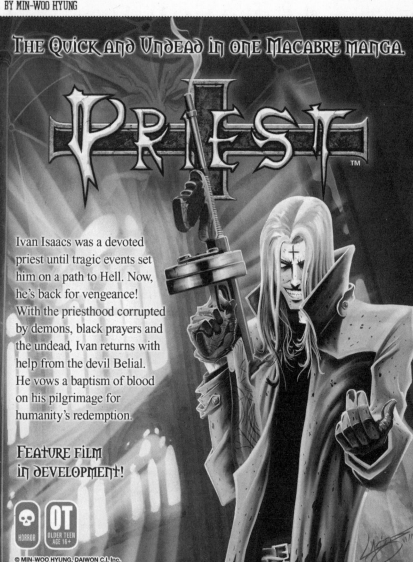

STOP!

This is the back of the book.
You wouldn't want to spoil a great ending!

This book is printed "manga-style," in the authentic Japanese right-to-left format. Since none of the artwork has been flipped or altered, readers get to experience the story just as the creator intended. You've been asking for it, so TOKYOPOP® delivered: authentic, hot-off-the-press, and far more fun!

DIRECTIONS

If this is your first time reading manga-style, here's a quick guide to help you understand how it works.

It's easy... just start in the top right panel and follow the numbers. Have fun, and look for more 100% authentic manga from TOKYOPOP®!